THE LIGHTLESS SKY

My Journey to Safety
as a Child Refugee

Gulwali Passarlay

WITH NADENE GHOURI

THE
LIGHTLESS
SKY

MY JOURNEY TO SAFETY
AS A CHILD REFUGEE

Atlantic Books

LONDON

First published in hardback in Great Britain in 2015
by Atlantic Books, an imprint of Atlantic Books Ltd.

This paperback edition published in 2016 by Atlantic Books.

10 9 8 7 6 5 4 3 2 1

A CIP catalogue record for this book is available
from the British Library.

Paperback ISBN: 978 178 2398479
E-book ISBN: 978 178 2398462

Printed and bound by CPI Group (UK) Ltd, Croydon, CR0 4YY

Atlantic Books
An Imprint of Atlantic Books Ltd
Ormond House
26–27 Boswell Street
London
WC1N 3JZ

www.atlantic-books.co.uk

For my Mother.

And for the 60 million refugees and internally
displaced people who are out there somewhere in
the world today, risking their lives to reach safety.

ILLUSTRATIONS

Map: Gulwali's Journey. Credit: Jamie Whyte

Images

1: Gulwali, aged 8, selling tailor supplies
2: Gulwali, aged 10, and his younger brother Nasir in Afghanistan
3: Laghman Province, Afghanistan. Credit: Naveed Yousafzai
4: Gulwali, aged 10, with his family in Afghanistan
5: Gulwali's Afghan passport photo, 2008
6: Gulwali with his foster father, Sean
7: Gulwali's proudest moment so far: carrying the Olympic torch in 2012. Credit: Capture the Event

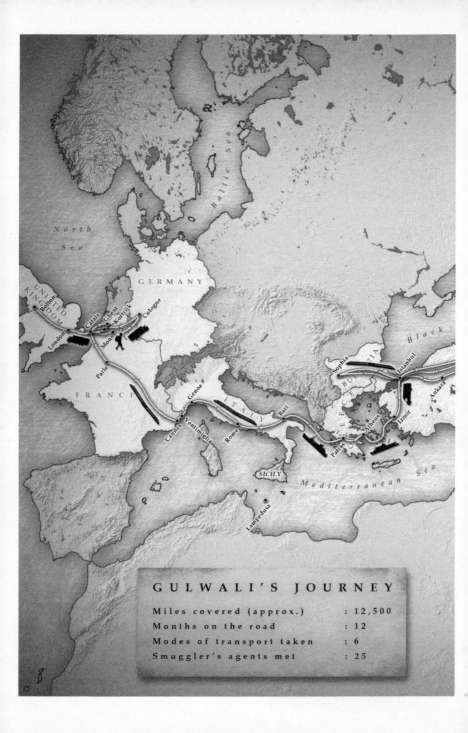

GULWALI'S JOURNEY

Miles covered (approx.)	: 12,500
Months on the road	: 12
Modes of transport taken	: 6
Smuggler's agents met	: 25

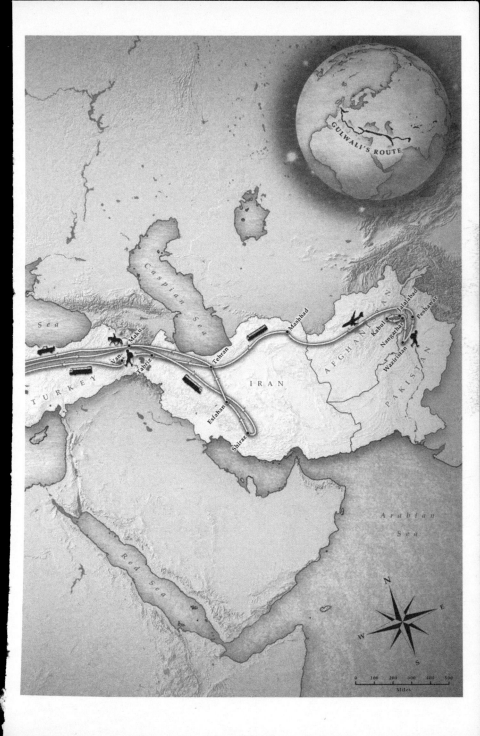

THE LIGHTLESS SKY

My Journey to Safety
as a Child Refugee

PROLOGUE

Before I died, I contemplated how drowning would feel.

It was clear to me now; this was how I would go: away from my mother's warmth, my father's strength and my family's love. The white waves were going to devour me, swallow me whole in their terrifying jaws and cast my young body aside to drift down into the cold, black depths.

'*Morya, Morya*,' I screamed, imploring my mother to come and snatch up her twelve-year-old son and lift him to safety.

The journey was supposed to be the beginning of my life, not the end of it.

I have heard somewhere that drowning is a peaceful death. Whoever said that hasn't watched grown men soil themselves with fear aboard an overcrowded, broken-down boat in the middle of a raging Mediterranean storm.

We'd eaten what little food and water the captain had on the boat within the first few hours. That had been more than a day ago. Now, fear, nausea and human filth were the only things in abundance. Hope had sunk some time during the endless night, dragging courage down with it. Despair filled my pockets like stones.

When we had set sail from Turkey, the white-haired Kurdish smuggler had promised we would reach Greece in a couple of hours. The man worked for a powerful, national-level agent, one of the shadowy businessmen who own and control the trade flow of desperate migrants moving through their countries. Money exchanges hands and deals are struck through a series of regional agents and local middle men. A powerful agent might have several junior agents and hundreds of local-level smugglers, drivers and guides in his employ, dealing with hundreds or even thousands of migrants and refugees at any time.

Yet, despite the Kurdish man's promises, it had been two days since we had set sail and we were still at sea.

On the morning of the second day, far out to sea, the captain changed the boat's flag from Turkish to Greek. This should have been a good sign, but something felt wrong. If we were in Greek waters, why hadn't we docked yet?

Everyone guessed that something had gone awry and the majority of the men, many of whom were locked below in the hull, began to panic. These were the men who had been first to board, the ones who had shoved weaker men aside so that they might be guaranteed a place on the boat. As they had got on, the captain had instructed them to go below. How could they have known that they would then be locked in behind a metal door? They hadn't expected to be trapped in a floating coffin, and had been screaming half the night, desperate to get out. I thanked the Creator I wasn't in there with them.

I had been one of the last to get on and I had been worried that I wouldn't get a space. By the time I was aboard, the hull had been already full and I was placed on the open deck – a lucky stroke of fate. As the only child on the boat, my chances of survival weren't great even at the best of times, but at least being on the open top deck allowed me a fighting chance.

There was no toilet anywhere on board. Men had soiled their clothes; others urinated into empty water bottles – some even saving the yellow liquid to drink. Desperation can be a great motivator. A foul mix of sea water, urine and faeces constantly lapped at our feet and, even in the open air, the stench burned my nose. Added to this, my bottom ached from sleeping and sitting on the hard wooden bench that ran around the edge of the deck. It was impossible to snatch more than a couple of minutes' sleep at a time. We were wedged so tightly together the only way to sleep was sitting up.

Hamid, a youth in his early twenties I had met just six days earlier, as we had hidden in a forest waiting for this boat journey, was sitting next to me. We took it in turns to rest our heads on each other's shoulders. My only other friend, Mehran, was one of the unfortunates trapped below deck. During the nights I heard him screaming in terror: 'Allah, please help us. Allah.'

The only reprieve came on the second night, when the captain allowed me and Hamid to go on to the roof of the boat. I don't know why I was chosen – maybe he felt a bit sorry for me because I was a small boy travelling alone.

Big waves rocked the boat incessantly, but being high up felt safer, somehow. It was such a relief to get fresh air and to be able to stretch my arms and legs, but at the same time I was terrifyingly conscious that even the slightest wrong movement could see me topple over the side and into the waves. I had no idea how to swim: if I fell in I'd be dead. I didn't expect that anyone would jump in to save me.

By dawn of our third day at sea our captain had become extremely agitated, constantly shouting into his radio in Turkish. I suppose he knew we couldn't stay out there for much longer without food or water.

I overheard a couple of the passengers, both Afghans like me, discussing whether it made sense to take control of the boat.

'Let's attack him and tie him up,' said one.

His friend shook his head. 'You fool. Who would get us into Greece if we did?'

The second man was right.

Like it or not, we were at the captain's, and the sea's, mercy.

By this point, I was beginning to feel delirious from lack of food and fresh water, and had started to hallucinate. My throat was so parched with thirst I was unable to breathe through my dry mouth. I kept thinking how nice it would be in Greece – just to wash my body, and not stink of piss and vomit. It sounds so stupid but rather than food, I began to fantasize about new clothes and how good they would feel on clean skin.

I was too focused on trying to stay alive to think much about the family I had left behind. Remembering them made me so unbearably sad, especially when I thought about my thirteen-year-old older brother, Hazrat. We had fled Afghanistan together, in fear for our lives, but he had been ripped away from me by the smugglers just days after we'd escaped.

It helped to try and focus on my mother's steely determination and imagine her voice urging me not to give up: 'Be safe, and do not come back.' They had been her last words to me and my brother before she had sent us both away to find sanctuary in strange lands. She had done it to try and save our lives, to help us escape from men who had wanted us dead.

But so many times I wished she hadn't.

Sometime in the afternoon of the third day, the engine started to choke and splutter, and then it cut out completely. The captain pretended for a while that everything was OK, but as time wore on he became even angrier, sweating and swearing as he tried to restart the ancient diesel motor. Eventually he got on to his radio again and started shouting at someone, this time in a language I didn't recognize.

Finally, after one particularly heated conversation, he asked a Turkish speaker to translate to us all.

'They are sending a new boat to get you. Don't worry.'

The captain smiled around at us all, displaying black, decaying teeth, but the look in his eyes gave the truth away, filling me with intense dread. Not all of us were going to survive, of this I was certain. I felt rage swell inside me at the slippery lies that had come so easily from him.

My fears were confirmed when the weather worsened. Curling tails of wind whipped the waves into frenzy, wailing like demonic beasts.

'*Morya, Morya.* I want *Morya.*' I screamed for my mother, the mother who was far away in Afghanistan. I was a lost little boy, about to meet his death in a cold, foreign sea.

Before getting on this boat, I had never even seen the sea before; the only knowledge I had had of it was from pictures in school text books. The reality was beyond the wildest reaches of my imagination. For me, those waves were truly the entrance to the gates of hell.

I managed to get into a higher position – on the roof of the wheel house. The move gave me air and space, but now each rushing wave swung me back and forth like a rag doll. My skinny fingers gripped the railings, my knuckles white and bloodless.

After a couple of hours of this, the boat began taking in water. Everyone started screaming, the people trapped below frantically pummelling at the locked door with fists and shoes.

'We are going to drown, let us out. For God's sake, let us out. We will die here.'

The captain waved a pistol and fired in the air, but no one paid him any attention. It seemed sure that the boat would overturn.

For a brief, strange moment I was calm, resigned: 'So, Gulwali, this is how you will die.' I imagined it – drowning – in explicit detail: the clean coolness of the water as darkness closed overhead, my life starting to flash before my eyes: my grandparents' wizened, wise faces; me at four years of age tending sheep by a mountain brook; walking proudly beside my father through the bazaar, him with his doctor's microscope tucked underneath his arm; sheltering from the baking sun under the grape vines with my brothers; the scent of hot steam as I helped to iron the clothes in my family's tailor shop; my mother's humming as she swept the yard.

No.

I wasn't giving up.

I had been travelling for almost a year. In that time, any childhood innocence had long since left me. I had suffered unspeakable indignities and dangers, watched men get beaten to a pulp, jumped from a speeding train, been left to suffocate for days on end in boiling-hot trucks, trekked over treacherous, mountainous border crossings, been imprisoned twice, and had bullets fired at me by border guards. There had rarely been a day when I hadn't witnessed man's inhumanity to man.

But, if I'd made it this far, I could make it now. A survival instinct deep within me spurred me on. I didn't want to die, not here, not like this, not gasping and choking for breath in the cold depths of the sea. How would anyone find my body?

My mother's face flashed before me again. 'It's not safe for you here, Gulwali. I'm sending you away for your own safety.'

How would she feel if she could see me now? Would she ever know what had happened to me?

That thought was enough to give me strength. I knew the captain had lied to us again – there was no other boat coming to get us, and this one was sinking fast. There was no way I was going to follow his orders to stay down and hide.

I searched in my bag and pulled out the red shirt I'd managed to buy in Istanbul, the one I was saving to wear as celebration for getting to Greece. I started waving and screaming: 'Help, help. Somebody help us.'

I hadn't realized it, but the captain was behind me. As I turned, he kicked me full in the face, sending me tumbling down to the deck and almost over the side. Dazed and in agony, I clung on to the railing for dear life. The boat rocked back and forth but still I held my hand as high I could, waving my shirt. The captain came for me again. I think he may have intended to push me overboard but by then others had followed my lead and had started screaming for help too, waving whatever they could to attract attention.

The boat gave a heavy belch and the bow dropped deeply into the water. Everyone screamed again and tried to move to the stern; I was still dazed from the captain's kick so could only try to protect myself from the stampeding legs.

The boat was finished, it was obvious. With a sickening wheeze, the stern settled heavily in the water too.

Now, we truly were sinking.

I closed my eyes and began to pray.

Goes from Gulwali's near death experience to his early childhood in Chapter 1.

CHAPTER ONE

'I found you in a box floating down the river.'

I eyed my grandmother suspiciously.

Her deep brown eyes danced mischievously, set within a face that was deeply lined and etched by a lifetime's toil in the harsh Afghan sun.

I was four years old, and had just asked the classic question of where I'd come from. 'You are joking with me, *Zhoola Abhai.*'

Calling her 'old mother' always made her smile.

'Why would an old woman lie? I found you in the river, and I made you mine.' With that she gave a toothless chuckle and wrapped me in her strong arms – the one place in all the world where I felt most safe, loved and content. I was my grandparents' second grandchild, born after my older brother, but I felt like I was their favourite, with a very special place in their hearts.

We are from the Pashtun tribe, which is known for both its loyalty and its fierceness. Home was the eastern Afghan province of Nangarhar, the most populated province in Afghanistan, and also a place of vast deserts and towering mountains. It is also a very traditional place, where local power structures run along feudal and tribal lines.

I was born in 1994, just as the Taliban government took control of Afghanistan. For many Afghans, and for my family, the ultra-conservative Taliban were a good thing. They were seen as bringing peace and security to a country that for over fifteen years had suffered a Russian invasion, followed by a brutal civil war.

For much of their marriage, my grandparents had lived in a refugee camp in the north-western Pakistani city of Peshawar. The refugee camp was also where my parents had met and been married. By the time I was born, Afghanistan was not at war, and relatively stable under Taliban rule.

My earliest memory is of being four years old and running with my grandfather's sheep high in the mountains. Grandfather, or *Zoor aba* ('old father'), as I called him in my native language of Pashtu, was a nomadic farmer and shepherd. He was a short man, made taller by the traditional grey turban he always wore. His hazel-flecked green eyes shone with a vital energy that belied his years.

Each spring he walked his flock of thickly fleeced sheep and spiral-horned cattle to the furthest reaches of the mountains in search of fresh and fertile pasture. My grandparents' home, a traditional tent made from wooden poles and embroidered cloth, went with them. Two donkeys carried the tent on their backs, along with the drums of cooking oil, sacks of rice, and the flour my grandmother needed to bake naan bread.

I would watch transfixed as my grandmother spread and kneaded sticky dough along a flat rock before baking it over the embers of an open fire. She cooked on a single metal pan which hung from chains slung over some branches balanced over the fire. I loved helping her gather armfuls of wild nettles which she boiled to make a delicately scented, delicious soup. I don't know how she did it, but everything she created in that pan tasted of pure heaven to a constantly hungry little boy like me.

Every year, as the leaves began to turn into autumn's colours, they would head back down to lower ground, making sure to return to civilization before the harsh snows of winter descended and trapped them on the mountains' slopes. There they joined the rest of their family, their six children and assorted grandchildren, in the rambling house that was home to our entire extended family. Our house then was a very simple but lovely, single-storey stone-built structure perched above a clear, flowing river.

I was my grandparents' shadow so I was thrilled when, aged three, they took me with them the next time they returned to the mountains. Their youngest daughter, my auntie, Khosala ('happy'), was also with us. She was fifteen and like a big sister to me.

For the next three and a half years I shared my grandparents' nomadic lifestyle, at night falling soundly asleep beneath a vast, star-filled mountain sky, safely tucked up inside the tent nestled between the pair of them.

Grandfather loved his family with a fierce passion, and laughter came easily to both him and my grandmother. I don't think I ever saw him angry. One time I accidentally almost took his eye out with a catapult. Blood was streaming down his cheek from where my badly aimed flying rock had cut it. It must have really hurt but he didn't chastise me. Instead, with characteristic humour, he managed to make a joke of it: 'Good shot, Gulwali.'

My grandmother was sturdily built and bigger than my grandfather. She was definitely the boss, but I could see they adored each other. Love isn't something people really discuss in Afghanistan. Families arrange marriage matches according to social structure, tribal structure or even to facilitate business deals; no one expects or even wants to be in love. You just do as your parents demand and make a marriage work the best you can – you have to, because divorce is culturally so very shameful that it is practically forbidden.

It was explained to me once – by my grandfather – that a woman is too flighty and unsure of her own mind to understand the consequences of leaving her marriage. Besides, who would look after her if she did? I knew only of one woman whose husband had divorced her. She'd been taken in by her brother but this was a great embarassment and shame to their family. She had been lucky that he had accepted her and hadn't turned her away on to the streets.

My grandparents would never have dreamt of breaking up, even if they could have done. They had married when she was fifteen and he eighteen, meeting for the first time on the day of their wedding, as is still often the norm. But anyone could see that their years together had given the pair a special bond.

By the time I was five I was already a skilled shepherd, able to shear off a fleece all on my own. I recognized every animal individually and loved how they knew the sound of my whistle. I particularly enjoyed watching my grandfather's two sheepdogs working. One was a large, thick-headed beast and the other a small, wiry terrier-type dog. They would run rings around the flock, corralling them into order. And when the local vet, a man who traversed the furthest reaches of the mountains to service his clients, came to treat the sheep, I remember thinking how brilliant it might be to be a vet myself when I grew up. I was fascinated by him and the various implements he used.

It was about as wonderfully simple and rural a life as you can possibly imagine.

In winter, I would be so proud of coming back down into town with Grandfather by my side. We carried with us precious bounty from the mountains: wild fruits, honey, and *koch* – a type of thick, unpasteurized butter that we would spread thickly on freshly baked naan for breakfast. And Grandfather would always take me to the bustling bazaar, where he would trade his wares for supplies of rice or a new farming implement. Everything was plentiful.

Coming back down to the family home meant I got to see my

parents and siblings, too. Although I loved being with the sheep,

I did miss my parents. And, of course, they'd missed me too, so I was very spoilt when I came home.

 As is the custom within our tribe, my parents were distantly related: my mother was my paternal grandfather's niece, his sister's daughter. My mother was fifteen and my father twenty when they married in the refugee camp to which my grandparents had fled after the 1979 Russian invasion of Afghanistan. During the fifteen or so long years of occupation and the civil war that followed, it is estimated that some 1.5 million people – a third of Afghanistan's population – died, and a similar number became refugees.

In the midst of all this chaos, my grandfather had somehow scrimped and struggled enough to ensure that my father, his eldest son, became the first man in the family to receive a higher education by studying to become a doctor. This caused a huge sense of family pride, and was something which really made my grandparents role-models for us all. They were the moral heart of our family.

My father's brothers, my two middle uncles, were also successes. They were both tailors who ran a large and profitable workshop in the bazaar. The fourth and youngest uncle, Lala, wasn't around as often. He had a senior role within the Taliban. He used to come to visit us, bringing Taliban soldiers with him. I thought he was cool and exuded power. I knew he was an important man but didn't really understand why or exactly what it was he did.

My mother's parents had stayed living in Pakistan, so at that time I didn't know them very well. My mother was one of twelve daughters. Her father was a very educated man – a mullah – and he had educated his daughters, something that was quite unusual among Pashtuns in those days. My mother was the only woman in our entire household who could read.

I think my parents were happy together: they certainly seemed it. But in Afghanistan a child knows better than to discuss or ask these things. There are certain boundaries you do not cross. I did

13

once ask my grandmother if she liked my grandfather. She just laughed and replied: 'I think he was the one who liked me.' As innocent as it sounds, in our conservative community that was quite a risky thing to say, even for an old lady.

My parents had three boys by then: myself; my brother Hazrat, who was a year older than I was; and Noor who was a year younger. Hazrat and Noor were very close, and used to pick on me a little bit. I was jealous of their little world of private jokes and unspoken communication. I think I was a bit of a loner, possibly because I was used to the solitude of the shepherding life.

My life changed completely when I was six, when my father and his three brothers ordered my grandparents back home. They worried the pair were getting too old for the nomadic life and wanted them to stay closer to the family so that they could be better looked after. There was also the matter of family honour: my father's profession as a doctor meant he was a highly respected man in our strictly conservative community. It didn't look good within the rigid mores of our tribal society to have the father of such a man living like a poor *kochi*, or nomad. Such was my father's standing, in fact, that my brothers and I were rarely referred to by outsiders by our names: we were known as 'the sons of the doctor'. Even Grandfather was known as 'father of the doctor'.

Both my grandparents loved their life, so were deeply resistant to the idea at first, but in the end they gave in. Grandfather sold his entire flock of sheep – more than 200 strong – for a combination of cash and a shiny new red tractor. The whole extended family – parents, two uncles with their wives, my father's unmarried sister Auntie Khosala, grandparents, myself and siblings – then moved to a new house in the district of Hisarak. This house was another single-storey building, made of mud and thatch, with lots of rooms running off a central, communal kitchen. Each night we

new setting

ate together sitting on the floor, a bounty of food – usually rice, meat, naan and spinach – spread out on a large tablecloth in the centre of the room. It was a happy home, full of chatter and noise. I still loved the company of my grandparents and insisted on sleeping in their room.

women's role

My mother, as the senior wife, managed the running of the home, while my uncle's wives, junior in both age and position, did the majority of the cooking and cleaning. Her outer nature, like most Afghan women, was steely and unemotional, and it was no wonder. Most women work from dawn until dusk doing housework. Washing is done by hand, while wood and fresh water must be collected daily. There is always bread to be baked and hot tea to be freshly brewed before husbands and children awake in the morning. It's also a land where two out of five Afghan children die before their fifth birthday, so it is easier not to show too much love to children. A year after Noor was born, my parents had twin boys, who sadly both died within a few days of their birth.

women discrimination

But love is hard to hide when it's a part of your very being, as it was for my mother. Under that commanding exterior, her survival mask, I often saw her gentle side – the way she would fuss over me when mending a scrape or bruise, her worry when one of us was ill, her obvious pride when recalling our accomplishments to a visitor or one of my aunts. She had a very deep voice for a woman but was tall and elegant, with a long nose and round, brown eyes. People said I looked like her. She smiled rarely, except for the secret grins that flashed across her features when I was naughty or did something funny. She was tough because she had to be but, underneath, there was an unmistakable warmness. Her family meant everything to her.

Culturally, it was a great shame to allow your women outside in case they were seen by other men, so my mother and aunts rarely left the house. On the rare occasions they did, they were completely covered by a burqa – as was the rule under the Taliban government. Inside the house they wore long shawls to cover their hair. It would have been seen as very bad for anyone outside of the immediate family, even a male cousin, to see their heads uncovered, even in the house.

I was an extremely pious child, and this was a rule I took upon myself to enforce: 'The wrath of Allah will be upon you – go and cover your head,' I used to say to my aunties. The young wives worked hard all day baking naan bread, and cooking over the open fire. If I wasn't playing with my brothers or cousins, I often sat with them in the kitchen, bossing them around and ordering them to bring me tea. When my uncles were away, I would often refuse to let them walk to collect firewood, visit people or attend family weddings. I saw this as protecting the family honour. I would make a big show of insisting on collecting the wood for them so they didn't have to: 'Why do you need to go outside?' I would say. 'You are the queens of this house.' This was something I'd heard my uncles say many times. As was another saying in Pashtu: '*Khor yor ghor*', which was the two places for a woman: home or grave. Sometimes I would wake my aunts in the middle of the night to bring food for a newly arrived guest – my father's profession meant people looking for help would turn up at our house at all times of the night and day.

My father was much more relaxed with the women than his brothers were, but I think I must have absorbed more of my uncle's stricter attitudes. I was a bratty child, and I enjoyed exerting my power over my aunts. I know they loved me but I think I must have really got on their nerves at times. And if they complained about my behaviour, my uncles would tell them to be quiet and to obey me. It was not the best way to keep a child's ego in check, but this was how it was done. In our conservative culture, males have all the power, even little boys.

The only time I got seriously told off for picking on my aunts was by my mother. One of my uncle's wives couldn't have children, and this was a source of consternation to the whole family. 'If you don't get a baby soon, I will get my uncle a new wife,' I rudely said to her one day. The poor woman cried. My mother was absolutely furious with me and made me go and apologize at once. My aunt hugged me and I remember realizing I'd said something really mean, even though I didn't understand the severity of it at the time. It took nine years for her to get pregnant, but she went on to have six daughters.

Another of my aunts, my father's sister Meena, married a man who lived outside the district. This was a really big deal because it was the first time anyone in the family had married outside the tribe, and people were not happy about it.

Auntie Khosala was next to be married. She and I had a special bond because of all the time we'd spent together in the mountains, and I felt sad for her because although she couldn't read – she was naturally very smart – the man she married, her first cousin, was not only illiterate but obviously thick. But the match had been arranged when she was a baby: my grandmother had been pregnant at the same time as the wife of Grandfather's brother, and when the babies were born within days of each other, my grandfather and his brother had decreed that the two infants would marry when they were older. Within our culture these things are not said lightly; once said, they cannot be unsaid, and must go on to happen.

Aside from being a farmer's wife, my grandmother was also a traditional midwife. Pashtun men do not like to take their wives to a doctor – it's considered extremely shameful if anyone, especially a man, puts his hands on your wife. But the Taliban government had banned female doctors from practising. In those circumstances, it was not surprising that since coming back from the mountains, my grandmother's skills had been in great demand.

I often went with her to attend the births, but it was not something I enjoyed. I would be left to sit outside, helping to look after the family's children or talking to the woman's husband. Sometimes, if the family was poor, their house only had one room, so I would be forced to sit in the corner as the woman screamed and bled.

Childbirth horrified me. The labour could go on for hours. I would sit quietly, childishly willing and wishing the woman would get on and push the stupid thing out so we could go home.

My grandmother knew I was squeamish about the whole thing so she teased me mercilessly: 'Did you see all that blood, Gulwali? Did you look, you naughty child?'

'No, I did NOT.'

'Ahhh, you lie to me.' She'd give me a toothless grin and rub her fingers through my hair.

'Get off me. You were touching those women.'

That only made her cackle more as she grabbed me in a bear hug, wiping her hands all over my head as I squealed with horror.

Some men would have forbidden her from her midwifery work, especially because it often meant being out on the streets at all hours. But Grandfather was very proud of her and liked to joke about the hundreds of babies she'd 'given birth' to.

My family owned various shops in the bazaar, including the tailor's workshop run by my two middle uncles, and my father's doctor's surgery. Along the flat roofs ran a network of vines laden with fat grapes, which we sold commercially. We also had many fields out of town that grew wheat and different vegetables; at busy harvest times, we employed as many as 100 men locally. And before the Taliban took over and banned it, my grandfather had also farmed opium and cannabis – something that was entirely usual for Afghan farmers.

In warm weather, the whole town would become burningly hot, and the brown sandy dust of the town's desert landscape got everywhere, stinging eyes and blocking noses. My mother and aunts would fight a losing battle to keep it outside the house, seemingly spending all day sweeping with a stiff broom, or banging rugs against the walls to keep them clean. Their efforts were futile. The sand collected in little piles in the corners of the rooms, on door frames, behind chairs, and covered windowsills. And with the dusty sand came all manner of insects and bugs: dangerous scorpions, and the little black ants which, in particular, fascinated me. I loved to watch them mobilize into lines of activity and scurry towards the kitchen. Of course, keeping ants out of the rice stores was another lost battle. Whenever I heard my mother let out a long groan as she opened one of the earthenware containers which kept the grains cool, I chuckled because I knew how funny her angry face would be as she scowled at the infestation of ant invaders in our dinner-to-be.

Aged six, after my grandparents' nomadic activities were curtailed, I was enrolled in the same local school that my brothers already attended. I literally had to be dragged there on my first day by one of my uncles, as I yelled all the while: 'I'm not going. I don't want to go.' I wanted to go back to the mountains and run with the sheep, not be stuck in a classroom. But I soon settled in and became a very studious, hard-working pupil.

The most fun we had at school was in winter, when we had to fix the roof of our classroom. The building had been badly damaged in the war so none of the rooms had ceilings. In the summer that wasn't a problem, but in winter each class was dispatched to cut down trees and help drag them back to make a temporary roof. I loved it.

In Afghanistan, children aren't mollycoddled; they are expected to pitch in and work alongside the adults. Before mosque each morning there were duties in the fields: cutting hay for the cows, watering the crops, harvesting the vegetables, collecting firewood and jerry cans full of water from the nearby well. All the kids went,

women discrimination

even the two newest additions to our family, my little sisters Taja and Razia. As female education was banned by the Taliban government, during the day they helped my mother and aunts with the cooking and cleaning. In our culture, it's seen as important that girls learn these duties from a very young age, so that by the time they are married they know how to manage the running of a household. They also learned how to sew and embroider, as well as Quranic studies. After those chores, we went to the local mosque to pray, before getting ready for school.

We didn't really play outside on the street; the kids who played out were seen as the bad kids. My parents thought it showed bad manners and a lazy attitude. So, after walking home from school, my brothers used to hang out in the grape vines, making sure nobody tried to help themselves.

I preferred spending time with the tailor uncles. I was fascinated by the whirr of the sewing machines and the folds of the differently coloured woven cottons and wool they used to make *shalwar kameez*, the traditional, loose-fitting tunic and trousers worn by Afghan men. At times of celebration, they were overrun with orders, and my uncles would be at the shop day and night sewing wildly to get everything finished. I used to help by cutting out the fabrics and dealing with the customers.

Smart Kid

They were very proud of me when I devised my own system of numbering and organization, so that when people came to get their clothes I knew, among the hundreds of garments, where everything was. I took joy in the order and neatness of my system: to me, it was a little world of my own – a way of bringing a sense of order. A long day spent helping them checking off my lists and hanging the clothes ready for the next day was one of my biggest pleasures. By then, I knew I definitely wanted to become a tailor too. I was very enterprising – I even had my own little after-school stall outside their workshop, which sold threads and buttons.

The journey to and from school took us right past my father's surgery, so occasionally Hazrat, Noor and I would pop in to say hello to him. I used to sweep the floor for him or go and fill a jug with fresh water from the modern pump near the governor's house. I always felt sorry for him working so hard in his packed surgery, so I wanted to make sure he had fresh, cool water to drink.

In the early mornings, my father would do his rounds in the local hospital. Treating malaria, the mosquito-borne disease which blighted the local area, was his specialism. For the rest of the day he ran his surgery, and people came from miles around for him to treat their ailments.

His surgery was full of strange-looking equipment. I recall a little wooden box which used to store his dentistry tools – I remember watching in horrified fascination as he pulled a patient's head back and used metal pliers to prise out a rotten tooth. Whether it was stitching a wound, healing a snake or scorpion bite or setting a broken limb, my father's face was always a mask of studious concentration.

My father's most precious piece of kit was his microscope, a very rare thing in those days. It was too valuable to leave in the surgery so, at night, he used to carry it home under his arm, covered with a black cloth to keep it free from dust. He was immensely popular, and couldn't walk through the bazaar without people wanting to shake his hand or offer him gifts of fruit or sweets.

Sometimes, when the surgery was quiet, he used to sit outside in the sun on a wood-framed bench with a seat of knotted string, and chat with his friends or argue about politics. I used to love listening as he and his friends debated the ills of the world and would sit quietly, cross-legged on the ground, taking it all in.

I got the sense that he was a good man, a generous one. He had two big books in his office detailing the people to whom he had loaned money, and he never turned anyone anyway if they needed medicine and couldn't pay. The ledgers were very big – clearly, a lot of people owed him money.

The most intimate times I spent with my father were during the night, when patients who had walked from outlying villages with a medical emergency banged on our gate, hoping to be seen by him. To treat them he would have to take them to the surgery where his bandages and medicines were stored. In those days, electricity was scarce and only came via a generator, something we limited to using three or four hours a day. As my father helped the patient, I would walk ahead carrying a lantern to help light our path through the darkness. I felt of great consequence as I stepped through the pitch-black streets holding the lamp aloft. It was a source of pride to me to ensure that no one stepped into a puddle or twisted their ankle in a pothole.

One of my most treasured memories was when my grandfather ran away with me. My father had told me off for reasons I can't remember – I must have done something very naughty indeed, because my father rarely chastised me. My grandfather got really cross with my father, scooped me up into his arms and set off into the mountains.

'You don't deserve this boy. He's coming with me.'

In reality, I was a convenient excuse for the wily old man to get away for a few days. He had wanted to go on a trip to search for lapis lazuli, the blue semi-precious stone that is one of Afghanistan's most precious natural resources. But he knew that there was no way his sons would approve, so engineering a fight with my father over me had given him a convenient way out.

He and I had a truly wonderful week playing truant and searching for the stones. When we came back, my misdemeanours had been long forgotten – Grandfather was the one in trouble this time.

It was to be my last happy memory before my whole world changed for ever.

CHAPTER TWO

Even before the arrival of the Taliban, my family were religiously and culturally conservative in their outlook. We lived by *Pashtunwali* – the strict rules every Pashtun must abide by. The codes primarily govern social etiquette, such as how to treat a guest. Courage is a big part of the Pashtun code too, as is loyalty, and honouring your family and your women. No one writes it down for you – there's no book to learn it from; it's just a way of life that you are born into, which has remained unchanged for centuries. And, like all Pashtuns, I accepted them unquestioningly. They were – and still are – a source of cultural pride.

The Taliban government also saw it as their duty to keep the peace on the streets. My father told me that before the Taliban came to power, towards the end of the civil war, women and young girls were frequently raped if they went outside, while houses were robbed and children kidnapped and held for ransom. He said the country had been in ruins, but that the Taliban had returned order.

The Taliban position was simple: strong social controls and Sharia law was the true path to both peace and God. To me and the male members of my family this made perfect sense, because it wasn't really so different from *Pashtunwali*.

No one asked the women for their views, however – they didn't get to have a say in these kinds of political matters. But I think the

unreal

 # women discriminated

23

whole family was in unity. We all understood our different roles within the household.

I was aware that not everyone agreed with this, however. A very few of my friends at school told me their parents feared the Taliban and thought they were bad people. They said they were taking our country in the wrong direction and preventing development. They also said that they abused women.

When I heard this, it made me angry. My uncle, Lala was a very senior Taliban, so how could they possibly be bad? And yet their rules certainly were strict – men's beards had to be a certain length and they had to wear traditional, baggy clothes at all times, while women had to wear the burqa so their faces couldn't be seen, and soft-soled shoes so they couldn't be heard. In addition, you had to pray at fixed times of the day, and if you were seen on the streets or caught working when you should be praying, it was deemed a crime.

Fridays are the main day of prayer in Islam. When the mosque loudspeakers blasted out the hauntingly beautiful call to prayer, everyone in the whole town would stop whatever they were doing and go straight to mosque. The Taliban had a special team, called the Vice and Virtue Committee, who made sure everyone obeyed. They wore black turbans and patrolled the streets in four-wheel drives, pulling over and leaping out of the vehicle if they saw something amiss.

One sunny Monday afternoon we were in the tailor shop when we heard a big commotion outside. A man stuck his head through the shop door, his face ablaze with excitement: 'Come on. Twenty lashes.'

My uncles quickly locked up the shop and urged me to follow them to the bazaar. A large crowd had already gathered at the scene: two men in black turbans stood over a kneeling man, who was naked from the waist up.

'Speak. Admit your crime,' said one of the turbans.

The man said nothing.

'Speak.' The turban smacked the back of the man's head.

'I—'

'Louder.'

The man mumbled something, but it was impossible to hear it over the hum of the crowd.

The turban turned to the crowd with a smirk. 'This man did not attend prayer on Friday. He was found inside his home.'

The crowd jeered at this seemingly obscene crime.

'Do you have an excuse?'

This time the man looked up and spoke loudly. 'My wife was sick. I couldn't leave her. I thought she was dying.'

At this, both turbans roared with laughter. The crowd followed suit.

The second turban spoke this time, his voice ringing out as clear as a bell: 'The Islamic Emirates of Afghanistan gives the sentence of twenty lashes with justice to this man for his crime. May this sentence be an example for anyone else thinking of committing such a crime. Anyone who goes beyond the limits of God's law and against His rules, let it be known this will be their fate.'

He lifted a thin reed high into the air.

'By Allah the most merciful, you have been sentenced to a fitting punishment for your crime.'

As he brought the reed down on the man's back with a loud swish, the crowd roared and cheered.

The turban hit the man again and again and again.

By the time it was over, their victim had crumpled into a heap, his back a bloody mess. I don't know if anyone helped him or if they took him to prison after that, because my two uncles said it was time to get back to the shop.

Five minutes later, the sewing machines whirred into life and I was back to hanging clothes as if nothing had happened.

Many times after that I saw people get lashed. I once saw an old man beaten with a wire cable because his beard was too short: the black turbans would grab a beard with their hands to measure it – if the person measuring it had big hands and you had a wispy beard, then it was unlucky for you. Other times they gave out smaller punishments, such as painting someone's face black and marching them around, encouraging people to abuse them.

I suppose it sounds shocking, but this was all I knew. I had been taught by Uncle Lala that the Taliban only punished someone when they broke the law, so in my child's mind if someone was suffering this way they must have deserved it.

But one incident will always haunt me.

Grandfather and I were with a friend of his on our way to visit some relatives in a different district. We had stopped for *chai*, tea, in a small town. As we sat outside the tearoom, we watched several men begin walking and running in one direction. My grandfather stopped a man to ask what was happening.

'Justice, my friend. Justice.'

Curious to see what was happening, we followed. At the edge of the village, scores of men had gathered in a large clearing. Some of them were shouting, '*Allah akbhar*. Praise be to God,' while others were whooping with joy.

At first I thought it must be some kind of sporting event – maybe a dog- or cock-fight. I strained my head to see what they were looking at, and my grandfather's friend lifted me on to his shoulders.

I saw a woman. She was covered in a burqa with a black blindfold tied around her eyes. Her hands were tied behind her back with rope.

A man next to her – I guessed a Taliban official from the Justice Department – raised his hand. The crowd went silent. 'This woman is a dirty woman. She is an adulteress, a whore.'

The crowd roared insults at her.

Talibs 'The Islamic Emirates of Afghanistan gives the sentence of death to this woman for her crime. May this sentence be an example. She has been condemned to death by stoning. Let it begin.'

At that, he placed his hand on the woman's shoulder, almost tenderly, and walked her towards a dug-out area of earth. He took her arm and helped her get into it, so that she was standing in it, up to her waist. She didn't try to resist.

It was then that I noticed the rocks, sitting in a pile to the front of the crowd.

The Talib walked to the pile and picked up a large stone. He waved it above his head like a trophy. 'By Allah the most merciful, you have been sentenced to a fitting punishment for your crime.'

He walked back towards her, until he was a couple of feet away. Then he threw the stone hard, so that it smashed against her head.

Sick The crowd went wild. All at once men began picking up the rocks and throwing them at the woman. At first, she didn't seem to move, even as they hit her, but then one little rock caught the back of her head sharply, and she began to try to wriggle her way out of the pit. But as she did so, another hail of stones and rocks caught her and she fell backwards. After that, it was a bit of a blur for me, just a hail of rocks and a lot of shouting.

The whole thing only took a couple of minutes.

I don't think I really understood what I was seeing. The noise, the excitement of the crowd, the calm silence of my grandfather and his friend – I didn't enjoy it, but I didn't cry either. As I sat on the shoulders of Grandpa's friend, I looked around and saw other boys my age on shoulders too. Their expressions were blank but their eyes were confused, mirroring my own.

With hindsight, I can see what barbarity this was. But it has to be put into context. The country was recovering from a war in which brutality had known no bounds. Millions of people had been killed, thousands of women raped and children slaughtered. There had been a complete breakdown of law and order with no national governance. Their mantra was this: 'If you don't accept peace or our rules, we will force it on you.'

My grandfather called life under the Taliban: 'The best of times we are living in.' Given that he'd lived most of his life in the insanity of war, I don't think it is too surprising that he and many other Afghans felt this way.

 But, as is ever the case in the geopolitics of my country, we were about to get out of the frying pan and into the fire.

CHAPTER THREE

I was seven years old.

I remember running between the kitchen and the guest house, my mother handing me pots of tea to take to the assorted tribal elders and Taliban fighters who had amassed in our home. The air was thick with tension and heavy with discussion.

'We didn't have anything to do with it, so why should we bow down to the imperialists?'

'Bin Laden is our guest. *Pashtunwali* must prevail.'

'Our great country will never cede to this pressure.'

A Saudi man called Bin Laden, who Uncle Lala told me was a great freedom fighter, had attacked America. TV was banned under the Taliban so we didn't see any images of it, but the radio had been broadcasting non-stop news about it. Thousands of people had died in the attacks. They said people had been jumping from windows to escape. I had been told that Americans were infidels who didn't follow Islam but as I listened to these stories, I felt sad at the news and thinking about the families of the people who had died. Given my family history of living in refugee camps, I think I had an innate understanding that, wherever they were from, all people suffered in war and conflict.

Now, just days after the attack, the US was angry with Afghanistan, blaming us for it. This was because the Taliban were refusing to bow to American pressure and hand over Bin Laden, who was said to be sheltering in Tora Bora, a place only a couple of hours' drive away from where we lived. The US had threatened to attack if they didn't hand him over, but the Taliban refused because, under the rules of *Pashtunwali*, he was our guest, and a guest is under the protection of the host.

There was a swell of patriotism. No one really believed America's threats, mostly because everyone knew the Taliban had had nothing to do with the attack themselves, and we assumed the Americans accepted that too.

But, it turned out, this wasn't a view shared or understood by the world. Within days the US, supported by European countries, had invaded my country, and the Taliban began to retreat.

When it started, we could see US fighter jets overhead. For a day or so they only circled the skies, not doing anything. Taliban troops were everywhere, and lots of local people were volunteering to fight with them.

My father was expecting the worst and was busy trying to amass extra medical supplies. He had also ordered my mother to pack bags and food and prepare to take us children to the shelter of a nearby bunker. There were several concrete bunkers on the outskirts of town, a legacy of the civil war.

The following day, the US began to bomb Tora Bora. We could hear the sound but it was far enough away for us not to be at direct risk. Within days, however, bombs rained from the sky directly overhead.

It was terrifying.

It was never clear exactly where the planes would come from. We would hear the screech of Taliban anti-aircraft missiles attacking them as they approached, then there would be the sound of deafening, terrifying explosions. The whole ground used to shake with the force of the bombing. After each bombardment we would come outside for air and look up at the trails of smoke the B52 bombers left behind in the sky.

Pretty much every type of bomb except nuclear bombs rained down on my country. Even today, children are born with diseases and deformities caused by the toxic effects of that time, something that makes me very angry.

The children and aunts huddled in the bomb shelter with other families. Uncle Lala was the regional commander for the Taliban, leading the fight against the invaders. My father stayed in the hospital, treating the hundreds of wounded. My grandfather insisted on staying in the house to stop it being looted. I was proud of them all, for different reasons, but I was most worried about my father. I feared the bombs might hit the hospital.

I longed to run to the solace of my mountain paradise, but it wasn't safe. Fighting echoed across the hills. It seemed the whole of Afghanistan was under attack, and for days we couldn't sleep. I thought it was only a matter of time before our bunker hiding place was discovered.

I expected to die at any moment.

It was only later that I learned that the area around our home had been the last frontline; Uncle Lala had been one of the last local commanders of the Taliban to hold his position against the US-led coalition forces. We were told that his courage allowed busloads of fighters to escape Kabul into neighbouring Pakistan; in my childish eyes, this made him something of a hero. Soon after that final battle, he fled the country himself, and we didn't know where he had gone. I feared he'd been caught and killed, but we had no way of knowing.

For us, life then began under occupation. Suddenly, US troops were everywhere, convoys of armoured vehicles speeding down the road. The first time I saw Western troops on the ground, I was so scared of their big guns. They looked like something from another planet. From a safe distance, my brothers and I would throw stones at them.

After a while, seeing them became normal.

The pressure and political turmoil impacted on all of us. My father took the decision for the family to leave the district and go back to the neighbouring district where he had been born. Things were slightly safer there.

Not long after the US troops landed, the aid workers arrived – white Land Cruisers emblazoned with the blue UN sign were everywhere. They started to rebuild clinics and schools. My father conceded this was a good thing but he was still very disapproving that it was 'foreigners' who were building this new infrastructure, and not our own government.

Girls slowly started to return to school. Under the Taliban they had been banned, and that was all I had known. It was so strange to see them wearing their black uniforms and little white head-scarves, walking to school. They generally walked in groups for their own safety, because some of the boys used to take pleasure in cursing them and throwing stones at them as they walked. My two sisters did go school for a short while, but not for long. My father deemed it too unsafe. I was happy about this. Not because I wanted to deny them an education, but because I didn't want any of my friends telling me they had seen my sisters outside.

There is a religious *hadith*, or saying, that discourages gossip. It states that gossiping is *haram*, forbidden – *as though you eat the flesh of your brother*. But the reality is that it is rife. And most gossip in our community was about females – whether they deserved it or not. So damaging can this be, that if anyone says anything bad about a girl, harasses them or accuses them of misbehaving, some families either go and kill the person responsible for the slur, or move house or, in even more extreme cases, murder the girl, regardless of whether she was innocent of all wrongdoing. Either way, taking some form of action is seen as essential, otherwise the family reputation is destroyed.

As I didn't want any harm to befall my sisters, I genuinely thought that their staying away from school and safe from all of these risks was the best option. I was still as pious as I ever was; in some ways, even more so, since the arrival of the 'foreigners'.

Everything was still new, unsettled – we were still technically at war. The whole country was in a state of uncertainty. There were fights between different rival groups, some of whom supported the old Taliban regime, others who were now siding with the Americans.

The idea that the Taliban left and suddenly everything in my country improved overnight is nonsense. To many people, like my grandfather, it felt as if the world had collapsed into immorality.

And as bad as the Taliban might have been, the NATO forces were far from perfect too. I witnessed one incident, which, like the stoning, still gives me nightmares today.

We were driving to Jalalabad, the nearest city to us. US armoured vehicles were up ahead and the road was blocked on both sides, meaning no one could pass. Suddenly, a car – full of people, including children – swerved out and drove towards them from the oncoming side. I don't know why they did this – maybe someone was sick, perhaps they had another kind of emergency – but for whatever reason, they drove on.

There was a hail of gunfire from the American soldiers.

The car burst into flames, killing everyone inside the vehicle. I remember a silent scream filling my head as my father held me to him and tried to shield my eyes.

'Why? Why, why, *why*?'

There were so many incidents like this one that I lost track

33

of them. We used to hear the stories – accidental bombings of weddings, killings of innocent farmers, US soldiers shooting anyone they thought might be Taliban. People disappeared into the hands of the Special Forces and were not seen again for years. Women waited for husbands who never returned. Their crime – who knew?

There were also the petty humiliations of life under occupation. There were near-constant roadblocks. One poor woman gave birth by the side of the road because the soldiers refused to let her and her husband past.

I hated these people who had come to conquer us. I saw these latest invaders as worse than the Russians.

Politically, though, things became stable enough for Uncle Lala to return; it turned out he had been sheltering in Pakistan. He offered his services to the newly democratic Afghan government. The new district governor knew him well and knew what an intelligent man he was, and he gave him a very senior role running the prison service. But some local people feared and mistrusted him because he had been such a key figure in the Taliban. Others were jealous of my family's success, and saw denouncing my uncle as a way to get back at us. The Taliban were still thriving, only underground, in secret meetings and bunkers. The US military was hungry for information and people used old rivalries as an excuse to inform on others, whether or not the accusations were true. Because of my uncle's history, it became impossible for him to stay working for the government, so a few months later he left again, for Pakistan.

The US forces had a large base near our house, and they knew of my uncle's former role as head of Taliban intelligence for the east. They believed he had gone back to join the organization in a mountain hideout somewhere, and came regularly to our home to interview my father and uncles, even though my father didn't know where my uncle had gone – he hadn't heard from him since he'd left.

The men of the house, including me and my brothers, despised these visits. The soldiers had no understanding of our culture and stared directly at the women instead of turning their faces away, while my younger siblings were so scared they used to cry when they saw them.

'Gulwali, be polite and answer them. Better not to make trouble for ourselves,' my father used to insist.

But inside, I seethed.

'You are a year older now. Behave like it.' My mother's voice betrayed no maternal kindness, but after she spoke she broke into a rare smile.

It was my eleventh birthday – October 2005. In the Afghan calendar it was 1385. The Afghan calendar is based on the date that Islam became predominant in Afghanistan, around fifty years behind the main Islamic calendar.

We didn't celebrate birthdays. People say it's unIslamic to do so, but really it's more of a cultural thing: many Afghan kids from poor or uneducated families don't know what day they are born; if your family is educated, they will usually write it down somewhere so you know. So for my mother to make reference to it was something pretty special.

My chest swelled and I spent the rest of the day strutting around the compound. Our family had continued to grow, with the arrival of another younger brother, Nazir. My parents were delighted with the arrival of another boy, and his arrival softened their pain over losing their twin boys. But he was a sickly child who didn't eat much; I recall my father often injecting him with some kind of serum to help his appetite.

When I was ten, three years after the US occupation began, my mother's parents had returned from Pakistan, settling in a district about six hours' drive from us. My mother's father had two wives and a total of sixteen children, including my mother. Being a deeply devout man, he was fiercely opposed to violence of any nature.

My mother wanted us to get to know them better, so she sent us kids away to stay with her parents. I suspect the district where they lived was also safer than ours at that time, so sending us there was also a way to protect us. We were out of school, and it was fun spending time with this new set of grandparents and my other cousins, so I didn't mind.

We had just eaten a delicious dinner of home-reared lamb and rice when the news reached my grandfather. He took Hazrat and me outside. His voice was shaking, yet his words, as is the Afghan way, were brutally matter of fact: 'Boys, your father has been killed. You have to be strong. You are the men of the house now. Your father is gone.'

I recall my legs buckling underneath me, but after that I can't remember anything. I think I have blocked it out – my mind can't go back there.

The details of my father's death are sketchy, based on the little I was told. My mother didn't want us to know the full horror of what had happened and I didn't ask. I still don't want to know, because it won't bring my family back.

The night of my father's death, US troops came to our home. There had been an attack on their base that had resulted in several soldiers being killed, and they suspected the weapons used in the attack had been stored in our house. They were angry, and this time they didn't ask questions: they came with snarling dogs, kicking in the doors. They searched everything – even the women – throwing furniture, personal items, and the Quran on to the floor.

They came ready for a fight. And they got one.

Neighbours, relatives and extended family came to help drive

GULWALI PASSARLAY

the invaders out, all of them armed. By the time the shooting stopped, five of my relatives had been killed, including my father and my beloved grandfather. My two tailor uncles had survived, but were arrested and thrown into prison.

I honestly don't know if the weapons came from our house or not. I was just a child, and these things were never talked about in front of me.

Yes, my family were Taliban sympathizers, but I know my father would not have been happy putting his children at risk – he was never really happy when former Taliban members came to our house. But to refuse these visitors would have brought even more trouble on the family. The reality is that in war, ordinary families like ours are often left to make hard choices: appease one side and you make an enemy of the other side; try and placate the other side and the first side wants to know why. You can't win. The best you can do is try and negotiate a middle path and keep everybody happy, thus best ensuring those closest to you are kept safe. If indeed this was my father's strategy, and I will never know for sure, then tragically it failed.

I only knew one thing clearly. I had lost my father and grandfather, and so as was the tradition in my culture, I wanted revenge.

CHAPTER FOUR

Losing my father was the event that changed everything. Our family was plunged into turmoil. For a few months, my mother and my little siblings came to join us at her parents' house. My aunts also went to their respective parents' houses.

It wasn't just the shock of losing my father – money was in very short supply, too. In countries like Afghanistan, the reality is that if the breadwinner is killed, the family he leaves behind will be very hard put to live.

One solution was available to us: my father's big ledgers from his doctor's surgery – the ones detailing the debts owed to him for medical treatment. It fell to my brothers and me to call at the homes of the people listed in them, and ask, demand, then beg for the money my family was owed. I detested it. Often these families were in worse straits than our own, yet the ledger had it all there in black and white: it was where our next meals would come from.

After a while we went back to live in Hisarak, where we'd lived before the invasion. We had a huge extended family and people gave us a lot of support, with different relatives – including the husbands of my dad's sisters – coming to stay and support us. But with the men of our immediate family dead, imprisoned or, in the case of Uncle Lala, whereabouts unknown, it was left to my brothers and me to become the men of the house.

Revenge
opportunity

Other problems began to crop up, too. Taliban representatives began to visit more and more often. They wanted my brother and me to become fighters or even suicide bombers – martyrs – to avenge our father's death.

I was so angry that I wanted to do it. Hazrat and Noor were the same. The three of us didn't really talk about it but I think we had an innate brotherly understanding of each other's pain. But my mother knew that an angry and hurt child couldn't understand the consequences of such a drastic action and could be easily manipulated in his grief. She had been there for the horrific event and she too was filled with fury and pain – certainly a lot of Pashtun women would have wanted their sons to take revenge, even if it meant them losing their lives. Revenge is a central yet often lethal part of *Pashtunwali* – if you don't avenge yourself against your enemies, you have failed as a man.

But my mother was influenced by a different set of thinking – her deep and abiding faith. Thanks to my maternal grandfather, she had a genuine and strong understanding of true Islamic law, and it is a religion that prohibits the taking of life. She had been taught that killing anyone was wrong, even if the reasons might seem justified. She had been taught to try and forgive, to show compassion and to accept tragic events as God's will. It wasn't easy for her, but her faith helped her get through losing my father.

My mother was also doubly scared for me and Hazrat, because the US forces had also turned their attention to us two elder boys, urging us to become informants. They wanted information about my uncle's contacts and where Taliban weapons might be stored. She feared that if we followed that route and got involved with the NATO forces, or even the Afghan authorities who were cooperating with them, then we would be seen as traitors and killed.

It was a genuine fear. We knew other families where this had happened.

The approach from the US forces was all very carefully done: there wasn't really any direct contact. It was more indirect – through letters or messengers. We had a family friend who revealed himself to be a US informant. He had survived so far because he was a very powerful man; so powerful, we'd been told he had the ability to call in US airstrikes if he needed to.

Hazrat and I visited him at his house to try and find out information about my uncles: we still didn't know to which prison they had been taken or what their charges were.

We sat on an ornate gilded French-style rococo couch and drank tea.

'Do you know the saying, boys? "The enemy of your enemy is your friend?"' Of course we did. It was a very common Pashtu saying. 'You would be wise to remember it now. I will do whatever I can within my power to support you and help you, but you would also be wise to think of who your new friends might be.'

I was suspicious of him. As we all knew he was working with the US military, advising them on local intelligence issues, I was worried that he could be double-crossing us. But I also knew he'd known our family for a long time and had known my father very well, so I hoped that stood for something.

At the end of the meeting, he warned us both to be careful, telling us flatly that the NATO forces wanted us to work with them. He said if we didn't do what they said, there would be a danger we'd be killed or end up in Bagram prison. They had impunity. He knew it and we knew it. He also made clear that if we made any moves towards the Taliban side, he would know about it.

And, in that circumstance, he was more than clear that he couldn't and wouldn't help us.

In the weeks following our father's death, our house was full of visitors, all with lots of advice, and all of it conflicting.

Senior elders told us to get involved with the Taliban, insisting it would be for our own safety. A messenger arrived, a stranger, who said he was there to offer condolences. He said that he was representing the Taliban shadow governor for the province, a man who had been appointed by Mullah Omar himself. He told us the Taliban authorities were happy to take revenge on our family's behalf, but that before doing so he needed our cooperation in the form of my brothers and me joining the movement as fighters.

'Work with us, not against us. Join us to fight the infidels and expel them from Afghanistan.'

He went on to say that he understood we had family duties and could understand why we might want to stay out of things, but he still hoped we'd play our part.

'This isn't just about revenge for your father, boys. We want you to be part of a bigger and greater mission – expelling the invaders.'

For me this message made sense. Of all the different people advising us, he was probably the most persuasive – to me, at least. Hazrat hadn't liked him.

Later, the messages took a more sinister and threatening turn in the form of so-called 'night letters': a handwritten letter would be thrown over our compound wall or through the doorway. The words on the page were stark: Be martyred, or die.

Added to this, when we went to school, we were followed home by bearded men on motorbikes. Some of them were cajoling; others directly threatening; some of them even tried to grab us and make us go with them to a Taliban training camp there and then. It got to the point that as soon as we heard the sound of an engine we ran to hide.

All this terrified me. It got so bad that we had to have body-guards guarding the house.

So many different people were offering protection and support, but the reality was that we didn't know who we could trust.

41

I doubt that the Taliban would have killed us for not joining them – this was about threatening persuasion. But I think if we had collaborated with the US military they certainly would have. While my brother and I were just two little boys, in the political and moral whirlwind of that time we were pawns in the two sides' deadly game of chess: easily played and easily lost.

In the end, highly unusually, a woman – my mother – decided our fate. One night, she sat Hazrat and me down. She was very composed. 'Gulwali, Hazrat, you need to leave. You have to go somewhere far from here, where no one knows you. Noor is too little, so he will stay with me. We are working on a plan.'

That was it. She didn't say where, for how long, or when. She didn't ask our opinion or how we felt about it. I wanted to ask a hundred questions but she was already busy making tea, her tight-lipped look making it clear the conversation was over.

Never did I imagine that her plan would involve paying human smugglers thousands of dollars to take us to Europe.

In my head I thought the journey – in as much as I knew about it – would only take a few weeks.

Hazrat and I were sent first to my maternal aunt's house in Waziristan. I assumed we'd be coming home at some point, so there were no big goodbyes, no tears of sadness. Even when I hugged Grandma and my little siblings goodbye, I didn't make a fuss because I thought I'd see them all again soon. We'd been moving around so much since the conflict began, none of it seemed unusual. And I didn't question my mother, because in my culture, as a child, there are things you just do when you are told to – you don't ask why or require an explanation. We never thought about ourselves individually, just about the family.

My uncle (the husband of my mother's sister), came to collect Hazrat and me. The journey to Waziristan took us across the area that is the lawless heartland of the Pashtu tribes, a place that has been described as the most dangerous and controversial border in the world. Although recognized internationally as the western border of Pakistan, the area is not recognized by the Afghan government. It's known as the Durand Line, named after Sir Mortimer Durand, a British diplomat who, in 1893, after two Anglo-Afghan wars, negotiated the 2,640-kilometre-long boundary between what was then British India and Afghanistan. The idea was to create a neutral buffer-zone to both improve diplomatic relations with Afghanistan, but also to limit Russian expansion – a battle for the control of central Asia known as the Great Game.

Pasthuns refer to the Durand Line as: 'A line through our heart.' For us it is a remnant of colonial oppression, and the sense of injustice had been instilled in me for as long as I could remember. Pashtuns see the real border as further into what is now Pakistan, where the river Indus separates both the Pashtun and Baloch lands – Balochistan – from Punjab and Sindh. The Baloch people, who the Pashtuns see as cousins, have been fighting for independence from Pakistan for nearly sixty years.

As we journeyed over mountains, rivers and lakes, my heart stirred, both with the pride of being a Pashtun, and with the happy, nomadic memories of my early childhood. How I longed to be in the fields again, tending sheep with my grandfather. I was still grieving so very badly for both him and my father, the two men I had loved so much.

It took over a day and a half of travelling, and I was very happy to reach Waziristan. It was so exciting. The town was ringed with beautiful, snow-covered peaks crisscrossed with sparkling rivers.

My uncle took us straight to the main bazaar. It was filled with merchants, all shouting their wares in a guttural tribal dialect I could barely understand. They crouched on the ground drinking green tea, arguing loudly, or comparing wild birds kept in long rows of cages. Most of the shops were either selling guns, making guns or testing guns – by firing them into the air. I jumped constantly every time I heard a gunshot. Everywhere there were semi-wild street dogs, while the smell of sizzling kebabs, sold by roadside vendors, made my stomach rumble with hunger.

I was mesmerized, particularly by the piercing green eyes of the locals. The people of that district are famous for their beautifully coloured eyes. Even when they are happy they manage to look fierce and other-worldly.

My aunt's house was small and surrounded by fields of opium, wheat and cannabis. I was desperate to run free in the fields, but it wasn't safe because the Pakistan military were fighting local Taliban militants nearby. Mostly my brother and I sat in my aunt's house, doing nothing, getting bored and feeling homesick, annoyed at not knowing how long we would be there or what was going to happen to us. We were only really allowed out to go to the village mosque to pray. I loved being there, as it helped settle my mind. I prayed that all of the pain to hit my family was for a purpose: I was beginning to understand that life was a test, and that it was important not to give up. I was also pretty depressed at not being in school any more.

After a week or so, my uncle took us to buy clothes. I was furious when he made us try on pairs of jeans. 'Uncle, I'm not wearing these. It's what the invaders wear.'

At home, we only wore the traditional *shalwar kameez*. I was so anti-Western, it felt like a complete betrayal to even consider wearing these devil jeans. I couldn't understand why he was making us do it: denim was the cultural uniform of my enemy.

But my uncle was in no mood to argue. 'Put them on. Do you think I am wasting my money here?'

Sulking, I did as I was told but I hated the way the stiff cotton felt on my skin. He also bought us a small rucksack each, T-shirts, underwear, and woollen gloves, strong boots and warm jackets. By the time we'd finished shopping, the rucksacks were full.

No one had yet spelled it out to us, but it was fast becoming obvious what might be happening.

Hazrat and I were far closer now than we had been in our early childhood. The trauma of the past couple of years had bonded us, but like all brothers we still got on each other's nerves. Things weren't helped by the fact that even though he was a year older than me and very clever, I always saw myself as the leader. ✷ Leader

'They're sending us away, aren't they?' I said to him that evening. He nodded.

I saw how he was trying to look wise and mature about it, but blurted out the only feeling I had on the subject: 'Let's not go. Let's go home. We're needed. We run the businesses and look after the women. I can take over the tailor shop. I'm a good tailor.'

'*No*, Gulwali.' My brother looked at me. 'This is our mother's decision, and we must respect it.'

'She's wrong,' I insisted.

'Listen, if she's made this decision, it has to be serious.'

'You're a *khazanouka*.' Calling my brother a feminist didn't help matters, and I still felt angry. It wasn't just my mother I was upset with; it felt as though the whole family was involved in this plot.

That feeling only intensified when, the next day, my uncle took us to a kebab restaurant. He greeted the owner of the restaurant, who took us to a back table away from the crowds.

'So, these are the boys?'

'Yes. And they will travel together? Their mother insists on this.'

'You have my word,' said the man.

I sat there nervously listening to my uncle and the man debate money, paperwork and routes. Nobody had said anything explicitly to Hazrat or me, but it was now becoming obvious that my family had been making arrangements for some time. For most of that meeting, in fact, my uncle and the man talked about us as if we weren't there. Maybe it was too dangerous to share information, or perhaps they didn't want to scare us even more. I don't know. I just remember feeling a lot of confusion and despair.

In late October 2006, when we'd been staying with my auntie for around three weeks, my mother arrived for a visit.

I was happy to see her as I'd really missed her, but at that time I was also very angry with my mother. I felt betrayed. I had been the child who had prided himself on responsibility and protecting our family honour: it was a role I relished. Being stuck in Waziristan, I felt as though I didn't have that status any more. And, unfair as it was, I blamed her.

She kissed me on the forehead when we greeted her, then went straight to talk to my uncle. The pair of them sat talking in hushed tones, and I wanted to shout at them. Why were they doing this?

The next night, Hazrat and I were told that we, my mother, aunt and uncle were going to visit someone's house for dinner. This was to be expected: if you are visiting a new place, local people will invite you for dinner – it's a key part of *Pashtunwali* – so I didn't think anything out of the ordinary, assuming it might be one of my mother's distant relatives or some old friends we were seeing.

The house was about a ten- to fifteen-minute walk away. My mother and aunt walked alongside us, both wearing their blue burqas. On arrival, Hazrat and I were ushered into the main quarters, where a few men of different ages sat on striped kelim-covered cushions on the floor, drinking green tea.

As I stuffed some naan into my mouth, I listened to the men debate politics.

'The war over the border has reached us here now.'

'The government will never win this.'

'*Pashtunwali* itself is at stake.'

'These foreign fighters need to go home. It's because of them the US are dropping drones on our head.'

'How can you say that? The US are the ones who occupied our brothers' country.'

'Yes, but isn't it because of them that these Chechens and Arabs are in our midst?'

'These Chechens and Arabs are our guests. They came here to fight the holy war. They are our brothers.'

'Some brothers. Marrying our women and bringing danger to our villages. What good is this doing for our people?'

'There are thousands living in camps now. We are refugees in our own homeland.'

After the food and the debate were over, we drank hot, sweet green tea and ate dried apricots, mulberries and almonds. I was beginning to feel relaxed and sleepy when my uncle and the host stood up and told Hazrat and me to follow them.

They walked us to the door, where my mother was waiting for us, in her burqa. I was aghast to see she had our rucksacks next to her. I had last seen them at my aunt's house: I had no idea who had brought them here. It didn't feel right.

Hazrat looked at me, as shocked as I was. I glanced at my mother for reassurance.

As she stood there, her knees seemed to give way slightly. I thought she might fall down.

She looked at my brother and me. 'You must hold on to each other's hands. Never let go of each other. Do you understand?'

'What? *Morya.* I'm not ready. Please—'

'I said, DO YOU UNDERSTAND?' She stared at us so hard through the mesh of her burqa I thought her eyes would burn through my skull. —Imagery

We both nodded.

47

'Be brave. This is for your own good.' And then she said something that froze my heart. 'However bad it gets, *don't come back.*'

I started shouting. 'I am not going anywhere. I am *not* leaving my family. I am needed here.'

'Gulwali, this is for the good of the family. Do as we say.'

'No.'

I looked over at Hazrat. He looked stricken.

My mother started speaking again. 'Listen to me, both of you. These people will take care of you, but you must take care of each other. Hold each other's hands. *Always.*' She looked at us both again, hard, holding our eyes. Then she took something from the folds of her burqa.

She handed us each US$200; my uncle gave us a handful of Iranian currency.

Our host looked at his watch. 'We should move. Long drive ahead.' He began to herd us outside, to where a car was parked.

I started to feel sick. '*Morya*, I don't want to go. Let's go home now. Please take me home.'

She glared at me and, for a split second, I thought she was going to hit me.

'*Morya*, please.' I said, absolutely desperate now.

The man shifted impatiently, looking at his watch again. 'We need to hurry, madam.'

My mother began to visibly shake. I could see her eyes through the mesh of the burqa flitting from the man and back to us.

'Where are we going, *Morya*?'

'To safety. To Europe.'

'They will be there in a few weeks,' the man assured my mother. 'It will be like a holiday for them, an adventure.' And with that he literally bundled us into the car.

My mother stood watching as we got in, standing tall, proud

and resolute. I don't know how she would have reacted as the tail lights of the car rounded the corner: did she collapse, screaming and howling, finally allowing the trauma and grief of losing her husband and now her two older sons to finally flood through her?

More likely, given what a strong woman she was, she simply stayed quiet and locked her pain deep inside.

I was too traumatized to speak. My only comfort was my brother's hand gently squeezing mine when he noticed my tears threaten to fall.

'We'll be OK. We're together. I am going to look after you.'

That night we were driven to a city. I think it was Peshawar, but no one told us. We were taken to stay with a family, complete strangers, but given food and mattresses to sleep on.

In the morning, two new people arrived: a man and a woman. They were Dari-speaking Afghans.

Dari and Pashtu are the two main languages of Afghanistan. Pashtu is my mother tongue, and I'd lived in an exclusively Pashtu area, so my Dari was in no way good, but I could make myself understood – most Afghan kids speak both.

The woman explained that they would take us to the airport and fly with us to Iran. In the airport, we were to be on our best behaviour and pretend they were our relatives. She told us to make no noise and not to attract the security guards' attention. From there we would go to Europe.

'Where in Europe?' I demanded to know.

The woman shrugged. 'I don't know. Don't ask me. I'm just an agent. Your family made the arrangements with people in Kabul.' She reached into a bag. 'Here. Take this.'

She handed my brother and me an Afghan passport each. I had never had one before. I stared at it in surprise as my photograph peered back at me from the page.

When had my family arranged this?

On arrival at Peshawar's international airport, I momentarily forgot my sadness. It felt so huge, with people, cars, queues and machinery everywhere, and I stood gaping in wonder at the scanning machine as our little rucksacks went through it.

I was brought back to reality with a jolt when the man we were with picked up Hazrat's bag and led him through the gate. I went to follow, but the woman held me back. Hazrat didn't give me a backwards glace – I assume because he thought I was right behind him.

I wanted to yell his name but the woman's earlier warnings about not attracting attention still loomed large in my mind. 'I want to go with him.' I spoke to her as forcefully as possible and in the best Dari that I could muster. I had to make her understand what I said.

She ignored me, grabbing my arm so tight it hurt. I started to cry and she looked around nervously. 'Be quiet.' A guard glanced over in our direction. 'It's OK, it's OK,' she said quickly. 'Later. You will see him on the plane.'

I stopped crying because I believed her. But when we boarded the plane, my brother and the man were nowhere to be seen. 'Where is he? Where is Hazrat?' I demanded.

'Quiet,' she hissed. 'Different plane. You will see him on the other side.'

This time I knew she was lying.

By the time we arrived at our destination, I was a terrified, lonely and sobbing mess. As we went through Immigration, the reality that I was now in a foreign country hit me. Waziristan and Peshawar, although technically in Pakistan, still felt familiar because they were Pashtun areas. But Iran was completely alien.

Outside the airport, the woman simply pulled me over to a taxi without saying a word. I was begging for my brother and desperately straining my eyes in all directions in the hope that I would see him.

The female agent and the taxi driver spoke in Farsi, the main language of Iran. It's very similar to Dari – the two languages are virtually the same, but the dialect and accent are quite different – so most Afghan Dari speakers can converse in it. But to a Pashtu speaker like me, Dari was hard enough, and my mental anguish and their strange accents made it hard for me to understand anything.

I tugged at the woman's sleeve, trying to get her attention, but she flicked my hand away as if I were an annoying fly. Still weeping, I was bundled into a car and driven out of the airport into the surrounding countryside. I wanted so badly to see my mother or my grandmother – to have one of them hold me and reassure me and tell me it had all been a bad dream. I prayed that Hazrat was going to be wherever it was they were taking me.

The taxi driver, a skinny man with a big, hairy nose, glanced over at me as I sat on the back seat, snot and tears dribbling down my dirty, exhausted face.

'Welcome to the holy city of Mashhad.'

This made me furious. Iranians were Shias. Muslims are split into two main branches – the Sunnis and Shia. My family were Sunni, and I had always been taught in the local mosque and at school that the Shia weren't true Muslims, something that as a child I had accepted unquestioningly.

But I had to admit that Mashhad was very beautiful. It looked new and shiny and clean; the pavements were so sparklingly clean they seemed to glow. And the tall skyscrapers and shopping malls I had seen in books were everywhere; even the roundabouts had decorations in the centre of them. I marvelled at one that had a pair of hands holding the Quran carved in pink marble.

As I peered out of the car window in wonder at this modern paradise, I almost forgot my situation – until I saw an Iranian family walking down the street. The parents were holding the hands of their two children, a little boy and girl. The girl was wearing a white, lacy dress with a stiff petticoat and frills, while ankle socks and black patent shoes adorned her feet. The little boy had on a smart black suit and a red bow tie. The parents were clasping their kids' hands tightly and swinging them up into the air. The sight of their carefree happiness cut like a knife as images of my little sisters and brothers rushed into my head.

Quickly, I blocked them out. I was already learning that in order to keep going I had to stop loving, stop remembering. Thinking about those I had left behind was too painful.

I was taken to a smart little hotel in the centre of the city. The manager came out to the taxi and asked if I had luggage – I had to concentrate really hard to understand the question. I answered by shaking my head and clinging on to my rucksack: it was all I possessed in the world.

Once inside, the manager took me to one side. 'Are you the person of Qubat?'

I had no idea what he was talking about. What was 'Qubat'?

'Where is the other one? I thought there were supposed to be two of you?'

'My brother? Is he here?'

'Maybe. There are some others belonging to Qubat here. He might be with them. Let me show you the room.'

He led me along a hallway and into a lift. As he pushed some buttons, it began to move. I was fascinated – I'd never been in one before.

'OK, you guys are in room fifteen,' the manager said, jangling his keys as the lift door opened.

Outside the room, he knocked on the door. Anticipation ran through me. I prayed Hazrat would open it.

Instead, a skinny, tall youth with protruding teeth and messy hair poked his head round the half-opened door. 'Yes?'

'The new arrival is here. He's little. Introduce yourselves and look after him. He's asking for his brother.'

The youth gave me a toothy smile and introduced himself as Mehran. '*Salaam alaikum.*' He welcomed me in Pashtu. — new boy

I smiled back with relief to hear another Pashtu speaker. From that time on, being around other Pashtuns would always make the experience of being in a strange country feel a little bit easier.

The room had four single beds, one in each corner; in the centre was an Iranian-style carpet with a peacock design. Two other figures sitting on the floor got up as I walked in.

They both came over and hugged me. One, a clean-shaven, fit-looking man, who looked to be in his late thirties, introduced himself as Baryalai. The other said his name was Abdul. He was in his mid-twenties and seemed a bit shy.

'You are too young to be here, little man. Let me get you some tea.'

'No, no, I'll get it,' said Mehran.

This made me smile – typical Afghans, fighting over each other to show hospitality. These three made me feel instantly welcome.

As we sat on the rug drinking tea from tiny Iranian-style cups and saucers, I learned more about them. Baryalai was from Nangarhar, the same province I was from. He had grown up in a refugee camp in Peshawar. Mehran was also from Nangarhar and from Hisarak, the same district I'd grown up in. Abdul was the son of an army officer from Kabul.

They explained they'd travelled by coach from Kabul to the city of Herat in western Afghanistan. From there, they had crossed the border into Iran, where they swapped coaches to travel here.

We didn't really get into the details of why we'd all had to flee; I think there was an unspoken assumption that there must have been good reasons, otherwise why would we be there?

'Have you eaten yet?' Baryalai smiled at me warmly. There was something about him that made me feel safe.

I hadn't eaten since Peshawar. I was starving.

'We have some food. Come, eat.' Mehran was already piling fried rice from a steel container on to a plate. The food looked reassuringly similar to Afghan food.

I had so many questions in my head: how long were we staying there? What was happening next? Just one passed my lips: 'Where is my brother?'

'Your brother?'

'Hazrat. He should be here. Is he in a different room?'

Baryalai looked at me and frowned.

'There are ten other Afghans. They are with different agents – we are the only ones belonging to Qubat. But none of them is called Hazrat.'

'But they promised.'

'"They" make a lot of promises, Gulwali.'

I went silent. I think they could see I was scared and depressed, so they suggested we go for a walk. I was surprised we were allowed to go out by ourselves, and I jumped at the chance.

We wandered through a nearby park eating watermelon. Finally, I was able to ask all the questions I needed, including one which had been perplexing me ever since I arrived at the hotel: 'What is "Qubat"? Is it Farsi for "kebab"?'

They all roared with laughter.

'What's so funny?'

Mehran wiped tears from his eyes. 'I thought I was stupid, but this kid is *really* dumb.'

Baryalai spoke next. 'Gulwali, "Qubat" is the main agent from Kabul who we paid to get us here.'

'But I didn't pay anyone.'

'No, but your family did. Qubat is a people-smuggler. A big guy. I think I met one of your uncles when I was there in Kabul. I heard him arranging for Qubat to take his two nephews.'

'Is Qubat here? He'll know where Hazrat is.'

'No, Gulwali.' Baryalai's tone softened. 'As I explained, he's the big guy. He lives in Kabul. I only met him once. He has guys working for him over here. He organized it all, and he's got our money. He's got every rupee I ever had. That's all I know.'

'But what about Hazrat?'

Facing me, Baryalai put his hand on my shoulder and stooped slightly so that he was looking straight into my eyes. 'Little man, I think they lied to you. You have to forget your brother for the time being. We're your brothers now.'

I didn't want to embarrass myself by crying in front of my new friends, so I bit hard on my lip.

But Baryalai had noticed. 'Try not to cry. Your uncle paid for you both, so he'll be somewhere on the same journey. I am sure you'll meet him again soon.'

Brothers were separated
– can't imagine being split up
from my brother

CHAPTER FIVE

Early the next evening, we left the temporary security of the hotel. We had a long coach journey ahead, driving to the city of Esfahan, then on to the Iranian capital, Tehran.

While I was reassured by my new travelling companions, I still felt very lost and scared. Every time I thought of home, my grandmother or my little brothers and sisters, I couldn't stop my tears. And when I thought of Hazrat – taken God only knew where – I felt physically sick.

The hotel manager drove us to the coach station and bought us our tickets. The bus tickets had assigned seats; ours were the long back row.

Baryalai wasn't happy. 'This is dodgy. If the police come on board they will see us straight away. Get us a different seat.'

The manager looked exasperated. 'It was full. These were the last seats.'

'So we'll take the next bus,' insisted Baryalai.

'It's not for six hours. They are expecting you in Tehran tomorrow evening. If you delay, you'll miss your pick-up.'

Baryalai still wasn't pleased.

I didn't want him to be sad, so I tried to reassure him: 'It's OK. We'll manage.' But as the coach left Mashhad for Tehran, I felt as if I was driving further and further away from everything I knew.

*

I was small enough to find some small measure of comfort on the vinyl seats of the bus. When not sleeping, I snacked from a packet of salted sunflower seeds and watched as Iran unfolded outside the window. It looked so clean and organized. Unlike back home, the roads were asphalted and smooth, and I loved how many of the modern-looking buildings were festooned with strings of coloured lights.

Every few hours the driver stopped to refuel, or for meals. We would pile out, grateful to stretch our legs and visit the bathroom. At some point during the night, I woke as the bus pulled into a larger terminus. Dozy and confused, I stumbled into the cool air. The depot was overflowing with tired travellers blinking away sleep. Their clothing and hats marked them out as decidedly Persian. There were few women around, but those who were tended to fall into two categories: the older ones wore full black robes that covered their heads and bodies but left their faces showing; the younger ones wore jeans and long tunics or belted coats, with brightly coloured scarves covering their hair.

Being the pious twelve-year-old that I was, I found it unsettling to see so many women outside without their faces covered. I was still thinking of my province, where women were rarely outside the home, and when they were, they wore the traditional blue burqa.

The depot was full of enterprising stall-owners, all selling their wares to hungry and thirsty travellers. Decorated stalls sold rows of tempting dates, mangoes, apricots and oranges; others displayed myriad different-coloured marzipan sweets and decorated little cakes, along with cans of Coke and cups of sweet black tea.

I was entranced, and started walking between the rows. I was so busy, in fact, looking at the mouthwatering wares, that I lost all track of time – I came to with a sudden realization: the driver had told us to be no more than ten minutes.

I ran back to where the coach was and opened the door with a puff of relief. Only to see an unfamiliar driver.

Panicking, I stepped back and looked left and right. There was row upon row of identical-looking coaches. Where was mine?

My heart was pounding. My passport was on the bus, along with most of my money. I ran up and down the rows of coaches searching for mine, but they all looked the same.

My face was becoming hot and tearful; I pushed people out of the way.

'Hey, kid, watch what you're doing.'

I glared back though teary eyes. 'I've got to find my bus,' I said, forcing my way through a gap in the crowd. Blind panic was setting in. What if they'd gone without me? Surely the others wouldn't let that happen?

My tears were flowing so much now I could hardly see; my heart was pounding so hard I thought my chest would explode. Where was I? What town were we in?

I realized I didn't even know that.

I had no idea how to survive in a foreign country. I was just a little boy. How could this be happening to me? Where would I go? What would I do?

I let out an angry sob. '*Morya*. I want my *morya*.' In my panic, I continued to run, shoving my way past the back of the next bus. And straight into a familiar form.

'Gulwali. Where the hell have you been?' Mehran looked truly furious.

'I got lost. I'm sorry. I thought you'd gone.'

'We nearly did. The driver wanted to leave. Come on, we have to get back on now.'

As I slumped into my seat, I could barely look the others in the eye.

'Are you all right?' asked Baryalai.

I couldn't show them weakness. 'Yes. Fine.'

'Make sure you stick close to us in future.'

I tried to rest as the bus roared through the night, and eventually sank into a fitful sleep.

When I next opened my eyes, I thought my journey to freedom might be over before it had begun: an Iranian soldier was sitting right next to me. Had we been arrested?

I opened my mouth to speak, but Baryalai quickly spoke for me. He was talking in Dari, the Afghan language very close to the soldier's Farsi. It meant that it was obvious we were Afghans, but at least he and the soldier could converse easily.

'Good morning, Gulwali.' His eyes implored mine not to say anything.

I couldn't quite work out what was going on. The solider was chatting to my friends casually, as if it was the most normal thing in the world. If he'd come to arrest us, why hadn't he already done it?

I sat as quiet as a mouse, not daring to say a word.

As they conversed, however, I realized the soldier wasn't there to harm us. It turned out that he'd just finished his duties and was on his way home to see his parents, just a bus passenger like us. He asked us polite questions about how we were finding Iran and did we like the scenery. He seemed very proud of his country. I guess he just assumed we were on holiday, or working there. It's not unusual to see Afghans in Iran; many Afghans go there for business or to find work in the Iranian construction boom.

As nice as he was, though, I was still very relieved when he got off the bus.

Later on in the morning, we stopped again for breakfast, pulling into a service station. There were a couple of assorted restaurants and a small mosque. This time I made sure to stay with the others.

At the ablutions area, a row of benches and taps was surrounded by men preparing themselves for prayer. Ablution is the ritual

Muslims do before prayer, which involves washing the hands, arms, face and feet. We joined them as the *azzan* – the Islamic call to prayer – stirred my soul. Even as a small child, it was the most wonderful sound in the world to me, filling me with a sense of peace.

I had been taught from a young age to fear the Shia as apostates – yet the *azzan*, the ablution…everything seemed to be the same as my own rituals. As we went inside the mosque to pray, I realized that we also said the same prayers. The only real difference I noticed was that when I prayed, I placed my hands in front of me; they had their hands by their sides. They also prayed out loud, whereas I was used to worshipping silently. But, apart from that, everything seemed normal.

As I looked around me, I did not see heretics or disbelievers, as I had been led to believe Shias were. All I saw were faithful men.

We arrived in Tehran early that evening, after a full night and day on the road. Compared to cities like Peshawar and Kabul, it was a hugely modern and clean place. There were endless concrete suburbs. The traffic was bumper to bumper, with yellow taxis everywhere. Diesel fumes made the air chokingly thick.

The moment we stepped off the coach was chaos. The terminus was massive, and as we descended the bus steps, taxi drivers were grabbing at our sleeves.

'Taxi.'

'Come with me.'

'This way, sirs.'

It was so bewildering. We'd been told someone would be there to meet us but we had no idea what they looked like or who they were. Fortunately, we did have a phone number.

We managed to break away from the taxi touts and find a public pay phone.

'I'm here. Outside the station. Come out.' The man's voice rang out in clear Farsi.

We walked into the street but still had no way of recognizing the man. It was up to him to work out who we were. It clearly took him a while because we were standing there nervously for twenty minutes before he found us.

A young man in jeans and a sports jacket approached us. '*Salaam*. Are you Qubat's guys?'

We nodded.

He apologized for being late, explaining there had been delays on the metro. I had no idea what a metro was.

'Let's walk along the street. The taxis here are too expensive.'

As we followed him, I looked around and marvelled at the city. The roads were lined with beautiful flowerbeds, all different colours. There was a lot of noise and traffic still, but the city seemed so calm and ordered. Most consumer goods in Afghanistan come from Iran so I had had an idea it was a developed place, but the reality was something else. Our capital city of Kabul was once a famous tourist destination known for its gardens and parks, but the years of conflict had damaged it terribly. Although still very beautiful in its own way, these days open sewers run down the sides of pot-holed roads, and rubbish piles up in the rivers. To me, Tehran was the epitome of what a capital city should look like.

We then got into a taxi, which took us through winding back-streets to our destination, a small *musafir khanna*, a traveller's guest house, located above the top of a hardware store in a busy bazaar.

There were a few Afghans already there. And it was clear they weren't happy with the guest-house owner, even though he was also Afghan.

'We were supposed to leave Tehran two days ago, but this guy is forcing us to stay here,' complained a large, chubby man who introduced himself as Shah. He was from central Afghanistan, home of the Hazara people. The Hazara make up about 10 per cent of the Afghan population, but throughout history they have been treated as second-class citizens and had their lands taken away, in part because they are Shia. Back then, all I really knew about the Hazara was that they opposed the Taliban ideology, something that at the tender age of twelve I couldn't understand anyone wanting to do. Shah was sharing a room with Faizal, a younger man from Balochistan in Pakistan.

As we ate dinner, they told us more of their stories. Shah couldn't believe we'd flown into Iran legally. He'd walked. 'I didn't think I'd live to see Tehran. We left Afghanistan at Nimroz and trekked for so long into a city called Zahedan. The damned Iranians shot at us. I saw a child fall and die right in front of me. His brother was screaming. We were running like scared chickens.'

Hearing this made me think my experience on the plane hadn't been so bad after all.

Faizal – a journalist – had also faced great danger crossing on foot from Pakistan into Iran. He was clearly very disturbed. 'You don't understand what's happening to my people. The military are disappearing us. I found my cousin's body with wire round his neck. He was only nineteen. I left my whole family, my two kids behind. I don't know when I will see them again.'

The situation at the *musafir khanna* was really unsettling: the owner told us he was Qubat's business partner in Iran, but then started yelling at us. 'Qubat was supposed to send enough to get you to Turkey. But where is the money? Where is it?'

None of us had any idea what he was talking about.

'I'm not buying your tickets out of my own pocket. You don't go anywhere till I get paid. It's bad enough you all have hungry mouths to feed.' The manager pointed at Shah. 'This fat Hazara has cost me too much money already. I should throw him on the street.'

Shah threw his hands in the air and rolled his eyes, before saying an old Hazara expression: 'Hazara also have God.'

I liked Shah – even when he was angry he was still funny.

That night I lay on a lumpy, metal-framed bed watching cockroaches scuttling around on the dirty walls. This place, which stank of boiled meat and stale cigarette smoke, couldn't have been more different from the smart, clean hotel in Mashhad. For a long time I stared at the ceiling waiting for sleep to come.

Even though the people around me were being nice, they were still strangers. I ached for my family. All I wanted to do was get back on the coach and find a way home.

But my mother's words, '*Don't come back*', echoed through my head.

CHAPTER SIX

'I. am. not. giving. you. my. passport.'

Mehran looked so angry I thought he was going to hit the guy.

'None of us are handing them over,' Baryalai chimed in.

Qubat's guy, the guest-house manager, had come into our room to tell us his money had finally arrived and that we were to take a bus on to the city of Tabriz that night. But he'd demanded that we hand him our passports.

'If the police catch you with your passports then it will go badly for all of us. Better to turn them over to me, then there's no evidence for the police.'

'Maybe you want to sell them and leave us here to rot?' Mehran was becoming hysterical, yelling at the top of his voice.

'Shut up, you foolish boy. Do you want people in the street to hear us? It's for your own good.'

'NO.'

But the guest-house manager was getting irritated by our refusal now. 'You were supposed to be here for a few hours, but you stay for days – and now you try to tell me how to do my job. Don't you think I have done this hundreds of times before?'

Baryalai wasn't buying it. 'I bet you've tricked men like us a hundred times before.'

'A thousand times,' muttered Shah.

'Fine.' The manager finally snapped. 'Don't give them to me. Stay here in Tehran and rot. No passport, no ticket. No Europe. Your choice.'

This threat scared me more than anything, and I found the courage to speak. 'What guarantees do we have that we'll be safe?'

'Shut up, boy – don't speak of things you know nothing about.' Faizal shouted me down.

'Leave Gulwali alone.' Baryalai clearly didn't like Faizal.

'The boy is blind to everything except his little crush.'

The manager saw his opportunity to reason with us. 'The boy can see enough to know I am right. The only guarantee I can make you is that you don't go anywhere until you give me those documents. But you know what? Perhaps I will turn you over to the police – you have cost me too much money already.'

I couldn't help myself. 'No, please, don't. We'll think about it, OK?'

'Think about it? You think you have a choice?' The man snorted with derision. 'You really are wasting my time now. I am not an unkind man, but this is my home, and my rules. You are going to need fake papers – but that won't happen until you get closer to Turkey. Until then, you are safer not having any papers at all.'

Mehran shook his head. 'Look, these are *our* passports.'

'"Our" passports? Weren't they provided by Qubat? These are his property, not yours. They served their purpose to get you here, but you don't need them now. Give them to me.'

'No.'

We were clearly getting nowhere. I didn't want to hand over my passport either, but nor did I want to stay in that stinking guest house a moment longer. 'I don't think he's lying. If it's for our safety, we should.'

*

A couple of hours later and four brand-new Afghan passports were in an envelope on the reception desk, weighted down by an illegal bottle of Johnnie Walker Black Label.

We all hated the man and his smelly guest house. Everyone was really worried about what had happened, and Mehran wasn't speaking to me because he said it was my fault that we had given in.

But, as good as his word, the man dropped us at the coach station and gave us tickets for the bus to Tabriz.

It was another overnight journey, but this time I was too scared to get any sleep. When we finally arrived, it was into a much smaller bus station, and it was a relief not to be hassled by taxi touts on arrival.

A heavy-set Iranian Kurd approached us. 'Qubat?'

By now we knew the ropes. 'Yes.'

He issued instructions to the others in a mixture of Farsi and a language I had never heard before, which I assumed to be Kurdish.

'It's time to go. We still have a long drive.' He looked down at me and my little backpack. 'Is that everything you have?'

I nodded.

'So then ... *yallah* – let's be going.'

I have no idea how, but six of us and our bags managed to squeeze into his Toyota. We rattled out of Tabriz and into the Iranian hinterland.

After an hour or so, the Toyota started to work harder as we curled up arid foothills. Our driver hummed along to loud pop music; he hadn't spoken a word to us since we'd set off. My legs had long since gone numb.

The road eventually straightened and I could see that, up ahead, it seemed to go right through the centre of a large lake. Big black rocks covered in wire formed a barrier on either side of the road, and the traffic had begun to form a large queue.

I started to feel a sense of rising panic. Was this a border?

'What's happening?' I whispered to Abdul, who was sitting to my left.

He shrugged. He very rarely spoke.

The Kurd suddenly pulled over to the side of the road, got out and opened the nearest passenger door. '*Yallah.* Get out. Let's move it.'

On foot, we followed him, making our way alongside the traffic. Up ahead I could see that the lake widened and stretched out into the horizon. The queues of cars were easing on to a large ferry.

The Kurd had gone over to some machines and now came back with a handful of tickets. He spoke in Farsi. 'Act normally. Try and behave like tourists. Enjoy the view.' He pointed to a gangplank where a handful of foot passengers were boarding. When I next turned around, he'd disappeared.

This was my first time on board a boat. And even though Afghanistan has lots of lakes, I had never seen one this big or wide. To me it looked as I imagined the ocean would – something else I had never seen.

Most passengers stayed in their cars. There were no seats for foot passengers, and my legs swayed beneath me once we had found a place to stand, by the edge of the boat. The water was flat and placid but, as I looked over the edge into the deep, blue water I found myself having another attack of acute homesickness, and I wished I had someone to hold my hand and comfort me. But I didn't want the others to think I was a baby so I tried to act brave and nonchalant, as if I did this sort of thing every day.

home-
sick

The crossing took about fifteen minutes. As we approached the shoreline on the opposite side, the driver mysteriously reappeared by our side and hissed to us to board a green minibus that was sitting in the centre of the ferry. Behind its steering wheel sat a different man.

We got in and, as the ferry came to a standstill, our new chauffeur drove off. About an hour later, in the middle of some quiet countryside, he pulled over behind a blue off-road vehicle.

'Please change cars.'

They were the first and only words he spoke to us the whole time we were with him.

A third man drove us on. The road was good and as we travelled down an empty, winding road, the terrain began to change: trees dressed in October's autumn hues of gold and burnt orange lined our way. I was taking the first driver at his word and trying my best to enjoy the view.

'We should be there soon.'

It was nice of the driver to reassure us, except he failed to mention where 'there' was. Mehran asked him where we were going but no reply was forthcoming. At some point, the driver took a call on his mobile phone. He spoke in short, hurried bursts of Farsi mixed with Kurdish, and so quickly that I could barely understand even the Farsi words. But I did notice that after the call his mood changed, and he became sweaty and nervous.

As a car approached on the other side of the road, he flashed it to stop and wound down his window. He spoke in Farsi to the other driver, so this time I could work out the gist of it: 'Are they checking cars ahead?'

'No, I just drove straight through.'

A few minutes later we cruised through an unguarded police checkpoint.

'Allah was on our side today. They usually check the vehicles here.' His relief was short-lived, however. Fifteen minutes later, as we wound uphill into a village, the engine cut dead.

'Shit. This isn't good.'

We could see what he meant: there was a police station to the right, just a few hundred yards ahead.

'Stay inside and try and keep your heads low.' He got out and lifted up the bonnet, fiddling around inside, then he came around to the driver's window. 'It should be OK, but we need to jump-start it. All of you get out and push. Let's just be fast and get out of here.'

We managed to get moving again just as two policemen ambled down the road towards us. Thankfully, they barely paid attention as the engine barked into life and we piled into the car.

It was late afternoon when, a few miles later, we turned into a cluster of low, concrete-block and traditional stone buildings, surrounded by fruit trees and high fencing.

Dozens of cars were lined nose-to-tail in front of a dilapidated cow shed. An imposing-looking man stood in the yard waiting for us.

'I am Black Wolf,' he said, shaking our hands as we got out of the vehicle.

His eyes were as dark as the colour of his name, but they seemed kinder than the name suggested. He shook down a large gold watch from beneath the sleeve of his white tunic, making a show of checking the time.

'Welcome to my house.' He gesticulated with a sweeping arm. 'I apologize for your inconvenience with the different vehicles. But you are here now.' He smiled, showing near-perfect white teeth. 'Welcome to our Kurdish heartland. I will show you where to sleep, and bring you some water.'

He spoke beautifully articulated, crystal-clear Farsi, even though he, like the driver, was obviously Kurdish.

'Ignore these men,' he continued, waving his arm at three men busily syphoning fuel from various vehicles' petrol tanks into battered orange fuel drums. 'They will not bother you, and it is none of your business, anyway.'

Whatever Black Wolf was up to, I got the impression business was good.

69

'Come, gentleman,' he said. 'Follow me.'

We followed him past a pile of car parts and scrap metal, between two further stone buildings and towards a large, very modern looking house, entering beneath a smart looking porch.

As Black Wolf gesticulated to a door just to our right, I noticed a large diamond and emerald ring glinting on his finger. 'Here,' he said. 'This is your room.'

It was well furnished, with traditional mattresses around the sides and Iranian carpets on the floor.

'You can help yourselves to fruit any time,' he said, pointing towards a large orchard. 'But be quiet, and discreet.'

Through the net curtains of the window I could see trees heavy with apples, oranges and pears – the likes of which I hadn't eaten since I had left home. My stomach went into a frenzy of rumbling.

'There is a tap on the side of the building and a toilet around the side.' Black Wolf smiled and ruffled my hair. 'Don't look so worried, boy. No one is going to hurt you. You are going to rest here for a few days until I get word it's time to move on.' He looked up at the rest of the group. 'The next part of the journey is hard. You will need strong legs, so I expect you all to behave with good manners and sleep as much as you can. If you see that I have other guests, please stay in your room. You definitely do not want to make any trouble for me.'

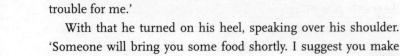

With that he turned on his heel, speaking over his shoulder. 'Someone will bring you some food shortly. I suggest you make yourselves comfortable.'

Too exhausted to talk, we flopped down on to the mattresses.

I was shaken awake.

'Hey, Gulwali.' It was Mehran. 'Wake up, man. It's food time.'

I was confused by the half-light.

'It's almost dark. You've been snoring for hours.'

A lanky, teenage boy was in the room. He placed a large dish of rice, a steaming roast chicken, a pot of lentil stew and a traditional Kurdish salad of olives, cheese, cucumber, tomatoes, lemon and cabbage on a cloth in the centre of the room. It was a feast.

Black Wolf strode in carrying a pile of plates. 'This is Rizgar, my brother's son.' He nodded at the boy. 'Come on, then. Take a plate – get eating.'

He smiled in my direction. 'Don't delay, little boy. Get eating before the fat one beats you to it.'

Shah glowered at him as we all laughed.

As six hungry people sat eating cross-legged in silence, I found myself staring out of the window into a star-filled sky. The stars shone almost as brightly as they did in the mountains of my childhood.

It had been just over a week since I had been ripped away from my family and everything I had known, but the pain of each hour had made it feel like months. After the meal, when we said our late evening prayers, I asked Allah to keep my family safe.

I woke very early the next morning. It was still dark. The others were fast asleep, so I stepped around them quietly and went out to visit a beautiful horse I had spotted in a field next to the orchard the previous evening.

I took a pink apple from a tree and held it over the fence. There was a large shadow in the distance. I clicked my tongue against the roof of my mouth and the shadow moved closer.

The mare was a beautiful chestnut with a shiny coat that glowed even in the pale light. Her muzzle twitched as she scented my offering, and large white teeth crunched up the apple in two easy bites.

It felt peaceful being alone with this graceful animal, and I couldn't help but be reminded yet again of my early years living with my grandparents in the mountains. How could I have had any idea then of the pain and suffering that was to come to me and my family?

The strains of the dawn call to prayer floated across the trees from a distant mosque as a softly pink light began to melt the clouds. I hurried back through the orchard back towards the main house.

'Little boy.'

The voice felt loud in the still morning air.

'Hey, little boy.'

Black Wolf loomed over a low wall that marked the entrance to the back of the house. 'Are you coming to pray?'

'Where?' I really wasn't sure about this.

'Come, boy. Come inside.' He waved a hand, his jewelled ring glinting in the dawn, beckoning me towards him.

I did as I was told, stepping through the back door into the inner sanctum of the family quarters. A group of figures stood in the middle of the central courtyard, faces towards Mecca.

'Little boy, this is my brother and my cousin. My nephew you already know.' He nodded to me, and then addressed everyone. 'Let's pray, brothers.'

I joined them as they fell on their knees. I thanked Allah for a merciful journey and prayed for his blessing on my mother. I asked him to keep my brother safe until we were together again. And I thanked him that Black Wolf was a kind man.

When we finished I felt much better – very calm and comforted.

Black Wolf looked over at me. 'Will you take some breakfast with us?'

I beamed. 'Thank you.' It was a great act of generosity by Black Wolf to allow a male who wasn't a direct relative to meet his family. I was nervous. This was the first time I'd been in the company of Kurdish people.

I knew from geography classes at school that the Kurds are the largest ethnicity in the world without a country of their own.

They historically inhabit the border regions of Iran, Turkey, Syria and Iraq, but they don't recognize the boundaries between these countries. Like the Pashtuns, they also have a very strong sense of identity.

Perhaps I should have been more careful, but Black Wolf had a relaxed manner and an easy charm, and I was fascinated by him. The way he moved had a confidence about it – as if he knew with absolute certainty he was the lord of all he surveyed. He reminded me of the tenth-century merchants I had read about in history books – the men who made this region famous for its rich trade routes.

If I still had any misgivings, they evaporated the moment his wife and her sisters-in-law caught sight of me.

For a moment I was taken aback at his wife's beauty: she wore a loose scarf around her neck, allowing her long black hair to escape on to her shoulders, but then the little boy who had taken family honour so to heart back at home became outraged – I wanted to tell her to cover her hair more carefully.

But my childish moralizing flew right out the window as his wife gushed: 'Oh, isn't he adorable? How cute.' As she spoke, she tousled my hair in a way that was intended to both embarrass and delight me in equal measure.

The women's teasing continued even as the men sat to eat first – the women would eat once we had finished. We ate flat bread, rich with olive oil, dunked in smoky baba ghanoush and some of the dhal I recognised from the previous evening's meal. We finished with delicate glasses of sweet, black tea.

Black Wolf sat back and lit a cigarette, picking a fleck of breakfast from his teeth. Tendrils of smoke oozed from his nostrils. 'So,' he said, cocking an eyebrow at me. 'Are you recovered from your journey so far?'

'Yes, thank you.' Then, to my horror, I suddenly felt tears spring to my eyes – perhaps because his family reminded me so much of my own. I chastised myself for being so silly and tried to hold them back, but it was too late. Black Wolf had seen them.

'I wish I could say I hadn't seen many children like you on this path, but I have. Too, too many. It's a sad world.'

other boys have done the same journey as Gulwali

My tears flowed unchecked now, and when his wife dabbed at my eyes with a tissue, the act of maternal kindness was just too much. I grabbed the tissue from her and looked at the floor as I struggled to find the right words in Farsi to make myself understood: 'My mother sent us away. I don't know where my brother is.' At that, a series of big, gulping sobs escaped me.

Black Wolf and his wife looked at each other and shook their heads sadly.

'This is unfortunate. But I am sure you will find him again. You have a long way to go and will no doubt cross paths with many unscrupulous men. Take my advice, little boy – do not trust these people, these so-called people-smugglers.'

'But aren't you a people-smuggler?' I blurted out, immediately regretting the way it sounded.

Black Wolf bristled for a moment, taking another pull on his cigarette. 'Me? You do me an injustice, boy – and under my own roof, too.'

His family laughed at my obvious discomfort.

He waved a hand for dramatic affect. 'I am a mere facilitator. My business interests lie in other directions.'

His brother, cousin and nephew laughed again.

'No, I am merely a man who has a well-located farm where people like you can stay until the smugglers are ready to move you on. I provide a service, and offer a level of discretion these men find comforting.' With that, he sent another cloud of smoke billowing up to the yellowed ceiling. 'More tea?'

When I rejoined my friends, I wasn't their favourite person.

'Gulwali, you idiot, where the hell have you been? You missed prayers.' Mehran did not look happy.

Even Baryalai raised his voice. 'I told you to stay with the group. Do you think we need the drama of worrying about you as well as ourselves?'

I tried to joke my way out of the situation. 'What? Did you guys eat breakfast without waiting for me?'

Even Abdul said a rare word: 'Gulwali, you haven't answered their questions.'

I was about to tell them, but then something stopped me. I had a sense that, however nice they were, they'd resent the fact that I'd just been given special treatment.

'I was seeing the horse.'

'A horse? In the dark? Do you want to get arrested?'

I felt a bit ashamed. 'I did pray. I prayed outside.'

They refused to speak to me all day.

For the next four days we settled into a fairly relaxed routine of eating, sleeping, praying and playing cards. Or rather, the others played cards – no one offered to teach me, and I felt too embarrassed to ask.

There were a couple of Kurdish story books on a shelf in the room. Like Pashtu, Dari and Farsi, the Kurdish language originates from Arabic; and, like most Afghan kids, I'd been taught to read the Quran in Arabic from a very young age. So I reckoned if I tried, I might be able to make out a few words.

I spent hours poring over the book trying to comprehend a few meanings.

On the fifth day, Black Wolf came to see us in the morning, clearly troubled by something. 'I can't make contact with the agent in Turkey. He's supposed to be meeting you there.'

Abdul was the first to speak: 'So, what does mean for us?'

75

'I can't make my arrangements to get you safely over the border until he makes contact. This has never happened before. I've only been paid to have you here for three days.'

I was beginning to learn that everything came down to money with these people.

Black Wolf must have read my thoughts because he looked straight at me. 'I'm not a greedy man. You can continue to stay here. And you will be taken care of. But, understand, this is causing me inconvenience. I have various meetings with business associates over the next few days. I need you to stay out of sight. After breakfast, you will stay in the furthest back orchards until it is dark. One of my men will bring your food there, and you will not return to this room until you are given instructions to do so.'

We sat listening in silence. I supposed it could have been worse.

For the first day it wasn't so bad. The late autumn sun still carried warmth, the trees offered dappled shade and they had laid out a large, woven-plastic mat for us to sleep on. Whenever my stomach started to rumble in the afternoon, Mehran and I took turns to pluck fruit from the trees.

Black Wolf entrusted me to collect our food from the women in the kitchen. I didn't mind in the least – it felt special to be trusted by the family, and the women insisted on doting on me in a way that made my insides bloom with butterflies.

 By now we'd been there ten days, and our relaxed routine was beginning to feel like a prison. We wanted to move on as much as Black Wolf clearly wanted us out of there – and it only got worse with the arrival of another five migrants. They were also Afghans, but mostly older men from the north.

The room was already squashed with the six of us; with five more bodies it became impossible to sleep without having to lie on someone's legs or end up with a foot in your face. I didn't like the newcomers, while my friends were growing more sullen and angry by the day. I tried to avoid everyone by going to the furthest reaches of the orchard where I could be alone.

It was a heavy dusk when Baryalai came running through the orchard to find me. 'Let's go. Get your stuff. We're going.'

'We're really going?' I asked, not quite believing my ears.

'What did I just say? Now, get your stuff, little man.'

I jumped to my feet.

The whole thing was like a military operation: within minutes, all eleven of us were crammed into the back of a high-sided pick-up truck. Black Wolf told us he'd sent two of his men ahead on horseback to check the way was clear.

'Stay down and shut up. And don't move for anything.'

CHAPTER SEVEN

The pick-up rattled on to the road. For most of the journey we drove with the headlights off. I was convinced we were going to crash but I could tell that Black Wolf was a skilled driver. The sky was carpeted with stars, giving enough light to see the splintered rocks that studded the dim contours of the surrounding hills. We were heading into a terrifying blackness along mountain roads, towards the crossing into Turkey.

It was cold on the back of the truck – the slipstream rushed down my back and made me shiver. But the air smelled sweet with the scent of wild grasses and herbs.

Before long, the truck slowed. 'Keep calm. We are coming to the police checkpoint,' Black Wolf called back to us softly.

The eleven of us were squashed together tightly, but I pressed myself down to be even smaller.

The driver's window squeaked indignantly as Black Wolf wound it down. Then, the scorching beam of a torch swept into the truck.

I can only guess that this policeman – whoever he was – had been paid off by Black Wolf in advance: there would have been no mistaking the eleven cowering bodies in the back. But he shook Black Wolf's hand and simply acted as if we weren't there.

A sudden metallic clicking sent my heart to my throat: I was convinced it was the guard moving the safety catch on his rifle.

Instead, Black Wolf made a low curse as he wrestled with the gear lever, before over-revving the engine and lurching us forward with a roar of tyres spinning on gravel.

I must have nodded off because my next memory is of waking up with the truck bouncing violently over broken ground.

'We are here.'

Waiting for us were the two horsemen who had been sent on ahead. As we got out of the pick-up, I looked curiously at the oil drums hanging on each side of their saddles.

One turned his horse towards the mountains. 'Follow me. Stay close. And don't fall back.'

As we prepared to follow them I turned to say goodbye to Black Wolf. To my disappointment he was already in his truck, pulling away without so much as a backward glance in our direction. It hurt me. Gulwali hurt again

We started walking, the second horseman bringing up the rear. I could make out the shapes of other horses and people walking parallel to us in the distance. Coming from the other direction, we passed a group of sad-faced donkeys pulling rickety carts piled high with goods: boxes, crates, sacks. As we continued further up the slopes we saw yet more people going back and forth, some with horses slipping and straining beneath heavy loads.

We stopped to drink from a little brook. The night air was so still, the mountains acted like an echo chamber. The unmistakable sounds of people singing folk songs drifted over to us.

I was amazed by the scene. Was this a border? It reminded me of the lands I'd travelled through to reach Waziristan. I had thought of Black Wolf as a tenth-century merchant, and this sight was even more fittingly incredible. It was like an ancient caravan of traders.

A familiar voice rang out: 'It as if King Darius himself is assembling his army tonight, yes?'

Black Wolf's lanky nephew, Rizgar, was walking towards us,

leading a horse. It struggled beneath bulging saddle bags. Whatever was inside them, I assumed, was in exchange for the oil Black Wolf was so clearly smuggling into Turkey.

'All of humanity is here,' he said, as he high-fived me. 'We have cheap labour, cheap fuel' – he knocked theatrically on one of the oil drums – 'and let's not forget cheap thrills – how much of your famous Afghan opium can a camel carry, do you think? This, my friends, is where the real business of the capitalist world is done.'

And with that he was gone.

We walked the whole night. I'd never walked that far or on such rough terrain. I was exhausted. It was made worse by not knowing how much longer we'd be walking for, or where exactly we were going. I knew we were walking towards Turkey, but no more than that.

Just before dawn we clambered across some stones that bridged a little river bed, and rounded a bend. My stomach went into little fits as heavenly wafts of chargrilled meat floated through the air, while the strained notes of Turkish pop music competed with a growing hubbub of voices and the sound of braying donkeys.

On a small flood plain at the bottom of a mountain was a makeshift bazaar. It was alive with hundreds of people and their pack horses, while battered trucks honked their way through the crowds. Everything was being sold in bulk, like an open air warehouse: cooking oil in drums, flour by the sack, raw wool, hessian bags of corn and beans. Some meat was for sale – mutton, mostly – and all still on the hoof. Men haggled, waving fists of grubby notes at each other with an intensity that suggested a punch might be thrown at any moment. A woman was busy loading a goat into a truck as her husband yelled instructions at her.

Our horse-riding guides led us to a small guest house that was built into a stone cliff. They told us to wait inside, then left us.

A Kurdish woman with a face as crinkled as a walnut shell directed customers with the no-nonsense manner of my beloved grandmother. She too spoke the local Kurdish dialect, and she kept trying to talk to us even though it was obvious none of us could understand a word. Eventually she worked this out and, using sign language, told us to follow her. We were delighted when she showed us a small bathroom where we could wash.

When we came back she had produced a large platter of bread, olives and a type of feta cheese. Happy to be clean, I set about the food. I had never tasted such sweet bread, while the olives and cheese were salty and rich. I could feel my body thanking my mouth, expanding in gratitude.

After we'd eaten, our guides came back and told us to follow them outside. The horsemen walked us a little way up a hill, then simply trotted off. 'We leave you here,' one called over his shoulder. 'God be with you.'

We stood there perplexed, not knowing what to do next. Thankfully, a small red pick-up truck was waiting nearby, and the driver gestured us over: 'You. Qubat people. Get in please.'

The back of the vehicle was packed with rolled-up carpets – he tried to squash the eleven of us in too. I was thinking how stupid it was. With such a heavy load I couldn't see how it would go anywhere. Somehow we crammed inside and the driver put blankets over our head. It was torture. The pick-up grumbled along slowly and painfully.

From my vantage point I could see some of the road and my heart was in my mouth as we passed a roundabout. A man in uniform, I think a local militia, was directing traffic. He had a rocket propelled grenade launcher strapped to his back.

It was as we began trundling down a rocky valley that we, unsurprisingly, broke down. We all got out while the driver tried to fix it. There was so much dust on the road; on my feet, it felt like walking through snow, only warmer. Even in the desert landscape of my home I hadn't seen anything quite like this.

We suddenly became aware of the sound of a car approaching. Further along the valley, we could see a vehicle snaking towards us.

'It's a police car. What shall we do?' Faizal yelled in panic. 'We have to get out of here.'

We tried to push the pick-up, but it was too heavy due to the carpets. We pushed and pushed with all our might until finally it spluttered into life. Trying to squeeze ourselves in a second time, this time with real urgency, was even harder.

After driving for a few more miles we arrived at a small guest house. There was a group of six other Afghans there already. They didn't speak to us much other than to tell us they were all from the province of Kandahar.

All I really remember about that stay was that my feet were so hot from being half-smothered by blankets, that I almost expected steam to come off them when I rinsed them under the outside tap. I was so grateful for the water – the way it cooled my body and helped settle my mind. As I sank into sleep, I didn't care that the tiny room I was in was cramped or that the mattresses were alive with fleas.

We were rudely awoken less than thirty minutes later by the guest-house owner. He was carrying a handful of disposable razors, while with his other hand he gestured to his chin, making a shaving motion.

The men were on their feet in a flash.

'You can't be serious,' said one of the guys from the other group, pulling at his thick grey beard to emphasize its length. 'I have grown this since I was his age,' he said, pointing at me.

The manager didn't understood his Pashtu; he just continued to make the same shaving motion.

The old man turned to the rest of us. 'He cannot be serious.

What if we are caught and I am sent home? How can I stand in front of my family with a shaven face?'

I was much too young to shave, although I could sympathize. All of my male relatives were proud of their facial hair. A long and full beard had not only been the law in Taliban-controlled Afghanistan, for many it is a key aspect of what it means to be an Muslim man.

They soon returned from the bathroom with faces like plucked chickens.

'Don't you dare laugh,' said Faizal, holding his fist to my nose. Abdul couldn't stop giggling. 'I'm serious. One more laugh and I'll cave your heads in with a brick.'

A turbaned old man sat in silence, running his fingers over his smooth chin. Silent tears dripped down his face.

There was nothing I could do for him. I decided to go back to sleep.

The next day, a face peered around the door and spoke to us in a mixture of Kurdish, Arabic and Farsi: 'Good morning. I'm glad you arrived safely.' He looked around the room. 'Ah, that's good,' he exclaimed. 'Before, they were only Afghan goat herders – now, they are taxi drivers.'

I seethed inside. Not only was he disrespecting the elders, he was making offensive comments about shepherds. Hadn't my grandfather been one?

'Now,' he continued, holding out a battered Polaroid camera. 'Let's capture that beauty for the ages. You need new documents.'

The rude camera operator told us he was an agent working for Qubat, and that he would be responsible for the next leg of our journey. He explained we were in the first small Turkish town in the Kurdish region, literally just over the border.

According to him, there were two different ways to a place

called Van, which was the nearest city. Neither option sounded very appealing. The first was to walk – it was less risky but much longer and more difficult. The second option was to go by car. This was obviously much easier – but the risk of arrest was much higher. If we wanted to take the second option, which he intended for us to do, that required new fake passports.

It took another day to get the documents made but it was, we all agreed, worth it. No one had wanted to walk.

I was ordered into a red Toyota Corolla along with Baryalai, Mehran and Abdul. I made sure I held Baryalai's hand. The others, including Faizal and Shah, got into different vehicles, which drove off in different directions.

'I have a feeling that is the last we'll see of them,' said Baryalai sadly.

We drove a few miles around the town before swapping to yet another car. The agent had told us secrecy was necessary because in a small town like that one, outsiders were easy to spot and people were inclined to talk.

The driver of the second car was a bit cocky. I felt uncomfortable the moment we got in.

'My car is fast,' he said, stroking the carpeted dashboard. 'We will arrive soon, *In'shallah*.' By now I had picked up a few words of Kurdish and could make out most of what he said. Invoking the will of Allah was normal in such conversations; his sales patter was less orthodox: 'Pay and pray. That's the way to make your stay,' he sang to us, as if it were a radio jingle.

It didn't really make sense to me. But then we were only paying for his car, not his conversation.

The scenery was wild and beautiful. Jagged ridgelines of the steep hills plunged into wooded pockets in the narrow valleys and gorges. I was very pleased we weren't walking.

The winding road had a constant military presence – we passed a long convoy of armoured vehicles and earth-moving machinery atop trucks, all heading towards the border. Turkish infantry marched along the road, too. I recognized the uniforms from home, where Turkish troops were part of the NATO mission.

As we rounded a bend, suddenly, on the road ahead, was a manned roadblock. Cars were being pulled over to the side and searched by soldiers.

'Say nothing,' the driver ordered, staring at us in the rear-view mirror.

An officer stood in the middle of the road, directing traffic towards his waiting men. An AK-47 hung around his neck, its muzzle tracking at windscreen height. He signalled to us to pull over.

The car slowed, coming to a rest in front of a sandbagged machine-gun position. Our driver lowered his window and volunteered our passports, speaking in Turkish.

My heart thundered in my ears. I knew that if the officer spoke to me then the game would be up. I put my hand over my mouth to stop myself blurting out something in fear.

The officer took his time, reading each one and staring into the car. We hadn't seen the fake passports until this moment. I was surprised to see they weren't Turkish, as we had assumed, but the familiar Afghan blue. Why would they give us Afghan passports again, when they had taken away from us the ones we already had in Iran? And how would an Afghan passport work here? None of it made sense.

More exchanges.

And then the soldier handed the passports back. He smiled into the back seat. 'Enjoy your holiday.'

'Praise to Allah,' the driver shouted with a laugh as we gathered speed away from the roadblock. He held out one of the passports and pointed at what looked like an entry stamp. 'Potato. We make with potato. It's visa *aloo*.'

85

He thought this was hilarious.

But it seemed the potato stamp had fooled the soldier into believing we'd entered Turkey legally.

'Two more checkpoints,' said the driver happily. And then he put out his hand, gesturing that he wanted money. 'Pay, please pay.'

'The agent has already paid,' Baryalai protested.

'You've paid me? No. Not me.'

'We paid Qubat. He paid the agent. You've been paid.'

'Really? Maybe you think of my cousin? People say we look the same.'

We all knew this guy was just trying to scam us, but we were resigned to the fact that we had to give him something.

One by one we pulled a few dollars from our pockets. I had spent most of my Iranian currency on snacks and drinks in Iran, but I still had the US$200 my mother had given me.

I took a couple of my smallest notes from my wallet – the most rumpled and filthy ones – and added them to the little stack on the driver's elbow rest.

'Yes,' said the Kurd. 'Pray and pay. Very good.'

He put the passports firmly back into his glovebox. Clearly his next passengers would need the potato stamp.

I felt sick. Everybody was out for money in this game, and we were very easy targets.

After about half a day we arrived at Van. We drove through a series of dilapidated neighbourhoods before pulling into a complex of abandoned workshops. We all climbed out and waited in the shade as the driver approached a tall, thin man in a Western-style pin-stripe suit.

They shook hands and had a short conversation before the driver got back in his car and departed. 'Pray and pay,' he shouted, by way of farewell.

The tall man looked very Turkish, yet he spoke to us in Iranian Farsi. 'I am Malik. This is my operation. In a few minutes, one of my men will transfer you to a minibus, which will take you to a house in the suburbs. There you will be able to rest, before your journey continues.'

I thought he looked very impressive. He carried a leather brief-case and exuded the air of a man who was very much the boss. In fact, I realized he was a Turkish version of Black Wolf. I started to imagine how nice it would be to stay in a decent place again.

I got very excited when we saw the house. It was large, sitting behind a high wall, and there were many shady trees in the garden. It looked beautiful. I was already planning to lie beneath a tree on the cool grass.

Our driver pulled up right outside. 'Go quickly – but don't run.'

As I stepped through the small visitor's door on the main gate, however, my heart sank. There were two burly guys standing there, neither of whom looked friendly.

'Come. Around the back.'

The two guys manhandled us, pushing us along a narrow passage that ran between the house and the high brick wall. At the rear of the property stood a little shack.

Baryalai was the first to speak.

'It's a bloody chicken coop.'

DANGER

CHAPTER EIGHT

Fifteen people were to sleep in that chicken coop – cramped, filthy and starving. The four of us, and the eleven dead-eyed others who were already there.

'Welcome to hell,' said a red-haired man with a straggly beard as we entered.

A few mattresses covered the floor, but there was not enough room for all of us to lie down. There was barely even room to sit, but we squashed ourselves in anyway. A tiny, plastic-covered window gave a blurry view of the trees in the garden.

Previous residents had written on the broken door which swung despondently, hanging off its hinges. Some had chosen to write their names and the dates they had been there, using the Afghan calendar. All the entries were written in either Pashtu or Dari.

Hamid Shah. Herat. 1384.

Khalid Kakar. Kabul.

Others offered advice or warnings:

'Trust no one.'

'Do not pay ferry man.'

'Life is cheap and so are smugglers.'

'Malik is a bastard.'

In the coming days, I learned the truths on that door.

A scruffy, bald man in a dressing gown brought us some food:

boiled rice and Turkish bread. The rice was dry and the bread looked stale; nor was there nearly enough to go around. He didn't speak a word as he roughly plonked the dishes on the doorstep.

After he left, the others let rip.

'This bastard has no manners.'

'He treats us like animals. Get used to it.'

'He's a filthy drunk.'

They said they'd been there for three weeks, yet Malik had promised them it was only supposed to be overnight. They were waiting to go to Istanbul, on the next leg of the journey. I assumed from this that Istanbul was to be our next destination too.

We were not allowed outside that chicken coop. We had a single pipe that only dribbled water for half an hour twice a day; we never knew what times it would be turned on so when it did splutter to life we would scramble to wash our faces and rub a toothbrush through our stale mouths.

A lot of time was spent trying to control our bodily functions. Just once every twenty-four hours we were taken in groups of three to use a stinking toilet. There was never toilet paper, and the tap for washing yourself often didn't work, forcing desperate men to wipe themselves clean on the streaked walls. It wasn't long before people started to get sick. I don't know what was worse – the horror of watching someone vomit in such close confines, or the embarrassment of the man who soils himself in front of his travel companions.

For the entire time we were there, we got very little food – a few mouthfuls of rice each per day, if we were lucky. When we complained, the bald man said he'd bring us a roast chicken if we paid him. He charged the equivalent of US$5. I was shocked – my mother could have fed our family for days with that money. But I was starving, and my body was craving protein, so I spent some of my precious money and ate my little share of the chicken greedily.

I did my best to cheer everyone up by trying to tell jokes or reminding them of one of my favourite Pashtu sayings: 'If the heart is big enough, the space is never too small.' I can't say my efforts really worked.

From our few toilet breaks, we worked out that the bald man lived with his elderly mother. Occasionally there were a few kids about. I could see, too, why the others had called the man a drunk: he stank of stale alcohol and was always wearing his dressing gown. This made me dislike him even more – I completely disapproved of any Muslim drinking alcohol. His speech was permanently mumbled and he seemed strangely blind to the appalling situation we were in. This man was capable of such cruelty, but the odd thing was that he seemed numb to what he was doing.

Fortunately for me, the elderly mother noticed how young I was. She did not shy from showing her affections, and I had already learned at Black Wolf's compound the benefits of ingratiating myself with the women of the house.

We had no means of communication, however, so without a common language we resorted to a kind of sign language.

I pointed at myself. 'I am Gulwali.'

'Gulwali,' she repeated, struggling with my accent. Then, 'Gu-wal-i,' she said again, breaking it into syllables.

I nodded enthusiastically.

She smiled a toothy smile and pointed at her chest. 'Ma-ree-ammm. Ma-reee-ammm.'

'Mariam?'

She seemed pleased with my progress. Then she pointed at the bald man. 'My son.' At that, she rolled her eyes then pointed to her temple and twirled her finger in a circular motion, as if to show he was mad.

I sensed an ally. 'I am twelve years old,' I said, explaining it by pointing at my chest flashing first ten, then two fingers.

Her face erupted with concern and surprise. She pointed at the dilapidated shed and waved her index finger horizontally to show the universal sign of matriarchal displeasure. Then she drew her finger towards the back door of the house and pointed to a small patch of carpet in the family living room. She stabbed her finger at the floor, then placed her hands palm-together and rested her cheek upon them.

'You want me to sleep in there?' I asked, repeating the gestures back at her.

She nodded enthusiastically.

I broke into a huge smile and, without a moment's thought, gave her a huge hug. 'Thank you.'

I will never forget the kindness and gentleness that old lady showed me. In addition to the safe place to sleep away from the hell of the chicken coop, she also sneaked me into her kitchen and forced bowls of rice and vegetables, Turkish bread and steaming sweet tea into my hands.

Those left in the coop were furious that I was allowed to sleep inside; it made no difference to them that I was a child. I'm sure they suspected I was getting fed well too. They thought I was manipulating the family to get special privileges. Maybe I was. But would those men have done any differently in my situation? I was a little boy, and I was fast learning it was the only card I had to play.

I think the truth was that we were all so desperate that we quickly came to resent anybody who had something we did not – the extra mouthful of water, a tiny bit more floor space, a filthy pillow or a few grains of rice. Our humanity was slipping away – being stolen away. Perhaps that was the real price of this journey.

The resentment grew as the situation inside the chicken coop deteriorated. We had been there more than a week and some of the men were beginning to reach breaking point. Starved, thirsty and packed into filthy conditions, they became increasingly desperate.

At least I was able to use my position inside the house to help my friends a little bit, sneaking in extra food and water.

Early one morning, a man turned up in the yard carrying several lengths of heavy polythene sheeting. He balanced on an old chair and began to cast the sheeting on to the roof of the shed, like a fisherman casting his net. Satisfied with how he had laid it, he then lobbed half-a-dozen broken bricks on top to hold it in place.

The *thump-thump-thump* on the flimsy structure woke several of the occupants inside.

The bald man, who had come down to watch him work, grunted and pointed, directing their gaze to the new roof covering. The builder wore the half-smile of a man who has done a good job. 'Now that I have fixed your dog kennel, I will be able to get another twenty or thirty dogs to join you, no problem.'

It was too much for the men to hear. One of them lunged forwards, grabbing a brick from the pile on the floor. 'Where is that liar, Malik?' He grabbed our drunken host by the wrist, turning the half-brick towards his face. 'Maybe I should knock some sense into you instead?'

Two other men surrounded the builder.

There was a short pause and then, without warning, the builder suddenly crouched into a ball and flew at them, sending them flying on to their backs.

Everyone else began kicking and punching.

It was madness. We would be discovered, I was sure of it, so I shouted at the top of my lungs: 'Stop it. Stop it.'

'Stay out of it, boy, or you'll get a slap too.'

I backed away just as two other men – the ones in charge of the main gate – ran into the yard. They both had sticks, which they used to beat my friends until they lay whimpering on the ground. They were about to come for me but Mariam pulled my face into her bosom and wagged her finger at them.

They shouted something back at her in Turkish, waved their sticks once more then took out cigarettes, lit them, and swaggered back to their guard post.

Mariam took me inside and insisted I drink some tea.

A little later one of the guards came and thrust a mobile phone into my hands.

'*Salaam*, Gulwali. This is Malik.'

I held the phone in silence.

He continued to elaborate, in Farsi: 'Gulwali. I heard about what happened this morning. And I hear you have all been complaining. This is not good. I want you to talk to the others and inform everyone that I am trying to get you out of there as soon as I can.'

'OK,' I said, unsure about why I needed to be the messenger.

'I am arranging a luxury coach for the next leg of your journey. Lots of room, air conditioning, comfortable seats. But such luxury does not come easy here – I need a little more time to organize this. So tell everyone to be patient, because otherwise they will have to travel in the back of a smelly truck.'

'OK,' I repeated. 'I will tell them.'

'Good boy. And don't forget – it will be a luxury bus. Air conditioning and all that.'

I soon realized why Malik hadn't wanted to deliver his news in person: the men glared at me with pure hatred.

'And you believed him? You stupid, foolish boy.'

'I don't care how we travel. I just want to get out of this stinking, shit-filled cage. But I suppose you didn't tell him that?'

'And besides, what do you care? Tucked up inside with your foster mother dropping morsels down your scheming little throat. I should choke you like a chicken.'

'Leave the boy alone,' said Baryalai. 'Can't you see he's no more to blame for this than ourselves? Until we reach our destination, we are at the mercy of these people. They own us, and can treat us as they will. You'd better get used to that.'

'Easy for you to say,' snapped one of the eleven. 'You've only been here one week. We've been here for almost a month now. And it's more than half a year since I last saw my wife and children.'

Later that day, Malik himself strolled into the yard. He was all smiles and greasy charisma. 'And how has the food been, boys? Has the man been feeding you properly? You look as though you've put on weight.'

At that, the men couldn't contain themselves a moment longer. They railed at Malik, listing their grievances one by one, careful to highlight the near-starvation conditions we had been forced to endure.

'I am as shocked as you are,' exclaimed Malik, holding his hand to his heart. He loosed a storm of abuse at the bald man, who had come out to the yard with him. He was clearly drunk again, and you could see he was confused. I found it hard to believe that Malik didn't know exactly what was going on – he struck me as the kind of man who kept a close eye on his business.

I concluded that Malik was shifting the blame. He clearly liked to protect his self-image of a successful, maybe even legitimate, businessman. Any failings were out of his hands – he was trying to do right by us. But even in my child's mind I knew our misery paid for those expensive suits.

As he left, he gave a curt promise: 'The situation is urgent and I will deal with it accordingly.'

The following afternoon we were ordered out of the property.

CHAPTER NINE

Our departure was so sudden I didn't even have time to say a proper goodbye to Mariam.

I owe her so much – her kindness may have literally saved my life, as I'm not sure I could have survived in the shed with the men. I also felt sorry for her: she clearly wasn't pleased with having a bunch of undocumented migrants in her backyard, but with a useless, alcoholic son in charge, what power did she have to say no?

We were driven to the outskirts of the city. By now, I understood fully that behind all the noble talk, the only thing that mattered to any of these people was money. This was a business, where profit was the only motive and people were of value only for as long as they could keep on paying. But there is more than one way to make money out of migrants – as I was about to discover when we pulled up outside a large, ramshackle hostel building, just off a ring road.

'I think I have died and gone to heaven,' joked Mehran. He stood, slack-jawed, staring at three girls bending over tables collecting dirty plastic plates and cups.

I had never seen a blonde woman before. It shocked me – not so much the colour of her hair, but rather that she made so little effort to keep herself covered. She was wearing a skirt that barely reached her knees, and a tight T-shirt that left nothing to the imagination. To me she was as good as naked.

'I doubt these women are virgins,' snorted Abdul. He looked at the women in a way I thought was very bad, and I shot him an admonishing look.

As we walked down a long corridor inside, I could see various rooms off to the side. There must have been over a hundred people staying there – the cacophony of different languages filled the air.

Dozens, perhaps more than fifty people, sat on the floor of one of the largest rooms. Mostly men and boys like ourselves, they ate with a concentration that comes from constant hunger.

A young Persian woman with eyes the colour of Turkish coffee and an elegant oval face called out to us in Farsi: 'Come. Sit and eat.' There was a sadness to her, and a heavy layer of make-up did little to hide the swelling under her eye. The bruising on her upper arm also spoke of violence.

'These women are filthy whores,' said a man loudly, as if condemning their morality might make him a better human.

'Then don't eat their food,' said Baryalai. He smiled graciously at a woman as she handed him a heaped plate of delicious-looking red peppers stuffed with vegetables and rice. She was a little older than the others – fairer than most, too.

'She's European, I am sure of it,' he said, as if he could read my mind.

'They should cover their hair,' I said. 'Are they not ashamed to disgrace their families by dressing in such a way?' For me, modesty and honour were two sides of the same coin.

As we crossed our legs and began shovelling in food – I hadn't eaten properly in weeks – Abdul looked at me thoughtfully. 'Gulwali,' he said, through a mouthful of food. 'How did you come to be here?'

'You know this. My mother sent me and my brother. We had to leave.'

'Yet you think these girls are here by their own choice?'

'No, I'm just saying they should cover themselves. Their families—'

'We're a long way from home now, Gulwali. This is not Afghanistan. None of us have families. Are these women not showing you kindness?'

'Yes.'

'But still you would condemn them as immoral?'

Abdul didn't speak much, but when he did, I have to admit it was usually with wisdom.

Mehran sat himself down next to us. 'I can't decide which one to marry first. The Persian is kind and beautiful.' He took a mouthful and continued: 'She is sweet and a little shy. She would make a good wife, I think.'

Baryalai looked at him. 'I don't think these women are open to marriage. Or, more likely, whoever owns them has plans for them that don't involve marrying a penniless Afghan sneaking his way to Europe.'

I smiled. 'You sound like my grandmother.'

We all laughed.

'Clearly a wise woman.'

As I ate, I remembered how the sheep used to know the sound of my whistle. I had been their master. Now we were the sheep, and our master's voice was currently the lilting baritone of Malik and his purring lies. Was he also the master to these women? Did the business of prostitution pay for his smart suits and leather briefcase? I couldn't have hated him more at that moment if I had tried; he was the epitome of immorality to me. This was everything my family and my culture stood against.

We spent twelve hours there – long enough to realize that there were other women. Some were Africans, one who looked definitely Middle Eastern, a Chinese woman and a couple more who looked Eastern European.

Mulling over Abdul's words afterwards, I realized he was right.

I had no grounds to judge them. I was too young to fully understand what hell they were in or on their way to, but I had an idea.

At about 10 o'clock that night the place emptied out, with the men in the front rooms leaving. A couple of hours later, and my little group of four and the other fifty people in the room with us were told we too were on our way.

Outside the building was a large cattle truck with a canvas roof. It certainly didn't look big enough for fifty-four people but we were ordered in anyway. Climbing up was hard because it was so high, but I didn't want to show I was scared so I didn't ask anyone to help me. All sad thoughts of the poor women had vanished. I was too busy worrying about my own safety.

We crammed inside. Men were squashed into every free space, guards using fists and sticks to make sure no room was wasted. The four of us clung to each other so we didn't get separated. I balled down into a shape as tiny as I could make between Mehran's knees among a forest of legs and fetid feet.

I only knew Istanbul was the destination, but how far that was I had no idea.

After five sweaty, painful and cramped hours, the lorry pulled over. A heavy-set Kurd in his mid-twenties got out of the passenger's side of the cab, adjusting his sunglasses and trucker's cap. He opened the canvas. '*Yallah.*'

Men started jumping off, and we were pushed towards some nearby trees, where some guides were waiting. The chief guide carried a large staff, just like a shepherd. 'Follow me. Walk fast.' He started walking uphill. And, just like sheep, we followed him.

I wanted to be sure my friends and I stayed close. It was around 3 a.m., and still dark. I took it upon myself to be the organizer: 'Baryalai, I'll hold your hand. Abdul, you hold Mehran's. And let's stay to the front.'

I looked back to see the truck driving off into the distance.

We didn't know why we were walking or what was coming next. The mental anxiety of not knowing where I was going or when the walking would end made every step harder: it's easier to walk for miles on end if you know where you are heading.

The terrain was a bit like the border-crossing from Iran into Turkey – very rocky and steep. I had the distinct feeling that we could be ambushed and arrested – or even worse – at any moment.

We stopped to rest and drink from a little stream. It was so brief that those following up at the rear didn't have time to sit down; by the time they caught up, we'd already been ordered to get up and keep moving. My instinct to stay close to the guide at the front had been the right one.

After two hours of a forced march, we came down a little gulley into some farmland. The lorry was there waiting for us, and we were ordered back into it.

I was too tired to work out how the lorry knew where we were, or how the guides had managed to bring us to the right spot.

We drove the whole of that day. It was baking hot under the canvas, and we were so thirsty and hungry. Occasionally the driver would stop and throw a couple of bottles of water into the back. They didn't give us any food.

I was grateful for the water, but the driver didn't seem willing to stop for toilet breaks – presumably because we'd have been seen. I tried to drink as little as possible so that I didn't need to go. Some men, however, were so desperate they were peeing into the empty bottle. It smelled so bad. Eventually I had to try too, as my bladder was really hurting, but I just couldn't do it.

'Get over it, Gulwali. What's your problem? Just do it in the bottle.'

'I can't.'

Baryalai laughed at me. 'In our company, you will become knowledgeable.' Another old Pashtu saying.

I tried to smile. But I still couldn't do it in that bottle.

Thirty hours later, and we were on our third truck drop and hike. To the side of us we had been able to see that we were walking past some kind of checkpoint: we could hear dogs barking and make out queues of vehicles and soldiers. We were walking in order to skirt past them.

I understood what was happening now: the trucks drove as far as they could along the roads without meeting the police. As we got close to the police posts, they ordered us out and into the woods so that we could walk around the checkpoint. The driver would pass through the checkpoint with an empty vehicle and all his official paperwork intact. He would then drive a safe distance away, pull over and wait for us to find him again. Then we would climb back into the truck and continue driving.

I was so thirsty and weak now that only Baryalai kept me going. He kept urging me on, taking my hand when I couldn't put another foot in front of the other. My feet were bleeding and I just wanted to lie down next to the path and sleep. But that would have been fatal. 'Come on, little man.'

'I can't.'

'You must.'

I could not.

Our column had thinned out; I had dropped right to the back of it. Only the weakest and oldest hobbled past us now. I knew my situation was getting critical when one of the eldest men in the group wheezed by.

'*Kaka*, uncle, help me with the child.' Baryalai's voice was desperate.

'I can't.'

'Help us. Look at him. He's almost done.'

'I can't. If I help him, who will help me?'

'Come on, Gulwali. Get up. We've got to go. Up. Move. Move. Move.'

'I'm sorry,' gasped the old man, shuffling off.

Baryalai exhaled a long breath. 'Here, drink.' He presented the last mouthful of grey liquid from a creased Sprite bottle. 'Come on, boy. You must. What would your mother say if she saw you being so weak?'

That was the right thing to say to me. I started to gather what few mental resources I had left and I kept going. One footstep at a time. Left, right, left, right – I just concentrated on the rough ground immediately beneath my feet. Left, right, left, right.

On and on and on.

After walking for four hours we came to a place where the truck was waiting for us again. This time we drove for three hours before getting out and walking again.

I don't know how I kept going.

I was so grateful to Baryalai looking out for me the way he did – I couldn't have made it otherwise.

In total we did the drop and walk four times. On the penultimate drop, we sat and waited for so long for the truck to return that the sky went from late afternoon gold to the stars punctuating the sky. I stared up at the beauty of the twinkling pinpoints of light, wondering if the truck would ever return and if that night would be the night I died of cold.

The next morning, our driver dropped us by the side of a fast-flowing river and told us to drink and relieve ourselves. No sooner had we got out than two more trucks roared up in a cloud of dust. Five men climbed out and started shouting in Kurdish.

For a minute I thought their anger was directed at us, but then our driver and his mate pulled knives and ran at them. A fight broke out. We just stood and stared as those seven men punched and lunged at each other. They were like wild animals – ripping off their shirts to reveal huge, hairy chests and pulling off studded leather belts, which they waved over their heads like lassos. There was a lot of shouting, screaming of insults and blades glinting in the air. I was certain someone would get stabbed.

It appeared to be over when our driver screamed at us all to get back in the truck. I'd never been so happy to oblige.

This was a turf war. It turned out the smuggling gangs would occasionally hijack each other's groups, especially when they wanted to settle a score.

The driver got back in with a second man, who told us to be quiet and stay calm. This man said that Malik and he had had a disagreement and so he was taking us as his revenge. He told us to sit tight until he was ready to order our driver where to go.

We sat there inside the truck, parked by the river, for maybe four or five hours. Waiting, expecting the worst at any second. We didn't know what to think. We thought that maybe because we'd complained to Malik about the chicken coop he'd set the whole thing up. Or maybe the second man was lying? Perhaps Malik had sold us to him? Perhaps the driver was in on it?

We all huddled in the back whispering frantically to each other.

'Should we kill them?'

'Let's run for it, while we still can.'

'Just wait. Don't do anything rash.'

I didn't know which way to turn. I could only hold Baryalai's hand for comfort.

In the end, after what seemed like for ever, the second man got out and we continued on our way as if nothing had happened. We didn't know how the dispute had been resolved.

We were still very afraid and shaken when, a couple of hours later, the driver pulled into a remote set of farm buildings. We were told to bed down in a dirty cow shed where huddled groups of other migrants already lay. There must have been over 300 people already there, plus our truckload. I had absolutely no idea where we were.

There were no mattresses, just straw on the floor. We were human cattle. It was a beautiful, bright autumn day but inside the sheds it was dark and dank, smelling of cow dung. We didn't understand why we were there or for how long we'd have to stay.

It had echoes of the chicken coop all over again.

My life couldn't have felt any more out of control. Just over a month ago, I had been an ordinary schoolboy interested in my books, looking after my family, collecting firewood, teasing my aunts and sleeping in my grandparents' bed. Those happy days already felt like a lifetime ago.

But at least my original companions, Mehran, Abdul and Baryalai, were still with me. We'd made friends with Shah and Faizal but lost them so quickly. I was beginning to learn that people came and went, and there was no way of controlling that. And so, while I was determined to stay close to my friends for my own safety, I was also steeling myself for the inevitable loss. I didn't see the point of trying to make new friends. I didn't have the energy.

In the afternoon of the next day, one of the drivers made an announcement in the cow shed over a loudhailer: 'Stay ready and alert. Your trucks are coming back this evening.'

Sure enough, that evening we continued onwards, driving past the outskirts of a city someone told me was the Turkish capital, Ankara. Finally, after three very long days and nights, we reached Istanbul – the city that bridges east and west.

CHAPTER TEN

Struggling to balance on top of a flaking steel-framed school chair, the glory of Istanbul – the city famed for being a melting pot of ancient and modern – lay like a patchwork blanket before me.

I was hoping to catch a glimpse of the Blue Mosque – one of the city's iconic sights, and a place Black Wolf had told me about. His eyes had misted over when he'd described it as one of the most beautiful things he'd ever seen. But I had no idea if we were even anywhere near the mosque. All I had been able to see of Turkey's largest city for the past two days was a narrow segment of it, through a small, greasy window, a segment that was visible only when I stood on the chair. Mostly I could see just satellite dishes, television aerials, air-conditioning vents and clothes strung across crudely erected rooftop washing-lines. I could just about make out a few minarets, but they seemed too small.

'Get off there, kid. I'm not going to tell you again.'

It was the Turkish owner of the apartment we were staying in.

I hurriedly jumped down.

The night we had arrived in Istanbul, we had been taken to what looked like a shanty town. As we had disembarked from the truck, we had been greeted with the question: 'People of Malik?'

I supposed that meant we were under Malik's ultimate control now that we were in Turkey.

The area was a clutter of temporary shelters made with metal poles, tin roofs and tarpaulins. It was situated near quite a busy road and wasn't hidden by fences, so was in clear view of any passing motorists. I was amazed that undocumented migrants would be left to wait in so obvious a place – but at least there we were able to pray, go to the toilet and walk around the space quite freely.

We waited in the shanty town for a whole day – it seems the business of smuggling takes time to organize. Malik apparently needed confirmation that we had arrived in Istanbul before he paid the drivers; then the agent in Istanbul needed to get the OK that it was his turn to move us. Abdul, who was good at using his quietly calm ways to obtain information from people, had managed to glean this from the driver who had brought us here.

Once all was in order, the fifty-four people who had been in the truck were split up into smaller groups and moved off to various safe houses. Luckily, I was grouped with the three men who had been my friends since Mashhad.

The apartment Baryalai, Mehran, Abdul and I stayed in was an anonymous-looking, two-bedroom flat in a medium-sized block in a quiet suburb. We four shared one room, and another group of five shared the other. We stayed there for two weeks, not going out and getting very bored and frustrated until, without warning, we four were moved on again, to a not-dissimilar apartment a couple of blocks away.

This time it seemed we'd been passed on to three Afghan business partners who lived in Istanbul. They didn't give us much information about our situation. 'We're working on a plan. You'll be in Greece soon – that's all you need to worry about.'

I was even more confused when they gave me US$150. 'Qubat sent it, for your expenses.'

To date, Black Wolf had been the only agent who had ever bothered to take the time to try and explain things – I often fantasized about how nice it would have been to stay at his farm. I could have helped him with the dodgy oil business and made myself useful. Even if I'd had to muck out his horses, it would have been preferable to the situation in which I now found myself.

By this time I was in a perpetual state of confusion that made relaxing properly, even for one night, impossible. We just never knew when we'd be told to be on the move again. I was constantly exhausted, living on adrenalin and fear.

For the first few days we were locked inside that apartment on our own, but the three Afghans had left a few basic groceries – rice, salt, oil, tinned chickpeas – which we cooked for ourselves on a little electric stove in the kitchen. I had never so much as boiled an egg before – male children weren't expected to know how to cook in my family. Thankfully Baryalai, who had lived for several years in a refugee camp, was a master at creating a tasty meal out of nothing.

The trio of Afghan agents popped in every couple of days to check on us:

'Are you men staying quiet? Do not alert the neighbours.'

On their third visit, one of them took me outside with him to get the shopping.

I was delighted to have a taste of freedom, even if only for an hour. Istanbul was enthralling, more diverse and exciting than Tehran, which now felt sterile by contrast: the vibrant noise of the city; the smell of grilling kebabs; long rows of high piles of spices and fresh herbs and vegetables outside the shops; large, smart modern blocks situated next to preserved historical buildings; and thumping pop music booming from cars. Music had been banned in Afghanistan under the Taliban as unIslamic; after they fell, pop music – mostly Indian or American – had exploded in popularity in Afghanistan. But this Turkish music was different: it was a real mixture of Arabic and Western sounds.

I was able to change a small amount of the dollars my mother had given me into Turkish lira, and I used a little to buy some treats: a new T-shirt for me, and a box of delicious dates and a bag of Turkish sweets to share with the others. I was so disappointed when the shopping trip ended and I had to go back to the house.

Climbing the stairs, I could feel the walls closing in on me once more.

The following day, we were all dozing when the mobile phone the agents had left us for emergencies started shrilling.

Baryalai picked it up.

I could hear yelling down the line. 'The police are coming for you. You all have to get out of there. Now.'

We were given an address, told to split into pairs, and walk calmly down the street to it. We shoved our meagre belongings into our bags and rushed to leave the flat. I walked with Abdul, and Mehran was with Baryalai.

The new address wasn't far away. I wondered how many other houses and apartments across Istanbul were also hiding the displaced and desperate.

For the next month we were moved around a lot. Everywhere we stayed there was always a succession of bitter, angry, tearful migrants who found themselves sliding downwards on this game of Snakes and Ladders, on journeys that that had stalled or gone awry, or were going backwards as they were forced to return to their homelands. They couldn't wait to share their tales of woe and warnings of what was to come for the fresher-faced hopefuls.

One man we met in the basement told us he'd recently escaped from a kidnap situation in Kurdish Iran – where we'd just come from. He had been forced to write home to ask for more money, but no one had replied and the smuggler wouldn't release him. It had taken three months for him to sort it out so that he could reach Istanbul and continue the journey. Others had been tricked

THE LIGHTLESS SKY

into paying whatever cash they had left to take fake routes, or pay for transport that never arrived, leaving them stranded. Others had faced arrest and deportation. Some had been immersed in this nightmare for so long they had almost forgotten who they were or where it was they were supposed to be going.

I listened to truly terrible tales of beatings, blackmail, women and children suffocating in trucks, or men being shot at point-blank range when they argued with their handlers. In some ways, I suppose it was helpful to be warned, but it only made me more scared – knowing that I might be tricked or physically hurt didn't mean that I could prevent it. I was at the mercy of the drivers, guest-house owners and their bosses – the agents of the actual smugglers. And there was nothing I could do about it.

Our current three agents continued to tell us they were working on a plan to get us to Greece. Every time they checked in on us we heard the same promise: 'Tomorrow you will go to Greece.'

But tomorrow was taking an awfully long time to come.

Greece was a mythical, magical country I had read about in school. I knew it as an ancient civilization and the home of Alexander the Great, a man respected in Afghan history as a great warrior after marching through central Afghanistan in 330 BC. He famously wrote a letter to his mother about the bravery of the Afghan warriors he fought: 'You have brought only one son into the world, but every man in this land could be called an Alexander.' His blond-haired, blue-eyed descendants are still very visible in the areas where he and his men made camp.

As a schoolboy, the idea of my visiting such an historic place as Greece would have been the dream of a lifetime.

But not like this.

Other migrants told us that from Istanbul the smugglers might take us one of three ways to Greece, and then on to mainland Europe.

The easiest was across the Aegean Sea by boat. I heard that if you were lucky it would only take three hours, yet the journey was fraught with terrible dangers on overcrowded and unseaworthy vessels. As a child from a landlocked country who had no idea how to swim, this was beyond the wilds of my imagination. But if that sounded bad to me, the second route was worse – one hollow-eyed migrant described it to me as 'the pathway to hell itself'. This route had to be done on foot, marching over dangerous mountains, hiding near borders, and crossing three countries, from Turkey into Bulgaria, then on to Macedonia, and finally into Greece. The third path was also an overground route, crossing a narrow, 12.5 kilometre strip of heavily militarized land which forms the direct border between Turkey and Greece.

Everywhere we stayed, other migrants filled us with fear about the overground routes.

'No roads, no tracks, only rocks and mountains.'

'No way to get food when it runs out.'

'Bodies were littered all along the pathway. No one will ever find them.'

'It's a wasteland of death.'

I heard so many terrifying descriptions from those who had tried to make it, but had either been turned back by Bulgarian border guards or forced to retreat by the vicious weather, that I must have crossed both overground routes hundreds of times in my head. As scared as I was of the thought of a sea crossing, these other two routes filled me with absolute dread. I was told that both these routes could take weeks or even months to navigate, and that there were many rivers with terrible currents. Some you could only cross with a small speedboat, but the boats the smugglers provided were very old and they often capsized – and that meant certain death, dashed on the rocks by the fast-flowing waters. If there was no boat you had to try and cross on foot. I was told of smugglers who had forced screaming women and children into the water at gunpoint, only to watch them drown. Moreover, portions of both routes were said to have deadly land- or anti-vehicle mines. I knew all about landmines; they were one of the tragic legacies of the Afghan civil war: some 10–15 million mines were said to still litter the country in the year I was born. One of my closest friends at school only had one leg – the other had been blown off after he had stepped on a mine during a football game. And, according to pretty much everyone who had been that way, Bulgarian border guards were notorious for shooting at migrants. If you were lucky enough not to be shot, they might beat you before stealing your possessions and forcing you to walk back to Turkey.

The worst story of all was told to me by a Pakistani man. He and his brother had attempted the third route in the middle of winter. They had become separated from their group and wandered through the snow until they were rescued by Greek soldiers. His brother had had such bad frostbite he had been taken to hospital by the soldiers, where his fingers were amputated. After he recovered, both brothers were deported back to Pakistan. And now the one telling me the story was here again, attempting the journey for the second time. 'When we went home, my brother wasn't sad for the loss of his hand. He was sad because he became useless, unable to support our family. I have to try again because if I don't make it, who will feed us?'

Hearing this story caused my brother Hazrat to haunt my dreams more than ever. Where was he now? Had he been tricked into taking one of the overground routes? Was my brother's broken body lying on the bottom of a river bed somewhere? Had he been shot?

Was he lying out there bleeding, calling for me?

CHAPTER ELEVEN

I was almost beginning to want to be caught: being deported surely had to be better than getting killed. But the thought that Hazrat was out there somewhere, lost and alone, stopped me. Hazrat would be looking for me too, I was certain of that. Besides, if I went home without him, I knew my mother would never forgive me.

The only solace in my existence was that by now the three Istanbul-based Afghan agents trusted our little group and gave us more freedom, so we were able to go outside for a few hours a day. We walked through parks or drank Turkish coffee in pavement cafés – anything to help pass the time. On one of our walks we discovered an Afghan-run DVD rental and sale store, something that had Baryalai and Mehran practically whooping with joy. Films had also been banned under the Taliban but, once they had gone, bootleg movies had flooded the bazaar in our town. I hadn't been able to see them, however, because my family didn't have a TV, and my father didn't approve of such things anyway.

After chatting to the friendly shopkeeper at the store, Baryalai used some of his precious cash to purchase three copies of Bollywood movies. He was as excited as a little kid. 'I saw this one three times in Peshawar. It's so good. Trust me, little man, you are going to love it.'

When we got back to the *musafir khanna*, he fiddled with the

Chinese-made TV and DVD player that stood in one corner. It had a label on it which read: 'Sonysonic'. Baryalai told me that was the maker. 'Don't you get it? It's brilliant. The Chinese are so enterprising.' He laughed, but I couldn't understand why he found it so funny.

The films were OK. They were in Hindi with English subtitles, so I couldn't understand what was being said. There was a lot of singing and dancing and a big fight scene. I couldn't really work out what was going on except that it was some kind of love story. I very nearly nodded off. When the closing credits rolled I looked over at my friend. He had tears running down his face.

The next film was a historical action movie. Even though I still couldn't understand the words I quite liked the fight scenes, and I much preferred this movie – so much so that by the time it ended, I was so utterly engrossed in it I had completely forgotten it was make-believe. The final epic battle had seen so many brave warriors fall that I turned to Mehran and said, 'Is everyone in India dead now?'

He bopped me over the head.

Those few moments of light relief were rare. By now all four of us were completely fed up with the constant moving and changing of locations, and the anxiety and uncertainty it created. We complained to one of the Afghan trio. I begged them to contact Qubat and see how my family was.

'We'll try, but he'll probably be too busy.'

'But I need to tell them how I am.'

They wouldn't make the call for me but they did reassure me my family would know I was safe and where I was. They told me that every time I crossed into a new country my family would be informed by Qubat or one of his representatives. This was because his next instalment of payment would be due. They explained that the money my family had paid was held by a mutually trusted third party, a kind of smuggling lay-away plan. Each time I crossed a new border, the third party handed over a little more to Qubat.

That didn't make me feel better, and I suspected they could have been lying to me. In fact, we complained so much that the trio said they were sick of us and were passing us on to a different Istanbul agent. We had little choice but to do as they said. All we knew – all they told us – was that we were expected to meet the new agent in a certain café.

The new agent was another Afghan: Zamir. He was young, and smartly dressed in Western-style clothes. He wore a casual, open-necked shirt and gel in his fashionable haircut. Leather bracelets were wrapped around his wrists.

'I'm taking you to a really good place. It's the best *musafir khanna* in all of Istanbul.'

I was coming to realize that the agents were the salesmen of the smuggling world. They have to sell their fat lies and thin hope to convince you to keep going – it's in their interest, because if they don't get you to the next location they don't get paid. They will say anything to persuade you. But it's the people below them – the employees, the drivers, the farmers with the cow sheds where the agents hid us – these were the ones who were the most brutal. They had already been paid by the agents, and so had nothing to lose. Often they subcontracted their work to family members or friends. That's when it got really messy and you had no idea who was whom.

Having to work out all of that was making me grow up very fast.

There are exaggerations and then there are complete lies. As soon as Zamir delivered us to the new address, I knew it was a bad place. Our new hideout was guarded day and night by three nasty-looking Turks, who glowered at us menacingly. We didn't see weapons but I am sure they had them, because one of them kept fingering the bulge in his pocket.

It was another basement, already packed with twenty to thirty Afghans, who didn't waste a second in letting us know what a mistake we'd made by coming there.

'This man is a liar. Everything he says is pure bullshit.'

'Months. I've been here for months.'

'We are less than human.'

Every time someone tried to speak, the thugs ordered silence.

I was so depressed to be there. The basement had tiny, locked windows. There was no fan and it was brutally hot inside. So many times I thought I was going to faint. No one was allowed outside and the only food was takeaways, brought in daily by the thugs. And we had to pay for those with our own money. The others had been borrowing money from each other just to live.

After one particularly noisy and restless night one guy got up and announced he'd had enough. 'Fuck this, I'm leaving.'

The guards punched him to the floor. 'Think we'll let you go and call the police?'

My exit came when Zamir arrived one day and read out a list of ten names. He called my name, but not those of my three friends.

'Don't go, Gulwali,' they all urged. 'Stay with us so we can look after you.'

I didn't want to go, but I didn't want to get stuck there for months either. I swallowed hard and summoned my courage. Looking Zamir square in the eye, I said, 'If they don't go, then I don't go.'

'Fine, it's up to you,' he replied, calling my bluff. 'They're not going. Stay if you want. But let me tell you, this is a guaranteed trip.'

That made me stop and think. This was *my* journey. I *had* to continue. And I also wanted to prove something to myself: I had heard people whispering behind my back, saying how my friends had to look after me and what a little boy I was. It made me defensive and angry. I was determined to show I could manage on my own – to prove I was grown up.

I went.

Zamir's men shoved us roughly into the back of a van and drove us to a train station. I had a very bad feeling that this was not the way to Greece – not by boat anyway. The train station was closed for the night but the railway security guards opened some gates at the back to allow our van in. They greeted our agents as if they were old friends and ushered us towards the rear of the station, where an empty train sat in the sidings.

We hadn't had food or water all day and I was wobbly with hunger.

'You. The small one. Come here.' A guard motioned me towards the train and into the driver's cab. I clambered inside and took a seat.

'No, not there. Here.' He pointed to the ceiling.

'What? I don't understand.'

He laughed long and hard, clutching his fat belly with a scaly hand. Then he stood on the seat and unscrewed a large acrylic panel which covered the ceiling light. 'Up here.'

How was I was supposed to fit in *there*?

Warily, I climbed on to the seat. I tried to haul myself up as the guard gave me a vigorous shove up my backside. The cavity was pitch black and chokingly full of dust. My eyes could just about make out a tiny hollow next to the wiring of the light box. Surely not?

'Get in. Hurry up.'

With that he gave me another hard shove. By wiggling, I just about got my torso in. 'I can't get my legs in. It's too small.'

Another belly laugh. 'Get in.'

Somehow I managed to twist at the waist, contorting my legs in behind me. My eyes and nose filled with choking black dust and grime. It felt like a coffin. My coffin.

I cried out in pain and fear as the guard stood on the chair again and began to screw the ceiling panel firmly back in place. 'Please. No. Let me out. Please.'

'Shut up, boy.' He replaced the last screw, locking me firmly into the claustrophobic, filthy blackness.

'Breathe, Gulwali. Keep breathing.' Talking to myself made me feel calmer. 'Stay alive. You can do it. Breathe.'

I realized I was heading to Bulgaria.

The train had begun to move. I didn't know if any passengers had come on board because I couldn't hear anything save for my own panicked breaths.

I think I managed to breathe myself into some kind of trance because I don't really know how long I was up there. I think it was a long time. The next thing I knew, the conductor was unscrewing the panel, revealing a dark landscape flashing past. 'Get down. Come on. Down.'

I tried to move my legs but they were stiff with cramp. 'I can't.'

'For God's sake, boy. Hurry.' He grabbed at my legs, yanking me back through the tiny space.

I fell out, bashing my torso on the sharp edge of the seat before hitting the floor. My body went into shock. I was gulping for air, hyperventilating.

The train was still moving. But where were the others?

'Hurry. Jump. Jump when I say.'

'Jump? What—? I don't...'

Grabbing my shoulder, he yanked me up and towards the door of the driver's cab. He flung the door open to reveal the ground moving swiftly beneath us. Rocks, grass and fields swam by my blurred vision in the twilight.

If I jumped I'd surely die.

I looked to my right and saw the others, all standing in the doorways of the next carriage. I could read the terror on their faces.

'I can't. Please, no. Don't make me,' I pleaded to the conductor.

'There's a checkpoint coming up, you stupid little fool. Get off my train.'

As the train rounded a bend it slowed slightly. He tried to push me out. I fought back, trying desperately to cling on to both him and the train.

'Gulwali, look out. Jump.'

One of others was pointing up the tracks ahead of us. The landscape was changing. Grass and trees gave way to large, jagged rocks.

Someone shouted, 'In the name of Allah, jump now. Everybody jump now.'

I don't know if I jumped of my own accord, or if the conductor pushed me. All I remember is hurtling through the air and seeing the earth moving underneath me before crashing down in an agonized heap.

I think I must have blacked out. When I came to, my head hurt so much I could barely lift it. Everyone else was screaming. It was still dark, and my eyes struggled to make out the shapes.

'My leg. Allah. Help me. My leg.'

Slowly I eased myself up. The train was hurtling into the distance. Scattered along the track were nine bodies in various states of brokenness.

'Gulwali, help me. My leg.'

I staggered over to Zia, an Iraqi. His leg was twisted at a sickening angle.

I retched before collapsing and started to cry. My head hurt so much I thought I was dying.

Two of the others appeared by our side. 'Where is everyone else?'

People were still screaming uncontrollably. Some of them looked really badly injured.

After that it all became a blur. The police arrived with an

ambulance at some point. The badly injured were taken away and I never saw any of them again.

I was semi-conscious as I was bundled into a police car.

CHAPTER TWELVE

When I awoke, I was alone in a Bulgarian police cell. Someone had placed me on a rickety iron bed with just a thin mattress and no bedding. Through the bars of my cell I could see others from the train lying in similar beds, in other cells.

Istanbul had been so hot and stuffy; here, the air was freezing, but stank of rotting flesh. And it wasn't just migrants in there; some of the other prisoners looked local and really scary. I don't know if they were mad or drunk, but a few of them shouted out all night long.

My head was hurting so much I could barely move. If I tried to stand I felt dizzy and had to lie back down. I tried using hand gestures and a mixture of different languages to appeal for help. 'Please. I need a doctor. Help me. I'm begging you.'

The guard who brought my meagre rations of food refused to even look at me.

After a couple of days, they told us we were going back to Turkey. I knew what to expect because I'd heard it all already from the stories: the Bulgarians sent people back over the border without the knowledge of the Turkish authorities.

From Sofia, we were put on a police bus and driven for several hours to a forest. Half-a-dozen guards pointed to the trees – we were expected to walk back to Turkey.

I think it was probably around January or February by then, and there was heavy snow on the ground.

We hesitated. They pointed their rifles at us.

It was pretty clear we had no choice but to move.

We walked into the trees, not knowing what direction to take. It was so very cold. My boots – 'my best friends' as I jokingly called them – were holding up well, but my thin clothes were filthy and ripped after jumping from the train and our stay in the cells.

Of our party, there were three who had leapt from the train with me, some of the least injured. I didn't know about the others from the train – most likely they were in hospital, but I couldn't say for sure. The rest of the shambling column was made up of other migrants from the prison.

How I missed my three friends. I missed their company, and their help and support. Maybe I wasn't as grown up as I had tried to convince myself I was.

We walked through the snow for several hours. My toes went numb, along with my face and fingers. I wondered if my fate would be that of the Pakistani man who lost his fingers. Would I go home to my mother with some terrible injury, rendering me a burden for the rest of my life?

Eventually, the trees began to thin out and we reached a small village. A flag above one of the rooftops told us we were back in Turkey. Although I was going backwards not forwards, I didn't mind; I wanted to cry with relief at having escaped Bulgaria: the train had clearly been the first step of that notorious overland route to Greece via Bulgaria and Macedonia that I'd been warned about. The train had almost killed me; I'm certain that I would not have survived the rest of the journey.

At the village, the three of us from the train separated from the rest and got a taxi to a larger town. From there, we used my Turkish lira – the money I had exchanged on the shopping trip with the

Afghan agents – to buy bus tickets. The other two only had dollars, but they promised to pay me back once we reached Istanbul.

Before we got on the bus, I used a pay phone to call Zamir. I had his number written in my pocket on a piece of paper he'd given me. He had said he'd send someone to the station to meet us.

'But why aren't you in Bulgaria?'

This made me so angry. 'Why aren't I in Bulgaria? Because one of your friends threw me off the train. Then we got put in prison. Then we marched through the snow like the Soviet army retreating from Afghanistan. How could you send me on my own like that? That was not good of you.'

'Calm down, Gulwali. You're all right now, aren't you? You did agree to go. Don't you remember?'

'I agreed to go to Greece. Now I am in Turkey.'

'Well. This was the way to Greece. So it didn't work. Not a big deal. We'll try it again.'

'I am not going that way again. People were hurt.'

'Really? I must say that is very unusual. Let's not discuss it now. We'll talk about it when you return.'

He sent one of his thugs to pick us up, and we were taken back to the same place as before. Baryalai, Mehran and Abdul were still there.

I was so relieved to see them.

The day after my return from Bulgaria, Zamir passed us on to another agent, an associate of his, a Turkish Kurd.

He came to pick the four of us up in a taxi. I was just grateful I wasn't being separated from my friends again.

This new agent didn't bother to tell us his name. He was about the same age as Zamir and similarly dressed, in a tight open-necked shirt, denim jeans and pointy leather shoes. He reeked of cheap aftershave.

In the taxi, he spoke to us in what was by now becoming a typical mixture of Farsi and Kurdish: 'We need to wait until night. Then I will take you to a place where you can get the boat to Greece. We will wait at a place I know.'

Given what had happened to me in Bulgaria, I did not trust a word he said. And I knew for sure we'd been lied to when he directed the taxi to a shop in the middle of town, opposite a petrol station. This exact location had been described in minute detail to us by other migrants. It was the smugglers' holding centre everyone dreaded the most, one of the places they kept you before sending you overland on the second route – the journey which took you over the heavily militarized Turkish–Greek border.

We were led up a metal staircase at the back of the shop to a scruffy apartment. There were already forty or so migrants there, who looked to be a mix of nationalities. Everyone was sitting on the floor in silence, their heads down.

We tried to get away before we got trapped: as we neared the door and saw the scene inside, those at the front turned to go back down the stairs – but the agent was standing behind them, blocking their way. Abdul had grabbed my sleeve to try and pull me back when a guard by the doorway yanked me inside by my arm.

We were pretty much forced in and told to take our places on the floor with the other people. The Kurdish agent spoke briefly to the guards, then left us. We never saw him again.

There was no food or water, and it was freezing cold despite the number of densely packed bodies. The atmosphere was awful, depression and sadness hanging in the air like a black cloud. I think every man in the room had an idea of the fate that was about to befall us.

I sat as close to my three friends as I could; no way was I being separated from them now. We sat in silence, lost in our thoughts, for a couple of hours. I tried to perk myself up, telling myself I might survive this, and that I had to try, at least. But it didn't really work: my thoughts kept taking me back home – I thought of my little siblings and how they were growing up without me; I thought of my second brother Noor, so close in age to Hazrat and me, but who had been left behind to become the man of the house, aged just eleven. How had he reacted when he was finally told that Hazrat and I weren't coming back from our trip to Waziristan? How betrayed had he felt when he was told he'd never see his older brothers again?

'Psst.'

I looked up. Abdul was trying to get my attention.

'Shut up.' The guard glanced at him in warning.

Abdul ignored him and continued to whisper: 'What are we doing, sitting here like dead men? Let's just go. They can't force us to stay here.'

He was right. My eyes met Baryalai's questioningly. He nodded.

I stood up first. I almost wanted to laugh. Abdul was right. Were we lambs to the slaughter? No. We were human beings, free to choose our own destiny. We would stroll out of there and find a way to manage on our own.

The cupped palm collided with my ear, sending a shockwave of pain through my skull. I fell on to a patch of dirty carpet and rolled into a ball, seeing, through watering eyes, the guard slump back down heavily on to his chair.

'Leave the boy alone,' said Baryalai.

I lifted my head just as the guard's leg flashed like a cobra, sinking its teeth in the small of my friend's back. He let out a yelp of pain and writhed on the floor, clutching a hand to his spine.

'Sit down.'

Bang. Bang. Bang.

The room was suddenly flooded with panic.

Bang. Bang. Bang.

'Someone's at the door.'

'Shut up – they'll hear you.'

A hollow voice boomed in Turkish. We were trying to stay quiet so no one translated for me, but I could read the others' reactions and knew enough words of Turkish by now to work it out.

'This is the police. We know you are in there. Open the door now.'

The guard replied in Kurdish: 'I can't. I, er, I lost my key.' He turned wide-eyed to his colleagues, shrugging his shoulders. They nodded at him, gesturing at him to carry on. 'My friend locked it when he went out, forgetting that I am still in here. He is a bit stupid like that sometimes. He will be back later tonight – you really shouldn't trouble yourselves to wait so long.'

There was no answer. Instead, an axe head split the door in two, and then a dozen men stormed into the room, shouting, 'Police. Don't move. Lie on the floor.'

They had guns and wore bulletproof vests, but weren't in uniform, which only compounded the sense of panic.

'Kidnappers.'

Some people tried to escape through the back, or get to the window. The men screamed and pointed their guns at them, telling them not to move.

Uniformed officers then flooded into the flat, adding to the chaos.

Men flung themselves out of the way in terror, but there was nowhere to move to. I half expected the police to start shooting at any second.

I'd just been in a Bulgarian prison, and I didn't want to be jailed again but, as I placed my hands on my head as they demanded, I felt a surge of pure relief and gratitude. I definitely hadn't wanted to go on the overland route.

We sat on the floor, arms on our heads, for an hour or so.

Eventually, we were loaded into the back of a police van and driven to a large police station and prison complex somewhere near the centre of Istanbul.

We were asked our name, age and country of origin, then taken up two flights of stairs, where we were seated in a large hallway. There were no chairs so we sat on the floor, tightly packed together. A couple of officers stood watch.

With the lack of space, the way we were sitting in silence and the guards, it didn't feel much different to the place from which we'd just been rescued.

Six hours later I was quivering, alone and afraid, in an interrogation room. Somewhere over my head a striplight made a little *plink-plink-pink* sound, a bit like my grandfather tuning his *rabab*, an Afghan lute. I could see the stuttering bulb in the interrogation room's mirrored walls, and jumped each time I caught my own reflection looking at me – as if the red-eyed stranger staring back at me might take offence.

A young, uniformed officer entered the room. 'So,' he said, scraping his chair on the floor as he pulled it out, and slapping a notebook down. He spoke in Turkish, but the basic questions I could understand.

'What is your name?'

'Gulwali.'

'How old are you?'

'Twelve and a half.'

'Where are you from?'

'Mauritania.'

He sighed. Then he turned to a second man, who was not in uniform, and shook his head.

The second man spoke to me in Farsi. 'You are our seventeenth interview this morning. Are you going to waste our time with lies, too? Or are you going to be a good boy and tell me the truth?'

I understood the translator perfectly well, but I had to stick to my story. Other migrants had warned me that if I ever got arrested in Turkey, I should say I was from Mauritania. I didn't know why, or even where the place was, but word was that they might let you stay in Turkey if that's what you said.

I pretended I didn't understand him and started waving my arms around, as if I was doing sign language.

Now it was the translator's turn to shake his head. 'I know you understand me. Where are you from?'

'Mauritania.'

The notebook slapped me in the face. Suddenly, I could feel tears coming. I was a young boy searching for safety – my only crime was to be travelling without the right documents. He let out a little laugh. 'Mauritania, you say? So, let's continue this conversation in French. *Je parle assez pour vous comprendre.*'

Why was he saying that? I didn't speak a single word of French.

I just continued to wave my arms. I hoped, if I was lucky, he might think I was mentally ill.

He paused, gave a sneer at my obvious incomprehension, and called out sharply to the mirrored wall.

The door opened. I watched in the mirrors as two more uniformed officers, tall men with hard faces, walked in and stood behind me.

My mouth went dry.

'Take him outside.'

The pair walked me back up the stairs to where the others were sitting. I made to sit back down.

'No. Keep walking.'

They walked me up another two flights until we stood at the very top of the stairwell. There, they spun me around, and while I was still fighting for balance, shoved me backwards. 'Look down.'

Three strong hands gripped my skull; the fourth grabbed a fistful of my hair at my temples and twisted hard.

It felt as if they were peeling the skin from my head and I screamed – more in shock and fear than pain.

Then they marched me back down to the interrogation room to face the first two officers. But this time the second pair stayed, standing over me.

I told them the truth. 'I'm from Afghanistan. I am Gulwali from Afghanistan.'

One of the men behind me threw me forward suddenly so that my cheekbone crunched on to the tabletop.

I looked up at the two interviewing officers, dazed and petrified. There was no holding back the tears. I mopped my eyes and nose with the back of my grubby sleeve.

'Tell me about the smugglers.'

'What?' I said. The question didn't seem to make sense.

'Where did you stay?'

'I don't know. I don't know, I promise.'

The hands locked themselves to my head again, twisting my hair so hard it came out.

'Please. Stop it. It hurts.'

'Who were the men? Who did you pay?'

'I don't know. Please. I don't know.'

They released their grip and my head fell forward again. I spluttered tears and snot all over the table.

'Get him out of here. Let's see what the next idiot has to say.'

I was taken back to the waiting area, where several of the men had swelling to their faces or bleeding lips.

Every so often, the officers would drop a sweaty man off and pick a fresh candidate to take with them.

*

Mehran was sitting next to me. He hadn't been interviewed yet. 'Did you say Mauritania?' he whispered.

'Yes, but it doesn't work. Don't even say it.'

'Oh, so you don't want me to be free?'

'Go ahead then, say it. Tell them that. If you like pain.'

It was several hours later, almost morning, by the time all the interviews had finished. We had been sitting there without food, water or sleep all night.

A young man in a shiny blue suit appeared on the stairwell, flanked by the Farsi-speaking officer. 'I am from the Afghan embassy.' Hopeful eyes turned to look at him. 'You are to be taken to prison, where you will be held until the Turkish authorities are ready to deport you.'

'Please,' someone said, 'can't you help us?'

'You are here illegally, without documentation,' said the diplomat, adjusting his dark grey pencil tie. 'What do you expect the embassy to do?'

'We expect you to do your job. We are Afghans, your citizens. You are sworn to serve the nation,' Baryalai spoke up suddenly, his face flushing with anger.

'Don't,' I hissed, mindful of the interrogation room and the hovering guards.

The diplomat swallowed hard. He looked at Baryalai. 'I am sorry, my friend. But do you have an Afghan passport on you?'

Baryalai said nothing.

Satisfied his tie was straight, the diplomat spun on his leather heel and clattered off down the corridor.

The guards waited a moment, then grabbed Baryalai by the shoulders, pulling him to his feet.

He struggled for a moment. 'Get your hands off me.'

This didn't feel good. We had no idea where he was being taken.

'We'll be thinking of you. Please be careful,' I called to him. A guard looked over his shoulder at me and I dropped my eyes, rubbing my throbbing scalp.

Baryalai was our unofficial leader. Abdul, Mehran and I stared at each other helplessly.

We were then ordered to stand up and told we would be taken to the cell block next door.

The holding cell was huge. It was packed with men of many different nationalities, who sat huddled in ethnic groups of African, Arab, Persian or Asian descent. There were a few bunk beds around the corners, all occupied.

Many of the faces bore witness to recent questioning.

We found a small piece of empty cell near the door, the only floor space available.

'Please, can we have blankets?'

'No.'

As I tried to go to sleep on the concrete floor, my head still aching from the interrogation, misery began to creep in. Was this really what my mother had sent me away for? How could this be better, or safer, than what I had left behind? Would the foreign forces in Afghanistan have treated me worse if they had been questioning me? I wanted to believe so, but the cold floor sucked any certainty from me.

In the morning, I woke to feet stumbling over me. Food was being served right where we were lying. We had to get out of the way, fast.

I looked around the cell properly for the first time. I could see the faces of the whole world there, each nation sitting in its own area of the room.

'Get some food before it goes.' Mehran handed me a little metal bowl of rice.

I fell on it, wolfing it down gratefully.

For the next few days we were told nothing. I had no idea what was happening, but some of the prisoners did seem to show genuine concern for me.

'You should be in the kids' prison.'

'What are you doing here with us?'

One of the prisoners, an Iranian called Bernard, was small, dark haired and kind. He told us he was sometimes asked to help translate during interrogations. As such, he had information for us.

'Your friend. He has been taken to another prison.'

'Baryalai?'

'Yes. The guards suspect he is an agent. It is very serious for him.'

'Are you sure?' I asked.

'This is what one of the guards told me. Maybe he lies, but...' He paused. 'I thought you would want to know.'

A few days later, we were taken to a shower room. There were only a handful of them and we had to queue for ages. It was the first time I had seen a Western-style toilet – the type you sit on. This one was filthy.

None of the shower doors had locks, so Mehran and I took turns standing guard for each other. In my culture, this was a very humiliating thing. I was so embarrassed having to do such private things surrounded by so many people. It was the first shower I'd had for two weeks, but it wasn't enjoyable. In the end it was a matter of necessity, rather than pleasure.

The water was freezing cold and there wasn't any soap, but it did feel healing. My skin tingled. I washed my bruised face and head with care, and rinsed my mouth repeatedly, running a finger over my teeth and gums.

Back in the cell I did a little mental audit. I had about US$250 left. Some had gone in Turkey – a haircut, some new clothes. More clothes in Iran. I had spent money in Turkey and in Istanbul – mostly on food.

The prison was overflowing with refugees, the overwhelming majority of whom were Sudanese or Somalian. I hadn't been around very many black people in my life; in Afghanistan there aren't any, and although I'd seen a few Africans around Istanbul, I hadn't got to know any. I felt so sorry for the ones in this prison – some of them had been here for years. I was told a few were there on drug charges.

I was managing to hide my money in my underwear, and I had some in my pocket. I had also given $50 to Mehran to look after for me. That got stolen.

Mehran was upset and angry. He thought maybe I believed he was lying to me and that he'd taken it. Of course I didn't. I totally trusted him.

We went to see Bernard, the kindly Iranian. He shrugged his shoulders sadly. 'These things happen in here. You have to accept your money has gone.'

After the horrible beating, days of little food and even less sleep, the disappearance of my money was too much. They were dollars my mother had given me. They had been a symbol of her hope for me, and the future she wished me to have. And now I had lost it. I couldn't stop crying.

'What's up?'

I stared into a round, black face and a pair of the deepest, kindest eyes I had seen in a long time. Seeing a black person was still very unusual for me.

'Why are you crying?'

'It's nothing,' snapped Mehran. 'Leave us alone.'

'It doesn't look like nothing. Tell me.'

The shock of him speaking a Persian language made me forget my tears. 'How can you speak Farsi?'

He laughed and threw his arms wide. 'I study here at this fine university. Nothing else to do. So, tell me. Why do you cry?'

'Someone took my money.'

'Who?'

'I don't know.' I began to sob louder. 'My mother gave me that money.'

'I see. How much?'

'Fifty dollars.'

'I see. I'll sort it out.' He gave me a concerned stare. 'What's your name?'

'Gulwali.'

'I am Marrion. Don't cry, little one. No more tears, OK? I will sort this out. I promise.'

I stared at the floor and bit my lip. When I looked up again, I was surprised to see Marrion's tall form already striding back across the cell.

'Do you think he'll get it back?'

Mehran seemed unconvinced.

To be honest, so was I.

I lay down and fell into a depressed slumber. Proper sleep was all but impossible on that cold floor.

'Gulwali.'

The voice crashed into my lovely daydream, in which it was Eid, and I was breaking fast with all my family. We were eating fat, juicy fresh dates. I was happy. We all were.

At the sound of my name, my family vanished.

My new friend Marrion stood over me. 'Here,' he said. 'I found it for you.' He tossed a crumpled ball of green-grey paper to me, and I clutched my money to my chest. 'The thief says he is very sorry.'

'Thank you.' I nodded and smiled at him with gratitude.

'It was my pleasure. See you later. No more crying, OK boss?' He strode back to the African corner of the cell without another word.

I was so happy; suddenly, the world felt a good place. Mehran had cheered up, we had a new friend in the horrible prison, and I had my money. This money – the exact note that my mother had given me – was my last connection to her. And now I had it back. That was all that mattered.

There was some kind of commotion going on with the guards outside in the corridor, but I ignored it. I was exhausted from all my crying so I tried to sleep again. I was just managing to nod off when I heard some Pakistani prisoners telling Mehran about something.

'No one could believe it.'

'I know. When he started hitting his head on the sink I thought he was going to kill him.'

One of them threw me a glance. 'You missed out on all the fun, boy.'

'What happened?'

'Two African guys had a massive fight in the showers.'

'What? Just now?'

'Yeah. Only, it wasn't so much a fight. One of them beat the living shit out of the other. Only stopped to take something out of his pocket and then went.'

'The guards did nothing. We were waiting outside and they stood there watching, like us. '

I was too scared to ask.

'Gulwali? Weren't you listening?' Mehran had clearly worked it out.

'The big guy really gave it to him. He didn't look good at the end.'

I felt vomit rising in my throat.

Marrion.

CHAPTER THIRTEEN

The news spread like wildfire throughout the block.

We couldn't have known it before because we hadn't been there long enough, but it turned out that Marrion was one of the longest-serving prisoners there, and pretty much ran the place. He was in on drug-smuggling charges and no one dared cross him, not even the guards. He claimed he'd killed hundreds of people. He came from the Democratic Republic of Congo, where it was rumoured he was wanted for war crimes, although some people said this was a whisper he himself had put about, so I don't know for sure if that was true. He also spoke seven languages fluently.

I was sick to my stomach at the knowledge that a man had been beaten because of me. The money burned in my pocket like acid. Was this what a man's life was worth? Fifty dollars?

Marrion was now a bad man in my eyes. He shouldn't have hit the thief. And yet, he'd got my money back for me. And he'd been so kind to me...I couldn't believe I'd imagined the softness and concern in his eyes.

Not only had the story of the beating spread, but also the reasons for it. It meant that every man in the cell knew I had money on me – but now that it was known I was under Marrion's protection, no one dared touch me. I spent most of the next day on my knees, praying for the other man and asking for forgiveness.

*

Prison was an angry and frustrating time. The boredom was terrible – a waiting game for something unknown. Most of the men
played card games or chatted. Bernard had kindly lent me a Quran,
from which I took great comfort whilst reading it. I spent much of
my time praying, walking around the cell thinking about life and
reflecting on the purpose Allah had for me. It felt like a test of my
faith.

I met men from Iraq, Iran, India and Pakistan, and from all
across Africa. Some of them, especially the Africans, told such terrible tales of poverty and hardship it made my own life sound easy
by comparison.

Many were dirt-poor fishermen or farmers. They had left behind
their wives and children because they couldn't make enough money
to feed their families. I heard stories of toddlers dying of hunger
in their parents' arms, of wives falling sick with a simple fever
and dying for lack of medicine, of babies stillborn to malnourished
mothers. The only chance of their family surviving was if these
men made it to Europe and found enough work to send money
back home.

But not all were poor like that. Many of them were very inspirational people to me: lawyers, doctors, teachers, journalists or
engineers. Often these were people who had been denied work or
persecuted because of their political beliefs.

The most tragic story was that of my friend Bernard. He was a
university professor from Shiraz. He told us he had helped to run
an underground school, without government permission, educating Afghan refugee children. He had written a paper which was
critical of the government and he'd been arrested and tortured.
After being released he had fled the country, to Turkey.

I heard him crying on his bunk one day and I asked him what
was wrong. Normally if you saw someone upset you wouldn't say

anything to them. Everyone kept respectful distances from emotion: we all knew we had our problems and prying wasn't the done thing. I didn't mean to be rude by intruding, though – I just wanted to know. I'd never heard a man cry before, not in this way. He was sobbing so softly, yet as if the world was utterly without hope.

'Why do you cry, uncle?'

'They are sending me back to Iran.'

'But you will be going home and out of this jail ... maybe that's a good thing—?'

'They say that I damage the minds of my students. They made me confess – electrocuted me – and made me sign my name, like a criminal. I escaped once. This time I won't. They will hurt me again. They might even kill me.'

'Tell the guards this. They cannot send you back.'

'I have told them and begged them, with a lawyer. There are such lawyers here who would help me.' He sighed. 'And you'd think after all the help I give the guards they'd do something for me, wouldn't you? But no. They laugh, and pretend that I should be packing for a long holiday.'

He wept tears of fear, not self-pity.

'I'm sorry, uncle.'

He sat up on the bunk and offered me a dignified handshake. 'Thank you. So am I.'

The next morning I watched as the guards led Bernard out of the cell block. He didn't look at me. He just stared at the ground mumbling to himself.

I don't know what happened to him, or if he is a free man today. Maybe he's dead. I wish I knew, because I think of him often. There was something about him that reminded me of my father.

I began to make plans – I was not going to end up like Bernard: I had to get out, to survive. The authorities could not be trusted any more than the people-smugglers. They were all liars, and were only looking to take advantage of the human river that ran beneath their feet. My greatest fear was to be sent back home: it would have felt like such failure. As much as I longed to see my mother and family, I did not want to shame myself or them. As hard as my journey was, they had invested everything in my success.

I thought maybe I could try again: I could walk to Afghanistan's western border with Iran, as my old friend Shah had done. Maybe I could even still get to Europe and find Hazrat. I could find a job and save money. Find Black Wolf – maybe he would help me? My mind was racing, none of my thoughts realistic.

Several of the Afghan prisoners who had arrived in jail at the same time as me had already been given the paperwork confirming their deportations, but there was a catch: the Afghan embassy would help arrange their flights, but they had to pay for it themselves. If they couldn't, they stayed in prison. There was a single pay phone near the toilets. From my sleeping space so close to the cell doorway, I could hear snippets of conversation as imprisoned men apologized to families already in debt to people-smugglers, and asked them to find the money to pay for an international flight. Listening to them talking to loved ones was like a double stab through my heart: their plight could so easily be my own – and yet I had no phone numbers or way of contacting my family.

Some of the men wept like babies as they came back. It was through this I learned that people-smugglers don't pay refunds for failure. If you get caught and finish the game early, you still have to pay in full. The agents will normally offer a discounted deal to let you try for a second time, but if you don't take that deal, your family's money is forfeited.

As yet, I hadn't been given any papers, so I had some hope that things might work out.

What I did have, however, was a piece of paper with a phone

number for Zamir, the flashy young Afghan who had been our last agent but one. Abdul suggested we try calling him for help.

Mehran and I stood by the phone expectantly as Abdul spoke to him. We could see from his face it wasn't going well.

'What did he say?' Mehran asked impatiently, as Abdul hung up.

'He told me not to call him from prison. He was worried the police would trace his phone. Said it was our fault we got arrested.'

We had no way of contacting Qubat, the so-called 'big guy' in Kabul.

Abdul had asked Zamir to at least call him on our behalf and let him know where we were, but Zamir had said it wasn't his responsibility before telling Abdul never to call him again and hanging up.

We also tried Malik, the besuited very first agent in Turkey, the one who had made us live in the chicken coop. But the number we had for him was now unobtainable.

I think I had been in prison for around two or three weeks – time dragged so slowly it was hard to know for sure – when the man from the embassy came again.

He explained that those of us who couldn't afford flights were to be deported to Iran by coach the next day.

Just after breakfast the following day, the guards came to get us. 'You men on the bus to Iran. Get ready. You have two minutes.'

I jumped up in a panic, as if I had lots to pack. Then I remembered I only had my small bag, containing all my possessions. 'I'm ready.'

Before we left, Mehran, Abdul and I tried to ask the guards about Baryalai, saying we didn't want to go without him.

'Shut up, you'll make them suspicious. It will be worse for him,' another prisoner warned us.

Leaving without him and not knowing whether he was still in a different prison somewhere, or had already been deported, was horrible. But what choice did we have but to go?

Yet again I was going backwards on this twisted board game that had become my life – but part of me was happy, because at least I was getting out of prison. The confinement had been beginning to make me lose my mind.

CHAPTER FOURTEEN

After four days, I was starting to wish I was back in prison. Around fifty of us were packed into a large coach, two to a small seat, our sweat and breath intermingling. I sat next to Mehran. Every six hours we pulled over to go to the toilet. They gave us very little water, so it was hard to go.

I had lost all hope. I was going back to war and back to Afghanistan – where the Taliban would be waiting for me.

Some of the men started grumbling.

'There are only four of them, and fifty of us. We can take them easily.'

'At the next stop, five of us can grab each one – another five the driver.'

Maybe this sort of dissent was common at this point in the journey, because the guards, plain-clothed immigration officers with guns, seemed to know what was going on.

A guard pushed his way to the back of the bus, an anxious look on his face. 'We're almost there. Don't get any clever ideas. Things can always get worse.'

He didn't even bother to pat his gun. He didn't have to. We'd all heard the stories from other prisoners. It was alleged that sometimes Turkish border guards sold migrants to the Kurdish criminal gangs. These gangs, which everyone referred to as mafia, would imprison you somewhere and then make you contact your family to demand they pay a ransom. We were told they always asked for a ridiculously high price, like $5,000 dollars, which you had to try and negotiate down. If you didn't cooperate and refused to call your family, they made you walk barefoot into the mountains, where they beat you. In extreme cases, I'd heard of men having their noses or ears cut off because their relatives either couldn't or wouldn't pay. As ever, the ransoms were paid to a middleman with a bank account somewhere in Europe or Iran. Nothing could be linked back to the kidnappers directly.

For me at least, this meant I was on my best behaviour with the immigration officers. I didn't want to be sold on like that. Aside from Black Wolf, my experiences of Kurdish smugglers and criminals so far had not been positive.

On the fourth day, when we were very close to the border, we were ordered off the bus to sit and wait for a few hours in what looked like some abandoned former military buildings. The whole area was covered with tiny bits of sharp gravel. It was too tiring to stand up all afternoon but it was painful to sit on, and I was like a chicken on a hot plate, constantly shifting and fidgeting as the gravel pricked my bottom and thighs.

As we boarded the bus, the count came back one person short. 'Who is missing?'

Somehow one of us had managed to disappear. I looked around, but it was hard to tell who it was.

The guards stayed with us on the now stationary bus, but they informed the police in the local area.

Three hours later, the police returned with a guy called Zabi. He was also a Pashtun, from the city of Kandahar, and only a couple of years older than I was. He was bleeding and bruised, but still had some fight left in him: 'Let me go, you bastards.'

The local police who had caught him shoved him hard into the side of the bus. 'You stupid fool. Did you really think you could run away from us?'

He carried on screaming insults at them, which one of them took as justification to punch him in the guts.

Satisfied, they shook hands with our guards and drove away in their blue and white Hilux.

Zabi told us his story: 'When I went to pee, I just ran. I walked for ages. People kept looking at me but I carried on. I was trying to find the bus station.'

Everyone had questions for him.

'Did you have money?'

'Why didn't you ask me too? I would have run with you.'

'You fool. Now you've put us all at risk. They will be angry and sell us to the mafia.'

The guards weren't happy. 'Shut up. Don't talk to him.'

It was late when we got to the actual border. We didn't go to one of the main border crossings; this one was just some kind of a military checkpoint. There was no traffic – a single man on a motorcycle droned through like a blowfly. Other than the half-dozen Turkish soldiers standing around, there were no people there.

The guards came towards the bus, carrying a large a box of *zataar* – hot Turkish flat bread sprinkled with fresh thyme. It smelled delicious. 'We can give you this now, or you can eat it before you cross. Your choice, but we suggest you eat it later.'

In my world 'later' could mean anything, but the general consensus was to go with the guards' advice. Bad idea, because we never did get to eat it.

We were put into a series of army jeeps and driven along a road, down one side of which ran a very high, barbed-wire and electric fence. Every so often along it there were lookout posts with bored-looking solders inside. We were told to get out of the jeeps and wait by the fence. Suddenly, a lot of chatter and noise came through our guards' radios, and the soldiers who had been driving the jeeps rushed to the wire, unclipping a long strip of electric fencing. They told us to wait but get ready.

It was dark by now, made more so by heavy clouds which obscured the stars and moon. Then the soldiers turned the jeep headlights off, making it even scarier.

Mehran turned to Abdul and me. 'Why would they do that? Do you think the Iranians know we are coming?'

Abdul looked tight-lipped and grim. 'Maybe they know the mafia are there.'

There was one man on the bus who spoke fluent Turkish, an elderly Pakistani man from Peshawar. He'd spent most of the bus journey chatting happily to the immigration officers. They clearly liked him and, I suspect, felt a bit sorry for him. As we prepared to move, one of them handed him a large knife in a leather sheath.

'Here. You take this. Be safe.'

It was a nice act but it didn't make the rest of us feel any better. They clearly knew full well they were sending us into danger.

'Go. Go. Go.'

When the order came to walk, Mehran held me back.

'Don't be first across.'

A few men had already started to walk through the gap in the barbed wire into Iran.

I had no idea what was waiting for us out there in the dark. My legs were like jelly.

'Go. Move.'

It was all I could do to make my feet move. Mehran took one of my hands and Abdul the other. I was slightly reassured to see that the old Pakistani with the knife was right next to the three of us.

Everyone by now had started walking. We were in small groups but in a disciplined horizontal line, like soldiers coming out of the trenches in the First World War into no-man's land.

People walked slowly at first, gingerly, carefully. Then suddenly they started running, going in all directions.

We broke into a run with them.

Then we saw some police waving at us. 'Come this way. Over here.' There were eight of them, all carrying horsewhips.

We started to run towards them, but then we heard other voices, shouting at us. 'No. Not that way. We are the police. Come here. Over here.'

'It's the mafia.' a frightened voice shouted. 'The Kurds. They're in police uniforms. Run.'

'Where do we go?' I was panting both from fear and from the running – the weeks in the prison had left me exhausted and weak.

As everyone ran in panic, I lost hold of the others' hands as we were knocked and buffeted, swept along with the frightened herd. The ground was rough and rocky, and I thought I would fall and be trampled. My chest was hurting so much I couldn't catch my breath.

Headlights appeared, then a few men wearing uniforms and carrying torches walked towards us. Suddenly there were more cars, trucks, motorbikes. The men with the horsewhips were upon us, their whips making cracking, splintering sounds as they struck at the running bodies. They managed to corral maybe half of us into a semi-circle.

'We were informed you were coming. Stay calm. Do not move.'

Some people tried to break free. A whip cracked through the air. 'Do not run. Do not run.'

I had no idea who these men were but I truly hoped they really were the police. One of the motorbikes moved round behind us, as the half-dozen men with the whips ordered us to walk forwards.

As we walked on, dawn began to break and it was possible to see a little more clearly. Up ahead I could make out a one-storey building. There was an Iranian flag flying above it, and soldiers standing outside.

My breathing began to return to normal. We were with the right men.

As we approached the building, I realized for the first time how cold it was. We had been in a stuffy bus for days, but now on this flat, rocky plain with spiky bushes and mountains ringing the distant landscape, I shivered. It was definitely winter, maybe February by now. It could even be March. I really had no idea.

The one storey-building appeared to be the first Iranian checkpoint on this side of the barbed wire border. Watch towers stood to either side of it. It was still semi-dark, and moths fluttered around a fluorescent light above the doorway. As we arrived, three more police officers spilled outside.

'Line up. Now. Hands on your head. Faces to the wall.'

We placed our hands on the front of the building.

'Slowly turn around. Empty your pockets, take everything out.'

They spoke to us in Farsi but their accents were heavily Kurdish. I guessed we'd crossed the border back into another Kurdish dominated area.

Some people were not cooperating with the order and didn't want to empty their pockets. As a result of that, we were all ordered to take off our shirts, even though it was freezing cold.

The old Pakistani man had tried to hide his knife but he was rumbled.

'Where did you get this?'

'In Turkey. The police gave it to me.'

'Liar.' The slap rang out clear in the crisp air.

Why was it that every time I thought I was about to feel safer, the opposite happened?

I had $250 dollars still: $50 was in my bag; $100 was hidden in my underwear; and another $80 in my socks.

From my pocket I took out a $20 bill.

A policeman looked at it, took it, pushed me then put it in his pocket.

His friend began rifling through my bag. 'Got any drugs or guns in here?'

The policeman who had taken the $20 laughed. 'Don't you know it's good manners to bring gifts when visiting others?'

I was furious. We might as well have been taken by the criminals.

'Look at this,' his friend exclaimed. 'What a little discovery. Green's my favourite colour.'

My heart sank.

He scrunched the $50 note like an autumn leaf. It was the very same note I had had stolen from me in prison, the note that had only been returned to me because Congolese Marrion had beaten another man on my behalf.

I knew I wasn't getting it back, but this time I didn't care. It felt toxic to me now. Maybe this was God's punishment for what had happened.

And at least my $180 was safe in my pants and socks.

We were still standing there, freezing and half-naked, when a series of cars arrived and parked by the entrance. Several men jumped out. The police officers walked over to them as if they were old friends. All of them stood by the cars, speaking in rapid-fire Kurdish as they argued and negotiated something.

'They are bloody plotting to sell us. These guys are mafia,' someone whispered.

My Kurdish was good enough by now to pick up a few awful words.

'...depends how much...'

'Let them rot in...'

'...risk...'

'Families pay...'

'Your share...'

I felt sick with fear.

Mehran was trying to reassure me. 'It doesn't make sense. If they wanted to sell us, why did they bother to come and save us?'

'Money,' said Abdul. 'Why does anybody do anything to us? We are just another dollar for these people.'

I wanted to run: 'We have to escape.' But even as I said it, I knew there was no way to escape. They all had guns and I was not physically strong enough to risk anything stupid. I'd barely eaten anything in days.

Abdul read my mind: 'How? Even if we could get out of here, do we just run into the hills? No water, no food? We would be dead in two days – even if they didn't just capture us again.'

Just then, the low hum of an approaching vehicle could be heard. The voices at the entrance changed, becoming more urgent.

I tensed. This was bad.

A young man with epaulettes on his shoulders got out of his car. He looked like a boss. His smart officer's uniform strained around his belly as he shouted at the other policemen.

He spoke in Farsi: 'You think I don't know what you are doing? Meeting your gangster friends in the middle of the night. This lot' – he waved his hand in our direction – 'like chickens ready for market.'

My legs started to shake with relief.

'Tell your other friends to leave. If I see them here again, they too will be in the cells. Is my order clear?'

With that he strode inside. The men in the cars left, but only after handshakes, hugs and apologetic looks from their police-officer friends.

We stood waiting by the wall for over an hour in the cold, but at least we were allowed to put our shirts back on.

I think the boss must have called people he knew personally to take us, because different cars came. Not police cars, but what looked like local people on their way to market. We were ordered into them. A couple of the police officers came with us.

The car I got into had a trussed-up goat in the back. It bleated at me pleadingly as we drove away. I knew just how it felt.

CHAPTER FIFTEEN

The mountains.

After a while they start to look like bones. Jagged knuckles, bare of flesh.

I felt as though all life had been stripped from me.

My face felt like granite, sharp and hard – washed clean by storm after storm. I tried to sleep – I was exhausted but, as ever, I was the smallest person in an overcrowded car.

From the border we had been taken to an Iranian town called Maku where we spent the night in a local police station. We still hadn't eaten and I was faint with hunger.

In the morning we were put into police cars and told we were going to court.

The land around Maku was crisscrossed with apricot orchards and vineyards, watered by a network of irrigation canals.

'It is very ancient here,' said the police officer in the back. 'It is very beautiful, do you not think?

I didn't care. I ignored him.

We drove through a gate in a high stone wall.

'Look,' the driver spoke. 'Look at this tower.'

A seven-sided tower loomed, ornate and strong; maybe a grave for a whole dynasty.

'Maku is famous for its architecture, as you will see.' Then the driver laughed until he coughed.

They took us to a golden-brown coloured court building – it made me think of bread. My knees wobbled as we were led inside. I didn't think I could face another interrogation like the one in Turkey.

Many of the court officials and local police spoke only in Kurdish, not Farsi. We were given documents to read in Farsi, but the language was so complicated I couldn't really work it out. I was just about to ask Abdul to try and explain it to me when we were told to get up and walk over to a counter. There, we were told to write our names, ages and countries of origin in a big blue ledger.

I wrote my age, twelve, in big clear letters. I hoped they might take notice of it.

The whole court process was over in a few minutes, however. Escorted by the police, we were made to walk from there to a prison nearby. There, the police did some kind of official handover to the prison officials, showing them the court papers. Abdul said he thought the court papers were permission to detain us. I prayed someone would notice my age and do something to help me.

The prison was some kind of old military barracks made of mud and stone. Now I understood why the driver had laughed so hard. The barracks were indeed ancient, with no running water. We had to file under a carved archway and down a little step to get into the dungeon-like cells. On the border it had been so very cold, but now it felt so hot in the airless cell I was assigned to, sharing with ten others. There were no beds, only mattresses on the floor, packed in such a tight row that you had to step over them to reach the ones closest to the far wall.

There were about twenty-five prisoners, all migrants, already there.

'Welcome to the luxury hotel.'

It was what was by now becoming a familiar story: they told us if you couldn't afford to pay for your own deportation, you rotted in that jail. Some of them had been there weeks, some months.

The governor was a fat man with a uniform that looked fit to burst whenever he moved. To cheer myself up, I imagined how funny it would be if it did, his buttons popping everywhere.

He issued us our instructions: 'During the day you will be outside exercising or resting in the yard. At night you stay in your cells. If you want to get out of here, you can pay from amongst yourselves for the cost of a coach to the city of Zahedan, on the border with Afghanistan. The authorities will help return you to the hands of your government. The Pakistanis among you can go home from there.'

This caused consternation among the Pakistanis of the group. Afghanistan was not a safe place for them, especially with no papers.

'There is no food for you here. If you are hungry give us money, and the guards will go and get it for you.'

The first thing we did was pool some resources and send out for some chicken and rice. I was delighted to finally get something to eat.

Each morning the guards turned us out into the yard. There was no shade, and this fact was made worse by hundreds of dive bombing mosquitoes, which filled in the gaps of misery the sun could not reach.

The guards sat and watched us bake from the shade of their watch towers. They made us do endlessly humiliating squat jumps with our hands on our heads. My head swam in the heat. Each breath scorched my lungs so painfully that I felt my whole body might burst into flames. My arms and thighs sang from the pain, but they kept forcing us to do more and more until we were on the point of collapse. Only then did they let us rest.

We had little food the week we stayed there. I had money and so did Mehran and Abdul, but we couldn't afford to use all our cash to buy food for everybody. As we felt guilty eating in front of hungry people, we mostly stayed hungry ourselves. One afternoon, after the forced exercise, a guard threw a crust of bread – the remains of his lunch – into the yard. Two desperate men jumped on it.

I knew I had to get out of there as fast as I could. I took it upon myself to try and find enough people with money to help pay for the coach to Zahedan. The governor had made clear that the coach to freedom was only permissible if it was full; the journey to Zahedan was far, and he would need to send guards with us. He said it would cost us US$20 per person.

A man named Raheem and I began to negotiate with him. In the end, the governor agreed on $10 per person.

As there were fifty-two of us in total, that made $520 dollars for him, minus the bus fee, of course. But there was one condition: 'You take everyone. I cannot listen to the complaining a moment longer.'

With Raheem's help, I became the organizer. As a child, people were more trusting of me not to cheat them. I walked around the yard trying to get people to cough up. Some were genuinely penniless, begging me to help them; others had money, but wouldn't admit to it. Some were willing to pay for themselves and a friend only. Others refused to pay at all.

I had to use all of my powers of persuasion.

By the end of it, I was $50 dollars short of the $520 we needed. I used my own money to make it up. That left me with just $150 to my name.

It was worth it, though, the moment we boarded that coach.

From Maku, the coach headed to the city of Shiraz; from there it would go on to Zahedan and the border with Afghanistan.

It was a very long way but I didn't care – at least I was out of that prison. The bus was ancient, fiercely hot with no air conditioning, but the windows opened and we were in the shade most of the time. Two prison guards were assigned to travel with us.

'Behave and cooperate, and we will treat you with respect,' they told us curtly.

Every now and then we stopped at a small town along the way for food and toilet breaks. A guard went around collecting money and returned shortly with tea and bread for all of us. I was touched when one of them paid for our food himself on one occasion.

They usually let us get out of the bus when they were eating themselves. I think they felt embarrassed to be eating in front of us because they had nicer food than we did, and they knew we were hungry.

We had stopped to rest in some small public gardens. We stretched out in the shade of a low tree and ate hungrily. As usual Mehran, Abdul and I stuck close to each other.

As we sat chewing in silence, we all looked at each other. The same thought – escape – passed between us unspoken.

'If we are going to do this, then we must do it right,' I said, knowing that failure meant the police would probably shoot us.

'It is madness,' said Abdul. 'Don't be so stupid as to even try.'

I looked at Mehran.

He nodded to me. 'I'm with you.'

I can't remember how many days we had been on the road by then. I think maybe three days and two nights. We had a feeling this could be our last stop before we arrived at Shiraz, so this was as good a chance as we would get.

'Raheem is a brilliant Farsi speaker. He can help us get across Iran.'

I looked over at Raheem. He nodded in agreement.

'I'm not helping you get yourselves killed,' said Abdul.

'Come on, man. Let's stick together,' Mehran pleaded with him.

'Nor me,' said the old Pakistani man, the one who had been given the knife in Turkey. 'I am too sick to run. But I can distract the guards for you.'

'But that's the point – they don't expect us to run. They think we are far too exhausted and hungry,' said Raheem.

My mother's disappointed face was scarier than the police and their guns. For the first time since I had set off on this journey, I knew exactly what I needed to do.

'And that,' I said, 'is exactly why we must run. We must run now.'

CHAPTER SIXTEEN

I really didn't want to be deported, but I could sense the others were unsure. After all, I was a twelve-year-old trying to persuade grown men to escape a prison bus with me.

I knew I had to convince them that this was a risk we needed to take; I tried by pushing the most obvious button you can with Afghan males: by calling their bravery into question.

'If I am not scared, why are you? Isn't it better to try than regret?'

Mehran nodded enthusiastically. He was as keen as I was.

No one else said a word. A couple of people looked at their feet or picked at the grass.

Abdul was still adamantly against it. 'Are you crazy? You'll be shot.'

Mehran sat quietly for a few seconds before weighing up his options: 'If they send me home to Afghanistan, I am dead. If they keep me starving in one of their prisons, I am dead. Europe is the only chance I have.'

Our kindly decoy, the old Pakistani, climbed to his feet, brushing his trousers clean. 'May Allah be with you. Are you ready, boys?'

'Are you sure?' I asked him. We all knew he was risking punishment for us.

'Yes. I'll try and make sure you get a head start.'

'How will we know?'

'Don't worry, you'll know. Just run as soon as I reach the bus.'

He walked towards the parked bus, screened from our view by a bed of tall shrubs. The prison officers were sitting on the other side of it, eating. We had all behaved so well for the past few days that they had begun to relax and let their guard down a bit more than they should have done.

And then it happened. 'Guards,' our old friend cried. 'A dog just stole my bread. Tried to attack me.'

'What are you talking about, old man?'

'I think he might have rabies, sir.'

'Rabies?' said the officer. 'Show me where it went.'

And the old Pakistani gentleman led the guards in the other direction.

We seized our chance.

I looked around at the nervous faces. Abdul shook his head. Raheem stood up.

'Let's go.'

This was it.

Mehran and I both sprang to our feet and ran through the park with Raheem following right behind us. We dashed out of it and into a narrow side street.

My one abiding regret is that it all happened too fast to say a proper goodbye to Abdul – until the very last second, I don't think he believed we were really going to do it.

Until we ran, I wasn't sure I had believed it myself.

'Where are we going?' Mehran cried.

'The fields,' I shouted. It was the first thing that came to mind. 'We've got to get away. They'll never find us in the fields.'

We ran through a series of narrow alleys lined with tightly packed houses, trying to avoid the main streets where there was more traffic, and a group of sprinting, breathless, wild-eyed males would be quickly noticed.

It wasn't a big town, but there was much confusion about which way to go. There were fields ringing the town, which we'd seen from the bus window, but we had no idea how to get there. I half expected to feel a bullet in my back at any moment.

I was pretty confident the prison officers would not come after us because they had to stay with the rest of the group, but I knew they'd call the local police, who could be waiting for us around any corner. Suddenly, I realized that the houses were giving way to shops and there were more people around.

We were running into the centre of town, not out of it.

'Wrong way,' Mehran panted breathlessly, his eyes wide with the dawning realization of what we'd done. 'Where now?'

'Look normal,' Raheem murmured to us both.

We slowed to a walk, trying to look as casual as possible, but it was hard, and my heart was pumping with fear. It was clear we were distressed, dirty and scared – we looked like the escaped con- victs we were.

Quick-thinking Raheem asked a passer-by where we could find a taxi. Luckily, we got one almost straight away and, to our joy, the driver was an Afghan immigrant.

'Please take us to Shiraz.'

I think he guessed something was up, possibly even realized we were illegal migrants. He reassured us with a single sentence. 'I understand. You are lucky to have found me.'

The city of Shiraz was where the prison bus was headed for an overnight stop before moving on to the border town of Zahedan and the planned deportations, but we knew it was a big enough city not to be seen, and with a lot of non-Iranians, especially Afghans, wandering around, it would be easy for us to blend in. It was also the nearest city to this little town we were in, which we had to get away from fast if we stood any chance at all.

I breathed a sigh of relief as I sank into the black vinyl back seat of the taxi with Mehran.

Raheem got into the front and spoke to the driver. '*Kaka*, we don't have any Iranian money. We only have US dollars.'

The driver looked slightly frustrated but was still kind: 'Give me your dollars. I will exchange them for you.'

Raheem gave him $250.

At the bus station in Shiraz, the driver exchanged Raheem's money at a little kiosk. As he drove off, he offered us some sound advice: 'Don't get lost again. You might not be so lucky twice.'

The station was buzzing with people. We were able to relax a little bit because there were migrants everywhere. Shiraz is a little bit like an Iranian version of Dubai, with lots of people from neighbouring countries going there to work.

We weren't really sure what to do next.

'Do you know anyone in Iran?' I asked Raheem.

'Not anyone I can call. You?'

'No.'

'Yes, we do,' said Mehran. 'What about the place we stayed in when we first came here, in Tehran? Where we met Shah and Faizal. The place was run by that nasty guy – the one who took our passports.'

'Why would we call him?' I still had bad memories of that guest house, which stank of boiled meat.

Remarkably, Mehran had the phone number: he had meticulously stored all of the different agents' numbers in a notebook in his backpack. I was amazed – he was the joker of our pack; he'd never struck me as particularly organized, or even that intelligent.

I didn't think for a second it would work. It had been several months ago that we had stayed there, at the end of October 2006. Now it was late spring in 2007. I didn't think the man would even remember us.

The only other place we had stayed in this country, aside from the Maku prison, was the smart hotel in Mashhad when we had first arrived from Afghanistan last October. Mehran had written down the telephone number for that too, but not the name of it. Besides, Mashhad was at the opposite side of Iran to Shiraz. If we were to avoid deportation and make it to Europe, we needed to get away from border cities and to the north of Iran, to Tehran.

I stood lookout with Raheem as Mehran made the call from a public phone booth. He spoke as loudly as he dared to make himself understood over the noise of the street. 'We are people of Qubat.' His eyes darted around nervously as he spoke. 'Three of us. Escaped from the prison bus. We need help.'

I shifted anxiously and scanned the street for police or anybody who might be taking an interest in us. It was the early evening rush hour, and tired commuters were busy rushing home from work or running for buses. Thankfully, no one took notice of three paranoid illegals.

After Mehran had hung up, we walked to a quiet corner where he repeated the conversation to me and Raheem: 'He said we have two options. If we go there, he'll send a friend to get us. He says he is too busy to help us himself. Or he says he knows someone in Shiraz we can stay with, but he said that would be more risky.'

'I don't trust a word he says,' I said. I hated that man.

'Me neither, but he's all we have,' continued Mehran. 'The good news is that he told me he'd call Kabul and inform Qubat of the bad news that we are back in Iran. He said it was up to Qubat to decide what the next plan was. If Qubat agrees to pay him, he can help us himself, and we can go to stay at his place again.'

'I will look forward to that,' I said sarcastically. 'Maybe we can get our passports back.'

'I think they were sold for a tidy profit long ago, my friend.'

The day was fast disappearing into a warm and sultry night. We used some of Raheem's newly exchanged Iranian money to buy tickets for an overnight sleeper coach to Tehran. It wasn't leaving until midnight, some six hours away.

We were absolutely filthy. We had spent a week in the prison at Maku, and three days on the hot and sticky bus journey, all in the same set of clothes. I worked out that I hadn't had a shower since the prison cell in Istanbul, about fifteen days ago.

Raheem was worried that the state of us might arouse suspicion. I got his point. Mehran and I sat on a bench and waited while Raheem wandered across the street to a small shopping mall. He came back with three new shirts and trousers for us all, as well as socks and underwear. With a look of triumph, he then produced a small glass bottle from a plastic bag. 'We can't shower, but I brought some cologne. It might help.'

We managed a quick wash as we changed in the public toilets. The cologne, a cheap musky sandalwood, might have made us smell stronger but it certainly didn't make us smell any sweeter. But I felt quite grown up as I looked in the mirror and copied Raheem, who was splashing it all over his neck and behind his ears. I had never worn cologne or aftershave before.

We threw our old clothes in the bin. It was so good to wear new clothes – but Raheem had managed to bring me jeans one size too big. I didn't have a belt, so I kept having to hook them up as I walked.

'You two look like Bollywood stars – especially you, Gulwali.' With that, Mehran did a silly dance of the type we'd seen in the Indian DVDs we'd bought.

'Shut up. I do not.' My face burned red. I was a bit sensitive about the fact I had watched and enjoyed the movies back in Istanbul. For me, it still felt a bit *haram*, forbidden. Remembering the films also made me think of Baryalai, who we had left behind in a Turkish prison, accused of being an agent.

Feeling more secure in our new clothes, we ventured out of the bus station to try and find a restaurant. The last time I had had proper food had been back in Istanbul, before I went to prison there. That had been well over a month ago. In that time, I'd been to two different jails in two different countries and survived on either tiny amounts of rations or nothing.

To our delight we found a tiny Afghan restaurant tucked away behind the station. It looked just like the restaurants in Jalalabad used to: Formica tables, metal chairs, plastic roses in vases and mirrored tiles on the wall in angular patterns. For the first time since leaving home we had proper Afghan food: Kabuli *pilau* (rice fried with onions and raisins); kebab and *bolani* (a type of fried pasty); all with freshly baked naan, washed down with salty lassi (yoghurt) with cucumber and mint.

I so badly wanted to enjoy this rare treat, but my stomach had shrunk and was painful from the previous lack of food. I had to force down every mouthful, and eating it made me feel instantly bloated. I was so disappointed, and soon in a lot of pain. We wrapped some of the kebab in napkins to take with us for the journey.

The bus journey to Tehran from Shiraz took about eight hours. Iranian coach services are generally of superb quality – air conditioned and comfortable. We were thrilled to discover that this one was a proper sleeper, with seats that reclined into beds. It even had a TV screen above the driver's seat showing movies. It was the most luxury I had seen in months.

I slept soundly, only waking when we stopped in Isfahan for breakfast. Esfahan is famous for its architecture, with many beautiful palaces, covered bridges, mosques and minarets. There is a famous saying about it, '*Esfahān nesf-e jahān ast.*' ('Esfahan is half of the world.') It was a place I had seen in picture books as a child, and while I was scared of being arrested any second, I did still enjoy seeing this wonderful place.

When we reached Tehran, we called the number Mehran had

been given for the man who was supposed to come and pick us up. I was so scared that the number might be a hoax, and that no such man existed. But, thankfully, someone did turn up.

He was Afghan and said he worked in Tehran legally, labouring in a warehouse. I got the impression he wasn't used to dealing in this migrant business – I think he'd been co-opted in to help us by the guest-house owner.

He took us on the metro. This was truly exciting: I had never seen such a magical thing before. The carriage was made of glass, and I was amazed by how it was we were standing in the same place but the carriage was moving. It was beautiful.

After half an hour on a couple of different trains, we arrived at the other side of Tehran. The man walked with us to a local park where he left us and told us to spend the day. He said he needed to go to work and would come and pick us up in the evening.

We spent the day trying to relax but it wasn't easy. Every time someone walked past us we were nervous because we thought they were staring at us. I felt as if I had the words 'Escaped convict' tattooed on my forehead. Fortunately, Raheem still had some Iranian currency left so we were able to buy drinks and snacks to keep us going. My stomach was still not used to normal food, though.

When the man returned in the evening, as promised, he took us to his house. It was a very basic one-room hut on a scruffy farm on the outskirts of the city. He explained that the farm belonged to an Iranian friend of his and that he was allowed to stay there in return for keeping an eye on the place when the man was away.

We ate and slept on the hut's flat roof. It was the only place where there was enough room for four people, but it had the added advantage of offering us a good vantage point should police cars come looking for us.

Our benefactor was, as we had suspected, neither a paid smuggler nor an agent: he was helping us as a favour to his friend. I don't know if he'd been put under pressure to do so, but he was very gracious about it and we were grateful to him for putting himself at risk to shelter us.

He told us most Afghans living there, even the ones who were legally allowed to work, lived in poverty and struggled to survive. 'It's tough, but it's better than home. At least we are free from bombs.'

In the morning his friend, the guest-house manager, called and asked him to let us stay another few days. It seems that he had contacted Qubat, who refused to pay him for the intervention or hire him to move us on again. Qubat wanted us to go to one of his different – we assumed more efficient – agents. But this guy was refusing to let us go. He insisted that because we'd called him from Shiraz we were now de facto 'his' for as long as we were in Tehran. He insisted Qubat owed him money, at least for the help he'd given us so far.

In our minds, if anyone deserved money it was the man whose hut we were sitting in, not the guest-house owner. But, of course, our host had no direct connection to Qubat himself – he was just a poor Afghan caught up in the middle of all this.

The whole thing got even more confusing when two other migrants arrived. They had only just left Afghanistan and this was the first step in their journey to Europe. Jawad, in his forties, was from Nangarhar, the same province Mehran and I came from. Because of that we nicknamed him 'cousin'.

Jawad was very sad. Usually people didn't say too much about their background stories or personal reasons for leaving, and he didn't tell us the full whys and wherefores. But he often spoke of his little son who was just six. He was missing him and his wife like mad.

'Will I see them again? I can't bear it.'

The other person was Tamim. He was very young but had lost

all his hair due to stress, although he liked to joke it was because 'I think too much.' He was a tailor from Jalalabad. Somehow, he and Mehran worked out they were distant relatives by marriage. They decided to call each other 'cousin' too, which meant overnight Mehran and I suddenly had not one but two new relatives.

Tamim told us he had been threatened by the Taliban and that's why he'd left. Why exactly, I don't know.

On the fourth day it seemed the argument with Qubat had been settled because our host was instructed to take us to the side of the field running alongside the farm, later that night, when it was dark. A deal had been struck with a bus conductor who would stop to pick us up.

As ours wasn't a proper bus stop we rather assumed the bus would be empty, but when it arrived it was packed with locals. We were fuming. How obvious could it be that this was a dodgy pick-up? We were certain we'd be caught.

Raheem stayed behind. Our host had reassured him that, even without papers, he could work in Iran. He knew enough about the country and had such good language skills he figured he'd be better off trying to survive there than continuing to risk all to get to Europe. I was sad to leave him, but I understood his reasons.

The new group of four: me and Mehran, and now Jawad and Tamim too, travelled on the bus for the whole night, until we were the only passengers left on board. We had no idea where we were going, only that we were driving away from Tehran. I hoped, prayed, that the bus was going somewhere in the direction of the Turkish border, which was what we needed to do in order to keep moving forwards.

If I made it, it would now be the third time I had crossed the border into Turkey.

CHAPTER SEVENTEEN

'Get out.'

It was 10 o'clock in the morning. The driver had just stopped the bus, without warning.

'What? Where are we?'

He was dropping us in the middle of the road, in the middle of nowhere.

'Get out.'

We did as we were told.

'Now what?' Jawad and Tamim looked at Mehran as the bus drove off.

He shrugged.

'Have you got a plan?' They turned to me next.

'Nope.'

'Oh, that's just great,' snapped Jawad. These two were new at this. They had yet to realize that this kind of stuff was normal.

Not knowing where I was, where I was going or when I'd get there had almost become routine for me now. It never stopped being stressful, but I was used to it.

We stood by the road not knowing what to do. Less than five minutes later, a car approached us.

It was the most amazing car I had ever seen. It was silver, with tinted windows and looked like a racing car, of the type I had only ever seen in pictures. As the driver pulled over, it sat crouched low to the broken ground, like a wild animal ready to pounce.

A young, clean-shaven man in jeans, a grey Western-style suit jacket and red shirt opened the door. He looked very nervous as he spoke: 'Qubat's people?'

I couldn't contain my smile. It was so wide I thought my face might crack – even as hungry, tired and scared as I was, that car gave me a thrill. If my friends back home could see me now. Imagine driving through the streets of Jalalabad in this.

'What are you grinning at?' said the man, who was dabbing sweat from his brow with a handkerchief.

'Nothing,' I replied, swallowing my teeth.

He looked really annoyed. 'Why are there four? There should only be three of you. I can't take four.' He was right. The car had only one passenger seat and a very tiny back seat. He pointed at Tamim. 'You wait here. I'll come back for you.'

'No way. I am not staying.'

We looked at Tamim, feeling guilty. I looked the man pleadingly: 'We can try.'

Two minutes later, Mehran and I were crushed into the tiny back seat. Jawad, who was the eldest, was in the front – even in these strange circumstances we always gave our elders respect – and Tamim was in the boot.

The man was clearly not happy – sweat was now trickling down his temples. He didn't take us very far: along a couple of winding lanes and into a small hamlet, eventually pulling into the yard of a small brick house. In front of it was a woman sweeping, using one of the stick brooms my mother used.

The man ordered us out of the car. 'This is my parents' house. You –' he pointed to Tamim – 'will stay here, and I will come back for you.'

Tamim started arguing: 'Why me? Leave one of the others.'

I felt bad, but I wasn't about to give up my place for him. I'd been on this journey for over half a year now; Tamim had been on it for less than a week.

Mehran and I got in the tiny back seat again.

The engine roared into life as we pulled away on to some small and winding but smooth country roads. Tamim looked forlornly on from the yard. Mehran and I grinned in silence at each other as we pulled away.

After about an hour, the driver pulled over again. 'We are nearing a place where there are lots of police searches and checkpoints,' he said. 'I need to take some precautions.'

We all climbed out, and the driver opened the boot. Jawad and Mehran looked at me expectantly. I moved towards the boot: as the smallest and youngest in every situation, I accepted the treatment.

'No,' said the driver. 'The boy rides with me. You two – get in.'

My friends stared in shock at the tiny space.

'It's only a few miles. Then you can get out.'

Neither of them moved.

'Look, the boy can pass as my young brother. You two look like a pair of illegals, which is what you are. So, what do you suggest we do?'

I tried very hard not to burst out laughing.

Jawad went in legs first, tucking his back tightly to the back seats. Mehran followed – just: Jawad had to hold him in place by wrapping his arms around his chest so that they neatly spooned each other. I don't know how two grown men managed to fit in there, and it did not look at all comfortable.

The driver smirked. 'Such a cute couple.'

I could barely contain myself at that – I bit down hard on my lip and snorted.

Mehran looked up at me, his face red with discomfort and humiliation. 'You laugh one more time, Gulwali, and you'll pay for it when I get out of here.'

'Mind your heads,' said the driver, shoving the boot lid closed.

Barely able to contain my glee, I climbed into the passenger seat.

'Put your seat belt on,' the driver barked at me. 'We are relatives. So you must call me "brother" if the moment requires it.'

'Yes,' I said, flushing with guilt, anger and pain at the thought of Hazrat.

The driver took a pair of sunglasses and a magazine from the glove box. 'Put these on.'

I'd never worn sunglasses before. They felt fun to wear. And I really liked the way I didn't need to squint in the afternoon light.

'Read the magazine and ignore what's going on around you.'

'But I can't read Farsi very much,' I said, puzzled for a moment by the role the magazine was supposed to play.

'It doesn't matter. It's a car magazine – just look at the pictures and smile at the guards.'

'Um, OK,' I said, beginning to think it would be easier in the boot.

'*Salâm aleykom*,' he said, his Farsi accent strong. 'Now you say it.'

I knew this of course. Every Muslim knows the Arabic greeting, 'Peace be with you.' Most Muslims around the world use the simple, shortened version, '*Salaam*', peace, as a way to say hello.

'*Asal m-alaykom*,' I responded. I tried to say it in the best Farsi pronunciation I could muster, but clearly it came out with a Pashtu accent, with all the emphasis in the wrong places.

He groaned. 'Say it like that and we'll get arrested for certain. Try to sound like less of a peasant, and more like you belong both in this car and in Iran.'

I bristled at that. '*Asalâm aleykom*.'

'That's better. Not like an Iranian, but better. Please just smile and look at the magazine. Say nothing unless you are forced to.'

When the moment came at the checkpoint I was shaking so much I could barely hold my magazine still. Being in the car was no longer exciting – I just wanted it to be over.

I watched a truck full of migrant workers being searched in front of us. I could recognize them as Afghans. They had papers, which the police studied in detail. The police pushed them around and handled them roughly. I was terrified of what treatment we were surely about to get.

'Remember what I told you, boy,' said the driver, through the corner of his mouth.

The border guard approached his side of the car.

'*Salâm aleykom.*'

The steely faced police officer ignored the driver's greeting. 'What's your business?'

'My brother and I are visiting relatives for the day.'

'Oh, yes?' said the guard, as if he had his doubts.

I felt the guard's eyes on me. I lowered my magazine.

'*Salaam,*' I said, in as bright a tone as I could muster, hoping it came out the Iranian way. I was shaking inside and out, terrified. I tried to control my hands to hold the magazine steady.

'His mother wants me to discuss a wedding match for him, with my cousin. He is getting of an age. That's who we are going to see.'

'What's your favourite car, boy?' the guard demanded.

I pointed to a smart black police Land Cruiser parked by the gate.

He grunted with approval. 'If only choosing a wife was as easy, hey.'

The two men laughed.

'OK,' said the guard, sweeping his arm. 'You can go.'

I thought of my friends in the boot and said a silent prayer of thanks.

*

Shortly after getting a safe distance away from the police security check, the driver made a quick phone call to whoever was waiting up ahead. We drove on for another fifteen minutes or so before we came across a blue four-wheel drive, parked by the road. I recognized it as the type of vehicle commonly driven in the Kurdish inhabited mountainous regions. I guess it meant that that was where we were headed.

'Come on. Jump in,' the driver of the new vehicle urged.

I was first in, diving on to the back seat.

The others were struggling to get of the boot of the first car, and were not helped when the driver slammed the boot shut again as another car came around the corner. From my hiding place I looked on, horrified, convinced he'd just chopped my friend's hands off.

The car passed and he opened it again. 'For God's sake, get out of my bloody car.'

An angry Mehran snapped back at him, 'We were trying to do just that until you shut the lid on my head.'

I laughed with relief. If his mouth was working, that meant he was fine.

Mehran and Jawad got in next to me, both bitterly complaining about their bad backs and cramped legs.

'If I was afraid of coffins before, I really am right now,' Mehran said, rubbing the small of his back. 'That was awful.'

I started to snigger.

He threw me a furious look and waved a fist. 'I mean it, Gulwali. You laugh at me one more time—'

We were interrupted by the sound of the silver car and the rude young man disappearing into the distance. The sound of the engine still gave me a small thrill, even as the racing car vanished out of sight around a bend.

Ensconced in our new vehicle, we wound slowly upwards for the next few hours until the driver of the blue car dropped us off in a steep valley, the splintered hillsides sparsely thatched with coarse thorn bushes. A trail of pea-green willow trees marked the passage of a stream that tumbled below us.

'Hey.'

The voice drifted up on the cool dusk air.

'Hey. Over here.'

One of the strangest things about this journey was how whenever a smuggler or driver gave us an instruction, we simply followed it. Whether it was *get in the car, stay silent, follow me, eat this, shave your beard, hand over your passport* – we simply followed orders. Without questioning or really even thinking, we put our lives into the hands of strangers, time and again. We had no choice. When they said come, we little lost sheep had to follow.

It's very hard to explain the feeling of repeatedly putting your complete trust in the hands of strangers who see you as a commodity. Every time I did as one of these men asked, I had an acute awareness that this could be the last instruction I would ever follow. Each of these men had the power to take us to our deaths, at any time.

But I knew Allah was always with me. I prayed often, I talked to God, I found comfort in my faith. I don't even know if that was a choice I'd consciously made. I simply had to. Faith was all I had left.

We scrambled down a rocky embankment to see a fast-flowing stream, where a leather-jacketed man who owned the voice was standing. At the fork of the river, under a low-hanging willow tree, stood a tiny, crooked shepherd's hut. Its gnarled wooden door hung wide, clinging on by one remaining hinge.

'Wait in there.' He pointed at the hut. 'I will come soon.'

Nervously, we entered the dark interior of the hut. The dirty floor was uneven and scattered with leaves and the remains of cigarette butts, long since gutted for any scraps of tobacco. There were a few puddles of clothing in the corners that had been used as pillows, and ancient evidence of a fire in the crooked fireplace.

It was much colder in this mountainous valley. My T-shirt felt as thin as tissue paper, and I rubbed my shoulders to keep warm.

Mehran scrabbled about on the floor, trying to find a cigarette butt that still contained some tobacco. I rubbed and massaged my shins, knowing that we'd be on the move again before long. We were most definitely still in Iran, but where exactly I couldn't tell.

We spent several hours there, until the day turned to night. We were huddling together for warmth when two men carrying hissing, crackling walkie-talkies burst through the broken door. One of them started to jabber instructions at us in Farsi, but they spoke with the heavy accents we recognized as unmistakably Kurdish. 'Soon we go. Gather your things. But quietly. Very quietly. Many soldiers and police.'

The second man spoke into his walkie-talkie. The hiss and static made it almost impossible to hear. It sounded as if he was talking in code. 'The little birds are in the nest. When do they fly?'

We left the hut and formed into a small column. Again, we followed orders, unquestioning, readying ourselves for the next ordeal.

The pair of smugglers had a huddled conversation before the second man evaporated into the darkness.

'We wait,' the remaining man said, smoothing his moustache and lighting a cigarette.

Before long, his radio belched two bursts of static.

'Let's go,' he said, grinding his cigarette into the ground. 'Say nothing and do as I do. Many police looking for you. No talking, no smoking, no farting. You make noise, you go to prison.'

We nodded solemnly.

'Follow me. Where I walk, you walk. When I stop, you stop.'

We nodded again.

'Let's go.'

He moved a lot faster than his age and build suggested. My anxiety levels skyrocketed: if this guy was hurrying because we were at risk of being caught, then, I reasoned, we must really be in danger. I didn't want to go back to prison – any prison, but especially not an Iranian prison.

We snaked our way along a narrow sheep track that followed the stream. A crescent moon sliced through the cloud, giving enough light for me to see the second smuggler standing in silhouette a few hundred yards ahead, on higher ground. He was scanning the horizon behind and beyond us, issuing instructions to the man with us on the walkie-talkie. It felt like a well-organized military operation.

As we walked, all I could hear was the gentle padding of cautious steps on well-trodden dirt, and the occasional crack of twigs snapping underfoot. If the guide ducked we ducked, if he jogged we jogged too; when he stopped to hide so did we, and when he slowed to a more relaxed pace we breathed a little sigh of relief and did the same. We copied him as if it were a child's game of Follow My Leader. If we hadn't been so petrified it might have been funny.

The guide stopped suddenly, causing me to crash into Mehran's back, almost knocking him over.

'Gulwali. Watch it.'

'Quiet, you idiots.'

Somewhere ahead in the dark, a walkie-talkie rasped.

'Get down and shut up,' the guide whispered.

I fell down hard, knocking my hand painfully on a rock as I went. It was all I could do not to cry out in pain. As I lay in the black grass with just the sound of my own breathing in my ears, I stared up at the moon. I wondered if my mother could see the same moon right now. For a brief second, I wanted to scream at her, to tell her she shouldn't have sent me away. She shouldn't have put me through this agony.

'Get up. Move it.'

The guide seemed to be getting increasingly nervous as his walkie-talkie crackled out new instructions.

We continued in the same way, running and crouching like infantry soldiers entering enemy territory. At last, the guide led us off to the side of the track and under some trees.

I couldn't believe my eyes. Sitting under a tree were four young men, Iranians. I panicked – for a second, I thought they might be secret police. Then I realized they looked as scared as we did, maybe even more so.

'You are Ralph's people, yes?'

They nodded in confirmation of our guide's question. 'Who are you?'

'Never mind who I am. You need to get up and follow us.'

They looked at each other, hesitating.

'Hurry up. I won't wait for anyone. Stay if you want to stay, but the way you need is this way.'

They followed. Our column was now eight people strong: the guide, Jawad, Mehran, me and now the four young Iranians, who belonged to somebody called Ralph.

The narrow path we'd been following opened out into a wider, fertile valley. We had just set out across it, making our way directly through the centre, when suddenly gunfire rang out across the hills above us.

'Get down. Police. Police.'

It was chaos: we got down, but the Iranians ran back to the trees for cover. The shots rang out again. It was impossible to work out if they were shooting directly at us, or across the valley at each other.

'Get up. Fast. Run.'

We ran for so long through that valley I thought my chest was going to burst and my kidneys explode. Every single sinew, fibre and muscle in my body hummed with pain. I was desperate to stop and rest but I knew if I attempted to do so for even a second, the guide would leave me to the mercy of whoever was up there firing indiscriminately.

Not for the first time I expected to be shot and killed at any second. I ran like one of the frightened wild rabbits that burrowed along the edge of the valley path – I had no idea where I was running to, only that I had to get away from the immediate danger. I knew with complete certainty that I didn't want to die, not here, not like this. Running for my life was becoming all I knew.

Just when I thought I couldn't run any more and that I was going to fall behind, be shot and die alone on that path, we came to the end of the valley and on to a track where the same blue four-wheel drive we'd been in that morning was waiting. I could hardly breathe after so much running. My lungs felt as hot and tight as one of the brick kilns that scattered the countryside around my home in Nangarhar.

'Get in the vehicle,' a voice ordered.

We all ran, cramming seven bodies in as fast as we could.

CHAPTER EIGHTEEN

Even now, I have only half an understanding of the routes that I travelled; my memories are often a blur of faces, landscapes, half-formed thoughts, and then there are some moments that are etched on my mind for ever, ones I know I will never forget.

Running for my life along that valley in the dead of night is one of them.

As far as I could make out in the moonlight, as I gazed out of the car window, the landscape was very different from the terrain I'd seen when I first arrived in Iran from Afghanistan, and was taken to Black Wolf's farm. It was less populated, the buildings were simpler, and it was much more arid. I guessed that we were now approaching the Turkish border through a different region.

We spent a comfortable night hosted by a family who owned a fruit farm. The owner told us he was Afghan by descent but his family had lived in Iran for generations. His family may have been in Iran for a long time, but they still had the old ways: they made us proper Afghan-style eggs, served with delicious homemade bread and a salad of cucumber and tomatoes. It was some of the freshest, nicest food I had eaten in weeks.

My stomach was slowly recovering from the meagre prison rations, so this time I was able to wolf it all down with gusto. The farmer was warm and polite, treating us like guests – he gave us some delicious oranges from his trees. After all that running I was so very thirsty, so it was a joy to feel the juicy fruit exploding across my tongue.

It was surreal. One second I was being shot at; the next I was eating eggs and oranges.

It still didn't cease to amaze me how we had moments like this, or how many seemingly ordinary people and families along the way were involved in these smuggling operations, offering their homes for shelter or safe passage. I don't know if the farmer was paid to host us or if he was doing it because he was a relative or friend of one of the smugglers – they weren't questions we could ask.

I did discover more about our new Iranian associates. They told us they were students and were fleeing Iran due to the political situation there. They were obviously very scared, made more so by being shot at. They said they would only be able to relax a little bit once they were out of their country and across the border into Turkey. I felt the same way.

We got a decent night's sleep in a comfortable anteroom at the back of the farmer's house, and set off again in the middle of the next afternoon.

We drove up ever higher winding tracks for the rest of the day. Through the windows I could see people working and watering the irrigated fields that stretched as far as the eye could see. The lengthening shadows told me it was the crossover between late afternoon and early evening, the time of day when the sun graces the earth with a golden goodbye before turning in for the night. Entire families tilled the fields, the women wearing brightly coloured head scarves. Children played among the crops as their parents toiled. An elderly man and a little boy herded a flock of sheep across the top of a field. The sight of them made my breath catch in my throat like a stone of grief. In another life, that would have been me and my grandfather.

With a pang of guilt, I thought of my mother. During that last, awful twenty-four hours, running for my life, I had cursed her and questioned again and again why she had forced me to go away. Now I reminded myself that she had done it for me, for my safety. Once again I had survived, God had kept me safe. That had to be for a reason. I couldn't let her down now. This journey *had* to mean something. Besides, my brother Hazrat was still out there somewhere, and I had to find him. There was no going back until I did.

As the sun bowed its golden crown into a gloriously beautiful dusk, we continued up the rough gravel mountain roads until we reached a very small and pretty hamlet, nestled up high, with little stone houses carved into the rocks.

We were led into a house, where an intoxicating aroma of cooking tantalized our grateful senses. And, after a wonderful meal of roast chicken, rice and naan – our second great meal in less than twenty-four hours – I began to feel so much better. I had a sense that this family were gentle people, something that became clearer when, after the meal, they began to talk to us.

They told us we were in a village above Maku, in the remote mountains surrounding the city. This was news I didn't enjoy hearing – Maku was where I had been imprisoned. I hadn't expected to be going back there, not after that dramatic escape. But I reasoned that if it was where I had been deported back into Iran from Turkey, then it was also where I could get back across the very same border and into Europe again.

The family was made up of a youngish couple with their two small children, and the man's elderly mother. As the food had been served, I had noticed the old lady giving me glances of concern throughout. She spoke only a thickly accented Kurdish which I couldn't understand, and no Farsi, but her son, who did speak Farsi, translated for me.

'You are so young. Where are you going from here?' she asked.

That question threw me. I'd been running so long I had no idea. I had stopped thinking further ahead than the next minute. 'I don't know.'

She said something back to her son, who nodded at her, sadly. With that, she gathered up her robes and left the room as her son translated for me: 'My mother said you should not be travelling alone. It's not right for a child.'

There was nothing I could say to that. She was right, but how could I begin to explain? The man told us his name was Serbest, laughing when he said it meant 'royalty' in Kurdish. Serbest told us his mother didn't want him to do this type of work, explaining that it was very dangerous for him. Not only did he risk arrest from the authorities for sheltering illegals, he lived in fear of the powerful regional agents and the various local smugglers and drivers who worked for them. While it was the local-level smugglers who brought their charges to him, he knew they worked for the more powerful, wealthy people – people who could easily do him harm if they so wished.

He said the smugglers often tried to cheat him – paying for two guests but instead bringing ten. He said in those circumstances he was left with no choice but to feed the extra mouths. His mother would not allow it any other way.

Serbest's honesty and vulnerability made us all like him. We too knew what it was like to be tricked by the smiling liars in leather jackets and Land Cruisers. I thought back to our first ever Turkish agent, Malik, the liar in the smart suit who was also involved in trafficking women across borders to work in brothels. I recalled the awful chicken coop he'd kept us locked up in. I thought too of the family living there – the kind old lady who had been so nice to me, and her useless, drunken son. Both that old lady and her son, and Serbest and his family, were making their living from harbouring desperate migrants, but they were different, somehow, from the agents we had met. They certainly weren't getting rich from it. They were poor people who needed work and money. Were they really so different from us?

Serbest explained there was no other option for him. During harvest time there was some work on the farms, but it was occasional and didn't pay enough for him to save the money to see his family through the long, cold winters they endured. If a family didn't have enough wood, grain and rice stored, they would go hungry and cold.

It made me realize that life in the remote Kurdish-inhabited parts of Iran or Turkey was no different to that of rural Afghanistan. Yes, there were some bad people – criminals and kidnappers, but most people were decent. Living the same, hand-to-mouth existence, they put family, morality and duty first. And through that they survived.

We all said evening prayers together, then Serbest told us to get some rest because we'd be leaving within the hour.

I groaned inwardly – '*Please, not another journey into the dark.*' I was too nervous about what was to come to rest properly. Instead, I reflected on the people I had met over the past few months and all the things I had seen – the brutality, the injustice, the poverty, the kindnesses, the mixed objectives that most people had. The little rural and conservative boy from Afghanistan had seen and heard so much. This journey, as awful as it was, was certainly opening my eyes and my mind to the world.

Meeting nice people like Serbest helped. And all sorts of things, from seeing how other cultures lived, to hearing stories of poverty in Africa, and praying with Shia Muslims, had most certainly changed my views and opinions of the world for the better. I was no longer the baby fundamentalist I once was. The boy who used to boss his aunts around was long gone. If only they could see me now.

At that moment, for some inexplicable reason, my maternal

1 Selling tailor supplies at my stall in the bazaar, aged 8.

2 As an apprentice tailor aged 10, with my brother Nasir.
I am wearing clothes I made myself.

3 A familiar landscape: Laghman Province, Afghanistan. Credit: Naveed Yousafzai

4 With my brother Noor (left), my uncle and cousins, 2002.

5 Afghan passport photo 2008.
Kent Social Services were disputing my age at the time.

6 With foster carer Sean. This man has been
one of my greatest inspirations.

7 Carrying the Olympic Torch for my adopted homeland was the most amazing day for me. Burnley, June 2012. Credit: Capture the Event

grandfather's face came before me – the grandfather who was an imam. I heard his voice in my head so loudly and clearly I will never forget it: 'Life is an education, Gulwali. And all life must have a purpose.'

The wind was whistling through the trees outside when the old lady came to wake us. It was time to leave. As we left the house, she and Serbest's wife held a Quran above our heads which we walked underneath as they said prayers of supplication, asking for God to keep us safe, and for our return. My grandmother had said similar prayers, a tradition for travellers, before Hazrat and I had left our house for Waziristan and the start of our journey – when I had thought my journey was just for a holiday and that I would be home soon. The memory was heartbreaking but I was so touched by the fact that these people bothered to pray for strangers like us.

The old lady placed a work-coarsened, wizened hand to my cheek and stared at me with tears in her rheumy eyes.

I heard the sound of hooves and whinnying.

Serbest grinned. 'That will be your gift.' He slipped into the darkness. A few minutes later, he came back riding a grey horse, holding on to the reins of a second, sturdy-looking brown horse behind his. Both horses wore an embroidered bridle that brought back memories of my grandparents' *kuchi* 'gypsy' tent. He smiled at me. 'It's for you. You are too young – you will not be able to walk this path.'

'No way.'

'It will help. Trust me. But I am sorry, I cannot pay for him. He will cost you twenty-five dollars.'

'No. Forget the money. Forget the horse.'

I still had my dollars so I could pay for it, but in no way did I want to: I had been around donkeys and horses as a boy, but I had never really liked them. They scared me.

Everyone was laughing at me and my face burned red with angry humiliation as I backed away. 'No. No. *No.*'

Mehran just stood smiling, trying to hold back his laughter.

Serbest held out the reins again. 'Come on, I will help you up.'

'I said NO.'

An hour later I was sitting on the horse, filled with oceans of gratitude for Serbest and the animal.

The journey was brutal.

From the village we set off on our way, crisscrossing the landscape. The irrigated valleys and fields below had given way to sharp rocks and steep little donkey tracks that were barely passable by foot. The sure-footed hooves of my mount were far steadier than my boots, my so-called best friends, could ever have been.

'Get off for a bit, Gulwali. I need a turn.'

I turned to Mehran. 'Sure.'

As I got off, I tried not to let everyone see how the pain in the backs of my thighs was making me walk funnily.

It was only a couple of hours' walk before we reached what Serbest said was the meeting point.

It was like an ancient battle scene or, rather, a battle-preparation scene. Literally hundreds of people, men and women, were gathered in a clearing. Some were resting under trees, bundled clothing under their heads; others were preparing themselves – lacing up boots and putting on warm clothes.

It must have been close to midnight, but the moon was bright and I could tell that all of these people wore the same tired and confused expressions as I did. They were migrants. I tried to work out where they might be from. No Africans this time, but lots of Arabs and Asians – Afghans, Pakistanis, Iraqis and what looked like more Iranians. Their local guides, whoever their Serbests were, stood beside them, watering their horses, preparing saddles and packs for the journey ahead. I seemed to be the only migrant on horseback.

We waited there for over an hour, giving me time to absorb the whole scene. More and more people started to arrive on foot, a few on donkeys. The clearing was totally inaccessible by vehicle.

What I didn't understand was how so many people could be there without anyone seeing us; there was so much noise I was sure the whole city of Maku, somewhere below us, would hear. I was so scared the horsewhip-carrying police, or worse, the kidnappers, would come any second.

I also thought about the first time I crossed from Kurdish Iran into Turkey. Then, we had walked across the border on an ancient trading route. This time there were no jovial, singing merchants trading their wares. I recalled Black Wolf's nephew theatrically banging on his drum as he sat astride his horse like a tenth century warlord. This time, however, the mood matched the dry arid landscape. It felt sombre, almost doom-laden.

I don't know who gave the orders for when to set off, but it seemed that someone was in control because when we moved, everyone started walking together – a long line of bodies, mules and horses winding up the trails, across roads and rivers. We were quite close to the front of the group and, as I looked behind me, all I could make out was a long trail of exhausted people.

Serbest was a good and generous guide. He rode his own horse close to us, and kept checking to see if I was OK.

'Good boy. Thank you, boy.' I patted my horse. Without him, I am not sure I could have made it. At times the passes were so steep that people had to hold hands to avoid falling down on to the rocks below. Mehran, Jawad and I shared the horse; whoever wasn't riding him held on to his tail for safety.

The journey went on for most of the night as we wound around tracks that took us higher and higher, to where the air got so cold it was hard to breathe. Unbelievably, at some point in the night, we crossed over two busy roads, cars coming from both directions. How could these hundreds of the walking hopeless and hungry not be detected?

A frightened voice suddenly rang out in the darkness: 'Get back. Back. Everyone move back.'

There was no way back, other than down the narrow track – the way we'd come. All I could see behind me was more people. Confusion reigned. It was pitch black and no one could see anything as they tried to follow the order, scrambling to turn around. Miraculously, the horse found its way to the side, behind some rocks, where we both sheltered.

As quickly as the order had come to move back, a new order came to continue moving. I am absolutely sure some people got left behind in the confusion.

We had walked steadily for another thirty minutes or so when a shot rang out.

'Take cover. Cover.'

Most people managed to hide behind boulders. I was thankful the horse stayed calm – I suspected it wasn't the first time my trusty mount had heard gunfire. As we tried to shelter, some people said the shots were coming from quite far away, from the other side of the cliffs, on the Iranian side.

I couldn't understand that. Our army of the desperate was clearly walking away from Iran into Turkey, so why shoot at people who were leaving?

In the chaos, we lost Serbest. I panicked, trying to control the reins so I could find him. 'Serbest. Where are you? Help me.'

When his horse caught up with us, his face was ashen with worry. 'Little one, thank God you are safe – my mother would never have forgiven me. Keep your horse behind me and don't fall back.'

As the sun awoke to a new day and peeped through the veil of darkness to bring dawn, I saw that we were almost at the top of a mountain range.

'Here is Turkey, here is Iran.' Serbest gestured first to the east, then towards the west. All I could see was mountains and more mountains.

He told us we were only a few miles from Turkey now. Europe was once more in reach.

We had made it.

Serbest pulled the reins of my horse to a stop. He dismounted from his own and began shaking hands with his seven charges one by one. 'This is where I say goodbye. Farewell, my brothers. God will be with you. Stay on top of the game.' He turned to me. 'And especially you. Go well, little boy. Go well.'

I was sad to say goodbye to our new friend; I had liked Serbest very much indeed. But if I was sad to say goodbye to him, then I was surprised to learn that I felt even more sad to say farewell to my horse.

'Goodbye boy. Goodbye. I hope you get home safely.' I patted him on the neck as he peered at me with curious brown eyes. That horse, the simple creature that I had been angry at being forced to ride, had been my saviour that long night. He was so gentle with me, and so sure-footed, and sitting astride his back had been the closest thing to safe and secure that I had felt in a long time. Now I couldn't bear to see him go. I was annoyed to realize I was fighting back tears. 'Don't be a baby, Gulwali. It's just a horse,' I chastised myself.

We stood and watched as the various agents, smugglers and brigands walked back to Iran. Serbest stopped and turned to wave us a cheery goodbye. Then he and the horse were gone from view.

Those of us left behind paused to rest a little longer before walking forwards into Turkey. But I still couldn't understand just how this many people were supposed to walk right into Turkey undetected.

Spread out before me was a very different view to the one I had seen the first time I had stood in the no-man's land between Turkey and Iran. Then, just a couple of weeks into my journey and still a frightened child, I had been transfixed as I had looked to one side of the horizon and seen night, on the other side day. This time the rocky landscape looked the same, and it was impossible to tell how and where Turkey differed from Iran.

But I felt a new sensation, as though I was standing between two worlds – the old and the new.

My old and *my* new.

I calculated it must be close to seven months since I had left my home and my family. I was still no closer to Western Europe. But I had changed. I was no longer a little boy. I might still look like one, but I certainly wasn't one inside. How could I be? I had been beaten, abused, arrested. I had known hunger and fear and misery.

As I stood there, with Iran to one side of me and Turkey just a short walk on the other, I told myself that this was not a place I wanted to be in for the third time.

'This time, Gulwali, you will make it to safety. You *will*.'

CHAPTER NINETEEN

It was only when the Iranian guides and smugglers left that I had a chance to really see who else was with us.

There were a couple of hundred other people with us: most of them were huddled in small groups, just like Jawad, Mehran, me and the Iranians. Their ages spanned from teenagers to the elderly.

Many carried small shoulder bags and cases, no doubt filled with a lifetime's possessions. Others had nothing but the clothes on their backs – as if they'd left their houses that morning, and were now stuck in Turkey. Some had sturdy boots like mine, which they peeled off, allowing their wet, blistered feet to breathe. Others had plastic sandals – how they managed to walk any distance in those, I don't understand.

Most of the men were bearded. Shaving was an infrequent activity, and a low priority for most.

I was dismayed to see a couple of women with small children. The children were dirty, with runny noses and matted hair. One little girl wore a blue bobble hat, but only had a pair of leather sandals on her tiny frozen feet. My heart lurched when I saw that. I wanted to go and talk to her, to say something comforting. But the way her mother held her so close, so fiercely, stopped me. She watched the men around her with cold eyes. Like a lioness protecting her cubs, she just stared, looking for any signs of danger. I decided it was better to let the family have some privacy.

What quickly became very clear was that not a single person among us had any idea what would happen next. The Iranian guides had simply pointed down the mountainside and told us to continue the walk to Turkey.

'Is this familiar?' Jawad looked at me, as if I should know where we were.

'How should I know? It looks nothing like the last time I was in Turkey.'

'How do we find the agents?' he persisted.

'Why do you keep asking me? Do I look like I know?' I know he wanted answers, but he was getting on my nerves.

A couple of groups stood up and started to walk away. In an information vacuum, even the appearance of knowledge has power. I don't really recall anyone else saying much, but the rag-tag herd of human beings got in line and followed.

After a short distance, we could see men in brown uniforms approaching us on horses. They were armed.

I began to panic. Their uniforms didn't look like any I'd seen before – none of their clothing matched properly.

Mehran and I were right at the front of the column. We started to hold back, getting ready to run into the trees if things turned bad.

The riders waved and gestured us to come close.

I recoiled: Mafia kidnappers – I was certain of it.

They didn't introduce themselves. They didn't say a word – not even to check how many of us there were, or if we were safe. Neither did they wait to see if we followed – instead, they just turned their horses around and started down the hill.

I wanted to run. How could we trust them?

Jawad looked at Mehran and me, following our lead.

'Stop,' I said. 'They are kidnappers. Let's run back.'

He paused. 'I don't think so. This is all too organized.'

'Don't risk it. Let's go back. Come on.' I tugged at his hand, trying to pull him away.

'Gulwali, I think it's OK. If they were kidnappers, there would be more of them.'

'It's not OK. They will kill us. Do you want them to cut off your ears? Come on, let's go.'

As I made to leave, Mehran yanked my arm back so that I was standing in front of him. He was always quick to anger: 'Go back where, Gulwali?' he shouted, his face flushed.

He had a point.

'Do you want to go back to Iran? Walk back over the mountain? You have no horse now. We've just walked for a whole night, from only God knows where. So do you suggest we go back to God knows where?'

'I know. But if they kidnap us—'

I didn't like the fact that I was being held responsible for this decision. The truth was, I had no idea whether it was a good idea to follow them or not.

As the other men streamed slowly past us, reluctantly I fell into line behind them. Like lambs to the slaughter, we carried on down the mountain.

For the next couple of hours, 200 exhausted people walked behind the men in the homemade, fake-looking uniforms. The night had been so cold, but by now the harsh mountain light was beginning to sting my eyes. I was worried that the authorities would see so many people in broad daylight and arrest us, but the men leading didn't seem bothered at all.

We continued to walk, until we reached a handful of filthy cattle trucks. The waiting drivers herded us up the ramps and into the back. They pushed and shoved until the truck was so crammed there was standing room only. It was impossible to breathe and my ribs ached we were packed so tight. There was a huge diversity of nationalities among our number – the hundreds of people represented the collective enterprise of different agents: each one had their own little flock. As far as I knew, Qubat, back in Kabul, was still our main agent.

Whose hands we'd be passed into next, I had no idea.

The journey on the trucks quickly became unbearable. We'd had no food or clean water during the night – the only time we'd drunk was from mountain streams. I hadn't eaten properly since our final meal at Serbest's house in Iran. The drivers set off without giving us anything.

Our convoy wove through mountain passes and valleys. After a couple of hours, we pulled over into a lay-by and were ordered to get down. Many of the passengers were now so weak they could barely stand, let alone jump out of the stinking truck.

The Afghans, who formed the majority of the crowd, were separated from the rest of the group by the drivers, while the Kurdish, Iranians, Iraqis and Pakistanis, along with the couple of young families, were immediately put back into one of the trucks and driven off. I caught only the briefest glimpse of the little girl in the blue hat. Her grubby face was wet with tears and my heart broke for her.

The other two trucks drove away empty.

A little further along the road we could see twenty or so Afghan men already there, sitting cross-legged or lying on the ground. The drivers had left us without instructions, so we walked over to them, assuming that was what we were supposed to do.

'Brothers. Bad luck that they dropped you here,' one of the migrants shouted in our direction. He spoke Pashtu. 'We've been here a few days already. It's bad luck.'

The group looked depressed and particularly hungry.

We sat down next to them.

They were as confused as we were about where they were. They had been there for days, sitting outside during the day without food or water. At night, an old man had come on horseback and taken them down the valley to his farm. There, in a stable piled high with dung, they had slept on tattered blankets and been given a tiny portion of what they described as 'food so disgusting, just to look at it makes you sick'.

These guys were so dejected I felt sorry for them. But I was also irritated. We hadn't exactly been having it easy ourselves, and they seemed to think we should know what was going on. 'Who is in charge? How can we get out of here?'

I snapped, 'We have just walked over the mountains. How do we know?'

I went to the stream and washed my feet in ablution. I needed to pray. The water was icy cold and clean. I drank my fill, then washed. It made me feel better.

Back at the group, I knew what I needed to do. 'Brothers, who will lead us in prayer?'

No one offered. The first group looked at me blankly. Why was a kid asking this?

'Jawad, please can you?'

He nodded and stood up, leading us in *jammat*, or congregational prayer. Usually for this type of prayer you have a mat for prostration – for putting your forehead to the floor. Instead, we used our clothes or bags. We supplicated God with our palms outstretched together.

After the prayer, I like to think some of their hopelessness dissipated. We sat in a circle working out a plan. There was a lot of debate and argument about what to do. It almost felt like a *jirga* – the traditional gathering of elders and respected men to resolve disputes and make judgements. In happier days I had observed many *jirgas* held in our house, listening to the men talk and debate unresolved community or political issues.

'We have to get out of here as soon as we can,' said one of the first group.

'And how are we supposed to do that?' asked Mehran, rolling his eyes.

'Soon the old man will come. He will ask for money because he always does. Trust me, you don't want to argue with him. You will be beaten.'

His friend nodded in agreement. 'His men beat us when we disagree. Staying there at night is the worst thing that can happen to you.'

'Just pay him the money and don't argue with him. Whatever happens, you need to pay him.'

Mehran, Jawad and I were beginning to understand why these men looked so miserable. This was not a situation we wanted to be in any more than they did. But, through feeling calmer after my prayers, a sense of purpose came over me. Just as in the prison yard in Maku, when I had felt it my duty to negotiate our way out and take the people without money with me, I believed the three of us had come here for a reason: to rescue these men and take them with us.

On this journey everyone was out for themselves; in part that was because they were so helpless and powerless. No one ever believed they had the power to make change happen or influence the smugglers. I felt that by acting as a group we could make it through somehow. If we showed the old man a united front instead of everyone shouting, crying and pleading, we might get out of there. I wanted the old man to know we had nothing left to lose. And I wanted to look him in the eye and make him understand.

I was dozing when I heard the sound of hooves. A white-haired man appeared, sitting atop a grey horse. He looked old but strong, like a seasoned warrior. He reminded me of my grandfather. By his side were three or four younger men, also on sturdy horses.

The old man dismounted. From his saddle bag he took out a few pieces of bread and a couple of raw onions. He turned, about to throw the food in our direction. He wanted us to jump on it like animals.

'*Salaam*, uncle.'

He looked at me, surprised.

'Please give me the food. I will distribute it.'

He spoke back to me in a mixture of Kurdish and Farsi. 'You are the new people. You don't seem to know the rules.'

I glanced around: the others were all staring at the ground. I could feel the old man tensing with anger. I was truly scared, but I carried on. 'Apologies, uncle. I only sought to help you.'

He frowned, then passed me the bread.

I gave it to Mehran and Jawad, who started tearing off pieces and handing it around.

The old man continued to glare in my direction, before his voice erupted like thunder. 'You new people. You need to give me money for the food and shelter.'

At this Mehran snapped. 'What shelter? And you call this food?'

The old man stared at Mehran, but let the slight pass for the moment. 'Five dollars each man. No pay, no protection.'

That got the others started. Everyone started yelling at once, and several voices rose up in uproar.

'You've already been paid.'

'Why did you drop us here?'

'What kind of trick is this?'

'You are not getting a penny.'

'You fed us food that wasn't fit for animals.'

The old man looked completely unfazed. His men stood by, tensed like wild dogs about to pounce, waiting for instructions from their master.

'No pay, no protection,' he repeated, a calm menace in his voice.

Jawad reacted smartly to deflect the situation. 'OK, uncle,' he said. 'Let me collect the money for you.'

The three of us walked around taking money from everyone.

Some looked at us with a sense of betrayal. No one wanted to pay, but something inside me told me I was doing the right thing. I just needed to stay calm and I could get us all through this.

Uncle stood quietly, watching us. He seemed almost amused by the scene.

Jawad and I walked over to him with the bundle of cash. We smiled with as much respect and politeness as we could muster. 'Here you are, uncle.' In our best Farsi, we thanked him for giving us his protection and for bringing us the food.

He eyed us suspiciously. Such obsequious behaviour was clearly not the norm.

I took a deep breath and prayed my plan was going to work. 'Uncle, with respect, we would like to leave this place. Is it possible for you to arrange transport for us?'

For a few seconds he stared straight at me, then turned to his men. I was expecting the blows to come raining down at any second, but instead he burst out laughing. 'Well, that is something. In all these days, I never saw the animals behave so calmly or obediently.' He looked back at me. 'I don't know how you did that, child.'

He looked back at his men. They all laughed too, because he did. I got the sense that everyone, even his own people, were terrified of this old man.

'As it happens,' he continued, 'I had planned to send you all tomorrow anyway. But seeing as the boy asked so nicely, I will allow you to move today.' And with that, he and his men got back on their horses and cantered away.

As soon as they were out of earshot I turned to the others, expecting a round of applause.

'You stupid little boy. Now he's got our money and he won't come back.'

'You offended him. Now he'll sell us on to who knows what.'

'Are you so foolish as to believe his lies? He's been telling us this every day.'

I sat down, completely despondent. I'd done my best to help. Couldn't they see that?

As the hours wore on, the abuse continued.

'So, where is your truck, Gulwali?'

'I bet you made him so mad, we won't even be allowed into the stable tonight.'

It was getting to me, and I shoved my face into my arms so no one could see my tears. I didn't know why I had acted that way with the old man and, in hindsight, maybe I had been stupid. But, in the moment, it had felt so much like the right thing to do.

The sun was setting when the sound of engines rumbled over the horizon.

Trucks.

As they approached us, a few of the others stood up and cheered. I stayed crouched, quiet and calm.

With a roar of crunching pebbles, two cargo trucks pulled in before us.

CHAPTER TWENTY

We clambered on to the big trucks and headed off into the mountains.

I admit to feeling a little bit full of myself, but I was trying to stay humble.

Mehran was buzzing with excitement at what we'd managed to do. He slapped me on the back. 'We are learning this game fast, brother.'

He was right. This time we knew where to sit on the truck – right at the back, near the driver's seat. When the driver threw food and water into the back, we'd be the first to catch it.

Mehran started regaling some of the others with tales of our daring prison break: 'The police were everywhere. But we just kept running.' In his version, our bravery had increased somewhat. 'Yeah, we were scared but, you know, sometimes you just have to take the risk like a man.'

I looked affectionately at my friend. He was exaggerating, completely failing to mention how utterly terrified we'd really been. But after the events of the past few days, he deserved this moment of distraction.

'Any idea where we are, Gulwali?' Jawad turned to me. The guy was always asking me questions, like I was some kind of geographical expert.

In truth, I wasn't feeling relaxed either. Yes, we were moving.

Yes, the old man had brought the trucks as promised...but it's hard to describe the sense of confinement and worry as you are loaded on to a vehicle, locked in by a stranger, hungry, thirsty and with no idea where you were being taken, or for how long you might be confined.

I also knew that if anything went wrong on this journey, I'd be the one they'd blame. Some of this group were so angry at their fate I feared I'd be ripped apart if that happened. I also prayed I'd make it out of Turkey safe and sound this time. Having been on the road for nearly seven months, and still just on the very edge of Europe, I could only reflect how the very first smuggler, the man who had taken me to Peshawar, had promised my mother it would take a few weeks. I now knew it could be months, if not years.

That's if I made it at all.

For the next three or four days that truck became home, where we slept, ate and talked.

As we proceeded, I for once had a vague idea what was happening and where we were going: I was increasingly certain we were heading to the city of Van. That feeling intensified when we went back to the old routine of walking and driving. At various intervals along the route, the trucks would stop as the driver ordered us out to walk, then they met us ahead a couple of hours later. I had played this game the first time I had arrived in Turkey – it was all about avoiding the military or police checkpoints.

The tactics were the same now, but the countryside was different. The terrain was rockier, with slippery slopes and much longer periods of walking. And with two full trucks of people, it took longer too.

I think if it had been the first time I had done this I would have really struggled, but because I knew what to expect I was able to control my mind to push my body through. And, just as Baryalai had done before, Jawad was really helpful to me, holding my hand and pulling me along when I got too tired to put one foot in front of the other.

The only really risky moment came when our truck stopped on a roundabout, just outside the city of Van. Huddled under the tarpaulin of the open-roofed cargo truck, we knew it was morning rush hour.

When the driver stopped I couldn't believe it.

'This is madness. What is he doing?'

'Maybe there's a problem,' Jawad volunteered.

'Gulwali, why don't you try to look?'

'No way. I am not going back to prison.'

'Get ready to run again,' said Mehran. That seemed like good advice.

I couldn't believe this was happening. We heard the tarpaulin rustle and the driver's face appeared. He was pretending to look for something under it, and used the opportunity to whisper to us urgently: 'Stay quiet. We've broken down.' He looked white, as scared as we were.

Chinese Whispers-style, the message passed down the truck. Everyone held their breath in silence.

We could hear police arriving and talking to the driver. A couple of our group spoke Turkish, but the voices were too muffled to understand anything. We all knew that if the police wanted to search under the canvas we'd be rumbled.

To our amazement, they didn't even come around to the back of the truck. It was a miracle that we weren't caught.

Somehow we got moving again and were on our way.

By the third day, living inside the truck was becoming unbearable. The canvas roof made it suffocating, and the sickly sweet scent of sweat and urine permeated the little air we shared. The only time we could go to the toilet was at night, when we were walking, but even then we had to do it quickly to ensure we didn't get lost or left behind.

For the final twenty-four hours, we didn't walk at all: the driver didn't stop once, but just kept going. I was so thirsty, but I couldn't drink anything because my bladder was full to bursting. It was pure agony.

I had guessed correctly that we were driving towards Van, but we didn't stop there.

We continued on to Istanbul, some 1,200 kilometres away.

Just when I felt I couldn't take it any longer, we reached our destination – a small industrial suburb on the outermost outskirts of Istanbul. When we arrived in the evening of that fifth day, my stomach was distended, swollen and very painful. My relief as we unloaded was short-lived; I still couldn't pee.

We were taken to a huge sprawling complex of industrial buildings, situated by a noisy main road. Whatever industry had once happened in these buildings had long been replaced by a new trade in humanity, our bodies replacing the goods kept inside the store rooms. About eighty men, women and children were already inside, sitting on the floor, all with exhausted eyes. Most of them looked Iraqi. At that time – spring 2007 – it was the height of the conflict, following the Iraq invasion in 2003. Hundreds of thousands of Iraqi refugee families were on the move, seeking safety.

It was the second time in a few days I had encountered children. Seeing children was rare, because usually the agents and the smugglers who worked for them kept them separate from the men – I didn't count, I suppose, because I wasn't travelling with a woman. I wasn't much older than some of the kids there, but I was so sad for them and their lost innocence. I didn't see myself as the same as them – my journey and especially my three prison stints in Bulgaria, Turkey and Iran, had stopped me thinking of myself a child.

I stank. And I was soaked with sweat. I hadn't washed since leaving Iran. That was a whole week ago: one night and day to cross the border, a day with the old man just after entering Turkey, and then five days in the truck. In that week I had climbed mountains, fallen over in mud, ridden a horse for several hours and slept next to a hundred other unwashed bodies. All in the same set of clothes. No wonder I smelled so bad that even I gagged when I caught a whiff of myself.

For Muslims, being dirty is a great shame. The reason we take ablution before our five daily prayers is to stand clean before our Creator. Not being able to wash myself was a great source of distress for me, as I'm sure it was for all of the other human cattle kept in that vast, damp room.

At that moment, I felt less than human.

I wanted to run from that place as soon as I could. I did consider it, because by then I had a good idea of how to find my way around Istanbul, so I figured I'd be able to cope. I think I would have persuaded Mehran and Jawad to try and run with me, but the doors were blocked by burly guards carrying guns. All I could do was sit down and wait.

If my life wasn't about running, then it was about waiting.

My stomach was still in agony. An old man – an Iraqi Kurd – suggested that I eat yoghurt, as it might help. He offered to translate to the guards, who were clearly Turkish Kurds, to bring me some.

I watched as he approached them. 'Excuse me. The boy is sick. He is in a lot of pain. Can you please bring him some yoghurt?'

'This is not a shop.'

'Please. He needs help. He's a child.'

'Sit down, old man. You'll all be gone soon.'

There had been a total of about 130 men in both our trucks; with the 80 already there, we were a group of over 200 again. We weren't given any food, but there were a couple of toilets and one shower – between all of us. With so many people attempting to use the toilets they were overflowing with filth. I wanted to keep trying to make my bladder work, but I really couldn't face going in there. Besides, the queue was massive, and I wasn't sure anyone would have let a child go to the front.

Little by little, all of the other people left, including the other men from our truck, as a variety of different agents came to collect their property. By midnight only three of us – Mehran, Jawad and I – were left.

After a while, it seemed the guards wanted rid of us. The one in charge came over to speak to us. He spoke in Turkish, and one of the others translated for us: 'Your responsible person has been in contact. He says he cannot come tonight. You will have to stay here.'

I wasn't having it. I don't know what possessed me but I stood up and faced him. I shook my head firmly and made a telephone gesture to my ear, little finger and thumb extended. 'Call him. I want to speak to him.'

Remarkably he did. He came back with a mobile phone and passed it to me.

The guy on the other end of the phone was Afghan. I presumed he was supposed to be our agent.

'Are you the people of Qubat?' The usual question. And I could tell from his voice that he was drunk.

'Yes,' I replied. 'And may I ask who you are?'

'Are you four?'

The question perplexed me. Then I remembered Tamim.

'No, three. One was left in Iran.'

'I have no money to come and pick you up tonight. It is far, I need a taxi.'

'What are you saying? We need to leave here. Just give us the address and we will come to you ourselves.'

'Qubat hasn't paid me.'

Again, the usual. I was tired of hearing this.

'That's your problem, not ours. Our families paid him. We are getting out of here tonight. Tell me where to come.'

He slurred drunkenly. 'Be patient. I will come for you tomorrow. Let me talk to Qubat.'

This was unacceptable. 'No, I don't care what you do. But I want to come there tonight.'

'But it's the middle of the night. Go to sleep,' he slurred.

Eventually, he promised to send a taxi to pick us up, if we agreed to pay for it ourselves. None of us were happy about it but it was a better choice than staying there.

We used some of the US$100 we'd been given in Tehran to pay for it; the driver kindly exchanged what was left of our change into Turkish lira. We also stopped at an all-night café to get some food. Finally, I was able to go to the toilet, but the pain in my stomach hadn't gone away.

The drunken agent's *musafir khanna* was, at least, a clean and tidy two-bedroom fourth-floor apartment in yet another sprawling Istanbul suburb. It felt like déjà vu. As we entered, we woke up the other inhabitants, who weren't very happy with us.

In the morning we chatted to them properly – they were five young Afghans.

The agent, his breath reeking of cigarettes and marijuana, arrived not long after we'd all woken. 'I'm Amiri. You are the impatient ones. You were very rude last night.'

I couldn't believe this man was chastising us, but I let it go. I could see there was no point in arguing with him.

He told us to keep a low profile and not to make noise, and be alert at all times. He gave us permission to go outside, but only if we really needed to.

'Better to stay indoors for your own safety.'

The second time around, Istanbul felt more familiar. So too did the system. I fully expected to be moved around a lot. And I was right.

The good thing about that apartment was that it wasn't over-crowded. We were able to cook for ourselves and eat reasonably well. Jawad was a great cook and we used the rest of the shared money to buy simple but tasty supplies.

The agent, however, was a nightmare. He would visit daily, com-plaining about Qubat and threatening us: 'He still hasn't paid me. I am not letting you leave here until I have my money.'

'So what can we do?' Jawad tried to reason with him. 'We don't even know who this guy is. It's between you and him.'

He made me the most uncomfortable of all. Whenever he com-plained he looked at me directly, as if it was somehow my fault.

We got more worried when he moved us from the apartment into an overcrowded basement in a very rough suburb. Around fifteen people were housed in a one-bedroom apartment.

He told us Qubat still hadn't paid, and we were being moved there because it was cheaper for him.

The other men in the small apartment were all from north-ern Afghanistan, and native Dari speakers. They were angry that their already over-crowded space now had to fit in eight more: me, Jawad, Mehran and the five young Afghans. They were also resent-ful that we had permission to go out to the shops and that Jawad had been given a key. They had a different agent who had, until then, kept them locked in. The anger spilled over in disputes about rivalry and ethnicity.

'You Pashtuns represent the Taliban. It's because of your people that we had to leave Afghanistan.'

The Pashtun are the traditional rulers of Afghanistan and it's true the Taliban were predominantly Pashtuns. The leaders of the Northern Alliance, a group of non-Pashtun tribes in the north of the country, were resistant to the Taliban and it was they who helped the US to overthrow the Taliban.

These men saw the little apartment as a continuation of the war: 'Why did you leave your country? Life was perfect for you people.'

The apartment got so hot and with it, the tension in it was like a pressure cooker waiting to explode.

I tried my best to keep the peace: 'Look, we're just like you. We've all left our homes. And we're all Afghans. Do you think I left for no reason?'

'Forget it, Gulwali,' said Jawad. 'The Northern Alliance are the ones in control now. And they know it.'

The fights raged for hours. Everyone would be yelling and insulting each other. They refused to share their food with us, so we cooked for ourselves on a gas cylinder. It was ridiculous – with both groups cooking separately, the apartment got even hotter.

As the atmosphere in the apartment became more and more toxic, we couldn't handle it any more. Their agent was a friend of our agent, and both were called to try to resolve the situation.

They told us to put up and shut up. 'This is not Afghanistan. I don't want to hear this nonsense again.'

For once Amiri, a Hazara, was right. Here we were, all running for our lives, yet still arguing over the language and ethnic divisions that had destroyed our country and forced us to leave in the first place.

It actually got to the point where we were genuinely scared. We also knew Amiri was a cheat. Whenever we went to the shops, we discussed how to get away.

'This bastard is a joke. Not only do we have to deal with these Northerners, I don't believe he's going to take us to Greece,' Jawad complained.

'If he couldn't even pay for a taxi the first night, how can we expect anything from him?' agreed Mehran.

'But he won't let us leave,' I said. 'We've cost him money.'

We all knew there was an unspoken rule: if you ran away from the control of one agent, the others would refuse to take you. It seemed they all knew each other and were interlinked in some way.

As ever, Jawad looked to me to make a plan. 'So, Gulwali, what do you say we do?'

I really didn't have a clue.

For the next few days we felt increasingly determined but helpless; then an idea came to me. I remembered the nice shopkeeper in Istanbul – from the DVD shop. He might help us.

We went to see him. He was kind and helpful, and gave us contacts for a few people – but most said they couldn't help us without an agreement with Amiri.

In the end, we convinced one guy – Shir Aga – to help. He was really calm and considered, and was a Pashtu from Nangarhar, which also helped his sympathies for us. He suggested he speak to Qubat and persuade Qubat to pay him the money, instead of Amiri. I think Shir Aga knew Amiri was unreliable.

'Do you understand how risky it is for me to take you?' he asked. We did.

He told us to go to an address on the other side of the city.

Amiri was constantly trying to ring us on the phone. We tried switching it off, but every time we turned it back on he rang again. In the end we threw away the sim card but kept the mobile handset.

The address we'd been given was the best yet. It was an apartment belonging to a really nice Afghan man called Nour. He was a Hazara, a musician and artist who'd been living in Istanbul for years. He was a friend of Shir Aga, and said this was the first time he'd sheltered migrants. He was clear it was a one-off and a favour to his friend, but he seemed relaxed and laidback about it. He treated us like friends.

Nour's apartment was small – just one bedroom, a sitting room, bathroom and kitchen. But there was a television, and it was comfortable.

We stayed there for a week. Then Shir Aga arrived. He started by reminding us what a risk he was taking by allowing us to leave Amiri, and we were relieved to learn that Qubat had agreed the deal and paid him for our stay there – and for the next leg of the journey, to Greece.

'I'm working on a plan,' he promised. 'A guaranteed plan. *Insha'Allah.*'

Why was it that whenever an agent said something was guaranteed, I knew something was about to go wrong?

CHAPTER TWENTY-ONE

We were sitting on the floor watching a film one evening, when Shir Aga turned up, beaming a big smile. 'Good news. The game is direct to Greece.'

'How?'

'I'll tell you on the way.'

As the three of us got up to get our stuff, he pointed at Jawad. 'You stay back. Only these two for now.'

Jawad was furious: 'I am coming too. You will *not* leave me here.'

'Look, the boat is already overcrowded, and they only agreed to take the small two. But if they make it safely, you are definitely in the next game.'

Jawad was still not happy. 'No. I want to come.' He looked at both of us imploringly. 'Don't leave me alone. I want to stay with you.'

I gave Jawad a guilty look. I liked him and I didn't want to leave him there on his own either, but at times like this survival trumped friendship. The game dictated that if one player got a chance to move forward, then he took it.

Mehran and I went with Shir Aga to his car. He pointed to a large BMW parked in the street.

I had yet to meet a regional agent who didn't have a nice car.

We drove back into the city and on to another industrial estate, where we were led into a factory building. Inside were rows and rows of tables with sewing machines on them. Sitting at the tables were migrants, mostly Afghan men and women, making Western-style dresses.

I suddenly wasn't convinced he was telling us the truth about going to Greece. 'Shir Aga, are you honest with us? Are we definitely going in the boat?'

He wasn't annoyed by my doubts. 'Trust me. On this game, even my own brother will be going in the boat to Greece with you. You don't think I would betray my own brother, do you?'

This news did reassure me. But, of it were true, I had yet to see any evidence of a brother.

Before I knew it, a different man was ushering us into the back of a white transit van.

'Gulwali.'

I couldn't believe my eyes. Sitting there in a group of ten others was our old friend, Baryalai.

He was a little cool: 'You guys left me in prison. What kind of friends are you?' He looked at us, hurt. 'Because of you two I got myself into big trouble. I kept asking what was happening to you two, and they thought that made me an agent. I got six months.'

'Oh, no, I am sorry.' I felt awful for him.

He continued: 'I know you told the police officer I was your agent.' He held up a hand in the face of my denial. 'Don't lie, they told me. You two deceived me.'

Mehran and I were shocked he could think this. 'No, no. We didn't. We promise.'

'Don't lie.'

'We didn't.'

At this Baryalai couldn't contain himself any longer: he burst out laughing, giving us both a big bear hug. 'I'm so proud of you both. Tamim told me all about the prison escape.'

'Tamim? How do you—?'

A second voice spoke up from the gloom in the back of the van. 'You little traitors left me as well.'

Tamim was there too. I couldn't believe it. Two of my friends, there, in the van.

Mehran was already interrogating Tamim: 'How did you get to Turkey? Why are you with Baryalai?'

Tamim brushed away the questions. 'I walked, didn't I? But enough of your questions. Where's Jawad? You left him too, right?'

I looked at him guiltily. 'Er, yeah.'

As usual, I had no idea where the van was taking us, but at that precise moment I didn't really care. I couldn't have been happier to see Baryalai and Tamim again.

Next stop in our tour of Istanbul was an open-sided shelter tucked away in woodland. It was vile. Not far from it was an Afghan-style toilet. Judging from the smell of this spattered latrine drop, thousands of people had come and gone without it ever being filled in or cleared. The stench was overpowering.

Including the twelve from the van and those already there, we numbered around 130 – mainly Afghans, but with a smattering of Pakistanis and Iraqis. Baryalai introduced us to some of the men from the van: Engineer was a clever, geeky type of guy in his early twenties; Ahmad, who the others teased because he had some kind of skin disorder and spots all over his hands, was nicknamed *Gerasim*, 'germs'. There was also Hamid. He was a hugely charismatic, good-looking young man.

No one was happy to be in that shelter: it felt way too exposed and, as was so often the case, there was no food or water. Nothing made sense. Shir Aga had promised we were going on the boat, so why were we still on the outskirts of Istanbul in yet another filthy shelter? And where was Shir Aga's brother?

There were a couple of Pakistanis guarding us. They told us their boss would come soon.

This new agent introduced himself as Yassir. Instinctively, none of the Afghans liked being controlled by a Pakistani – our countries have long had an enmity and difficult history.

Mehran couldn't hide his distaste. 'Why would an Afghan hand us over to a dhal eater?'

It felt like a humiliation.

Yassir tried his best to convince us, and was polite. 'I understand your concerns. This place is not appropriate for a long stay. We were supposed to leave tonight but there has been a problem and we must stay here one day. You Afghans are always in a hurry – such impatient people. But please let me assure you your worries are unfounded. I am working in your interests.'

Everyone began trying to talk over him at once. He raised a hand and asked us to nominate one person to talk on our behalf.

'Baryalai, you do it,' I whispered to my friend.

Baryalai was just about to stand up and say something, but before he could get to his feet, Hamid had begun speaking to the guy in fluent English: 'We were promised to go straight to Izmir. We demand to travel tonight.'

The agent and Hamid conversed in English for a while. I was really annoyed – Baryalai was our spokesperson; this Hamid guy was half his age, not much older than me. Who did he think he was, speaking like this? And showing off with his English skills, too.

After he'd finished, Baryalai added a couple more points.

Yassir's response was curt: 'You will leave when I say it is suitable. Why are you Afghans so angry? I gave you my word, didn't I?'

A few people still complained.

'Fine. If any of you want to leave, be my guest. Go. There are too many people here anyway, which makes it dangerous for me.' He looked around at us in exasperation. 'Or you could be sensible and wait until the morning when, I guarantee you, you will be on your way to Izmir.'

Another day, another guarantee from an agent.

But this time, at least, he hadn't lied. After a sleepless, hungry night, the Afghans were loaded on to four different vans, thirty people in each. I was crushed into a tiny corner in the back, my body pressed up uncomfortably against the metal. The ten or so Iraqis and Pakistanis stayed behind. I assume they were given different transport.

We travelled most of the day in the darkest, hottest, most confined space imaginable. It was hell, and I honestly thought I might suffocate to death it was so hard to breathe. We were thrown out into a valley at one point, where we rested for a few hours.

In the evening some men came. One, a black-haired man with crazy looking eyes, said he was our new agent. The other three worked for him. They walked us through the trees, to the top of a cliff.

From there, I could see the sea.

We were exhausted and thirsty, in no fit state to trek for hours. Worse, the sun had just set, so we'd be slipping and sliding our way through a pitch-black forest. But what choice did we have?

As we walked, I tried to grab on to branches for support, but thorns ripped at my hands and made them bleed.

It was around 3 a.m. when we finally reached the edge of the forest and started making our way down a small, winding track that would take us to the Aegean sea. Out in the open air, I was reassured by the bright half-crescent moon in a cloudless sky.

As we snatched a few minutes' rest I stared up and, as I often did, wondered if my family was seeing the same moon that night. Were they also thinking of me? And what of Hazrat? Had he passed this way?

Tears sprang to my eyes. The past few weeks, since coming back into Turkey, had all been too much. I'd been on the move so often I really wasn't sure I could keep going. 'Stop it, Gulwali. Don't be soft,' I chastised myself. But I couldn't quell my overwhelming sadness: every particle of my being wished I was near home and hearth, food and comfort.

I got wearily to my feet as we all moved off again.

As we got closer to the seashore, I could occasionally make out the shape of moored boats, bobbing on dark water. This was my first time seeing the sea, and the size of it was terrifying to me, all inky blackness.

Hamid translated for us: we were to walk down to the sea, take off our shirts and get in the water when the time came.

We made our way down on to a small beach. As we waited there for three or four hours, we saw a police patrol boat. I sat in my dark hiding place, watching the red and green navigation lights go past. A piercing spotlight on the bow probed the shoreline for signs of life.

No boat came. Instead, I just listened to the terrible crashing of the waves on the shore.

I didn't want to get in the sea.

During that night, I found myself warming to Hamid. Even in the dark, he could tell that I was scared of getting in the water.

'Relax, I will take you on my shoulders. I am a good swimmer,' he said.

Then, 'Get down,' someone shouted.

The agent looked panicked as the lights of a police car flickered in the distance. We all crouched behind a wall. The car slowed, but kept on going. One man near me whispered that we should walk in the same direction as the car, rather than risk this terrible water.

'Shut up and do as I say,' hissed the black-haired agent. His manic eyes had a way of piercing through the darkness.

No boat came that night. Before dawn, we walked back up to our vantage point among the trees, cold and hungry, and exhausted from lack of sleep and spent adrenalin. No one knew when we would next have to do that again.

CHAPTER TWENTY-TWO

One thing about life on the run is, just when you think you're as miserable as you'll ever be, life manages to laugh yet more loudly in your face.

I shifted my head against the rock I was using for a pillow – it was a waste of time trying to get comfortable, but it was better than the ground, where insects might climb into my ears. A tree root jabbed me in the small of my back. I swallowed my frustration and tried to roll over, but accidentally knocked into one of the sleeping bodies lying near me.

My thin jacket and jeans were no match for the clammy, damp earth beneath me, despite it being a sunny afternoon. I reached into my little bag and pulled out a T-shirt, covering my face to block out the light.

'Gulwali, stop moving about. You'll wake them all up.'

'Sorry,' I whispered back to Baryalai. 'I'm cold.'

'I know. Try to rest. Don't make these guys angry, OK?'

He was right to warn me. Tempers had been really fraying. We were all desperate, hungry and increasingly angry. The nights were the worst. It was always hard to sleep. But, fearful as I was of the trees and unknown landscape, I was more fearful of the other men.

Since returning from the seashore, the Kurds had just disappeared and left us there, for three uncomfortable days and nights.

People were at their most cold and tired, so almost anything could set them off. Even if someone said something nice, the others shot him down. We were huddled in a small clearing, and there were a lot of fights about who would get the softest bit of ground.

During the daylight hours, we slept on the ground with only the trees for shelter; at night it was too cold to even attempt sleep, so instead we played cards. Tamim, Mehran, Baryalai and I huddled together for warmth. The only comfort I had now was being reunited with these friends, especially Baryalai, who had always looked out for me.

Since talking to Hamid that night at the sea, I had grown to like and trust him very much. He, Ahmad and Engineer had a bond, much as my little group had, but we all became kind of allies.

Everyone was too miserable to talk much but we gleaned little bits of information from each other. It turned out that Tamim, Ahmad and Engineer had been briefly kidnapped by our old nemesis, the drunken bully, Amiri. Our friendship was almost undone when we worked out that they'd paid the price for our running away: it seems Qubat had refused to pay him and had refused to send any more migrants his way. By way of revenge, he had held the three of them hostage for a few weeks.

Tamim didn't see the funny side. 'Not only did you little shits leave me on the border, you got me kidnapped too. If the Taliban don't kill you, I swear to God, I will.'

Mehran and I thought it was hilarious.

'We were just lucky. Stick close to us next time, and we'll keep you safe,' Mehran teased.

I couldn't help joining in: 'You bring us bad luck. Because of you three, we are stranded here. As much as we like you, are you guys really to our advantage?'

*

It was September 2007. I had left my home in October the year before, making me an undocumented migrant, an illegal, for nearly eleven months now. Only now was I getting closer to Western Europe.

At no point in this journey had I any idea how to go about claiming asylum, even if I had wanted to. None of the three countries I'd been stuck in for the past few months – Turkey, Iran or Bulgaria – had felt safe enough for me to want to stay. Prison or deportation was all they could offer me. I knew I had to keep going, keep moving – and hope that the promised lands ahead did actually offer safety and security.

I was glad my mother would never have any idea of the times I had felt so lonely or cried so hard and so often my eye sockets ached – full days lost to tears and headaches, sorrow and emptiness. But I think, on that cliff top, even among my friends, I started to feel sadder and lonelier than ever before. As I struggled to sleep on the hard ground, with a grizzling empty stomach, I couldn't help but let the memories flood in – memories I usually tried to block out. I'd dream I was back at home, teasing my cousins or listening to my mother hum softly as she folded our laundry, the house filled with morning light and smelling of freshly baked naan bread – only to wake cold and hungry to yet another lightless sky above the forest canopy.

What scared me most right then was that we'd been there for three days. The agent with the manic eyes and his trio of accomplices had failed to return.

The agent had thick black hair covering his hands. It matched the hair on his head and the little tufts poking out of his ears. Between the hair and those eyes, he reminded me of a spider.

Mehran and I decided to find out if Shir Aga's brother really was among us. We began by trying to find someone who looked like him – no one did. But we were so hungry, our vision was blurred anyway.

People tended to congregate in small groups. As a child it was easier for me to go and talk to others: 'Excuse me, I am looking for the brother of Shir Aga.'

No one seemed to know him.

Later, I was talking to Mehran when a young, green-eyed man with red hair approached us. 'Why are you looking for Shir Aga's brother? What's your business?' His tone was tough.

Baryalai noticed and bristled. 'Little man, is everything OK with you?'

I think I knew this was our guy. 'It's no problem. I know this man.'

Baryalai still looked suspicious. 'Then sit, my friend, and join us. Any friend of Gulwali's is a friend of mine.'

The young man sat down and spoke in an urgent whisper: 'Look, stop asking questions about me. If some of these guys know who I am, it will make big trouble for me.'

I used this to threaten him: 'If you don't do what I say, I'll make a public announcement. You need to contact your brother and find out what is happening.'

I noticed Baryalai giving me a surprised, but slightly admiring glance. I'd grown up a lot since we'd last been together.

The young man looked desperate. 'I don't have a phone.'

'So find one.'

We'd been warned by Yassir not to carry any mobiles with us because the police could use them to track us down. The only time I'd ever had a mobile in my possession was briefly in Istanbul – the one we'd stolen from Amiri. But that had been left with Jawad.

Somehow, the young man managed to find one and call his brother, Shir Aga. He came back with a slightly arrogant air: 'My brother says to relax. He's working on the plan. It's guaranteed. There is a new boat, and he's negotiating with the captain as we speak.'

I hoped he was telling the truth because, by the next day, people were beginning to think we'd been abandoned. There was talk of leaving, and everyone was arguing with each other. Some people wanted to try to walk to a road and find help; others told them not to risk being seen and arrested.

I knew for certain that turning ourselves in would be a huge mistake: 'Do you want to go to prison? Some of us here have been. It's no joke.'

'You know nothing, boy. Shut up. Children don't speak over their elders.' An older man raised a fist at me in warning.

I knew none of them would listen to a child, so it was better to let the others argue it out. I knew Hamid and Baryalai would make good decisions on our little group's behalf: I prided myself in making sure I made friends with the smart people. But I think, deep down, we all knew that if the Kurd didn't return by day four or five, we'd have no choice – it would be starve or surrender to the police.

Every hour that passed that day, I prayed and hoped he would return as I tried to quiet the rumbling pain in my stomach and quell my nauseating fear.

About eight o'clock on that third day, when we were sitting in silent hopelessness praying for a miracle, four or five of them came back. They were carrying crates of tomatoes and several loaves of bread, as well as two large 10-litre bottles of water.

I was so hungry I could have easily eaten several loaves all by myself. The crates of tomatoes might have looked a lot but after they were distributed, there was only one per person. While it was the best tomato I had ever tasted in my life, it did nothing to quiet the howling in my hungry stomach – just a pebble thrown into an empty well.

The Kurd watched us eat with a look of distaste. Filthy and starving, we snarled and whimpered like a pack of wild animals.

For him this was nothing new; every week he probably witnessed scenes like this, bringing in a new batch of dirty, hungry, desperate people – scum, in his mind. But we were the scum who would make him rich.

Finally, when the last crumbs had been sucked from beneath filthy fingernails, he gave us the news we'd been waiting for.

We were going to Greece.

When we reached the water's edge, it was close to midnight. The Kurdish guides started to push people in the direction of a small speedboat.

'Look.' Hamid translated for the smuggler as he pointed to a boat bobbing on the horizon. 'Get on the small boat and it will take us to the big boat.'

I didn't know much about boats, but even I could see that what he called the 'big' boat wasn't very big, and certainly was not large enough for 120 people.

Not one of us wanted to get into that water, nor into the tiny speedboat, or on to the so-called 'big boat' beyond it. In the dark, it was impossible to make out how deep the water was or what dangers lurked beneath. Soon, though, the speedboat began ferrying people – as many as they could squeeze in at a time – out to the other boat.

My new group of seven friends hung close together but somehow, in the crush, everyone but Mehran and I managed to get on the speedboat. I began to panic, thinking we'd be left behind. But the speedboat came back. It was my turn.

'Get in. We have to get in. Come on, Gulwali.'

My feet were stuck to the sand in fear. I could not get into that water.

Mehran literally dragged me into the sea and practically threw me into the boat. As the speedboat lurched into life I almost vomited with the strangeness of the sensation. I was absolutely terrified, but I also knew that if I could survive this, I was one step closer to Western Europe.

On the other side of this horrible water lay Greece.

'Stay in the game, Gulwali, stay in the game.' I tried to control my emotions.

When the speedboat reached the main boat, I was instantly glad we had been one of the last on board. The first arrivals had been shoved into the claustrophobic hull below deck, while the others were sitting on a wooden bench that ringed the main deck, which was also crammed with people. I could see Hamid sitting close to the steering wheel. Standing over him was a moustachioed man I assumed to be the captain.

Mehran and I didn't know where to go: there was no room anywhere. Suddenly, a young crew member, a pale-skinned teenager with pierced ears and a tight T-shirt, grabbed us both. 'You,' he ordered, pointing Mehran to the galley steps. 'Downstairs.' I went to follow. 'No. You, the small one, stay on top.'

I managed to squeeze past the bodies to where Hamid was sitting.

As the final people continued to climb aboard, we were sandwiched in tighter and tighter together until it became impossible to move my arms.

Breathing in the oniony smell of the men, I began to feel nauseated, and it took all my self-control not to vomit over my boots.

The captain, a burly looking, muscular man, stood close to Hamid and me by the steering wheel, looking increasingly tense. Finally he exploded at the Kurd, shouting in Turkish. Hamid translated for me in a whisper, pulling comical faces at the swear words: 'You told me we had sixty tonight. Why have you sent me so many? We can't take them all. This is a fucking pleasure boat, not a ferry.'

'Fuck you. Do you want the money? This is the cargo. Take it or leave it.'

The Kurd argued and argued with the captain, who demanded that half the people get off. Many on my deck looked like they wanted to. The captain had locked the hatch to the hull and those inside, including Baryalai, Mehran, Tamim, Ahmad and Engineer, were starting to shout, demanding to be let out.

'There's no room down here. Please.'

But the Kurd was having none of it: 'Shut up, stay still and keep quiet. If you just remain calm, you will be in Greece by the morning.' He then took a wad of cash and handed it to the unsmiling captain, who had a huddled conversation with the teenage crew member.

The Kurd got off the boat and sped away in his speedboat as the boat's engine coughed into life, sputtering out a greasy cloud of diesel smoke. I said a silent prayer, begging Allah not to let me die.

The boat had just begun to make progress, and we were starting to settle into our voyage, when chaos broke out: within a few moments, the boat was surrounded by a wire fence in the water. It was almost like a fishing net made of barbed wire – the boat was completely caught up in it. I can only think the weight of the boat had triggered some kind of trip wire that was hidden in the water.

Whatever it was, it alerted the coastguard: I saw flashing lights and heard sirens approaching in the distance. Despite everything, I felt a surge of relief. I was sickened by the crowd of bodies, the diesel smell and the rocking of the boat, which seemed as though it might capsize at any moment.

The captain, however, wrenched at the steering wheel, pushing the boat back and forth, while the crewman yelled at us to keep our heads down.

Somehow, in the dark, the captain found a way out of the mass of wire. Through the clattering roar of the engine, the sirens began to fade.

We were in the middle of the ocean.

The captain had turned off all the lights on the boat to avoid detection. I could make out nothing but endless black, while the only sounds were of the dreadful hiss and crack of waves slapping and sucking at our overloaded vessel. There was no joy at our escape, or sense of new hope. It was terrifying – like landing on an unknown planet.

The people in the hull started to bang on the door again. They were trying to move around and shouting that water was coming in below. The captain took out a gun and fired it into the air. They went quiet. I said a small prayer of thanks that I wasn't sitting down there. But I was really worried about my friends, and I said a prayer for them too.

After a couple of hours, land began to appear through the hazy dawn. It had to be Greece. I looked with blurred eyes, not having slept properly for several days, just staring out at the glimmer of land, listening to the hushed conversations of those around me.

The captain nosed the boat towards what I could just make out was a small, rocky beach.

'Greece. We made it to Greece,' someone called to the people below, who shouted their praise to Allah.

I shoved through the crowd to the side of the boat. Some from my deck had already jumped off and were picking their way over the rocks to the shore. The young crew member had unlocked the hull and was trying to quell the panic as people clambered up the stairs and off the boat, on to the beach.

'Slowly. One at a time.'

Baryalai reached the top deck and grabbed my arm. 'Get ready to jump, little man. Stay with me.'

I felt Hamid's hand on my other arm. 'Something isn't right. Wait.'

It was impossible to work out what was going on, or what to do. People were pushing and jumping, and the boat was lurching.

About forty people had got off when the crew member started pushing everyone back down the stairs and into the hull.

'Let us get off.'

'What are you doing? We're in Greece.'

The captain started up the engine again. As the boat chugged backwards, everyone started screaming, 'What are you doing? Let us off.'

One man started frantically trying to climb off. The captain clubbed him with his gun, then waved it menacingly towards the rest of us. 'Sit down.'

I was in shock, horrified to see that Baryalai had got off without me. I hoped the captain was going to drop the rest of us nearby. Maybe the group was too large to dock all at once?

Hamid put his hand on mine. 'Shush, Gulwali. We'll be OK.'

'I want to stay with Baryalai.'

'Gulwali, stop it. He'll catch us up. He'll be fine. And so will we. Really.'

As we got further out to sea, not to land, my heart began to sink. I glared angrily at Hamid.

'I told you it wasn't right, Gulwali. I don't think that was Greece.'

'Why didn't you warn Baryalai? Why did you let him get off?'

'I couldn't stop him. I wasn't really sure. I'm sorry, Gulwali.'

Tears burned my eyes. After finding Baryalai after so long, I couldn't believe I had lost him again. He'd been my protector for so many months.

Nor did I know whether Mehran and the others had got off or stayed on. Neither of us had seen them, so we hoped they might still be below.

*

Everyone expected the captain to throw us overboard.

We had been afloat for two days, seemingly drifting, although we'd been told the journey would only take a few hours. My whole body hurt from lack of sleep and the painful position I'd been sitting in.

We'd had no food since the first day.

I was sure now I would die. I would drown in this murky water; an icy, cold, lonely death – away from my mother's warmth, my father's strength and my family's love.

The journey was supposed to be the beginning of my life, not the end of it.

'Help us. Over here. Help us.'

I began to hear foreign voices over our own. I dared to look up, and couldn't believe my eyes. Four coastguard boats were circling our stricken vessel. People were cheering, shouting, 'Over here. Over here.'

My first, fleeting reaction was one of disappointment. I didn't want to be arrested and sent back, especially not to Turkey – again. But that thought passed in seconds – I was only thankful I wasn't going to die.

A voice from a loudspeaker boomed at us, words I couldn't understand. The police on the nearest boat were gesturing wildly. Everyone was screaming at them. Some men started to leap into the water, making the boat rock dangerously from side to side even more.

I hesitated. I didn't know if these people were lying to us too: if they were going to help us or if they'd let us die. But the boat was going down fast. If I jumped in I might drown, but if I didn't jump I would definitely drown.

As usual, there were no good options.

I held my breath and closed my eyes, preparing to jump. The waves were so big. I wondered how long I could stay afloat by flailing my legs. Then something fell beside me; it was a rope. The coastguards were throwing ropes up to the ship. Desperate hands lashed them to deck cleats as the police boats managed to lasso their boats to ours to keep us afloat.

The coastguard began fishing people out of the water, throwing those of us still on board life jackets. I had no idea how a life jacket worked, but I yanked it over my head. It felt safe.

And it was then that I realized that *I* felt safe – for the first time in days.

My body started to shake uncontrollably and my legs buckled beneath me as shock set in.

As our boat was righted and towed to the shore, shock seemed to spread through our crowd like a virus. Grown men started to cry and shake, thanking Allah, whooping and cheering, celebrating that we were alive. Hamid hugged me with relief.

After towing us to port, the police tied our boat to a large metal hoop fixed into the solid stone of the harbour wall. We were told to stay on board and not to move. I wanted so badly to get off that stinking boat, but I took solace in the fact that at least it was afloat, and not going anywhere.

A few people boarded, one of them a smartly dressed woman with flowing light brown hair, who came over to me and threw a blanket round my shoulders, then gave me a bottle of water. She had translucent olive skin and round blue eyes. She was wearing a fluffy white sweater and, in my delirious state, she looked just like an angel. She wasn't there with the police or the coastguard, but with a group of townspeople who had heard we had been brought ashore, and stood waiting with blankets and food. This I couldn't believe. It was the first act of human kindness I had witnessed in weeks. As she fussed over me, saying words I didn't understand,

I started to cry: all of the pain and fear and loneliness of the past three days coming out in great, big, hiccupping sobs.

The woman's face crumpled sympathetically, and she motioned to a friend, who brought over some fish with vegetables, and a bar of chocolate. She smiled at me with her big kind eyes peering into mine, continuing to speak to me in her soft voice. I just stared at her with tears rolling down my face, shoving the food into my hungry mouth.

After you've been hungry for so many days you can't imagine the joy of food. But I was so dehydrated and unaccustomed to eating, I could barely swallow. But, once I'd forced it down, my shrunken stomach couldn't cope, and I needed to go to the toilet almost immediately. I had to scream at the coastguard to make them understand that I needed to go – *now*. Two men escorted me off the boat and towards a toilet. But they stood guard, watching. As my bowels exploded, they were decent enough to wait a discreet distance away.

When I came back from the toilet, I was doubly relieved to see Mehran, Tamim and Ahmad were there and safe, even if they were as shaken and upset as I was.

The next twenty-four hours were confusing and scary.

The coastguards were recording everyone's name, age and the country we were from. Hamid was using his language skills again to translate for them, in English. After that, we were loaded on to a ferry and taken to the other side of the harbour, where there were two coaches waiting for us.

From there we drove for five hours to a big city.

We guessed correctly that it was Athens.

CHAPTER TWENTY-THREE

In Athens, we were taken to an immigration centre. It felt like I was entering a fortress: guards with guns and dogs stood looking at us behind a 3 metre high steel-mesh fence topped with razor wire; more guards stood by at several security barriers we had to pass.

Being imprisoned was fast becoming my way of life; for the fourth time in barely six months, I was back behind bars.

We were fingerprinted, and the police brought a doctor who gave me some medicine for my stomach. There was a Pashtu speaking Afghan translator at the centre, and they began to interview us again, asking our names and ages. They kept asking about the captain and where he was. I just said the same thing, over and over: 'I don't know.'

A few days later, I found out that the authorities had arrested him. As the boat went down, someone had handed him a *shalwar kameez* to wear so he could blend in with us. But, of course, he couldn't hide his ethnicity during interrogation. A police officer told me he could be jailed for twenty-five years.

It's very hard to say how that made me feel. He was paid a lot of money to take us to Greece and by agreeing to overload his boat, he nearly killed us. But I forgave him because at least we were alive – it was something to be grateful for. I also felt sorry for his family who would miss him if he were in prison.

I told the translator about Baryalai and the others left behind. He promised us someone would investigate, and that if they had been dropped on a Greek island near Turkey, it was likely they would have been deported back to Turkey.

I felt terrible about Baryalai. He had been there for me so many times, always sticking up for me, always protecting me, coming back for me, urging me to carry on, calming me with his words of wisdom. If I'd had one true friend on that whole awful journey it had been him.

But, as tough as it sounds, I resolved to move on and forget him. Those were the rules of the game: keep going, don't look back.

I'd heard whispers from other migrants that people being detained in Greece were being deported back to Turkey.

I was terrified that at any moment I could be sent back too. It would have been a bitter blow. I'd finally made it to Western Europe and I did not want to be sent back. I was still living the game of Snakes and Ladders. This was how my life was for now – I accepted the pitfalls and perils, but that didn't make them any easier to bear.

As ever, getting information on our legal situation was a constant source of stress and confusion. Officials at the immigration centre gave us papers detailing our case, but what were we supposed to do with them when they were written in Greek?

We were questioned again and again.

As Hamid spoke the best English out of all of us, after a while the police conscripted him to act as translator. In fact, Hamid's English was so good it was actually far in advance of that of the Greek interrogator's.

At one stage they interrogated a frail old man. He was weak and trembling, and I don't know how much he actually understood about what was happening to him. His answers certainly got Hamid into trouble.

The policemen were asking questions of the old man; Hamid translating them for him, and then translating his answers back to the officers. The police officers' reactions gave me some clues as to their response.

Hamid continued his role in the interrogation. 'Where are you trying to get to?'

'England.'

'What is your final destination?'

'England.'

'What is your preferred country in which to seek asylum?'

'England.'

The smaller of the two officers obviously thought Hamid was being insolent – with the third answer, he whipped his hand across Hamid's face.

We sat up in shock. The other officer screamed at his colleague in disgust.

That night, the guards put us in one large holding cell. It was incredibly cramped and we were all filthy, so the smell was horrible. They did feed us, though – lukewarm trays of mass-catering food like you get on board aeroplanes. When we lay down to sleep, we sprawled over each other, each man's body forming a pillow for another. I slept with my head on Hamid's legs.

The following morning the guards came and separated eleven of us from the others: Hamid, Ahmad, Engineer and myself were part of the smaller group. I assumed we were going to be questioned again, so I didn't bother saying farewell to Mehran and Tamim. But, instead of leading us along the now-familiar corridor to the interrogation room, we were taken to a different wing.

There, they issued us with new clothes. We also got towels and toiletries, and were allowed to take a hot shower.

I tried to ask one of the officials about Mehran – we managed enough English to just about have a conversation. After trial and error, it seemed that we had been separated according to age. But this didn't make sense to me, because Mehran was younger than Hamid. Mehran was tall for his age, so perhaps that's what had swayed their decision.

It was a bitter blow for me. Baryalai was gone, and now I was without Mehran too. We'd been together since those early days in Mashhad in Iran. He made me laugh, and could always be counted on to lift my spirits when I needed cheering up. It was hard to rely on these friends for so much, and to then have them taken away from me.

My brother was out there somewhere too. Thinking about him, where he might be or what difficulties he was going through, was like a raw, gaping wound in my mind. But at least I would have the support of the three new friends I had made in Hamid, Ahmad and Engineer.

When we first arrived on the wing we were put in separate cells, but after a day we showed we could behave well, so the guards relaxed a little bit and let us share rooms and have our meals together. Hamid and I became cellmates, while Ahmad and Engineer were just a few doors away.

When you are travelling, life becomes all about survival. Days and dates are of little importance when food, shelter and personal safety are the daily priority. But, one morning, we realized it was 12 September – the first day of Ramadan, the Islamic holy month.

The governor agreed to let us fast during daylight hours, as is the requirement during Ramadan, and we were allowed to eat our meals at night, when food is permitted.

I was greatly touched by this. Greece isn't a Muslim country, and even though we were in a prison or detention centre, I didn't really know which, the staff went out of their way to make us comfortable. It was very kind.

A group of young Albanians was also being detained in our

section. They were loud and noisy, and weren't allowed to eat their meals together. The guards seemed to take great care to keep them locked up. It didn't go down well with them that not only were we allowed to eat together, but we got special privileges too. I think we probably also woke them up when we were eating in the middle of the night. Each time we walked past their cell, they would scream and throw their shoes at us, or lunge at us if we walked too close. They were just bored, I think – picking fights and intimidating the Afghans seemed more fun than anything else they could do. A prison guard called Dimitri took it upon himself to stand up for us: he would tell them to shut up, and threaten to send them to the adult wing. I think he had real sympathy for our plight – as though he understood our pain and was genuinely concerned.

He became a regular and welcome feature of our day. Dimitri's English was good, so thanks to Hamid we could share stories of the lives we'd left behind in Afghanistan. He was genuinely interested. We were talking one day, and I told him about the events leading up to my journey. I couldn't help becoming very emotional and crying, while he listened carefully, his face etched with sadness. It felt good to talk to someone about what I had been through.

We showed him the case documents we had been given so he could explain them to us.

'Are we going to be deported to Turkey?' asked Hamid. This was the burning question.

Dimitri stared for a time, his eyes dancing over the paper, then he threw his hands in the air, and made a noise as though he was exasperated.

Hamid translated. 'Bureaucracy. It's idiotic,' he said.

'But what does it say?' I replied, desperate to get to the bottom of the paperwork.

Dimitri was speaking again.

'He says this is a permit allowing us to stay in Greece for one month. After that, we must leave the country or face deportation,' translated Hamid.

We shrugged. It could have been worse.

Dimitri left the cell promising to check our files to see if there was anything further he could do. The next time he was on duty, his face told me that we were in for bad news.

'He says we are sentenced to three months in jail,' said Hamid.

'But we haven't been to court,' I protested.

'It seems we were sentenced anyway. He says the court found us guilty of entering Greece illegally, and we need to stay in here for our own protection because we are young.'

'Protection? From what? The crazy Albanians who want to beat us up the first chance they get?' I was incensed. 'And after three months, what then? Can we stay in the country?' I asked.

Hamid and Dimitri resumed their conversation. It was frustrating doing it this way. I concentrated hard to see if I could pick up any of the English.

'He says he doesn't know. That we need to talk to a lawyer about that.'

'Oh, great,' I said. I was really angry now. 'You got a lawyer? Anyone? A lawyer going spare? Check under my bunk, I think I might have left one there.'

Hamid was more thoughtful. 'This doesn't make sense. Three months in prison, but the other letter says we have to leave Greece in one month.'

Dimitri said something.

'What did he say?' I demanded. I was cooling down a bit now – my mind beginning to focus on the problem in hand.

'He says it doesn't make sense.'

'I know that. Why are you telling me something I already know?'

We were just going round and round in circles.

*

My health was very poor in those days. My stomach had become distended through malnutrition, and my body was covered in pimples from the long periods of being unable to wash properly. At night, too, my sleep was filled with terrible dreams and flashbacks. I used to dream I was drowning, or wandering lost in the mountains. Sometimes I would wake just as I relived that terrifying leap from the moving train in Bulgaria. Night after night I would wake up shaking and so scared it took me minutes to realize where I was.

Dimitri arranged for us to see a doctor. Poor Ahmad's skin disorder was really bad – his hands looked as though they were falling off. My nightmares were common knowledge: when they happened I woke the whole cell block up with my screaming, so I was taken to see a psychologist.

Once I would have been horrified to sit and talk to a woman whose head was uncovered. But I had changed. Some things really weren't that important to me any more. And the nightmares were so bad that I knew I needed help.

Hamid came with me to translate. 'She says to tell her about your dreams.'

'Well,' I said, talking to Hamid. I found that strange, as though he was the psychiatrist, so I turned towards her instead. 'They happen almost every night. The dreams end the same – I wake up and I think I am at home, but I am screaming for my mother.'

She nodded the whole time I talked, even though I was speaking in my native Pashtun. She listened for about an hour. I'm sure it was as frustrating for her as it was for me. Hamid did his best, but it's very hard to talk freely and openly in a situation like that. Not that I had huge expectations of her: I was a twelve-year-old Afghan boy – in my culture, we don't go to psychologists. If something like that happened you'd either keep it quiet and tell no one, or go and see a religious scholar instead.

In the end she prescribed me some sleeping pills. They helped me sleep better, but I could still feel the demons in my head. A few pills weren't going to magically make them silent.

Another doctor gave me some cream for my spots and some other medicine for my stomach. All the medical people we saw in Greece were so helpful. We wore a uniform which was like a kind of tracksuit, but the doctors also gave us some second-hand clothes to wear for when we got out.

The best medicine, in fact, was talking to Dimitri. Even though Hamid had to translate, he always took the time to listen. I could talk freely to him, and he didn't mind when I cried occasionally. Sometimes he would tease me and rub his eyes, pretending to be me crying. The teasing didn't upset me; if anything, it made me feel more comfortable with him.

'I wish I could take you boys home with me,' he would say.

That made me cry even more.

Just over ten days had passed before Dimitri came in looking very pleased, and immediately started talking to Hamid.

'Good news. He says the doctors have convinced someone senior to let us go to a UN refugee camp,' Hamid translated. 'Dimitri says there's a football pitch and it's much better than here.'

He was only sort of right. A UN representative came to collect us from the prison. As we stood with our bags and new clothes in the car park, the UN official looked us all up and down, as if carefully checking us over. Then he turned to Dimitri and a second prison guard who were with us, and gestured to one of our group, a youth called Aman.

'I'm not taking this one. He's too old.'

Aman looked shocked; we all were. We all started arguing and trying to say we wouldn't go without him.

Dimitri reasoned with us. 'It was hard to persuade these people to take you. You others have to go. He has to stay here. I am sorry.'

Reluctantly, the remaining ten of us went. I hugged Dimitri, who promised us he'd come and try to visit us.

The camp was in a rural area about forty-five minutes outside Athens. There were some large communal buildings with a kitchen and offices, then row upon row of small container cabins for sleeping in, as well as shower and toilet blocks. The four of us good friends were able to share a cabin together.

It was comfortable, although I was aware that we had really only traded steel bars for wire mesh. The official had told us we were not allowed to leave the camp without his permission, and he made it clear that Dimitri had guaranteed we would behave ourselves.

Because we were still fasting they gave us a choice of either having pre-cooked food or to be given a daily allowance of ingredients which we could cook ourselves in a communal kitchen. We took the second option and shared the responsibilities between us.

Some of the residents – mainly Arabs and Afghans – had been in the camp for months and even years while they were waiting for their paperwork to be sorted out. Some were trying to claim asylum in Greece, while others were trying to claim asylum in European countries where they had family connections. They warned us that if we started the process there, it could take a very long time.

Although I knew I could get legal advice from the UN or claim asylum in Greece, I didn't want to get trapped anywhere. Hazrat was still out there somewhere, and I had to find him. The others didn't want to stay there either. Everyone was worried about the documents saying we had to leave Greece within one month – we'd decided we couldn't risk being sent back to Turkey if we were still in Greece when that time limit was up. Besides, no one had yet asked us if we had wanted to claim asylum, and without that security there was no way any of us were going to put trust in the system. We'd seen enough to know there was little logic to what happened, and even less effort to communicate it.

We'd been in the camp for two days when Dimitri brought his wife to visit us.

It was good to see him, if only for a little while. He sat with us in our cabin and seemed really concerned about how we were. We confided in him that we wanted to leave. Dimitri tried to dissuade us against leaving, assuring us the UN would sort out any problems. I didn't believe this but, by the end of his visit, we assured him we wouldn't leave.

As we waved him off he promised to come and visit us again soon. I suspect he knew our assurances not to try and leave were probably just to make him happy.

An hour after he left, we escaped from the camp.

We had it planned. We would go to the nearest bus stop, from where it would be back to Athens and then on to Patras, a shipping port where trucks and lorries go to Italy.

Late that afternoon, we walked to the volleyball pitch at the far end of the camp, near the outside gate. After messing around on the pitch for a while, we jumped over the wire barriers – they weren't very big – and ran into the surrounding trees. No one saw us or stopped us.

We made for Athens. One of our group had a relative in the capital who he had managed to call from the camp. He had told us where to go in Athens – a certain square where newly arrived migrants would congregate and be picked up by their agents. We'd been instructed to contact him again once there.

I think I had about US$150 left at this stage. I had a feeling that was not going to get me far; indeed, when I exchanged my remaining money for euros a few days later, I was dismayed to see that in the new currency it seemed a lot less.

In Athens, we managed to find the square we'd been told about; there were so many Afghans congregating there it felt almost like a street in Jalalabad. Our friend contacted his relative, who told us to wait there for a few hours.

It must have been obvious that we were newcomers, as all sorts of people approached us offering advice and help, such as arranging transport to Patras.

We didn't want to trust anyone at this stage. The whole scene seemed so bizarre. Even more worrying was that some of these people appeared to have information on us, asking us if we were the people from the boat that had sunk, or the boys who had left the prison. One man even told us he knew we had just come from the UN camp. I could not understand how these strangers seemed to know so much about us. It was really unsettling. But I don't know why I was surprised, given how tightly I knew these networks worked.

One man came up to me and took me aside. Hamid stood in discreet attendance, keeping me under his watchful eye.

'Are you one of Qubat's people?'

I couldn't believe it. I was scared. 'No. I don't know what you are talking about?'

'So you don't know the name "Shir Aga" then?'

At this I got even more worried. How the hell did this guy know all this? I clammed up completely.

He carried on talking: 'I am here to help. I am a representative of Qubat. Shir Aga is my relative. His brother, who I believe you know, is staying with me.'

This was beginning to make a bit more sense, but I still felt very wary.

'What happened to the others you were with on the boat?'

'I don't know. They were in the prison.'

'Some of the men haven't paid their bill to Qubat. Their families want confirmation they arrived safely before they pay the next due instalment. I need you to contact them and tell them to inform their families to pay.'

Why was this up to me? 'I can't. They are in the prison. What can I do? I just got here. Please leave me alone.'

His tone was threatening. He told me he needed to meet again here in two days, otherwise he would come and find me.

As I went back to Hamid I realized my hands were shaking.

Fortunately, our friend's relative arrived and took us all to a flat nearby. We had food and tea there. His relative stayed with him, and the others went their own way. He helped Hamid, Ahmad, Engineer and me find a cheap, Afghan-run guest house to stay in.

The guest house was populated by Afghan labourers. Their life was so tough. It was still Ramadan, and as soon as they had eaten *suhur*, while it was still dark, they would leave the building and go and wait by the side of a road to be picked up by locals who needed daily labour. They wouldn't return until very late in the night, exhausted and dirty. They earned only a few euros a day, barely enough to pay for their food and rent. Sometimes, even worse, they came back disappointed, because no one had picked them up.

For the first time on this journey I wasn't entirely illegal: the same paper telling me to leave Greece within a month also served the purpose of allowing me to stay. We had two weeks of it left. So, walking around didn't feel scary, and for the first time I could relax and be a tourist. We had proper haircuts and hot towel shaves – I didn't have any hair on my face to shave but the others did and I didn't want to be left out, so I insisted on having one too. We walked to all the famous sites and I distinctly remember going to Chinatown. I had never seen anything like it. For the first time in my life I tried Chinese food. We found some cheap clothes shops and bought ourselves new clothes and shoes. My boots – my old best friends – had served me well for the last ten months, but they had finally given up the ghost.

Two days later, even though I was really scared, I went back to the square to meet the man who had threatened me. He impressed on me that I do as he said, 'Look, boy, don't worry about them now. Now, what is your plan?' He pointed at Hamid and the others. 'Those people are your friends?'

'I don't know. But that's their business, not yours.' I felt like I had to stand up to this man.

He told me that he'd been instructed by Qubat as well as Shir Aga, to meet me and explain to me the different options I had now.

'Your family has paid eight thousand dollars for us to arrange passage to Italy, including your expenses.'

This was complete news to me. Until this moment, I had had no idea how much money had been paid, or for what. Now I realized why some agents had been giving me money along the way.

My family had paid all this up front. It was a huge amount. But all I could think about at that second was talking to them.

'Can you help me contact my family?'

'Do you have a number for them?'

'If I did, would I be asking you for help?'

'Don't give me cheek, boy.'

I checked myself and tried to be a bit politer, but I still didn't like this man. 'What about my brother? He was supposed to travel with me. I know my family wanted this. So where is he now?'

'I don't know about your brother. I was only informed about you.'

He went on to say that because my family had paid up to Italy, he would now arrange for me to get to Patras, and then to Italy.

'You can leave tomorrow. It's guaranteed you will be out in a lorry and in a ship. You will be in Italy in no time.'

That word again: 'guarantee'. It made me very wary. And the idea of getting back on a ship made me too terrified to even think about it.

'Do I have another option?'

'Yes, boy. I can give you some money back instead, and you can make your own way, which you will, no doubt, regret.'

I somehow doubted that. I definitely preferred to stay with my friends than to go with this creature.

'I'll go with my friends, thank you.'

'Your choice.' He sucked in his cheeks, fished in his pocket and handed me 300 euros.

I was shocked. 'What's this? This isn't enough for me to get to Italy. There's a guy over there who charges one thousand dollars to go. You just said my family had already given you the money. Give me back what they paid.'

He got very angry at that. 'I came here with my generosity. Shir Aga said you were a kid and I had to take care of you, but you are rude. If you want to take it, take it – if not, your choice.'

'But you said my family paid. I want their money back.'

Hamid, who had been keeping watch again, could see things were getting tense. He walked over.

'Give me the money. My family paid Qubat. I want their money.' I was becoming hysterical.

'Get out of my face, boy.'

'Is everything OK here?' Hamid was at my side.

'No. This stupid kid thinks he can take Qubat's money. We are generously giving him three hundred euros back, but he doesn't seem to want it.'

'But it's my family's money,' I persisted.

Hamid grabbed my arm and turned to the man. 'I'll take care of him. Thank you, sir.' With that he took the notes from the man and dragged me away. Once at a safe distance, he told me off: 'I thought you'd be a bit wiser by now. You don't argue with these people. He came to find you, to give you money, and you fight with him? Let's get out of here.'

That evening we got a train to Patras, but when we got there, we found the conditions terrible. There was a glut of migrants living on the streets, under bits of tarpaulin or in tents made from branches.

They cooked in the road. There was no clean water to drink and even less to wash with. It was raining the night we arrived and mud was everywhere, even where people were trying to sleep.

It was now the fifteenth day of Ramadan, halfway through the month-long fast. I had really wanted to continue fasting but there was no way it was possible in these circumstances. Food was scarce and, when and if we found it, we needed to eat it there and then.

I couldn't believe this was Europe. We had had no idea what it was going to look like but when we saw migrants, their clothes and faces totally black with filth, openly trying to climb on top of or under lorries, our hearts sank. We'd all been so pleased with our smart new clothes and the trendy sunglasses perched on top of our heads. How silly and naïve we'd allowed ourselves to be for those two days in Athens. We really regretted leaving the camp.

When I saw the scene, watching my fellow migrants jumping on to trucks like monkeys, I lost all hope. That night, we slept on the concrete floor of a partly constructed building that had been abandoned. The other migrants told us their stories.

'I've been here for a year now.'

'This place is crawling with agents. Every one of them a liar.'

'Trust no one.'

'The police have sticks. They will kick and beat you.'

'The police put my friend in hospital.'

'We are on the shores of Italy. So much for Europe.'

It was a cold, miserable night. The building was opposite a wire fence which separated the dock entrance from the road. That specific area was referred to by the migrants simply as 'The Fence'. All night long we could hear the shouts and screams of migrants being caught and thrown out of trucks.

In Athens, Ahmad and Engineer had been tipped off about a supposedly reliable local agent called Borat, operating in Patras. We asked around and it was easy to find him: his height and shaved head gave him a striking physical presence. We'd been told that for a price he could put us in a lorry and get us to Italy. He controlled a section of parking where the lorries waited to embark, and this was when he got his people on board. He claimed there was little security, and what guards there were didn't pay much attention anyway.

'It's a bit chaotic, but I get the job done,' he said proudly. 'Some people try for six months or more to cross, but not with me.'

He said he could offer us the best deal in the area: 'Five hundred euros each. I can accept an OK from Kabul or Europe.' What he meant was something that I'd learned already about how the system worked: 'Your family will keep the money with a third party acceptable to both sides. Only once you have passed through safely will the money come to me. If I fail you, your family don't pay anything.'

None of us had that much money and, besides, I had no way of contacting my family, but we didn't let him know that. We told him we'd think about it. As we prepared to leave and find somewhere to sleep for the night, Borat looked at me. 'You. I think I know you from somewhere,' he said.

'I don't think so,' I replied, fairly confident I would have remembered this man had I seen him before.

'Where are you from? You are very young to be making this journey.'

'Nangarhar,' I said, naming my province.

'Wait a minute. I met a guy from there. In fact, that's who I was thinking of. What was his name? You look like him. His name was Hazrat.'

'Hazrat is my brother.' This I couldn't believe. 'Where did you see him? When? Was he well? Where is he?'

'Whoa, whoa,' Borat said, laughing at my enthusiasm. 'Slow down for a moment.' He told me Hazrat had stayed with him for several months, about half a year previously.

'Are you certain it was my brother?'

'I am as certain as I can be,' he said. 'He had a picture of you, and I see the resemblance. I sent him to Italy. He was travelling with a friend of mine called Hodja. They got as far as Calais. I don't know where Hazrat is now, but Hodja now lives in Rome.'

Once he knew I was Hazrat's brother, everything changed. 'For the sake of your brother, I will help you. Get some rest. Come to fence area B in the morning and I will show you how it's done. Then maybe you will trust me and we can do business.'

That night we slept in the same building as before. In the morning, we could see people congregated in groups around the fence. It had been explained to us that each agent controlled a certain section. People were running everywhere, even after trucks that had stopped for petrol and climbing underneath. I couldn't believe my eyes. I was sure the truck would crush them.

Borat waved us all over to where he stood. 'OK, so today I will show you so you understand my methods. Tomorrow we'll do proper business together and soon after that, I will ensure that you will make Italy. It should only take a few days for you to learn this.'

He indicated to me, 'Come, Hazrat's brother.' He took me through a gap in the fence to where all the lorries were parked. He opened the back doors of a lorry which was full of furniture and put me and three others inside, then shut the door. Before long it started moving. Almost as soon as it did, it stopped again.

The police opened the door.

'Get out.'

The other guys ran; I followed. The police chased us. I didn't know how to get out of the fenced area so I just ran from side to side trying to escape the police. Hamid was still at the fence edge by the gap we had entered. He screamed for me to run towards him.

Borat was waiting to greet me. 'This is normal. Don't expect to be in Italy the first try. It's going to take a few days. But now you know how it's done.'

'I'm not doing that again. It's too dangerous.'

He laughed. 'OK, if you don't want to go inside, try the other way.'

A lorry had just parked outside the perimeter fence at the petrol station, and the driver had gone inside. Borat pulled me over to it and pointed underneath. 'There's a small space near the tyres. Go under and find it.'

'No way. I don't want to die. I'm not doing it.'

'Your choice.' Before I knew it another migrant had dived under the lorry and was heading for the spot I'd just refused.

Borat looked at me disappointedly. 'Your brother was more brave, Gulwali. If you don't practise, you don't learn, and you'll never make it.'

A few minutes later he called me again. I was getting tired already, and was really sick of this. He took me to another lorry and pointed to the gap between the driver's cabin and the trailer. There was a piece of metal connecting the two parts.

'OK, try this way. Sit on top of that.'

I looked at him in disgust. But his words about my brother being braver had stung me – the Pashtun pride runs deep. I squeezed myself into the space. The metal was unbearably hot, so I put my bag underneath my legs to keep from burning them.

I think there were other people in the trailer. Police officers or soldiers were shouting. I heard strains of Pashtu and doors slamming. No one came near my hiding place.

The lorry lurched forward. Hot engine fumes hurt my throat and eyes. As we moved, the tyre noise changed, and I could hear metal plates clanking beneath the wheels of the lorry.

The engine stopped and I could hear European voices.

I was on the boat. Borat had told me I could get out and rest at this point. But, despite a waft of the tempting smell of hot food, I didn't dare. Instead, I tried to sleep. At least my hiding place got cooler with every passing minute.

Two hours later, the lorry drove me into Italy. I couldn't believe I had made it. The stories I'd heard had been so discouraging, but here I was – all thanks to Borat, who was as good as his word. I was sad to think I'd left all my friends behind, but what choice had I had?

We were moving quite fast now; the engine was unbearably hot. I took a rock from my bag, which was now starting to smell scorched, and banged it hard against the engine casing, again and again. The truck slowed to a stop.

I scrambled out of my hiding place just as the driver climbed from the cab. The look of shock on his face at being confronted by a filthy child said it all.

I was dazed, and couldn't think clearly – perhaps it was the heat and fumes. Instead of running, I just wandered the verge, staring at the distant farmhouses, rolling pasture and neat rows of grapes.

Soon the police arrived, and led me to their car. They took me to a police station. They were gentle with me and treated me with decency. They were able to ask me some basic questions: what was my name? Where was I from?

They knew I had come from Greece, but had no proof of this. Otherwise they would have deported me back.

One of the officers made eating gestures. I nodded. We got back into the car and drove near the port. I thought they were going to send me back on a return ferry but, a moment later, we pulled up outside a café, where they bought me biscuits, croissants and milk.

CHAPTER TWENTY-FOUR

The sprawling outskirts of the port gave way to a recently built industrial estate. There were grey warehouses, and the biggest industrial supermarket I had ever seen.

I had seen plenty of deserts before – sparse, empty landscapes – but this felt altogether different. It was filled with signs of civilization, yet devoid of life at the same time.

It made me feel lonely.

Finally the police car stopped outside yet another featureless building. We were met inside it by two women. One was slightly older. She smiled and pointed to her chest. 'I am Sabina.' The other one was a bit younger, and greeted me with a broad smile. She was pretty, with dark hair tied back in a ponytail. After my childhood of seeing women cover their heads, I still found the way European women left their hair free a little strange.

'Ciao, Gulwali,' she said, holding out her hand. 'Alexandria.'

I smiled and pressed my palm to hers.

She was the first woman I ever shook hands with.

She took me into a large beige room with comfortable brown sofas and a television in the corner, which was showing some kind of strange-sounding game show. She smiled, sweeping her arms in high arcs to make me feel at home. She was very expressive, using gestures as we couldn't speak to one another.

'*Thenk-you*, Sabina.' I tried to communicate using the few words of English I knew by now.

Smiling once more, she ushered me down the broad hall. It was lined with doors, and light flooded in from a skylight above.

High-pitched laughter spilled out of a doorway the moment a door swung open. It revealed a slim, blonde girl just a few years older than me.

'Katia,' Sabina said. 'Gulwali.' She looked at us both. 'Katia, Russki. Gulwali, Afghanistan.'

I held a hand up.

A darker, fuller face appeared at the door.

'Ciao, Gabriella. *Permette che mi presenti Gulwali.*'

Suddenly I didn't want to shake this girl's hand. I didn't want to be introduced to anyone. I was depressed at being alone and having lost all my travel companions. It was still Ramadan and I wanted to be fasting. In fact, I wished I was back in the prison in Greece.

The two girls ducked back inside laughing, and shut the door. Hard.

Sabina smiled and gestured to me to come.

We walked to the end of the corridor, and into a bathroom. More gesturing followed as she directed my attention to the toilet and showers.

Doubling back into the hall, we entered a bedroom – I assumed much like the one the girls had slammed the door on. It was small, also beige, with a window looking on to a car park. There was a single bed with two white towels folded on the end. A wardrobe stood in the corner and there was a chair next to it with a neat pile of wash cloth, toothbrush, toothpaste, soap and deodorant.

'OK?' she said.

I nodded, and she began backing out of the room, pausing only to mime the option of having the door open or closed.

I returned in kind – closed.

When it shut with a secure clunk, I looked around the room once more. The wardrobe contained nothing but a few plastic clothes hangers. It didn't matter to me, I only had the clothes I wore and a couple of T-shirts in my backpack.

I picked up the soap and sniffed it. It smelled sickly sweet. Throwing the towels on to the chair, I collapsed on the bed and fell into a depressed sleep.

I awoke sharply and very disorientated in the half-light. It took me a few moments to place myself. I guessed it was early evening.

The hallway was deserted, but I could hear the television playing loudly. A cold floor could not spoil the pleasure of the clean, lockable toilet and shower. Although I had managed to wash my face in the police station I was still covered in grease from the lorry. The hot shower felt wonderful, washing away the grime, but it did not wash away my distress.

I was very hungry now, but was anxious about the common room. Making a cautious entrance, I found Katia and two teenage girls sprawled over the furniture. They were wearing tight jeans and cropped tops. Once that might have offended me, but I was so down I barely even noticed. And by now I was accepting that in Europe people dressed differently.

They barely noticed when I walked in. Instead, they were transfixed by a group of young men dancing and singing loudly across the television screen. The music sounded alien to me, and I felt oddly dehumanized, the way I entered and exited the room as if invisible.

I could smell food and hoped perhaps I might find Sabina or Alexandria.

My nose led me to an open-plan kitchen and dining room. A silver-haired man sat at a large wooden table, reading a newspaper. He looked up.

'Ciao, Gulwali.' He manoeuvred out of his seat and thrust a heavy palm at me. 'I am Davide.'

Ushering me to the table, he returned with a plate of pasta, chicken and salad. I nodded my thanks, then stared at the chicken. Using my few words of English, I tried to explain I couldn't eat it if it wasn't *halal*. 'I am Muslim.'

He understood, and gestured to me to only eat the pasta and salad.

After I'd scoffed that, he took the plate and returned with a sliced orange and a bowl of vanilla ice cream. That disappeared in seconds too.

When I had finished eating, Davide tried to engage me in conversation. Obviously I couldn't speak Italian, but he persisted, trying in English. But, really, I only had a couple of words so I couldn't make out anything he was saying.

It was kind of him to make the effort but I was not in the mood to communicate with anybody. We sat and stared at each other for a while. My stomach was full and heavy, and pretty soon it dragged my eyelids down.

When I woke in my bed, it was because of a nightmare, and I was screaming. Alexandria ran in to find me on the floor, having knocked the bedside table over. I was in a heap, crying and shaking.

She switched on the light.

'Gulwali.'

I was so embarrassed for her to find me like this but I hoped she understood that I had had a bad dream.

The next day Sabina – I think she was the manager – brought me some new clothes: new jeans, a T-shirt, several pairs of underwear and a pair of trainers two sizes too large for me. I put the clothes on, but chose to stick with my boots from Athens instead. They also brought me pyjamas for sleeping in. I thought they were a bit strange – the idea of a separate suit of clothing just to sleep in didn't really make sense to me.

I was safe, clean, clothed and well fed. These people were clearly trying to help me but I was as confused and anxious as I had ever been. No one could explain to me what was happening or how long I would be there. And I couldn't stop worrying about Hazrat. Since learning he was alive, all I could think about was finding Hodja, the man in Rome who Borat, my Greek agent, had told me had travelled with my brother. If I could find this man he might lead me to Hazrat.

Because of the language barrier, I couldn't explain any of this to these people, so what was supposed to be a kind of sanctuary actually felt like a prison to me.

The sad truth is, in my mind, the lack of information didn't make it feel that different to being with the smugglers – even though I know they truly tried their best for me.

Alexandria was in the living room talking to two teenage boys when I burst in and fired a string of questions at her in Pashtu: 'What am I doing here? How long will I be here? Are you going to deport me? I want to go to Rome. I need to find my brother.'

Alexandria just blinked at me, stunned by the ferocious onslaught of Pashtu. She must have registered my anxiety and frustration, which was quickly turning to anger. The two boys smirked, however, barely trying to hide their amusement. I disliked them immediately.

She gestured to them to leave the room. They laughed loudly all the way down the hall.

I could feel tears building behind my eyes. I was a coiled spring of confusion – I knew this was a safe place, but I couldn't relax. I didn't want to be there.

Alexandria beamed her kind smile and gestured to me to sit. She switched the television to Al Jazeera Arabic, and signalled that

I should watch and wait, while she made a phone call. I think she thought I understood Arabic, but aside from knowing the Quran in Arabic I didn't. But I watched the pictures.

She returned and leaned over me. 'Gulwali? Farsi?'

I smiled. Did this mean they were bringing someone to talk to me? 'Pashtu?' I looked up at her hopefully.

She shook her head.

I tried again. 'Dari?' I pointed to my chest. 'Gulwali. Pashtu. Dari.' I was trying to say to her that I spoke Pashtu and Dari.

She smiled ruefully and shook her head again. 'No. Farsi.'

I nodded, then shook my hand from side to side as if to say, 'OK, a little bit.'

She smiled and left the room. She soon returned, making steering wheel signs. Time for a drive.

'Where are you taking me?' I wanted to know.

She just smiled. I could feel my frustration growing again.

A short time later, I was sitting in another beige-coloured office in a local government building, with Sabina by my side.

A stern-looking woman in a tailored suit sat across the desk from us. To me she looked so smart and important I thought she might be the governor of the town. She and Sabina were talking in bouncy, rhythmic Italian. 'I am Fabiana,' she said to me. 'Hello, Gulwali.'

She spoke English, so I could make out a little bit of what she said. I couldn't help but like her, but that didn't change my feeling of mounting fear and anger. Physically, I was better off than I had been in months; emotionally, I was imploding.

Fabiana picked up her telephone receiver and dialled a number. She turned on the speaker phone, so we could all hear it ringing.

More Italian followed, before the voice on the line switched to Farsi. 'Salaam, Gulwali.'

I sat upright, jolted with surprise.

In my best Farsi I said hello back. I told him I was a Pashtu speaker but I could understand some Farsi. But I asked that if he couldn't speak my language of Pashtu, could he try speaking to me in Dari – the Afghan version of Farsi?

The speaker replied that he spoke zero Pashtu, but suggested that I should try and explain myself in Dari and he would respond in Farsi.

Throughout the journey and my time in Iran, my Farsi pronunciation had improved greatly, but on the road I'd got used to the different smugglers and agents speaking a bastardized version of Farsi mixed with Kurdish. I was mixing all my languages together. In a gabble of blurted-out Dari, Farsi and Kurdish in my native Pashtu accent, I tried to tell him everything. That I had lost my brother and was trying to find him; that I wanted to know how long I had to stay in the home; that I wanted to know what was going to happen to me; and that I wanted to know how long I had been on the road already.

Unsurprisingly, he struggled to understand a word. 'Calm down. Speak slowly. Calm.'

The whole thing was made even more frustrating because his Farsi was spoken with such a strong Italian accent, I couldn't really follow him either.

My head was bursting with questions and I desperately needed answers to stem the turmoil inside, but there was no way I was going to get them. I persisted for a while, but it soon became apparent we were making little headway.

When the call began, Sabina and Fabiana had looked expectantly hopeful; I think the dejected look on my face told them the real story. After I handed the receiver back to them, the man on the other end spoke in Italian, probably confirming we hadn't achieved much.

'Sorry, Gulwali,' said Fabiana I felt bad for them. I know they really wanted to help, but if we couldn't communicate, how could they explain the processes to me?

When we got back to the children's home, Davide was busy in the kitchen. Everybody was sitting around the dining table. They stared as I joined them, making me feel self-conscious.

Davide placed a large platter of spaghetti and meat sauce in the middle of the table. He returned with a basket of bread, and put a brimming bowl of pasta and vegetables in front of me.

'*Halal*,' he said triumphantly.

The three girls who had ignored me in the common room chatted in Italian. The Russian girl just stared at her plate. I ate in silence. It was lonely.

That night I settled down in my little room. Despite my exhaustion, I had trouble going to sleep. I had suffered fear, hunger, thirst, brutality, even cruelty through my travels, but I had never been alone. I had always been in a group of men and always had someone looking out for me. At home I had shared my grandparents' room.

This was the first time I had ever slept by myself.

Every day continued pretty much in the same boring, depressing way. They wouldn't let me go outside and at times I paced the floors like a caged animal. Every night I awoke to the nightmares.

It felt as though I had been there for ages. I started to get disruptive. They took me to see the lady in the smart suit, Fabiana, at her office a second time – something that made me even more furious, because it was patently obvious that although she was trying to further reassure me, it wasn't working.

The person to whom I felt the most connected was Alexandria. I used to stand on the third-floor balcony looking down at the car park, waiting for her to come to work. Whenever I saw her, I felt some measure of relief and comfort, but usually this came out in angry emotion. She bore the brunt of my frustration.

'I have been here one month,' I managed to say in English. 'One month. Why?'

She shook her head patiently and gestured me into the kitchen. There she poured me a glass of juice and sat me down. She took the calendar off the wall and pulled up a chair next to mine.

'Gulwali. No. Ten days you have been here. Ten. Only ten.' She gestured with ten fingers, then pointed at the date on the calendar. 'See? You came this day. Today is this day.'

I looked at her in disbelief. Could it really have only been ten days?

The following afternoon, Sabina ushered us all into a waiting minivan. The others seemed really happy and excited, but continued to ignore me. Sabina tried her usual mime routine, this time making her hands rise and fall, accompanied by spluttering sounds. Then she flapped her hand through the air, screeching so that the others all burst into fits of laughter.

I smiled and nodded as though I understood.

As we parked on the sea front, I worked out that Sabina had been trying to act out a beach scene for me. We had come to a nearby seaside town.

The beach was rocky, with large boulders. It was early October, and the wind was picking up and the waves were large. I froze with fear as flashbacks from the boat came flooding back. I didn't want to be anywhere near the water.

The others started running along the beach, chasing each other. All I remember is that I wanted to get away from there. I wanted to run. To get as far away as possible.

Later, up on the promenade, near some shops, Alexandria stopped me outside a clothing shop, and held a red sweatshirt to my chest.

'*Bella?*' she said, deliberately inflecting the word to convey her question.

I nodded.

The two Italian boys stood some distance away, laughing and aping my every movement. I shot them a self-conscious glare.

There were a lot of people walking around, with dogs on leads. I also looked at the pavement cafés, with people sitting outside drinking coffee. In the central square, teenagers were rushing past us on skateboards. I'd never seen these before and fully expected one of them to hit me or slice my feet off with it.

It should have been a pleasant, interesting afternoon out, but for me it was a trip filled with terror, confusion and loneliness.

I started plotting. I had decided I was going to run away.

Sabina returned with the girls, and ice creams. Mine was pistachio – it was delicious. In Jalalabad, the city near my childhood home, my grandfather used to take us to an ice-cream parlour where they made the best-ever homemade ice cream. The taste of this took me right back there, and to being six years old again and happy.

We walked back down to the beach, to where the minivan was parked.

I hung back from the others a little. A bus had caught my eye. I thought about trying to climb aboard. The driver was standing outside having a cigarette and chatting with some local people.

I could have easily sneaked on unnoticed. I had, thanks to the agent returning to me my family's 300 euros in Greece, more money than I'd ever had before.

I was torn. As desperate as I was to get away, I didn't really have a plan, and nor did I want to get Alexandria, Sabina or the other staff in trouble. If I ran, surely they'd be blamed.

We went home and I took a shower. Alexandria had made it her mission to get me washing every day. At first I had thought she was crazy: in an Afghan winter I might have washed my entire body once a week. Our winters were so cold none of the children wanted to wash much; it also took my mother and aunties a long time to heat the water over the fire. In summer, I would swim and bath every few days in one of the many rivers that flowed through our district. To me, showering every day seemed like a huge bad waste of water. 'But I'm clean,' I would protest to Alexandria in my best English. She would just shake her head and point at the bathroom door. I liked her so much that at these little moments, she did find a way to burst some of that boiling anger inside me. I think she may even have persuaded me to laugh.

Her persistence was such that I almost began to enjoy the daily ritual. And, as I grew more mentally withdrawn and trapped, the shower also became a good place to cry. I felt like tearing the world apart, just so it would know how I felt.

Another few days blended into more. I had a sense of time based on when I had last fasted: it had been Ramadan in Greece, and that meant that Eid, the celebration that comes after a month of fasting and is a bit like the Muslim Christmas, was just around the corner.

As a child, Eid had been something I looked forward to all year. We got new clothes and money as presents, and the whole family would dress up and go out to picnic sites for the day. Eid had been some of the happiest and best moments in my childhood. I called to mind bittersweet snapshots of playing egg fights – like playing conkers, but with a boiled egg – with my brothers. Whoever broke the egg got to eat it. Time and again Noor and Hazrat beat me. I remember glaring at them as they shamelessly stuffed my eggs into their mouths after winning. One time I had been so angry at Hazrat I thumped him, and my father had told us all off. Now all I could think about was finding him.

With the smugglers we had been like cattle, but at least we were cattle being herded, constantly on the move and in a group. This confinement was torture.

*

The night before I put my plan to escape into action, I had yet another nightmare. I stared at the ceiling, my whole body convulsing with sobs and shakes. I just couldn't cope with this any more.

I ate breakfast as normal, but inside my heart was racing. I was preparing myself. I was nervous, but I told myself if I could run away from the Iranian police, I could easily escape a children's home.

Back in my room I carefully packed my new clothes into my bag, along with the toiletries. Then I pushed my window as far open as it would go, and climbed on to a ledge that ran beneath it.

I had to do this. Anything to stop the feeling of being caged.

I took a big gulp, said a prayer and dropped three storeys to the car park.

I landed with a thump. The adrenalin was surging so much I didn't feel any pain. I looked up at my window, a little shocked at what I had just done. After a few seconds, however, the pain kicked in: the back of my heel was throbbing. But there was no time – I had to get away.

I exited the car park – the road ahead had three different junctions. I had no idea where I was going other than to try and find a bus or train station. I ran blindly down one of the roads.

Once I had gone some distance from the home, I slowed down and tried to act casually. I managed to make myself understood by using a bit of English: 'Excuse me. Where is station?'

An old man directed me to the left.

I saw train tracks and knew I was headed the right way. Escape was imminent. Crossing the roundabout at some traffic lights, I saw the station building just ahead.

Just then Alexandria screeched up in a car, screaming from the window: 'Gulwali. What are you doing?' She leapt out of the car and grabbed me by the shoulders, shouting at me in a stream of Italian. She was shaking as tears streamed down her cheeks, and I could see that she was as worried about me as she was angry. She kept pressing my shoulders and arms to feel if I was injured.

I had picked up a bit of Italian in the fifteen days I had been there, so I had a good sense now of her flurry of urgent words. I was a boy, I had nowhere to go. What would I have done?

I felt really guilty, but I still tried to resist getting in her car. 'No. I am leaving.'

At this she got really angry, making a telephone-to-the-ear gesture. '*Polizia*, Gulwali. I will call the police.'

I got in the car. She was still crying, and by now her tears set me off too. We both cried all the way back to the centre. She was shaking so much, in fact, that she lost grip of the steering wheel and we almost had an accident, bumping into another car.

When we walked back into the building, it was into a sea of shocked, ashen faces. I felt as if I was walking into the lions' den. They were all judging me, but none of them understood my pain.

I went back to my room from where not even Davide's cooking could lure me out. I lay on my bed trying to calm myself down, but my anger wouldn't subside. I felt humiliated. If anything, I was even more determined to leave. I could hear Alexandria on the phone. Her voice was nearly hysterical. I guessed she was either talking to Sabina or Fabiana about my attempted escape. I felt really guilty for putting her through that, but I also feared she wouldn't like me after this. Now I'd probably lost my only friend in this place too.

I *had* to go.

I came out of my room and into the main sitting room. Courage swelled inside me like a balloon. The other kids were in there, watching TV.

'I am going,' I shouted in Pashtu. The girls all looked at me like I was crazed. The two boys looked a little scared, which pleased me. 'I am leaving. Goodbye.'

So fuelled was I by a sense of righteous anger, I couldn't resist a final flourish in Italian for their benefit. 'Ciao.'

I unlatched the main door and stormed out.

I was in the car park when I heard Alexandria's voice shouting from the balcony above: 'Gulwali. Gulwali. Stop.'

I looked up at her briefly, imploring. I wanted her to let me go. In my head, I willed her not to come and look for me.

I knew she'd be following any second, so I broke into a sprint.

This time I knew where the train station was.

I think I had expected to see cars full of police waiting to arrest this escaped convict, but the station was quiet except for a couple of pensioners and a woman with two young children.

Breathlessly, I spoke to the man at the ticket desk, using a mixture of my limited English with the few words of Italian I had picked up in the home: 'Rome, please. I wish to go Rome.' It was the place I knew Hazrat had been – I could start there.

He printed me a timetable and, as I tried to calm my panicked breathing, he managed to explain to me that I needed to get a connection to a town called Bari, from where I could get a direct train to Rome.

He looked at me curiously as I handed him a 50 euro note for what was a 5 euro ticket to Bari. I feared he might try and stop me.

The train pulled into the platform. I ran and jumped on.

On the train I sank into the seat. As the Italian landscape sped past the window I was relieved to be free, but in the back of my mind I was worried about myself. I kind of knew that this was a silly thing to do – these people had been caring for me, so why couldn't I accept that? Why was I running away from the first genuinely safe place I had known? I felt oddly discombobulated, almost like a feral version of myself, trusting no one.

I think if they had outlined what had been happening to me, and what would continue to happen to me, it would have been easier.

It didn't take too long to get to Bari. Once there, I managed to buy myself a ticket to Rome, which cost me 40 euros. I also bought myself a sandwich, some chocolate and a drink. This little journey had cost me 50 euros so far, leaving me with 250.

There was a couple of hours to wait before the Rome train left. I cowered on a bench on the platform, feeling really scared. I was still expecting the police to come and find me at any second.

I regretted Rome almost the minute I arrived. It was late, and darkness had fallen. The station was huge and scary. People flowed back and forth in all directions; I so desperately wanted to ask someone for help, but I didn't dare.

I had been told in Greece that in Rome I needed to find the park, where all the migrants stayed. As I left the station I could see a few migrants – I think Eastern Europeans, but I wasn't sure – begging by the side of the road. I walked closer towards them and noticed a group of men, Afghans, walking down a side street. I followed them. They were stopping passers-by and showing them a piece of paper, asking for directions to whatever was written down. I had a hunch they were looking for the park too. A lady directed them to a certain bus stop. I followed. When they got on the bus, I did too.

This was my first time on a bus in Italy so I had no idea how to pay for a ticket. I had money, so buying it wasn't an issue, it was just the how. The Italian people seemed to have tickets already – they were pushing them into a slot in a machine by the door. The machine sucked the ticket in, then spat it back out.

The other Afghans just walked through and stood at the back. The driver didn't seem to be checking, so I did the same.

Ten minutes later, I was getting off the bus by a vast park. The scene was incredible.

The park was surrounded by beautiful, historic buildings that made me gasp in awe, but everywhere else were bodies. There were people lying on cardboard cartons, on the footpath, on the side of the road, by the carved marble monuments, in the park grounds, under the trees – it was a shanty town in the middle of Rome.

I had that sense again that every face in the world was there. I recognized Ethiopians, Eritreans, Sudanese, Congolese, Somalis, Iraqis and Afghans. There were probably many other nationalities I didn't recognize. But the overwhelming majority were Afghans or Iraqis.

I obviously looked a bit lost. 'What's the matter, boy?' a narrow faced man asked me in Pashtu.

It was such a relief to be able to understand what someone was saying to me, but I didn't feel I could reveal all to a total stranger. 'I just arrived, *kaka*.'

'Be careful, boy. This place is dangerous and there are some bad men here. Stay away from the police. They come at night.'

'Oh.' I really didn't want to meet the police.

He pointed to a small side street. 'There is an Afghan internet café there, where you can call home. There are many food places where you can eat. To sleep, come back here.'

'Thank you, *kaka*.'

'Where you going, boy?'

'Going to my brother.'

'Good. Keep moving. They don't like us here in Rome. You keep going, and don't stop until you make it.'

As I followed his directions, I was furious with myself. Why had I left that nice, safe home? What had I been thinking? Poor Alexandria must be in big trouble. I wished I could go back.

I found the nearby café. I could see the shop was more than an internet café: there were little booths with pay phones in them, and the man behind the counter seemed to be arranging transportation, and offering train tickets too. He was obviously Afghan.

He looked surprised to see a clean and well-dressed young Afghan walk in.

We started chatting.

'Do you live here?'

'No, I just arrived in Rome. I am hungry and I have no place to stay. What should I do?'

'Do you know anybody in Rome?'

I hesitated, then went for it. 'Yes, my brother's friend is here. I don't have his contact details, but his name is Hodja and he is from Nangarhar.'

I couldn't believe my ears at his next words.

'I know Hodja. If it's the same guy, then he's a good friend of mine.'

He told me his name was Marouf. He gestured to the phones. 'Do you want to call your family?'

I shook my head. I still didn't have any contact details for mine, but I didn't want to tell him this. 'I'll do it later.'

He was busy with customers, so suggested I go and eat somewhere. He promised that in the meantime, he'd try to contact Hodja for me.

I went to a Turkish café. I couldn't read the menu above the counter so I signed to the guy to make me something nice. He returned with a can of Coke and a lovely hot sandwich with egg, chicken, chips and cheese all mixed together. It was delicious.

When I went back to the internet café, my new friend was smiling. He'd already spoken to Hodja but got him back on the phone so I could talk to him and ensure it was indeed the right man.

'*Salaam*. Are you Hodja?'

'Yes. Are you Gulwali? Are you the son of the doctor?'

As soon as I heard this I was so happy. I knew it was the right guy.

We chatted some more. He assured me that Hazrat was well

but that he'd tell me everything he knew when we met face to face. He had already asked Marouf to give me a bed for the night, and would see me tomorrow.

I thanked him profusely.

By now it was very late. Marouf told me to go back to the park and come back when the shop was closing, around midnight.

As I walked around the park in the cold, late October air, I looked about me at the human misery. I was relieved to not be sleeping there, but worried about staying with a stranger.

When I got back to the shop it was locked and in the darkness. I banged on the door.

Marouf opened it. 'Shush.'

I felt scared – the situation didn't feel at all comfortable. I'd only met this man two hours ago.

I had assumed he had a flat above the shop or some rooms at the rear. Instead, he pointed to a small foam mattress behind the counter.

'We need to sleep here tonight.'

I felt like running. Why would this man help out a young boy? Suspicions bloomed in my mind.

'Apologies, Gulwali. My house is far from here. Tomorrow is Eid. We'll go to the mosque together for Eid prayer, and Hodja will meet us there.'

I was only slightly reassured. It still felt odd to me that he was letting me sleep there, and not with the hundreds of other desperate migrants in the cold park.

I knew some men took boys like myself as *bachas* – I'd already been warned about this. *Bachas*, traditionally, are Afghan dancing boys, although they offer a far wider range of entertainments for their masters, very little of which is consenting.

I told myself if he was Hodja's friend, maybe this was really just a stroke of luck.

I pulled a sweater from my bag for a pillow and tried to sleep, which wasn't easy, given how worried I was. Trying to calm myself, I realized that I had known Eid was soon but had had no idea it was tomorrow. I tried to feel happy about that at least.

It was still dark when we woke up. We went to a nearby supermarket which my host said was owned by a friend of his. There we showered and had breakfast. My host had a bag containing his new Eid clothes: a lovely, embroidered, proper Afghan *shalwar kameez*. This made me even sadder. It was my first Eid away from my family.

That thought came with a jolt of realization that I had been on the road for a whole year. That meant I was thirteen years old now. I had completely forgotten about my birthday – I had unwittingly marked my passage into teenhood by jumping from the children's home window in Italy barely twenty-four hours before.

I didn't really care about my birthday – it was, after all, just another date – but it did make me feel more lonely and isolated. 'Toughen up,' I told myself. 'You are a man now.'

Marouf took me to Rome's central mosque. It was magical – the largest mosque I had seen outside Istanbul. It was raining, but that didn't dim the Eid atmosphere: children in new clothes ran around outside, and there were food stalls selling all manner of deliciously scented kebabs, sweets and rice.

Inside the mosque I was thrilled to see the diversity of Muslims there – all colours, races and ages. I felt a strong sense of unity and brotherhood, something which eased the pain of not being with my family.

After prayers, we walked outside again, through some trees and flowerbeds. Marouf walked over to a bench and introduced me to a bearded man.

I was taken aback – Hodja reminded me so much of Uncle Lala. He embraced me. 'Welcome, Gulwali. Your brother told me so much about you, young man.' He peered at me. 'But you don't look like the little kid your brother said.'

To me, being in Rome, being at the mosque, the hug, that fact that he knew my brother – the whole thing felt like an Eid miracle.

'Let's eat, and then we'll talk.'

After we'd had our fill from the amazing food stalls, which offered an array of edibles that matched the nationalities of those inside – African, Arabic, Asian – we sat back down to talk.

Finally I heard the news I had been so desperate to hear.

Hodja told me that he had been with Hazrat a few months earlier. They had been travelling together from Turkey, to Calais in France. He had been looking out for Hazrat. 'He was always concerned about you. He never stopped talking about you or worrying about what had happened to you. He asked every agent or smuggler if they had seen you or to look out for you. He had a passport sized photo of you which he showed to everyone he met. He was determined to find you.' My heart sang to hear this. He went on to explain that after a few weeks in Calais, Hazrat had managed to get on a truck to England. 'He was so brave. It's hell in Calais. I only stayed as long as I did because he kept urging me not to give up. After he succeeded, I kept on failing. It's a terrible place. In the end, I couldn't take it any more so I gave up and came back to Italy.'

'So Hazrat is definitely in England?' I asked.

'Yes. Some of the guys shared a mobile phone, in Calais. He called to tell us he had safely arrived, but since then I've had no way of contacting him.'

I had mixed feelings on hearing all this. On the one hand I was very glad Hazrat was safe in Britain; on the other, I felt depressed that I was still en route, facing all this hardship and these challenges alone. I was really happy to know Hazrat had been as worried about me as I had him, if not even more so, but I wondered how, even if I did make it to England, I'd ever find him.

What I was absolutely certain of was that England was where I had to go if I had any hope of seeing my brother again.

For the first time since jumping out of that window, I was glad I had run away from the children's home. I still felt really guilty about Alexandria, Sabina and the other staff for letting them down, but I hoped if they knew my story they wouldn't be angry and might even understand why I'd run.

Marouf had to get back to his shop but made Hodja promise to bring me to say goodbye before I left. I thanked him from the bottom of my heart for letting me stay with him the night before. I felt guilty that I'd been so suspicious of his kindness.

After mosque, Hodja took me to his house, which he shared with two other Afghan men. I stayed there for two nights. He had a daytime job doing some kind of manual labour, I don't know what. He insisted on buying me new clothes: a really warm, bright yellow ski-type jacket and new jeans. He also went with me to the station to help me buy my train ticket to the French border.

He explained that I needed to get a train from Rome to Genoa, then from there to Ventimiglia on the French/Italian border. He paid for my ticket that far, but explained that from the border I'd have to buy new tickets for the French railway in the nearest French city, which was Cannes. And from there, to Paris.

'In Paris, talk to some other Afghans and make a wise decision,' he advised. 'Calais is very dangerous. Please try not to go there alone.'

As he handed me the tickets he gave me 150 euros.

'No, I can't take this. You've done so much for me already. This is too much.'

He insisted: 'Gulwali, you will need this in Calais. I have been there. Trust me.'

'No, I have money. I still have some dollars and two hundred euros. I have lots of money.'

He laughed. 'It might seem a lot to a child, but the train tickets in France will be more than one hundred euros. And there will be many people trying to part you from your money in Calais. You will need to survive there.'

He went on to advise me what to do when I finally got to Calais.

The most sensible thing, Hodja said, would be to find a good and trustworthy smuggler – well, the most trustworthy I could. I was to give them my cash but make sure they understood that it was all I had and that no more would be forthcoming.

If I could convince them, Hodja finished, they might guarantee to take me more quickly. He said the smuggling operations in Britain and France were highly organized, with networks everywhere. Where the system had gaps was that the smugglers on the ground were often short of cash, and someone waving a fresh 100 euro note in their face might get lucky.

He ended with a word of warning: 'Handing over your cash is more risky. An untrustworthy agent might run away with it – I know people this happened to. This is why people prefer the usual system, which is guaranteed.'

Guaranteed. That word again. In my experience, nothing on that journey was ever guaranteed.

The train wasn't for a couple of hours, so we went to say our goodbyes to Marouf at the internet café.

He was delighted to see us. But his next question threw me: 'Gulwali, can you do something for me? I'd like you to travel with my friend, Shafique.' He pointed to a teenage boy standing behind him, who looked as confused as I did.

'What?'

'Shafique needs to go to France. Travel together, and you will both be safer.'

'No way. I'm not some kind of agent. Why do you take me for a smuggler?'

Hodja intervened. 'Gulwali, no one is asking you to smuggle him. It's a good idea. You shouldn't be alone, and neither should he.'

I wasn't happy – I could barely look after myself, let alone someone else. But Shafique looked so worried my heart went out to him. People like Baryalai had looked out for me, so why couldn't I help someone else, now that I had been asked? I also felt that I owed Hodja and Marouf for their kindness.

So I agreed.

Shafique and I boarded a train to Genoa that night. There were a lot of Afghans on board, many of whom insisted on repeatedly asking the conductor how much longer it was until we got to Genoa. I told them to stop asking him. I was really worried it looked suspicious, and that we would end up getting detained.

On the train Shafique and I got to know each other a bit better. He was sixteen, and from Kabul. His reasons for running away were not dissimilar reasons from my own, arising from when his brother had been killed. He had been in Italy for a month, sleeping in the park. He had attempted to get to France once already, but had been sold the wrong ticket and ended up in Milan.

If you look like an illegal migrant, the Italian train staff normally refuse to sell you a ticket to the border unless you can show ID or a passport. For most people arriving in Rome, it's the first time they are without an agent. Like my family, most families only pay for the trafficking up to Greece, so the migrants are very vulnerable and have no idea how to even buy a ticket. Shafique told me that selling on tickets to migrants was big business in Rome. He had been tricked into handing over money for what he was told was a discounted ticket to France when in fact it was to Milan. After that, he'd managed to get back to Rome, where he'd slept rough.

The day before, he'd gone to the internet café to buy a ticket from Marouf – dodgy tickets being another of his side lines. Marouf had told him about me and suggested he wait for me so that we could go together.

After my initial displeasure, I was actually quite pleased to have a new friend. Once again, I was grateful for the stroke of fate that had brought me to him.

When we pulled into Genoa station, still in Italy, late at night, Shafique and I ran from the train. The other troublesome Afghans had fallen asleep. There was no time to wake them up.

The station was much bigger than I had expected; we had no idea how to find the connecting train we needed to go on to Ventimiglia and the border. We stared at the flashing words on the departure board but could make no sense of them. I took a deep breath and approached a conductor, who took the time to read my ticket and point to the right platform. He looked at his watch and urged us to hurry.

I smiled, waved and we ran. We couldn't find the way he'd described but we could see the platform on the other side of the tracks. There was no time. I then did possibly one of the stupidest things I've ever done: I leapt on to the tracks and ran across. 'Shafique. Come on.'

It was late so there weren't that many people around, but those who were watched in disbelief. It was idiotic of me, because it was a sure way to attract attention and get arrested.

Shafique followed me, but when we scrambled up the other side to the platform he was furious. 'What did you do that for?'

The worst thing was that we realized we were on the wrong platform. We ran to the end, then around a corner, where we spotted a train driver walking towards a train. I ran over and showed him my ticket. He smiled and nodded for us to follow him.

In the morning we arrived in Ventimiglia. Heading to the departure board to try and work out how to get the train to Cannes, we were deliberately trying to walk normally and casually, but still an

Italian police officer approached Shafique and me. He asked to check our ticket. When he had done so, he shook his finger at us. 'No France,' he said in broken English. 'No France. Go back or go outside.'

As we reluctantly walked outside I looked back and realized how we'd been caught. Less than twenty metres behind us were five Afghan men. They had been following us without us knowing.

'Why did you walk so close to us?' I was so angry. 'You got us caught.'

The policeman was walking behind them, escorting them out. He walked back and stood at the entrance to the platform where the train was leaving for Cannes and France. There was no way we were going to get past him.

The seven of us drifted around the streets until we found a café, where we bought some food. I was still pissed off with the other guys, not least because they now stuck to us like glue. Shafique and I were both kids, but they seemed to be completely useless at this.

As we ate, an argument broke out. It was clear we had to risk crossing from Italy to France without passports, and while buying tickets within Italy wasn't such a problem, the moment we tried to cross a border we needed to show a valid passport or ID to buy a ticket. None of us had any. Added to that, none of the men wanted to go to the ticket office.

'I'll go,' I said, confident of my ability to win the sales people over. Although Shafique was sixteen, three years older than I was, I had assumed the role of boss. I think because I had been on the journey longer than he had, I felt more experienced. But no way was I doing this for free: 'I'll sort it out, but you all have to contribute to pay for my ticket.'

I circled the station entrance, scouting for the policeman who had stopped me earlier. He wasn't there, although a number of his colleagues were patrolling.

Adopting my most nonchalant of walks, I strolled past the officers, being sure to keep my head low. In my new clothes and bright yellow ski jacket courtesy of Hodja, I was nothing more threatening than a sulky Italian pre-teen.

I approached a middle-aged lady sitting behind a glass screen and gave her a broad smile that I calculated was both charming and vulnerable. Women had been kind in the past, and I hoped this would prove to be true once more.

My Italian vocabulary was still very limited, but I did have the few phrases learned in the children's home. I also had a map of the rail network which Hodja had given me in Rome, which helped make the point.

After a lot of effort, I succeeded in making her understand that I wanted to know how much a ticket was to Cannes.

At first she wasn't willing to even tell me that: 'Sorry, ID please.'

I tried to gesture and explain my friends were waiting for me. She wasn't happy, but I just continued to give her my best pleading face and, in the end, she wrote down the price for me.

I left the station and found the others.

'Here's the deal,' I said. Their eyes were fixed on me. The simple act of buying tickets was very stressful for migrants, and I knew they couldn't do this without me. 'It's fifteen euros each for your tickets, plus the cost of my ticket spread over the five of you – but not Shafique – that's three euros. Think of it as a booking fee. Total eighteen euros each.'

There was some grumbling, but they had no choice.

I knew my little money-making scheme was immoral. I tried to justify it to myself, although it still troubled my conscience.

I went back to see the lady. I can't say she looked thrilled to see me.

I'm not sure if it was because I was persistent, or persuasive – probably it was my youth and vulnerability tugging on her heart-strings – but she began to soften slightly. I got the feeling she would sell me a ticket, but the issue was the other six.

'Why seven?' She shook her head. 'Too many people.'

I just shrugged and continued to give her my best pleading face and, in the end, amazingly, she sold me the tickets. Although, if I understood her Italian correctly, she did give a stern warning that we were likely to be arrested.

She pushed the tickets across the counter, looking around a little nervously. It was then that I realized that she was probably risking her job to help me. I gave her a genuine smile. She looked scared, but her eyes spoke of her emotion. I was beginning to realize that there were kind people around who were truly moved by the plight of us migrants.

I knew that a group of migrants was more likely to attract unwanted attention, so I took control and ordered everyone to board the train in pairs, and get on different carriages. My days of moving around the different *musafir khanna*s in Istanbul had taught me something.

When the conductor came into the carriage, he stopped and checked our tickets. I didn't like the way he looked at us, but he moved on quickly.

I panicked when two police officers walked through the carriage. 'Shafique, police.'

We dropped our heads. Shafique pretended to sleep.

I stared at the Italian countryside sliding past, all the while carefully checking their reflection in the window.

They went past us without a second look.

Shafique raised his head and grinned.

An announcement then crackled out over the speaker system. I didn't really pay any attention – my Italian was so limited I only understood a few words – but this time it was different. 'Shafique, I think he is talking French. I think we are in France.'

We sat and listened to the rhythm of the address.

'I think I love the sound of this language,' Shafique said.

We burst out with relieved laughter.

We weren't out of the woods yet, though. We listened for any announcements that mentioned our destination, Cannes, but neither of us could understand the accent.

I was puzzling what to do when we had a stroke of luck – a man entered our carriage. It was a young guy, with a rucksack slung over one shoulder. I didn't know him, but I could tell he was an Afghan Hazara.

'Hey,' I said in Dari.

He turned. '*Salaam.*'

'Do you speak Pashtu?' I ventured.

'Yeah. A bit.'

We beckoned him to join us.

He sat opposite us, his bag in his lap. He told us he was a university student studying in Marseilles.

He was generous with his advice, giving us a crash course on French pronunciation and useful phrases, telling us what time the train was expected in Cannes, and what to expect on the journey to Paris. As we slowed into Cannes, his final advice stuck in my mind: 'Be careful of the police. They will give you a very bad time.'

I wanted to know more, but we only had a few seconds before our stop.

'Will they put us in prison or deport us?' I said.

'Probably not – even if you want them to. Good luck.'

That confused me.

'Gulwali,' Shafique called from the train's open door. 'Let's go.'

The other guys had made it too. I half expected not to find them on the platform at Cannes, but I was happy they were.

The station was full of police. We headed outside and found a grimy Turkish café near the back.

'We met a guy on the train who said tickets to Paris are one hundred euros,' I said.

The others blew out their cheeks at the price. An argument erupted, with everybody shouting over each other, trying to be heard.

'Hey. Heeeeey.'

We all turned. The owner – a heavy Turkish man with impressive black caterpillars marching across his brows – leaned over the counter, waving a long kebab knife. 'Enough of your noise. Keep it down or get out of my restaurant,' he shouted, in a mix of English and Kurdish. 'And you can all buy some more food, too. I'm not running a charity. Bloody Afghans,' he muttered, turning his attention back to the rotating slab of grilling meat.

We lowered our heated bickering to a loud whisper.

Everybody would pool their finances, and I would buy the tickets again. I had hoped I could get another free ticket, but at 100 euros no one would agree to it.

We only had enough money for four tickets.

That was a major problem – but I had a plan. When the seven of us climbed aboard the train later that afternoon, three of the men went and hid in the toilets.

Shafique and I sat near the other two guys, trying to look innocent and unthreatening. A game of cat and mouse ensued with the conductor. We swapped seats and tickets on several occasions, the guys in the toilets trading places with those in the carriage.

I tried to look confident and relaxed when the conductor came past, knowing that although he had already checked my ticket, it was now in the hand of one of my travelling companions two carriages further along the train.

One of the guys got caught, though. As we pulled away from a rural station, there he was on the platform, looking horribly dejected, a policeman standing next to him.

It was a long journey.

CHAPTER TWENTY-FIVE

My gritty eyes slowly opened. We had been travelling for over half a day on this train, since leaving Rome around forty-eight hours ago.

'Paris,' said Shafique.

The train carriage rocked gently from side to side.

'Why is there so much writing on the walls?' I asked, as if Shafique might have an idea what the cartoonish images and words I saw through the carriage windows might mean. I had seen similar graffiti, although I didn't know what it was called, in the poorer parts of Greece, Turkey and Italy, but I hadn't expected to see it in Paris.

For some reason, I had a notion that Paris was the poshest and most beautiful city in the whole world. I don't recall from whom I had heard this – maybe one of my teachers at school – but as a child in Afghanistan I'd been told that every morning an aeroplane sprayed a fine rain of pure perfume over the city so that the air always smelled fresh and beautiful.

As the train slowed into the station approach, it hit me that this was a lie. We pulled into the biggest station I had ever seen – a vast, steel-framed hangar, bustling with people. In the public toilets, I looked in the mirror on the wall. The face staring back at me looked broken. I hardly recognized the boy in the reflection, his cheeks sunken, dark bags beneath his eyes. He needed a haircut.

As we made our way out of the station and on to the streets of Paris, we looked about us in wonder. The busy streets were lined with pale stone buildings with shiny shop fronts. There were restaurants and cafés everywhere, with smartly dressed people scurrying along so quickly it looked like a matter of life and death. Cars drove bumper to bumper as motorbikes buzzed past them like wasps.

'We need to find the park,' I said, unsure of how we might actually achieve that.

Hodja had counselled that when we reached Paris, we were to make our way from the Gare du Nord station to a park, where, just as in Rome, migrants gathered. We hoped we could make contact with people, possibly even agents, who would help us get to Calais.

I had half a mind to ask a passer-by the way. I hoped I could manage to communicate using a mix of sign language and English. But the Parisians who brushed past shot us looks as though we were something unpleasant to be avoided – a nasty smell that polluted the Parisian air, scented or not.

An older man, with the instantly recognizable craggy features of a life spent in the Afghan weather, squatted near one of the station entrances, rattling a paper coffee cup at the rushing commuters.

'*Salaam, kaka,*' I said in Pashtu. 'Where is the park, please?'

'That way,' he said, pointing to a busy intersection. 'Seven blocks away. But don't expect too much help, boys. It's every man for himself.'

He dismissed me with a shake of his cup, wrapping a blanket more tightly about him. It was cold, and I was beginning to shiver now, too – I was grateful for the jacket Hodja had bought me. The grey sky was heavy with fat clouds.

'Come on,' Shafique said. 'It's going to snow.'

I feared he was right as I stamped my feet to shake some blood into my cold toes. I felt wretched – exhausted and hungry. After twelve months of travelling, this was the reality of my existence, and the persistent discomfort didn't make it any easier. Lingering in my recent memory was the fact of the days spent in the children's home, where I had been clean, fed and slept in a warm bed. The memory seemed to mock me.

Tiny little flakes of something between rain and snow started to fall from the sky as we shuffled in the direction we'd been given. I should have felt excited: Paris meant that Great Britain was tantalizingly close now. Just a little further, and I would be there.

What 'there' meant in reality, I still wasn't sure, but all that mattered was that Hazrat was there, and I would be running no longer.

'Gulwali, look.'

I followed Shafique's gaze.

Three other Afghan-looking men had rounded the corner just ahead.

'Brothers,' Shafique yelled over the road. 'Where is the park?'

'Around the corner and you are there,' one shouted over the traffic. 'But you had better hurry – the charity people only serve the food until six.'

Food. We broke into a run. We hadn't really eaten on the train, and we'd only had snacks in the Turkish café.

We only just made it in time, as they were packing up. A few glorious minutes later, I was bathing my face in fragrant steam. The smell of white beans and chicken made me drool.

Shafique had almost finished his stew already.

'It's too hot to eat. You must have a stomach of iron.'

'It's too good not to,' replied Shafique, wiping broth from his lips. '*Très bien, monsieur.*'

'Nice French.'

Small groups of migrants were scattered around the park. A short line spilled from the tin shed that served as a soup kitchen.

'You finish your food,' said Shafique, throwing his empty plastic bowl into a bin. 'I'm going to see where we sleep.'

We had heard about a homeless shelter where they would let migrants stay overnight. Hodja had said that because we were so young, we might get lucky.

I was mopping the last juices up with a piece of bread when he returned.

'Bad news.'

'What?'

'I asked some people. The shelter is closed.'

This was a blow.

'So what do we do?'

'I'm not sure,' said Shafique. 'Some of the others are sleeping together at the far end of the park. We can go and join them.'

'In the snow?' I was inwardly groaning.

'It's not that cold,' Shafique said. 'Look, it's barely even snowing now.' I had begun to love Shafique for his optimism, which I knew was for my benefit. 'There's a tree over there,' he went on. 'It's practically dry underneath, and the branches will keep the weather out.'

We tried to get comfortable under our shelter. It smelled of ash and damp. Shafique was right: the earth beneath the tree was almost dry, but that was little cause for celebration as the temperature dropped over the coming hours, bringing bigger, fatter flakes of snow with it. We lay back to back, trying to preserve our body heat.

Shafique was soon snoring. My eyes got heavy a handful of times, but there was no way I could sleep. The cold and the strange sounds of the city kept me awake – sirens and traffic noise, voices calling out through the night, as though no one was sleeping and the great mass of humanity of the city was continuing to go about its business as I and the other homeless migrants lived like a sub-species.

I had had such high expectations of Paris, the city where perfume rained from the skies. And yet all I had witnessed was a dirty, smelly and cold city, filled with Parisians who shied away from us in horror.

I got up to go to the toilet. I guessed it was around midnight. My hips and shoulders ached with cold, and I limped with pain as I tried to get my blood moving.

I looked for somewhere to relieve myself. It felt good to be moving after the cold ground, so I wandered in no particular direction. Piles of bodies lay dotted around the park – mostly on benches, sheathed in cardboard. The low glow of a telephone box hung in the distance, snowflakes caught in its light like moths. It almost looked warm. I let its glass door slam shut behind me and my breath began to fill the space.

I leaned against the steel case of the telephone and closed my eyes.

Fleetingly, I imagined using this phone to ring someone – perhaps my mother. But I realized how stupid that was. She didn't have a phone, and I hadn't been able to contact her once on this journey.

A group of drunk young French men rolled past, talking boisterously and waving their glowing cigarettes around with extravagant flourishes.

I shrank down, trying to hide. They passed without seeing me.

I dozed for a little. I was warming up a bit now, as I crouched in the bottom of the phone box; despite being forced to squat with my arms across my chest, this was the most comfortable I had been all night. A snow-covered lump rattled along the street towards me, rousing me. A man in a heavy coat and hat pulled low shoved along a shopping trolley, his little dog trotting beside him. I watched him, puzzled. He didn't look like a migrant. I had seen other such homeless people throughout my journey, especially in Rome and Athens. I couldn't understand how this happened in European capitals.

The aluminium edge of the door suddenly crashed into my right ankle. Two black-clad figures loomed over me, the muzzles of their guns staring me down. For a second I thought I was back in Turkey or Iran.

Police.

I said nothing, frozen into silence.

The shorter one summoned me with a black-leather-clad finger, indicating that I should come out.

I rubbed my shoulders to try to make them understand I was cold and had nowhere else to go.

'*Halas*, finish,' the taller shouted, and shoved me down the street. '*Yallah*. Come.'

These were basic Arabic words, which he obviously thought all migrants might understand.

He shooed me away like a dog, making a *tksss tksss* sound with his tongue and teeth.

I put my wrists together and held them up. I was trying to gesture to them to arrest me. Right then, a warm cell seemed preferable to dying of cold.

'Go. Move.'

I skulked away like the animal I felt, retracing my fading footsteps in the snow. I made my way back to Shafique. He was still sleeping, but now shivering uncontrollably. I lay down next to him and tried to sleep.

When I woke up, Shafique was still sleeping. I sat there trying not to shake. I began to move around for warmth, eventually crossing the road to a sort of fire hydrant with a tap on top. People were washing their faces and hands in it. I did the same. The temperature of the water sucked the air out of my lungs.

About an hour later, the soup kitchen opened for breakfast. Shafique and I staggered over to join the queue of dozens of men, all shivering and moving about to try to warm themselves. Shafique was still shivering, his teeth chattering. I don't know how he'd managed to sleep.

At the soup kitchen shed, a sandy-haired Frenchman with a neat beard served me hot tea and a baguette with cheese. Gratefully, I cupped my hands around the mug of black tea. It was bitter and hot. I could feel it working its way down to my stomach, warming me from within. I loaded my cup with sugar until the lady behind the counter cleared her throat. Shafique savaged his piece of long bread.

'This is good,' he said, cheeks bulging.

'How can you be so happy? We nearly froze to death.'

'Yes, but we didn't, did we?'

I took a bite of my bread. 'Let's find out what to do. I don't think I can cope with another night here.'

We went over to where a group of migrants was huddled on boxes. The cardboard sheets were laid out in the same way that kilims and cushions would have been back home. This was the sunniest part of the park, and everyone was trying to get a little warmer from the few rays of wintry morning sun.

As we sat there, people who had been sleeping in different parts of the park, or the lucky ones from the shelter, came to join us. It took on a slightly jovial atmosphere despite the misery, reminding me of home, where people would congregate in the bazaar after breakfast, sitting with their backs against the walls of the shops as they caught up on the local gossip and politics of the day.

Shafique was talking to a fellow Afghan in a black woollen coat and jeans. I shuffled over to join them.

'Gulwali, this is my friend, Jan. We travelled together from Greece to Italy. I lost him in Rome, and here he is.'

'Pleased to meet you, Gulwali.' I shook his warm hand. 'Shafique told me about your night.'

'Yeah. It was something else,' I said, easing myself to the ground.

'Have some blanket,' Jan said, pulling a grubby white polyester cloth from beneath himself.

'Thank you.'

Jan looked at me. 'I feel like I know you from somewhere, Gulwali. Like I've seen your face at a wedding, or something. Where are you from? Who was your grandfather?'

I wasn't thrown by this. Afghan men asking about lineage was a perfectly normal thing – in Afghanistan, we did it all the time. It was how we identified people.

We traded relatives back and forth until we worked it out: my grandfather and his father were cousins.

I laughed: that meant we were cousins. I was picking up a few of those on this journey. I thought briefly of Jawad, and wondered if he'd managed to leave Istanbul yet.

'Nice to meet you. So what brings you here to Europe, cousin? Business or pleasure?' I joked.

'Ha ha.' His laughter was genuine. 'But I should be asking what *you* are doing here. You're so young.'

At that my humour evaporated. I stared at my toes as I tried to find the words. 'My mother sent me and my brother, Hazrat. It was too dangerous at home. My father and so many relatives are dead – killed by the Americans.'

'I heard. I'm sorry – I got the news when I was in Peshawar. May Allah rest their souls in peace.'

'Thank you.'

'So where is your brother? Is he with you?'

'I don't know. I think he is in the UK now. I want to get there to be with him.' It hurt me to say those words.

The events of the past drifted through my head like a strange dream. I think the others felt the same way, because we just sat in silence for the next few minutes.

'Are you boys hungry?' Jan clapped his hands together. 'I know a nice place which is not too expensive.'

The three of us walked to a Turkish café, where Jan bought us dinner. It felt so normal that for once we weren't looking over our shoulders, worrying if the police might appear. The locals went about their business without noticing us, and the man who ran the café served us kindly.

'So, what is your plan now?'

Shafique's cheeks bulged with chicken, so I answered for him: 'Shafique hasn't decided what he's going to do. Maybe he can stay in France—?'

'What about you, Gulwali?'

I knew what I was doing. While my family had only paid for me to get as far as Greece, I had learned enough from Hodja to realize that if I could make it to Calais on my own, I could figure it out from there.

'I will take a train to Calais.'

Jan raised his eyebrows. 'By yourself? You've heard how dangerous Calais is, right?'

I knew how it was – Hodja hadn't held back. And even that morning, when chatting to people in the park, some of them had recently returned from there because conditions were so bad. But I didn't see that I had a choice. And I didn't want Jan to think I was a little kid.

'Yes. So what?'

He raised an eyebrow at me. This made me annoyed.

'I've heard the stories. But so what? I'll go by myself if I have to. I can find help when I get there.'

The night before had made me more determined than ever to push on quickly. England felt close now. I was lucky that I wasn't in a Parisian jail, that the police from last night had simply moved me on.

'Why don't we go together, cousin?' Jan suggested. 'It was my plan to leave in the next few days anyway, but as you are here, I can come with you. I'm not happy about you going alone.'

His protective nature was getting on my nerves, but in a way I was touched. He saw me as family, and it was his duty to be there for me.

We tried to persuade Shafique to come with us too, but he insisted he wanted to wait in Paris a while longer. He had heard of a good agent that could arrange everything from there. He had had bad experiences of doing things without agents further back in his journey, and didn't want to risk it again.

'But don't you trust me, Shafique? I can sort it out for you. I got you to Paris, didn't I?'

'So why don't you stay here in Paris with me, and maybe in a few days we will have found an agent and we can move? Tonight we can find this shelter and have a warm bed,' he countered.

I did consider it, but I didn't want to. As much as I liked Shafique, I thought he was a bit naïve. He had only been on the road for six months, half as long as me. He'd got to Paris far faster than I had, but it meant he hadn't learned as much. That morning, as we had chatted to the others, he had been trying to find agents. I was worried he was going to get ripped off or tricked.

I had about 350 euros left: I'd had to buy tickets and food for Shafique and me. Hodja had given me 150, and the agent had given me 300 in Greece – the supposed change from what my family had paid up front. I also had about US$100 left. But Hodja had warned me Calais could be very expensive and I would need every penny. I didn't want to risk losing it to some dodgy agent here. Far better, I thought, to get there first and find out the lie of the land.

Shafique and I argued for a while longer. He kept trying to get me to stay, and Jan and I kept trying to persuade him to come with us to Calais.

It was no good.

Jan and I went to the train station to get two tickets. The next train was early afternoon. The train to Calais went from a different station, but I had no idea how to find it. We walked through Paris trying to find our way.

Surprisingly, it wasn't that hard – there were Afghans all over the city who helped us on our way.

CHAPTER TWENTY-SIX

By the time we found the station, we were close to missing the train. Jan and I sprinted along a polished platform. I realized now that I was relieved that he was coming too – despite my bluster, deep-down I hadn't wanted to go alone.

We boarded and snoozed comfortably during the ninety-minute journey.

We arrived just after lunch, and made our way out of the station. We weren't the only foreign faces getting off: dozens of us forced our way through the mêlée and outside. There were migrants everywhere. Filthy bodies were sitting wherever they could; others were standing around in little groups.

Jan approached a huddle of men. They were so dirty we couldn't really tell what nationality they were.

'Excuse me, friend...' he started.

'You newcomers need to go to the Jungle,' said a skinny, grey-haired man. He spoke to us in Pashtu, but his accent sounded a little odd.

'You from Afghanistan, brother?' asked Jan.

'Pakistan. Waziristan,' he said. I could hear it in his accent now.

'Is the Jungle so bad?' I asked hopefully.

I had heard stories in Rome of how awful the Jungle was – the name given to the port in Calais, the place where migrants gathered

and lived in order to try and get lorries to England. But I also suspected it might not be as bad as people made out; I thought maybe
the details were exaggerated to discourage people from going here.

'Whatever you've heard about the Jungle, it's worse than they
say.' He looked at us. 'The only thing you need to know is this –
they don't want us there. The West loves dogs, almost as much as
it loves war. Bush and Blair consummated their invasion, and we
are the unwanted puppies of their bombing. They don't want to let
us in to the warmth of their fire – but they don't have the stomach
to kill us. So, here we are, locked out in the rain and cold, fighting
over whatever scraps fall from their table.' It was obviously a favourite speech of his – and it wasn't what I wanted to hear. But I still
wasn't completely convinced. We were so close to England – how
bad could it be?

'What do you mean?'

'The people there are scum,' the man said. 'They are thieves and
liars. And the French police treat us like animals. To be hunted and
chased around and around, like it's just a big game.' He let out a
bitter little laugh. 'This is why they call it the Jungle, boy.'

'So, why should we go, then?' I wanted answers.

'Because, my boy, you have nowhere else to go. It's the same
reason all these miserable creatures are here. They've come this
far and now they cannot stop.'

'How long have you been here?' Jan asked.

'Six weeks.'

'So why did you not get on to a truck?'

'Oh, I've got on lots of trucks. Every day I am catching a truck.
But then the driver, or the police, or the security people, find me
and remove me.'

'They don't arrest you?'

'Like I said, to them it's just a game. If they arrest me, then they
have to put me in a nice warm cell, give me food. No, they prefer

to dump me on the side of the road and make me walk back to this miserable place. I think they want to teach me a lesson.'

Nothing this man was saying made sense to me.

'A lesson about what?'

'I don't know. Maybe they want to teach me that I was a fool to flee my home. That I would have been smarter to stay among the fighting. That it is better to watch your family and neighbours die than walk mile after mile along freezing roads with an empty stomach.'

'I never did like school,' said Jan, trying to lighten the mood.

'Then you will hate it here,' the man said.

Jan and I stared at each other, and then back at the man.

'So,' said Jan. 'Where is the Jungle? I can't work out which way it is.'

'Over there.' The man pointed down the street. 'Follow that road for an hour. You will smell it before you can see it.' He sighed. 'Do you have an agent here?'

We both shook our heads.

'No one does when they arrive. I wouldn't worry. Money talks. Take my advice and ask for the Kurd they call "Le Grande Fromage".'

'The what?'

Jan burst out laughing. 'It means "Big Cheese", Gulwali.'

Laughter erupted from my throat too. Big Cheese – it was the most ridiculous name I'd ever heard.

'Kurds,' said Jan. 'Forget Bush. I am beginning to think it's the Kurds who rule the world.'

I spotted a couple of women serving some immigrants tea from a large urn. We went and got a cup. A woman in a wool beanie handed me a steaming cup with a smile. It was nice to see a friendly face, even for a moment.

I saw familiar faces from the various countries and places I had stayed along the way – no one that I knew, but faces I recognized. It never ceased to amaze me that we could have crossed half the world, yet Afghans always seem to bump into each other. I supposed it was not too surprising given that we were all ultimately heading for the United Kingdom.

I knew that for the majority of the people there, the UK was their destination. It's the idea, the notion that, because it's the hardest to get to, it's the best place, the last stop, the end of the road.

The end of the game.

That's not the only reason, of course. Afghans have historical and cultural connections to Britain, either through the former empire or through war. Or language. Many have family already there. Also, the UK is seen as tolerant and fair to immigrants.

'Let's find some food,' I said. No matter what lay ahead, a full stomach would help.

Other migrants told us there was an evening food charity place twenty minutes' walk away. They were going that way. Apparently, the French police didn't make arrests near the various food distribution points, which were run by French charities, so these were safe places. Migrants tended to hang about at food places for that reason. They told us they also walked around in large groups. If the police spotted you alone or in a pair, they were more inclined to detain you; in a larger group, you tended to get left alone.

Being new here made me feel felt very vulnerable, so I was quickly learning how it all worked.

The line for dinner stretched for hundreds of metres. Jan and I stood in silence as we queued for about half an hour, and I watched the tide of people around me. What few women there were stayed close to their male companions. I saw the way some of the other men looked at them, and it made me angry to see this. These poor women looked scared enough, without strange men staring at them in a bad way. A few of the women had children with them –

filthy, snot-nosed little wretches with rattling coughs. Sometimes a migrant's life is about seizing what little dignity there is to be had – judging by the way these women kept their gazes low, they knew that too.

At the front of the queue now, I could see four older French women stirring the huge pots needed to feed so many hungry mouths. This wasn't a United Nations operation – I think perhaps it was a local church. The women dished out ladle after ladle of thick, white paste. I think it was supposed to be rice, but it looked nothing like it, while the lentils that went on top tasted of nothing. I ate it gratefully all the same. Around me, about 200 others were doing the same.

There were a lot of Afghans there. Some were clearly working – I suppose for different agents and smugglers. They would make their way through the crowds offering to guide people on to trucks and away to England – for a fee, of course.

'You are new.'

'I can help, I know a good agent.'

'I know a good Afghan agent, more trustworthy than the Kurds.'

Basically they were commission salesmen, and they were very good at spotting new arrivals.

We were suspicious of all of them, and determined to find an agent called Karwan. Hodja had told me about him and said he was the best of the bunch because he had a high success rate. He had also advised me to bargain hard.

Many of the people we spoke to were actually helpful; there was a genuine sense of camaraderie. We asked around and found some migrants who were 'his' people. They told us they would take us to him.

Nothing could have prepared me for what we saw as we walked. It looked as though the world's toilet had been flushed and the mess washed up here. We walked for an hour or so with these people, slowly making our way towards the port area. The Jungle was said to be a little further still. All along the way, migrants cluttered the roads. Some were in small groups, walking with purpose to an unknown destination; others merely sat or lay where they could find a comfortable space. Face upon face was deeply etched with hardship.

'There's no escape, boy,' a voice said to me in Pashtu from beneath a sleeping bag. It had been red once, but was now a sickly shade of green-brown. I didn't have a reply, but it did leave me feeling that as close as I was to Britain, I might be more distant than I had ever realized. All I could smell was human decay, and the diesel fumes from the stream of double-trailer lorries that crawled past us.

On the other side of the road were rows of warehouses made of corrugated iron, barren swathes of concrete between, all surrounded by huge fences. Impenetrable spinneys of coarse seaside scrub and willow trees made the place disorientating and bewildering. Black plastic shopping bags whispered from every sharp twig and thorn.

The place was so vast and so confusing, it really was no wonder they called it the Jungle.

CHAPTER TWENTY-SEVEN

As we neared the Jungle, I began to notice sapphire-blue tarpaulins everywhere. Each one marked a makeshift house or communal shelter, which were interlinked by a maze of tracks in the sandy soil. It was a temporary city of desperate human flotsam. There were huge piles of litter and human waste everywhere, full black plastic bags stacked as high as a man. White plastic water drums, fertilizer sacks, plastic cups, food wrappers, bottles, discarded clothing and worn-out shoes...the accumulated mess was abandoned, but ready for reuse, should the need arise.

We passed a small home built from a patchwork of three damaged tents – black, green and orange. A chimney made from discarded air-conditioning ducting peeped from the roof. Three Sudanese men in long black jackets with their hoods pulled up sat around a small fire, trying to boil eggs in a broken saucepan. A mouldy beige leather armchair, a broken office chair and an upturned supermarket trolley functioned as furniture.

Jan and I nodded a greeting to them and continued walking through what was essentially their living room, taking care to step over a shallow channel that had been cut across the ground to drain away rainwater. Now it functioned as an open sewer.

The people who were guiding us took us to a spot where several migrants sat huddled around a fire. An old man threw a plastic bottle on to the flames, which belched out clouds of sickly sweet chemicals as the plastic melted. At least it was momentarily warm.

A muscular man appeared.

'Gulwali, this is Karwan.'

We shook hands. His Farsi was good enough for me to understand him, but his Kurdish accent was still strong. He wore a shiny black ski jacket and faded jeans. Wrap-around sunglasses sat on his head, holding a long sweep of black fringe in place.

'You are the newcomers. I am told you want to get to England?'

'Yes,' I said. 'Tomorrow.'

He scratched at the patchy black stubble on his chin. 'Well,' he replied, taking his time, as if scratching for my benefit, 'have you put any money with anyone?'

I knew what he meant. Karwan wanted to know if I had any money lodged with one of the shadowy 'third party' individuals – did I have credit to travel? Most migrants reaching the Jungle have not paid in advance, as the national agents in places like Kabul and Pakistan only promise to get you as far as Greece, or maybe Paris, and that's all they take money for. After that, you need to use one of the specialist Calais agents, people like Karwan, to get you across on the ferry. This work – getting people on to trains and trucks – was all they did. The cashless people in the Jungle tended to pay for this part of the journey by having that third party somewhere in France or the UK act as guarantor. The third party was usually someone known to the agent, but critically was someone with a European bank account where funds could be lodged. If you had family or friends in Europe already, they could make the contacts on your behalf. There had even been people in the park in Paris who had promised they knew third parties who could help with this – if you paid for it in Paris (or at least lodged the funds), then in theory by the time you reached Calais the specialist agent would be expecting you.

Shafique had stayed in Paris trying to do just that. He had wanted to pay up front and sort it out in advance, not turn up here without plans as Jan and I had done.

The other option on offer in Calais was one where an agent would give you details of his own contact, with a bank account. These people would be complete strangers to you but they were still willing to guarantee for you, once they took some background details – the names of your family, and where they lived. The idea was that once you made it to England, you paid them back in full. Of course, you could just disappear and not pay them, but in reality this rarely happened. The strong tribal networks we had back home had tendrils that stretched into Europe, and if you didn't pay it was a safe bet that somehow the agent and their guarantor would find a way to hunt you or your family down and exact revenge.

It sounds like a crazy system but it works. If it didn't work, it wouldn't happen.

Karwan looked at me expectantly. 'I have contacts in the UK who can arrange your credit. I can give you their number and a phone to call them. You make the agreement and once that is arranged, I will ensure you reach the UK. Guaranteed. Five hundred euros each.'

He scratched his chin.

I stayed quiet and scratched my chin too. *Guaranteed.*

'We have cash.'

'If you want to pay me cash, pay me three hundred euros each.'

'That is too much. Where are we going to get that sort of money?'

He didn't answer.

'We don't have that much money.'

He continued to scratch his chin, this time with an air of annoyance.

'I can give you fifty euros,' I said, taking a thumbed note from my pocket and waving it at him. I had another fifty in there too, but I was determined not to let him see it.

He stared coldly. 'Don't waste my time with fifty euros.'

'Please, Karwan. You've got to help us.'

My hands wrapped around his wrist and I looked up at him, willing my eyes to fill with tears. If I concentrated hard on my mother's memory, I could get a fairly convincing hyperventilation going.

Under normal circumstances, Karwan might have pushed me away, or even hit me. I think he wanted to. I could sense the tension in his arms, but it was a risk I was willing to take.

'*Please*, Karwan.' I looked up into his eyes again. I was getting to him, I could tell.

He muttered something I didn't catch. He repeated himself: 'So, what about the fifty euros you still have hidden in your pocket?'

He'd seen. Reluctantly I gave him the money.

He looked over at Jan. 'And you. What have you got?'

Jan handed over another fifty.

'Please, Karwan. Take us.'

He shrugged his broad shoulders. 'All right, I'll take you,' he huffed, fixing me with a glare that told me he knew what I had done. 'But if anybody asks,' he hissed, drawing close to me, 'you'll tell them you paid £500 each. Into a British bank account. Got it? If you tell anyone the truth, I will kill you both.'

We nodded. 'We won't tell, we promise. Don't we, Jan?'

'People cannot think I'm a pushover,' he muttered.

Karwan told us we'd begin trying to get on a lorry that very night. He told us to come back to the fire and meet him there in one hour.

We walked around the Jungle, taking it in. We came across a group of Afghan and Pakistani men preparing to worship in a mosque made from wooden goods pallets and yet more tarpaulins. Someone had attempted to decorate the outside of the structure with stolen pot plants. I tried to pray whenever I could, and this seemed a perfect place to do so.

Jan and I splashed water from a split plastic bucket on to our faces, and left our shoes in a neat pile with the others.

It felt so good to pray. Afterwards, I felt calmer and less fearful about what lay ahead.

I was face down in the freezing mud, scrambling beneath a gap in a wire-mesh security fence.

Karwan leaned his weight back to hold the mesh up. 'Hurry up,' he urged, the strain showing on his face.

Jan, myself and four other Afghan men wiped ourselves off as well as we could and stared around at the large, brightly lit parking area filled with lorries. Through the sleet I could make out dozens of figures swarming around the backs of the high-sided trailers, or bowing beneath the wheels as if in search of an unknown goal.

'Come on,' said Karwan. 'You don't want to miss the best spots, do you?'

We jogged behind him. Groups of migrants, mostly in ethnic packs – Asian, African, Arab – roamed the park searching for any opportunity to board.

'Check underneath,' Karwan said. 'They are good spots, especially for a little guy like you, Gulwali.'

I had looked under one trailer before a hand caught my shoulder. It was a Pakistani man. Only his dark eyes showed from his balaclava. 'Don't listen to him, boy,' he said in Pashtu. 'It's too cold to ride underneath. If you don't freeze to death, you'll lose your grip and get crushed. Better to ride in the back.'

But as we searched, it became clear that there were simply too many people for the few hiding places.

'Let's go,' said Karwan. 'I have a better plan.'

Two hours later, Jan and I sat shivering back to back beneath a concrete motorway bridge. It was long past midnight. We'd walked along a snow-covered train line for around two hours to get there.

Karwan had gone on to make 'other arrangements'. He returned soon after, brandishing heavy grey bolt cutters. 'The keys to England, gentlemen,' he said, waving them at us.

He cut our way into another parking area. This one was a marshalling place for what Karwan told us was British-bound ferry traffic.

Unlike the first, this one was busy with truck drivers. We lay on the ground, trying to get a sense of the activity. Many drivers checked the doors on their trailers and searched the chassis. Others chatted, drank coffee and smoked cigarettes. Cars full of families and businessmen formed a series of orderly queues nearby.

Night was giving way to day now, and I could feel desperation rising inside me. Coming to a decision, Jan and I ran across the open car park, looking out all the while for the police or the sudden appearance of a driver.

We crouched beneath the tail of a lorry.

'There.' Karwan suddenly pointed towards a silver estate car parked to one side. The driver's door was open and we could make out a figure standing against the fence, steam billowing from around his feet as he peed.

We stalked forward, mindful of the heavy slopping noise our footsteps made. Jan opened the back door a tiny way. The passenger seats were full of suitcases and boxes, but the footwells were empty. My heart was racing. I slid into the tight space, crawling into the hole behind the driver's seat in an effort to make room for Jan. He squeezed in behind me and I heard the door click shut. I barely dared breathe as the driver returned from relieving himself.

My legs were beginning to cramp in such a small space, but the car was warm and I was thankful for that.

Before long, we started to move forwards. Jan patted my ankle as if to congratulate us – we were on our way to England.

The driver crept forward a few feet at a time, occasionally lighting a cigarette or adjusting his car radio. Suddenly I tensed, aware of voices at the driver's window. Torchlight probed the car's interior. A shout.

The driver turned, following the beam of torchlight. 'Hey,' he bellowed, throwing himself out of the car.

The door beside my head swung open and a strong hand dragged me on to the cold ground. Police stood over me, shouting.

Jan was on the other side of the car. 'Leave him alone, he's just a boy.'

The police shouted back. The driver, who had now recovered some of his composure following our discovery, shouted in my face and pushed me against his car before being held back by the police.

The police marched Jan and me down the line of cars, back towards the main entrance, near the ticket barriers.

'*Halas*,' they said, waving us away into the night. '*Allez*.'

We skulked away into the darkness.

'Why didn't they arrest us, Jan?'

'I don't know. A cell and a hot meal would be welcome right now, wouldn't it? Maybe that's why not.'

We found the train line and began the long, cold walk back to the Jungle. It was snowing more heavily now, and the freezing wind stuck my wet jeans to me, sucking the heat from my body. My stomach – knotted with tension for so long now – relaxed a little, so that the pain of its emptiness cut into me.

By the time we got back to the Jungle I was exhausted. We lay down on some sheets of cardboard and tried to sleep for a few hours, before Karwan came for us in the early evening to attempt it all over again.

And that became our routine.

We soon learned that each smuggler had their own area – a section of a car park or rail line that was theirs exclusively. Sometimes in one large park we'd see several groups of migrants all trying to board vehicles, yet no one wandered into another smuggler's area. It was, despite the chaos, very organized.

Occasionally the smugglers would settle their differences in a brawl. But most of the time we were alone, running from the police or truck drivers. It was easy enough to get on, in or under a truck or vehicle. It was impossible to go undetected by the police and border guards.

They had dogs, and cameras – and they knew all the best places to hide, just as we did. Whenever we got caught the police would just let us loose again – providing we were a long way from the Jungle. Or they would take the time to drive us to a remote location and dump us at the side of the road. They didn't want to take our liberty, only our time and precious energy.

Under Karwan's careful guidance, our little flock developed an economic hierarchy. Jan and I were always last to board when it came to enacting Karwan's nightly schemes. We had paid the least, and so we were his lowest priority. Eventually we blackmailed him.

'Stop putting us last, Karwan,' I complained. 'We can see what you're doing. Stop it, or I'll tell the others how much we paid.'

Karwan seethed at me, but Jan stood his ground.

'Do as Gulwali says, Karwan.'

He did.

'Karwan's Guys', as we now thought of ourselves, formed our own small camp, and we started to settle in as best we could. Jan and I befriended a quiet and thoughtful Afghan. I nicknamed him Qumandan – 'leader', or 'man in charge'. He was only a teenager, but he had a strength of character that we instantly warmed to. We made a little house using a tarpaulin and the branches of a willow tree; Jan and Qumandan found some pallets on a construction site after a long walk home one morning. The tarpaulin had been claimed in a similar manner. So too had a gas bottle, liberated from an unlocked shed in a beachside neighbourhood. The theft didn't sit well with me: theft is immoral. But we were acting out of desperation. No one was really trying to help us, so it was a simple choice of steal or die.

Life became a soul-destroying cycle of escape, capture, theft and construction. Only the physical necessities of eating at charity food points, the occasional wash and broken sleep disrupted the cycle.

As seemed the norm, the Jungle was ethnically divided into ad hoc nationality areas. The Africans seemed to be the poorest and slept nearest the fence to the car park. They didn't seem to have agents and appeared to be trying to get on trucks themselves. There were also Chinese – I didn't see where they slept, but they turned up at night with cans of beer and used to sit and talk to us. They may have been migrant workers – there were lots of factories nearby.

We tried to make the best of it. Someone found a tattered football in a playground. Having a kickabout with mates was a moment of normality – and was all too rare.

The police loved to raid during the day, when they knew we were likely to be resting. It was common to have my charity-donated blanket pulled from me, a screaming police officer shouting in French in my face. It was still a language I didn't understand, although their meaning was very clear. They would move us on, beating any guys who resisted. We would then be forced to stand shivering in the cold while they questioned us about things they didn't want answers to.

Sometimes activists came to the Jungle to form human shields between the police and ourselves. They tended to be young English and French men and women, although there were a few older people involved as well. They would stand outside our shelters shouting at the police, demanding they stop harassing us. They had loudspeakers which they used to try to embarrass the police into leaving us alone.

We were grateful for their empathy and support. Some of the

women used to like to hug me. If felt nice to have a moment of human comfort. Sometimes they brought fruit or other food with them – that was even better. But we knew they weren't going to be here all the time. As did the police. Sooner or later, the police would get their way.

A couple of times, officers detained me for twenty-four hours. I didn't mind – it was warm, and usually it offered the chance to see a doctor. There was a volunteer clinic where there was a young French-Afghan doctor who was nice to me. My face and body were covered in pimples – a consequence of poor hygiene – but there was little they could do. The medical clinic had showers, although you were only allowed to use them if you had a medical reason, but the doctor always let me sneak in and wash.

I lived in the same clothes for weeks at a time. I wore them until they were filthy rags – or until they became so infested with fleas and lice I couldn't stand it any more. Fortunately the charities that ran the food places were often giving away second-hand clothes. That became my definition of a good day – a hot meal, some new clothes, a visit to the doctor, and an illicit shower from which I emerged clean and dressed. I hated the filth – back home I was so clean. It gave me some small pleasure to throw my old rags on the fire, and watch as the bugs popped in the flames.

The humiliation was hard to bear. Many of the faces I saw spoke of the same thing. In their own countries, these people had power, even the respect of their communities. Here in the Jungle we were barely human. We were the beasts that gave this place its name.

I imagined myself running up to some high-ranking French official and shaking them to demand answers. It wasn't my fault I wasn't born in Europe. My home was a war zone – did that somehow make me less human?

I spent a lot of time just wandering the Jungle or the food area near the train station. It helped pass the day. The police would see me and often assume I was out stealing – pickpocketing or shop-lifting. Sometimes I was. They would drive past slowly, making a point of staring at me. Every so often an officer might take pity on me – I suppose some of them had children or relatives my own age. They would give me a few euros or perhaps some food. I always accepted it with a smile.

One night Karwan selected a high-sided truck. The driver had left the cab to use the toilet.

'I've already cut a hole in the top,' he told us proudly, as we lay in the grass on our stomachs, shivering on the cold ground.

When we finally got to our feet, I was pleased to be moving. But when we approached the lorry I wasn't so sure. 'What are those?' I asked, pointing at red signs with skulls on them on the lorry's side.

'Nothing to worry about, Gulwali,' said Karwan. 'Just don't eat anything you find inside. It's *haram*.' He boosted me up. 'You first, little man.'

I fell headfirst through the hole and into the darkness, where I landed heavily on what I thought was grain or beans. A cloud of soft powder blew into my face. I was sure it was agricultural. I crawled into a back corner and stayed still. Whatever this stuff was, it was soft to lie on, which made a nice change.

We stayed in the truck all night, not making a sound. In the morning the driver came and the truck started moving. We felt the lorry go in the direction of the port – you get used to judging distances – but, just before it should have turned right towards the port, it drove straight on for half a mile instead.

When the driver opened the door we ran, because we knew it wasn't the port.

He was screaming at us in English, only a few of words of which I understood: '...not run...ambulance, ambulance...' None of us had any idea what he was on about so, so we just kept going as fast as we could.

I was black from whatever had been in the truck, covered in fine dust. Maybe because I was the first in the truck, but for whatever reason, I had emerged far dirtier than anyone else.

We found a water pipe to wash some of the mess off, and I rubbed water over my face. It felt good to get it off. I felt clean again. I felt...burning.

The pain intensified. It felt as though my face was on fire. I screwed my eyes closed. 'Help. Help. Help,' I shouted, scrambling for more water.

Qumandan was there, splashing me down. 'That's it, Gulwali, wash it off.'

'Get my eyes. Rinse my eyes.'

More burning. The water only made it worse.

I screamed – the pain was beyond anything I'd ever felt, as harsh chemicals corroded me.

Qumandan dragged me like a dead goat, all the way past the food points, to where the medical clinic was.

The nice lady at the food point was there – she saw me and screamed in horror. 'We've got to take him to hospital.' She grabbed hold of me and put me in her car.

I passed out from pain.

When I awoke everything was black. Although I couldn't see it, I was in a real bed. The sheets were soft to the touch, and smelled clean.

'How are you feeling?'

It was a woman's voice. I thought I might be dead, but she had a French accent, therefore I was most likely alive. A hand rested on my shoulder, then it lifted, and began to peel my head. Slowly I could detect light. I felt gauze pads being lifted from my eyes. A blurry image hovered.

'Gulwali,' said the blur.

A bright light blinded me – first in my left eye, then the right. I blinked and the image grew clearer. A middle-aged woman stood over me – blonde hair, white gown, kind face.

Next to her was an Afghan man I didn't recognize. He stepped forward and addressed me in Dari. 'You are in Paris. In a hospital.'

I just blinked.

'The doctor says your eyes will be fine. They will give you drops for them, and cream for your skin, as well as some painkillers.'

I smiled, by way of thanks. My lips hurt. They felt blistered.

'We will discharge you now. We will take you back to where you want to go.'

Where I wanted to go? I had nowhere, only my temporary home in the Jungle.

The journey back was very strange. I lay in the rear of the ambulance, my face misted with ointment. The Afghan rode with me, but we said nothing. My mind was filled with relief about my eyesight, but I was equally concerned about what this new setback might mean for the rest of my journey. I was also furious at Karwan for making me get in the lorry. He must have known, suspected at least, that it was dangerous. Was that why he let me go first?

The rights and wrongs of the matter were no longer important. The only thing that mattered was my getting to England – by fair means or foul.

When I returned to the Jungle, things had changed. Karwan had disappeared. The agents were so secretive. The police were always asking us to reveal who they were. The truth is, we didn't really know. Secrecy was part of their business. They didn't tell us where they lived, or any other details about themselves. I couldn't figure it out – but it wasn't of major concern to me, any way. I was paying them to get me to England, not be my friend.

We found a new agent, a man called Pustiwan. We begged him

to take us on. We didn't have enough money, so we had to call one of his people in the UK to guarantee credit.

I found myself getting tired very quickly after I got burned. I still don't know what it was, only that it had some kind of chemical reaction with water.

Jan and Qumandan were kind and looked after me, bringing me food and insisting I stay in bed and rest. But when we went out to get on the trucks, the other people under Pustiwan's charge got very angry with me, accusing me of being too slow and spoiling their own chances. They looked at me now as if I were a weak link – as if what happened on the chemical truck that night was somehow my fault.

It just added to my sense of despair. I'd been there for so long, and I barely knew a single person who had made it to England. I prayed that we'd get news that someone had made it, just to give us hope. I was beginning to wonder if this was what the rest of my life would look like.

When I felt stronger, we tried jumping on trains heading for the tunnel. But it was just too dangerous – I knew the risks of trains first-hand, and even if you got on board, it was easy for security to find you. And that meant another long walk back to the pile of stinking rags we called home.

Over the time we were there, security became tighter, too. Some guys were detained and kept in jail for up to twenty days.

I'd got word that Shafique was in Dunkirk – he thought it might be easier to cross from there. I'd thought about going myself, but as bad as things were here, I couldn't quite believe there was an easier option that I'd been overlooking.

I was miserable, stressed beyond belief. I was a failure for coming all this way, only to be thwarted by a stretch of water I could almost picture swimming on a calm day.

One evening the others went out. I don't really remember what they said they were going to try. I just felt sick and tired. My face was still incredibly painful; it had blistered, turned black and was peeling. I wished Jan and Qumandan good luck, and buried my head under my dirty blanket.

They didn't come back.

I wanted to be happy for them, but it was the worst thing I could imagine. My one chance to escape had come and gone because I had been too tired. I cursed myself – told myself what a stupid little boy I had been. When I thought I couldn't feel any worse, their departure pushed me into a very dark place.

I was too scared to stay in the hut alone, but there were always newcomers looking for a place to sleep, so I found some Afghans who seemed nice enough and they were grateful to have the space.

Pustiwan tried to convince us to ride underneath some other trucks – those that had weighted suspension. When the lorry is empty, some of the wheels fold up to save on tyre wear. It's a good place to hide. But if the truck is loaded, you can be crushed to death in a moment. I knew someone who had died this way, and I didn't want it to be my fate – ground to bits in the suspension unit like lamb *kofte*.

Myself and a few of the others refused. A couple of guys knew the risks and went anyway.

'Brave, no?' saidPustiwan.

'Foolish,' I said, touching my cheek.

That Friday, Pustiwan appeared with a ladder under his arm. 'A new plan,' he proclaimed proudly, rubbing his belly.

We cut our way into a park full of trailers waiting to be hitched to a cab and driven off.

Pustiwan tutted and paced back and forth, making a great show of inspecting each trailer, until he found one he judged to be just right. 'Nice.'

He placed his ladder against the frame of the canvas siding and climbed to the roof. He used a razor to neatly slice a hole large enough to fit a man. My face throbbed as he did it – I was not going first on this occasion.

'This is a good one,' he declared. 'Come, quick.'

We climbed in one by one. The cargo was boxes of something heavy. I was relieved.

'Two days,' Pustiwan said, his head poking through the hole. 'Two days to England. Ha ha ha.'

He spent the next ten minutes repairing his opening, then left without a word.

There were five of us. We sat for two days. No food or water. We lay in silence waiting and waiting. I dozed a little, but my dreams were surreal and disturbing – my blistered face hung broken from the wheels of a lorry. I tried to lie still – to conserve energy, fluid, mental strength. After what felt like a week, the trailer shuddered into life as the cab hitched itself to us.

We were all suddenly wide awake.

'This is it,' someone hissed through the gloom.

As depressed, angry and exhausted as I felt, I got a rush of adrenalin. Perhaps this time I would make it. We began moving. Now came the sense of expectation. Either we would be making the long walk home, or we would be on a ferry bound for England.

I expected to turn left out of the park, towards the port. We'd made this attempt a thousand times. But, instead, the lorry turned right.

'Are we going the right way?' I asked.

No one was sure. I could handle the hunger and thirst as long as I thought we were heading in the right direction, but we weren't. Panic set in. Someone started banging in the dark.

'Stop, stop. Let us out.'

We all started shouting. I thumped my hand against a box – anything to get the driver's attention. Maybe he heard us, maybe he didn't. We kept driving. Further and further from the port.

After half a day the truck slowed to a halt. We heard voices outside. We were silent. The doors swung open, blinding us with daylight.

'*Halas.*'

It was the police. We climbed down on to the roadside. I had no idea where we were. None of us did.

'England?' someone ventured.

'Belgium,' the officer said. Then he burst out laughing.

The police tried to question us, but the language barrier made it impossible. In the end they made a great show of taking our names, then pointed to the nearest crossroads.

It was going to be a long walk.

We walked for twenty-four hours. More police stopped us. We tried to explain our situation, but I'm not sure they understood or cared. 'Calais,' they said, pointing to a nearby road. We kept walking.

I don't know how I kept going. I just stared at my feet – left foot, right foot, left foot, right foot. I thought it would never end.

I thought the Jungle was the most beautiful place I had ever seen when we finally staggered into camp. I flopped on to my pallet bed and fell straight to sleep. No lorries for us tonight.

At first I thought it was my mother, waking me for school – but the policeman was more persistent than my dreams. It was the weekly raid. I could have died. All I wanted to do was sleep. The horror of daily life now infiltrated my dreams. It was torture. The French police knew we didn't have any real options. All they wanted to do was humiliate us, take away what little dignity we had left. They wanted us to leave – to no longer be their problem – and so they left us no choice but to keep trying to go to Britain.

Each time I got caught, their taunts filled my ears: 'No chance this time, maybe the next.'

It was a perverse game, and I was trapped playing it for as long as it took – as long as I could keep going. It was the game without end. They thought it was funny. Every night was the same – cat and mouse with the police. Over and over.

Life only has value as long as you believe it is worth living. I was no longer sure. I was becoming detached from my surroundings. Nothing mattered any more. The instinct to survive is strong, but when survival is all that there is, you are left with the obvious question: 'Why go on?'

My life was a living nightmare. We kept trying trucks. The routine was the same. Break in, get caught, walk miles home.

One night the truck we were in took another right turn. I groaned inside. I no longer had the strength to fight it. The others banged and yelled, and then in desperation started to cut through the back of the trailer unit to escape. At that, the truck pulled over and the driver threw the doors open, glaring, baseball bat in his hands.

We had nothing to lose.

The six guys I was with leapt on the driver, kicking and beating him.

He dropped his bat and curled into a ball on the side of the road. '*Nein, nein. Halas... Bitte. Bitte.*'

I wanted to feel sorry for him. Part of me actually did. But ultimately I didn't care. He had a home, a family, a life. What did I have? Nothing.

Passing cars honked their horns. We stopped kicking and started running. We sprinted past a petrol station with a car dealership attached. It had Mercedes flags flying from masts, along with red, yellow and black ones.

'*Deutschland*,' someone puffed. 'We're in bloody Germany.'

I was glad I was running so hard, because if I'd been standing still I think I would have fallen down crying. Not that I wanted to keep going. Only the Jungle waited for me.

I slowed until I was jogging by the roadside, watching the traffic rush past. It would have been so easy to step out. No more hunger. No more fear. No more Jungle. No more England.

I thought of my mother. I kept running.

Our little group split up at that point. I was exhausted and, try as I might, I couldn't keep going. Two men agreed to stay with me. We plodded in silence for hours. My reserves of strength – mental and physical – were all but gone. I wanted to lie down in the soft grass on the side of the road and sleep, and, if I was lucky, maybe never wake up. I fought these thoughts, but I was simply too weak.

Perhaps I would have given up but at that moment, out of nowhere, a blue sedan pulled over in front of us. A middle-aged brunette woman got out. She smiled. It was genuine, and I smiled back at the uninvited warmth she radiated.

'Refugee?' she said, in English.

It was a word I knew.

'*Oui*,' we said.

She opened the passenger door and I flopped gratefully inside. I don't remember her name. I'm not sure we even asked, but she was very friendly and clearly sympathized with our situation. She gave us a baguette and a bottle of water. I devoured the bread in seconds, washing it down with the water.

I began to feel a little better almost immediately – I'm not sure whether it was the food, or just the simple act of caring she showed.

She dropped us off near the Jungle, where our makeshift shelter waited.

I should have been at rock bottom, but the act of kindness stayed with me. It sustained me psychologically for a few weeks, in fact – one small gesture from human to human. But the routine of life in the Jungle went on unchanged, and it wasn't long before I was lower than ever.

The burden was just too much. I was a young boy – I had no

natural business being in such a place. I should have been in school, playing with friends, or spending time with my family; instead, life was a constant struggle to live.

To survive, and whether I actually wanted to, was increasingly on my mind. And I suppose that's why, some time later, standing in front of a refrigerated lorry full of bananas, I didn't hesitate.

The six other guys I was with weren't so sure. 'We'll freeze to death in there,' one said.

I just kicked the mud off my worn-out boots and climbed up.

'Gulwali,' they asked. 'Are you sure?'

I shrugged. What difference did it make? Freeze in a banana truck, or freeze in the Jungle during this cold November? December would be even colder. Better to risk everything than to go on living like this. I couldn't do it any more – not another mouthful from the soup kitchen, not another mad sprint from the police or a driver, not another endless walk in the cold. My face was burned, blistered and blackened – just like my soul.

If the other guys knew my state of mind, I doubt they would have followed. But they did.

'The kid knows what he's doing.'

But I no longer knew anything.

CHAPTER TWENTY-EIGHT

As I got in the refrigerator lorry, I turned to the agent. 'Don't say it.'

Every time we got into a lorry he waved and said, '*Khodahafiz. Farhda Englise,*' which means, 'God be with you. Tomorrow, England.'

He was Kurdish of course, but he said the words in Farsi. At first I found it funny; then it wasn't any more. Now, it felt as though he was taunting me, jinxing me.

We knew the distance from the lorry park to the port entrance, we knew the sensation of going over the speed bumps that led to the port check-in, we knew how it felt when the truck slowed to join the queue for security checks. As each familiar sound or bump passed, I checked my mental map, plotting our course towards the elusive ferry.

The lorry stopped, and I heard the French police open the door at the French checkpoint. I was convinced it was over. In my mind I was beginning to climb down and into their custody, just as I had done a hundred times before. But somehow, this time, they didn't see us. We were hidden right at the back, behind boxes of bananas, and perhaps that night the police couldn't be bothered really looking inside. They closed the doors.

I had entered uncharted territory. This was the closest I had ever reached after a long month of trying – a month that had felt like three times as long.

The lorry drove slowly forward to what I knew would now be the English checkpoints, and the doors swung open again. I flattened my body as if trying to become one with the boxes of bananas. Through a crack I could see the guards playing their torches around the dark space. Then their boot soles slapped hard against the concrete, and the doors slammed shut, plunging us into the comfort of absolute darkness.

The lorry wobbled forwards. My heart raced with each new noise. A hollow, metallic *clank-clank-clank* as each axle passed over a ramp sent a chorus of excitement through the trailer.

'We're getting on the ferry.'

'Shhhh. We're not there yet.'

I said nothing. I barely dared breathe. The lorry went quiet as the driver turned off the engine, and for the next forty-five minutes the seven of us sat in absolute silence.

'Are we moving?' someone hissed.

I held my breath and concentrated. It was there – a discernible sway, a gentle rocking motion.

We were on our way to England.

I tried not to think of the deep black water sliding beneath us. This was a massive ferry – the biggest ship I had ever seen, let alone been on. I felt a little safer. These were professional sailors, not people-smugglers with a leaking tub overflowing with pathetic, desperate men.

We began to relax and talk freely.

'Thanks be to God that he didn't turn the refrigerator on.'

It was getting warm and stuffy in there, but at least it was tolerable. If he had turned it on, we could have frozen to death. There were many stories in the Jungle of people who had done so. That's why getting on to this lorry had been such a risk.

Just a few hours earlier I had been ready to die. I couldn't take it any more. I was going to make it, or they'd find my blue corpse curled up on top of the banana boxes. Either way, I would be out of that living hell they called the Jungle in the port of Calais.

'Yeah,' someone replied. 'I really don't want to die, huddled shivering in your stinking arms.'

We all laughed at that – migrant humour is dark. But without it we'd all have gone mad long ago.

'Hey,' came a voice from the blackness. 'George Bush, Tony Blair and Hamid Karzai are all in hell.'

'Is this a joke, or are you trying to cheer me up?'

We were really in a good mood now. It didn't quite feel real, and until I was safe and knew what my situation in England was, I couldn't relax. But at least, after months of trial and misery, I was on my way to Britain.

'Bush says to Satan, "Hey, Satan, I need to make a phone call to Dick Cheney, to check how the war is going." Satan replies, "Sure, George – that'll be a billion dollars, please." Bush isn't happy, but he pays the money and makes the call. Tony Blair then goes up to Satan. "Hey, Satan, I need to call the Queen in London – just to check on the war." Satan says, "Sure, Tony – no problem. That'll be a billion dollars please." Tony doesn't want to pay either, but what choice does he have? Finally, our glorious President Hamid Karzai goes up to Satan. "Hey, Satan, I need to call Kabul to check on how the invasion is going." Satan says, "No problem, Hamid. That'll be fifty cents, please." When Hamid goes to use the phone, George Bush and Tony Blair rush up to Satan: "Satan, Satan – why did you charge us a billion dollars, and Karzai only fifty cents? It's not fair." Satan turns to George and Tony: "Look, guys, it's totally fair. You're phoning Washington and London – that is long distance. Hamid's is only a local call."

I laughed and laughed. We all did. It felt good. My face itched a lot in the still air of the truck, as the burns were far from healed. I took my cream from my bag and smeared it on. It offered some relief.

After an hour or so, the lorry burst into life. The ferry engine changed note.

'We're in England.'

We started to talk more loudly then, because we had made it. It didn't matter if we got caught – we were there.

We'd been driving for an hour when a fight broke out. Several of the guys were arguing about whether we should try to open the door from the inside when the lorry stopped, or try to get the attention of the driver now by making a lot of noise by banging or trying to move the boxes around. The men knew they had to run for it as soon as they could, because otherwise they would be arrested and deported.

I was tired of running. I just wanted to wait until the doors were opened by the driver. I was so exhausted and sick I couldn't run anywhere. I didn't know if I'd be allowed to stay or not allowed to stay. I also feared I might be arrested and thrown in jail as I had been elsewhere.

I didn't think the UK would be like Iran, Bulgaria or even France. I knew there wouldn't be policemen with horsewhips or kidnappers waiting, so how bad could anything else be?

The others weren't happy, though.

'What do you care, kid? You'll be fine. Don't be selfish. You know they will take care of you. But what about us?'

'You run. I will stay here. I don't care,' I said.

In the end, we agreed to try knocking but the driver couldn't hear us. Eventually, when he stopped at his destination, he opened the door. The others were poised and ready to jump but the driver saw us, a look of total surprise on his face. But despite his shock he was fast, and slammed the doors shut before anybody could get out.

'No,' someone cried.

I had had my first glimpse of England, but now I was locked up in the dark again. We were scared. We didn't know what was going to happen now.

After a quarter of an hour, the doors swung wide open. Four police in blue uniforms stood there.

They ordered us out. I blinked in the bright daylight after so long in the truck. It all looked depressingly familiar. It was yet another warehouse complex, with parking for dozens of trucks.

I smelled British air for the first time in my life. It didn't smell of perfume or fish and chips or roast beef – as had been the joke among the Jungle migrants. But it wasn't bad, either. Maybe it smelled of freedom. The weather was good – surprisingly sunny for November, and much warmer than the day I had left France. Like everybody, I had heard it was always raining in England.

We stood in a huddle as the police questioned the driver. I think he was Dutch. They wanted to see his licence and they seemed to think he must have known we were in there. He was sweating and nervous.

I felt bad for him and wanted to tell the police he didn't know we were in his lorry, but I kept quiet. Eventually they loaded us into a police van and took us to a police station near Dartford, in Kent.

There were Pashtu translators there, to help the police with the questioning. We were under arrest, they explained. I had my fingerprints taken. I'd been arrested before, but never so politely – they explained that I was being arrested and told me what my rights were; they said I could stay silent and I didn't have to say anything unless I wanted to. It was as though they were asking my permission.

I hated the police by now, after all my experiences; but this felt different. I was scared of what would happen to me but I had stopped being afraid. I had seen it all, suffered it all already. What would these well-mannered English police do to me that the Iranian, Turkish, Bulgarian or French police had not done already?

I told them my age. 'Thirteen.'

They laughed at me. They laughed at me with humiliating, bitter, cynical laughter.

They did not believe me, even after the translator repeated the question several times.

After interrogation, they put us in small cells for twenty-four hours. It was the longest twenty-four hours ever. I was thinking, 'OK, I am in England – but what now? What if they deport me? Have I made it this far only to go all the way back to the start?'

Before, I hadn't thought that they would; now I wasn't sure. Being locked up felt like France, like Calais, back in the same police station. The food was horrible, and my anxieties came flooding back.

The following day they put us into a minibus. They didn't tell us where we were going. Everything was unclear again. I began to really think the worst when I realized they were taking us back to Dover. I could see ferries like the one I had just crossed on, cutting their way through grey wintry waves towards the distant French shoreline.

We were led into a building with the sign 'Immigration Removal Centre' over its main door – one of the men I was with explained to me what this meant. I was sure they would send us all back to France, or even Afghanistan – that made me scared like never before. I did not want to go that way. Going back now would be worse than death.

'Please, God. *No*,' I prayed.

At the vast migrant centre we were put in a featureless waiting room. It felt familiar, like so many places I'd seen before, filled as usual with all the faces of the world. We started talking to people, trying to get information about what was happening. Some were there to sign paperwork before being deported. They were finger-printed as they left, looking dejected and broken. Many of the others had just been arrested like us.

The atmosphere was distressing. Some people were crying. Others were just sitting huddled, their arms wrapped around themselves, as they rocked back and forth.

To have come all this way and to have fallen and failed at the last hurdle was just too much.

I shared their feelings – I was filled with dread. Clearly, England wasn't the welcoming place I'd been led to believe it was.

I was taken alone into a room and questioned by two immigration officers. With a translator, they interrogated me for hours. They kept asking about my face and why it was so badly burned. They insisted on looking at my tube of burn cream, and wanted to know exactly what it was. I was sent to see a doctor, who examined my face, and the suspect cream.

I talked to many different people, all government officials, and all through a translator. They all asked the same thing: 'Why did you come? How did you get here? When did you arrive?'

All day I was there. They asked detailed questions about my family and if I wanted to claim asylum. I told them I had left because my life had been at risk, so yes, I wanted to claim asylum.

It was the first time on my whole journey I had been asked about asylum.

It was strange. The question itself didn't feel comforting – not like I thought it might have. I had expected it to be like being handed a prize at the end of a race, but it didn't feel like that. I was in pain, I was tired and I was bewildered. I knew the process had to be done, but I was too traumatized to answer their questions properly. I had been awake for days and I hadn't had any food for the same length of time.

At least the immigration officials, when I told them my age, just wrote it down and didn't laugh in my face, the way the police had. I asked one man about my brother and whether they could find him for me. He did laugh at that, and told me there were 65,000,000 people in the country – so, no, they couldn't just find him. He didn't even write down his name.

That made me angry. I had seen some people being collected by relatives, so I knew that it must be possible to try to find people. Why could they not at least attempt to find Hazrat for me?

I seemed to spend hours in that waiting room. There was a coffee machine in one corner that squirted black liquid into little brown plastic cups. It was hot, there was plenty of sugar, and it was completely free. I must have had eight cups and it made my head feel a bit funny. But it still didn't make up for the lack of food – I was starving, and no one had offered me anything to eat.

Eventually, someone came to tell me that I was being assigned a social worker, and registered as an asylum seeker. I felt some relief – at least I wasn't being sent home straight away. An official gave me my ID card showing my name and date of birth, and a document showing my illegal entry status in Britain. I was told I had to return to the centre regularly and report in.

Seeing my picture on that ID was strange. There was little sign of the fresh-faced boy I had been just over one year before. My face was scarred and pock-marked, and I was thin and drawn.

But I was proud – I had done it. I was here, and they weren't sending me back – at least, not yet.

Later the same afternoon, a social worker took me to a hotel. I didn't see the others from the banana truck again. I still don't know what happened to them. The hotel was an old Victorian sea-front building. It was nice, clean. The hotel manager showed me to a small single room and told me to take a shower. I didn't need to be asked twice.

As I walked down the hall towards the communal bathroom, carrying a towel, I spotted a pair of shoes neatly placed outside a door. When you've used someone's feet for a pillow, you don't forget their shoes.

My friend Qumandan was there. I had last seen him when he and Jan had gone to try and board a truck the night I had been too tired, and never come back.

I banged on the door. His face broke into a familiar smile the moment it swung open. We hugged. It was so good to see him – and in England too. He told me Jan had been separated from him in the migrant centre, and he didn't know what the authorities had done with him.

That evening, in the hotel, we had long, hot showers and then a big supper of chilli con carne and rice. I slept like a log that night.

In the morning, I felt as though I had been born again.

'Let's go and see England,' Qumandan said, wiping the debris of his breakfast from his mouth with a paper napkin, like a proper English gentleman.

We walked into Dover town centre, following the sea front. The clean sea air felt great on my face – cooling, healing.

We climbed up the chalky cliffs towards the black stone castle that sits high above the town. From our vantage point I could see dozens of ships crisscrossing the English Channel.

It was very strange to see Calais on the horizon and know how much pain there was over there, in the Jungle. It was getting dark now, and I knew that not so far away, thousands of men, women and children would be getting ready to begin their futile, nightly task of trying to cross this unimpressive stretch of water. A shower, clean clothes, freedom and a place to stay. That was all I had, and I felt like a king. Why couldn't everyone have access to something so simple? Why were human beings given as little value as the fleas that bred in the makeshift tents that I had, less than forty-eight hours ago, called home?

Mentally, though, I was still a mess. I still felt completely alone and depressed. I needed my family – I needed to find Hazrat. There was only one way I knew how to do that.

And so, once again, I ran away.

I changed the last of my money – about 100 euros – into British pounds. I found my way to Dover train station and bought a ticket for London. I didn't know where Hazrat was, but I needed to start my search somewhere.

As the train pulled out I felt quietly confident. I had managed to work my way around Rome, Athens and Paris and find people I had a connection to. London couldn't be any different.

When I got to London Bridge station, I had second thoughts. London seemed so impersonal, so big and confusing. But I applied the formula I had used in every other European city I'd passed through: I walked the streets around the station and searched out Afghans, and asked them if they had seen Hazrat Passarlay. They all said the same thing – go to social services.

This made me realize how stupid I had been. There was a system here – I needed to learn how it worked. Walking the streets talking to Afghans was fine when I was trying to locate an agent or a smuggler, but here there was a different way of doing things.

It was time to return to Dover.

When I got back to my hotel, the manager was furious. Understandably.

The next day, a social worker came to see me. She was Eastern European. I hoped the fact that she was a migrant too might make her sympathetic to my situation.

I only knew a few phrases in English, basic questions such as 'What is your name?' – the French police had generally spoken in English to me when they arrested me and I found the language much easier to pick up than Greek, Italian or French. But her English was not much better than mine. I also found her very aggressive and abrupt. She refused to believe I was thirteen, and without proper evidence there was little I could do to persuade her otherwise. She looked at me as though I was something distasteful stuck to the bottom of her shoe. She told me she was from Kent Social Services, and that I needed to be interviewed so they could decide what to do with me. I would also be required to undertake an age-assessment test.

I spent the next few days waiting and worrying, spending time with Qumandan. Each day at the hotel people were interviewed, and often taken away afterwards. Qumandan told me that some went to Appledore, a special unit for migrants deemed to be young enough to be registered as unaccompanied children; other people were put in touch with relatives and allowed to go and stay with them. I wondered what would happen to me.

I was still terrified that I would be deported, and wondered every day what Hazrat was doing.

On the day of the age assessment, my social worker came to collect me. She took me to an office at Kent Social Services. I sat around a table with five different people – some were from social services, some were from Kent County Council, and one was a Pashtu-speaking translator.

They interrogated me for hours. None of them smiled. It was worse than the immigration centre.

Some questions were complete nonsense to me, such as asking me to name streets in Afghanistan. It was almost as if they didn't believe I was Afghan. They asked me the name of the main square in Jalalabad, and I gave them the answers they wanted.

Then the translator explained to me that they felt I was too clever and smart to be thirteen years old – as if correctly answering their stupid questions was evidence of my adulthood.

At the end of the meeting I was sent to a waiting room. After a long while, they called me back. A man with a face that looked as worn and grey as his suit, one of the council people, spoke, and the translator outlined what he was saying.

'Based on this interview, we come to the conclusion that you are sixteen and a half years of age. Therefore your date of birth is the first of May 1991.'

This was crazy, beyond the realms of make-believe. After all I had been though – the cruelty, mistreatment and abuse – to be assigned a new birth date by a committee stranger was more than I could take.

They gave me an age-assessment document with their findings, and my new date of birth on it. I couldn't read what it said, but I could make out the date of birth.

I tore it apart and threw it on the table. 'Thank you very much. I don't want this. You keep it,' I said, scattering the confetti in front of them. The translator relayed what I'd said in English but my actions made it obvious. They all looked completely stunned.

I may have looked older than my years, but what had I just gone through? My face had been very damaged by the burns, giving me a much older appearance and, besides, I had had to grow up fast and learn to act tough. How could these people not understand any of this? Had they not seen the record of my medical examination on arrival at Dover? Did they have no concept of what living outdoors in all weathers on a near-starvation diet might do to a person?

I stormed out in protest. I had no proof to dispute their absurd findings, and common sense wasn't a language these people spoke. I felt that instead of smugglers and agents, I was now in the hands of new strangers, and these bureaucrats were now in control of my life.

To be treated like a liar by this committee of officials was truly soul-destroying. After my outburst, I refused to say another word.

In the face of such stupidity, what did my cooperation count for, anyway?

A few days later, some officials arrived at the hotel.

'Gulwali,' said the manager, two unfamiliar faces standing behind him. 'These men have come to take you to Appledore.'

CHAPTER TWENTY-NINE

Appledore was like a large hostel, with twenty-nine shared bedrooms and a big communal kitchen and sitting room. There were around twenty or so under-sixteens in the building at the time I was there. The majority were Afghans, but there were Africans, Arabs and Kurds. All of them, like me, had travelled alone, without family.

We had care workers looking after us. They were very nice people. My key worker was Scott, the assistant manager of the centre. He was very young and had the ability to make me laugh, but he was so busy it was really hard to get any one-on-one time with him.

It was a very well-equipped place. The rooms were clean and tidy, with modern furniture. There was a table-tennis set and a football pitch outside. They really did try their best for us.

We were also expected to use the time to learn more about the UK. We had classes about British life: its history, monarchy, culture. One video we watched told us the UK was the father of democracy and a big leader in human rights.

We also had life-skills classes, such as time and money management, and how to use public transport. We won brownie points for cleaning our rooms and helping the staff in the kitchen. We used to go shopping for the kitchen – the idea was that we needed to allocate the budget accordingly.

I still preferred the company of older people – maybe my time spent with Baryalai and my other older friends en route had made me this way – so for me, hanging around the staff and offering to stack the dishwashing machine, unpack boxes of supplies or clean the shelves was preferable to talking to the other depressed, sad children like me. I didn't want to be reminded of my own story, let alone hear someone else's. I couldn't cope with it.

We were given a budget for clothes and had to write out lists about what would be appropriate for a particular location or weather. They needed to see that we could work out prices, and decide what was a good buy. It was all designed to ensure we could cope on our own in the UK when we left there. I think it was really useful.

The first time I went shopping was fun. I had been given a clothes allowance from my social worker – I think it was about £100. One of the care workers, Lorraine, took me shopping and helped me choose lots of things. She took me to a very big store she knew about which she said sold bargain goods at the very best prices. She said it was where all sensible English people shopped, but that rich people laughed at these kinds of places.

Inside, I was overwhelmed by all the choice – the shop sold everything, from household cleaning supplies to toys and clothes and bed sheets. We had so much fun as Lorraine helped me cruise the aisles finding discounted items and special offers. We managed to get so much – socks, towels, shirts and jeans. I'd never really had more than one change of clothes, at least since I'd left Afghanistan.

When Lorraine and I got back to the centre, we were both really proud of how much we'd managed to get for our money. I was so grateful to her. It gave me a real sense of achievement – the first I had had since getting here.

I had been there for just over two weeks when Qumandan was sent on from the Dover hotel to Appledore too. It was great to be allowed to share a room with him. He had been through a similar age-assessment process, but he had a different social worker to me, and different people assessing him. They believed him when he said he was fifteen. Eventually, he was sent to a foster family in a town called Hastings, leaving me feeling very alone. Why could I not be fostered too? I was still deeply unhappy about my own age assessment and dispute, but no one was willing to help me challenge it.

One of the things I liked best during my time at Appledore was that every Friday they dropped us at the train station and let us catch a train to Tunbridge Wells, to a local mosque. Meeting other Muslims was so good – a couple were other Afghans or Arabs. But Tunbridge Wells didn't seem like a place with very many immigrants: walking around there, where everyone looked very English indeed, made me feel quite self-conscious. But it was a really pretty town, and I enjoyed looking at the architecture.

Letting us go there on our own was a big deal for the staff – they had to trust us. Perhaps once or twice I considered running away, but I didn't because I really thought that by staying at Appledore I could sort out the age problem with social services, and begin the process of finding my brother. I also liked that I knew my way to the mosque and past a few of the nice sights, and I enjoyed the feeling of proudly showing off my newfound knowledge to some of the other new arrivals.

We even got taken to London, to the National Portrait Gallery. Art was a new thing to me. Images are not Islamic, and photography was banned by the Taliban, so portraits and pictures weren't something I had seen before. I found it a bit strange staring at the faces of people I was told had died hundreds of years before; to be honest, I found it a bit boring. I think, even despite it all, there was a little bit of me at that point that was a typical teenager. I did like the British Museum, though.

Every week we were given £10 pocket money by the care workers, which most people used to call their families. I was so sad that I couldn't do this. We also did community work, helping to clean a nearby steam train centre, and helping Kent County Council environmental agency with planting trees. This I loved. It reminded me of being a child again and cutting branches for the classroom roof. It was good, physical work. I know for sure today that there are fifteen trees in Kent that I planted, and I'm proud of this.

A month into my stay there, and I was beginning to wonder if I would ever leave Appledore. Once again, my mental health was not good – I was feeling isolated, alone. Unfeeling.

One day, I was sitting in the kitchen chatting to a boy called Kiran, a new arrival from Balochistan. He told me he had been arrested and hung from his feet and beaten with small canes. He said he didn't know why this had happened because no one in his family was involved in politics – unlike mine.

I wanted to support Kiran and show that I cared, but I felt only numb. I didn't honestly have the ability or energy to comfort him. I was just wondering how I could walk away without being rude when I heard a voice behind me.

'Gulwali.'

It was Shafique. I leapt from my chair so fast I nearly knocked it over.

Shafique hugged me and whooped so loudly that some residents came to see what was going on. Once we'd calmed down and talked, he told me his story. He'd managed to get across the English Channel by hiding in some kind of metal storage box attached to the side of a lorry. He said he had known it was very dangerous because there would be limited oxygen in the tiny space but, like me, he had reached such a point of desperation by then that he hadn't cared if he lived or died.

I was so happy he'd made it and didn't have to spend the rest of the winter freezing in France. I was still in the grip of despair but having him there helped so much – just knowing someone that I didn't have to explain myself to.

Not long after this, I was told I would have a Home Office interview. I was assigned a legal representative who came to see me at Appledore in advance of the interview, to go through my case. She seemed nice, and didn't argue when I told her how old I was. She seemed to believe me, and so I hoped she'd be able to do something. I also begged her to help me find Hazrat. She said that I needed to talk to the Home Office about this myself, but that she would put a note about it in my file.

By this stage, however, I was so angry and untrusting that I didn't tell her as many details about what had happened to me in Afghanistan as I should have done. Everyone kept asking me the same questions all the time, but it felt to me that no one was really listening, so I think I had just given up. I didn't have the energy to keep going over it.

I was not an adult, and I kept telling them I wasn't, but they were treating me like one. My feelings intensified when I realized that the Home Office had given me an adult interview and not a child's one – one where I would have been treated with more gentleness – because the social services had designated me an adult. I would eventually discover too, that though the Dover Immigration Removal Centre had believed my age in the first place, they had since changed it to be in line with the social services' assessments.

The day I went for my interview I felt sick inside – it took every ounce of motivation I had to make myself go. My feeling was that they wouldn't believe me, so what was the point?

I travelled to a place called Croydon in London for the interview. One of the care workers came with me. Croydon itself felt grey, impersonal and ugly – matching my mood completely. We arrived at a place called Lunar House. It was even more grey – there were queues snaking out of the door, while the scene inside set the tone: there were more long queues, and the sounds of people sobbing or arguing.

I was dismayed to discover my legal representative wasn't there, as she had promised me she would be. One of her colleagues came instead, but he knew hardly anything about me; it was obvious he had only read my notes ten minutes before.

I was taken to a room and, through a translator, I was grilled as though I was a criminal.

If I had thought the social services' assessment was bad, this was a whole different level of awful. It was as if they were deliberately trying to make me feel guilty and humiliated for having dared to come to the UK. I felt victimized and criminalized.

I tried to tell them that I was only thirteen, but a man at the table said, 'Sorry, we are not here to discuss your age today. That has already been done and dealt with.' They then told me that the information I was telling them was new and asked why I hadn't told them these things in my witness statement – a statement I had made for my solicitors. They also said there were differences in the account I had made when I spoke to the immigration centre in Dover.

Maybe there were, but it can hardly be surprising, surely? I had been traumatized: I had just got off a refrigerator lorry after a long journey, I hadn't eaten, and I was in shock. I didn't know then how the system worked, or that you were supposed to remember every key detail at the first interview lest you pay the price for it later. Couldn't they see that if I had made mistakes, they were genuine ones?

I just couldn't speak any more. I started crying, which made me feel even more humiliated. Then one of the men told me to stop acting.

At that I lost it. I started hitting the table, banging and banging it with my fist. No one said anything, they all just stared at me, as if this was also a sign of my criminality.

The whole process was so impersonal, so strange. Telling my life story to strangers was utterly at odds with my culture: we respected each other's privacy – it wasn't even something I had done during my time on the road. Now, here I was having to tell it to a bunch of strangers sitting around a table.

And it wasn't that I didn't want to tell anyone, but that I needed to feel safe and secure to be able to talk. This process was the opposite of that.

At the end of the four-hour interview, they told me they would make a decision on my application for asylum and that I would be informed.

I already knew it was over.

Back at the centre I was so depressed I couldn't function. But more bad news was to come: Shafique had had his age assessment, and they had decided he was eighteen, when in fact he was sixteen. Immediately after his interview he was taken by immigration officials to a detention centre. We didn't even have time to say goodbye to each other.

He remained there for a week and had been told that he would be deported to Afghanistan within thirty days, but he got lucky in the end. He had a very good legal advisor who fought Kent County Council about his age and the Home Office about his detention. The lawyer arranged for a doctor to examine him to reassess his age. The doctor accepted he was just under sixteen, and he was released back to Appledore. He was granted two years' leave to remain in the UK and placed with a foster family in Gillingham.

I was able to visit Shafique there once he got settled, but I don't think he liked it. The family were kind but he and I both got the sense they were doing it for the money, not out of love. Seeing this made me think that maybe it wasn't so bad I hadn't been fostered after all.

My depression could not have been worse at this point. I recalled the children's home in Italy and kind Alexandria, and I began to wish I had stayed there. At least they had treated me more kindly. Added to this, I despaired of ever finding my brother. No one would help me, and in a country of so many people, how did I even begin?

One day I got so angry I walked out of the centre in protest. I made my way to the station in the late afternoon; it was late November, so it was dark when I got there. I got a train to Tunbridge Wells and just walked around. I fully expected to be arrested. I think I had lost my mind. I was like a zombie, suicidal, walking in the middle of the road hoping a car would hit me.

After a few hours of walking around like this, I realized I had nowhere to go. I had to go back to Appledore. I called the centre to tell them I was at the station. One of the care workers answered the phone. If I had wanted understanding I didn't get it.

'Gulwali. I am disgusted at you. We have done so much for you – why are you so ungrateful? We were worried about you.'

When I got back I ran to my room. I couldn't look anyone in the eye. I felt as though I had done something very wrong and felt so guilty. I thought they would all hate me.

'Gulwali, we have lost all respect for you. You have lost the freedoms and privileges you had. Now you are not allowed to leave the centre.'

I understood my actions were wrong, but couldn't they see what a mess my mind was in?

The nightmares I had had in Italy and Greece returned. I would wake screaming, thinking that my bed was on fire, the burning sensation so real that I would run into the bathroom to douse myself in water. Sometimes I got so panicky I couldn't breathe or move; I could only lie on my bed willing myself to calm down. I missed my mother and grandmother so much. I longed for one of them to be there to comfort me in my night terrors, to hold me and tell me it was OK, that it was only a bad dream. Instead, I had to tell myself that. I was my only comfort.

A couple of days later, the others went on a day trip to London to the London Eye. I wasn't allowed to go as punishment for my escapade. I accepted why I couldn't go, but it made me feel even worse.

For the first time, I felt really suicidal. At Calais, I hadn't cared whether I lived. Now I wanted to die. Really die.

I was in my room when they all came back.

'Gulwali, open the door.' One of the other residents was banging on my bedroom door. I ignored him – the last thing I wanted to hear was about their fun trip. 'Gulwali. We need to tell you something.'

'Go away, leave me alone.' I hated the world, hated them all. I didn't want to see anyone. I just wanted the world to end. Life had no purpose for me any more.

He knocked again.

'Gulwali. We just met your brother. We found Hazrat.'

CHAPTER THIRTY

The next day my dreams came true. I was shaking as the care worker handed me the phone. I couldn't breathe.

'Gulwali?'

I started to sob. After that, it became a blur. Hazrat was almost hysterical with joy, babbling and blurting out his story. He told me he'd never given up hope and had shown my passport picture, the one the agent had given him in Peshawar, to everyone he met on the road.

He had arrived in England six months ago, and was living near Manchester. He was taking English language lessons at college and working in a shop. He was living with a friend, and had been granted two years' leave to remain as an asylum seeker.

Neither of us could believe the coincidence of how he'd found me. He had been in London on a college trip, walking along the South Bank. He and his friends had seen some fellow Afghans by the London Eye – my friends from Appledore. They had chatted and, during the conversation, one of the Appledore people had said there was a boy in the centre who looked just like him. Hazrat had asked the name of the boy and when they told him he began screaming, 'That's my little brother. That's my little brother.'

His social worker arranged for him to visit me a few days later. I was so nervous. Would my brother be the same person? I wondered if the indignities and traumas we had both suffered had changed him.

I hardly recognised him. He was so grown up. As he wrapped me in his arms I couldn't help tease my big brother, just as I had always done: 'Hey, you got fat. How did that happen?'

We spent the day together sharing stories of our journeys. His had been very similar to mine, with lots of going backwards and forwards, but he had spent less time in Istanbul and more in Greece. We also cried together as we thought of our family back in Afghanistan.

After he left, I thought my heart was going to break all over again. All I could think of now was two things: getting out of Appledore to be with him, and convincing the Home Office I was only thirteen. But bad news was to come.

I had been refused asylum.

I had initially been granted discretionary leave to remain for a year, starting from my arrival date of 17 November 2007, due to expire in November 2008. Then, as a result of the incorrect birth date they had given me, they told me I would be seventeen and therefore I would have to leave the country or be deported.

I was relieved to be able to stay for a year at least – it was better than nothing – but I was still so very angry that the age that was being forced on me was still the same.

And it had got worse – the latest documents given to me stated: 'Nationality Unknown.'

How could they say that?

The worst blow came when I was refused permission to stay with Hazrat, and told I had to stay in Kent.

The one piece of good news I received at this time was in March 2008, when I was given a new social worker. She was Iranian by descent, so we could communicate in Farsi as well as in my broken English. That helped. I also felt culturally comfortable with her.

I felt the social worker before her may have been a bit racist, and that was why she had been so abrupt with me. Nassi was more supportive, but even she said my situation wasn't good and that I would probably be deported.

Through her, social services found me a flat in Gravesend in an accommodation block with other asylum seekers. Mine was nice: a modern, two-bedroom flat. The other occupant was also Afghan, in his late twenties, but he seemed to see me as an annoyance and pretty much ignored me. Living there was noisy, because some of the others played music all night long, and my loneliness intensified. So did the nightmares.

My flatmate thought my night-time screaming was deliberate and complained about me to Nassi. The humiliation of being told off for something I couldn't help was the final straw; I had reached my limit.

The next day I calmly walked into a pharmacy and bought a bottle of paracetamol.

Then I swallowed them all.

CHAPTER THIRTY-ONE

My flatmate found me unconscious and called an ambulance. At the hospital they gave me something to make me vomit up the pills. My stomach, which had suffered so much already, was in agony as I heaved and retched time and again, vomiting up green bile into a bucket. The hospital staff were kind to me, and I appreciated it.

I stayed there a few days before being sent back home on my own. My lonely life continued.

I had no schooling, no work. Days just ran into endless, boring, lonely days. I bought a few books from the local charity shop and used the time to try and improve my English. I also read the Quran, something which always gave me comfort.

Nassi got me into North West Kent College on a part-time basis to study English, two days a week. I showed the teachers my first ID, which said I was thirteen, telling them I shouldn't be there and that I should be in school instead. But again, they said they couldn't help me.

I attended the college for a couple of months. The other students were, of course, older – all college age – but they too were struggling to adapt to life there. A couple of them were drinking heavily to quell the boredom, or maybe it was a way of self-medication to numb the trauma. One stopped coming to college suddenly, and we heard he'd been arrested for assaulting someone.

I think that after having grown up in a rigid cultural system like mine, it can be very tough for new arrivals to cope with the sudden social freedoms that Britain offers. And with no money, it's hard to keep busy. I received a young person's allowance of £94 per fortnight, with which I had to buy everything I needed, including bus fares to college. I was good at budgeting and I had learned to be a bargain hunter by seeking out special offers and discounted food in the supermarket, but it was still a struggle.

I was lucky to have friends. Shafique studied with me at the same college, and came over to visit me often, and that helped, but it had got to the point where I couldn't cope. I missed my brother so much. Being in the same country as him after all this time but not being near him was torture.

I used all of my allowance and bought myself a train ticket to Manchester. Once there, I called my social worker, Nassi, and said I wasn't coming back.

'You have to. You are registered in Kent. This will cause big problems for you. Go and visit your brother by all means, but if you don't come back I will report you as missing.'

I couldn't see how it could get worse.

I decided that if no one was going to help me, then I had to help myself. In Manchester, I literally walked into a couple of local schools and asked them to accept me. They said their hands were tied and they couldn't. Once again, I realized that this country has systems; systems I needed to understand before I could challenge them.

Proving my date of birth was the first step.

Hazrat and I went to the Afghan embassy in London. I applied for a new passport, giving them my immigration ID card as evidence – the very first one which had my real age on it. I also had to get letters from two other people who could verify who I was and how old I was.

When I got the passport I sent it to the Home Office as proof, but my plan backfired. The Home Office asked, if I was an asylum seeker, why I was going to my national embassy? But that was a silly question in my case – I hadn't been persecuted by my government (as many refugees from other places have been, causing them to leave their country and ask for asylum elsewhere). In my case, it had been a combination of the Taliban and the American military which had forced me to flee.

While I was in Manchester, some of my brother's friends told me about a place called Starting Point, in nearby Bolton. It was a special educational centre for children who had just arrived in the UK, offering intensive education in basic subjects and English language support.

I took the bus to Bolton and went there.

The head teacher, a woman called Katy Kellett, agreed to see me. As I sat in her office drinking a hot chocolate, a feeling of calm washed over me. She made me feel instantly safe as I explained to her my situation, and the age dispute.

The next words she said changed everything for me: 'Gulwali, I believe you. You can come here to study.'

She told me age disputes like mine happened all the time, especially to young asylum seekers in Kent. I could barely contain my joy as she asked the secretary to print me a letter confirming my place there, and get me a new uniform from the school shop.

I was told I could start the next day.

Mrs Kellett also promised she would contact Nassi and sort everything out. Her kindness was overwhelming. She then spoke to Manchester Social Services on my behalf and asked them to transfer my care from Kent to them. But they said they couldn't, telling her that they had had bad experiences of dealing with Kent in the past and wouldn't get involved. Eventually, I was allowed to stay in Manchester, but I was still officially under the care of Kent

– it was very confusing.

Mrs Kellett was successful in persuading Kent Social Services to get me a place to stay in Manchester. Hazrat had been living with friends, and they had got sick of me being there too. She arranged for me to stay in a place called Bedspace in Hulme, in the south of Manchester. It was similar to the first independent living accommodation in Gravesend – shared flats in a block, and this time my flatmate was a Kashmiri man in his thirties. Because the Home Office were still insisting I was sixteen and not thirteen, I had to be housed with adults. I had to catch two buses to get to Starting Point each day, but that didn't bother me. I was just so happy to be able to go there.

The year 2008 came to an end, and with it passed my fourteenth birthday. For the first time in two years I was beginning to feel like a child again. Starting Point made me school captain, which made me so proud.

The other children there were from all over the world: some were asylum seekers, others were from families who had moved to the UK to work. The numbers attending the place fluctuated, sometimes it was fifty, sometimes as few as ten. Starting Point became my family. Aside from Mrs Kellett, I had a teacher called Chris Brodie. I loved sitting at the front of her class and raising my hand to ask questions.

'Gulwali, can you keep quiet for just two minutes and let the other children ask a question for once,' she teased, smiling at my enthusiasm. But I was so determined to learn and to soak up every minute. During break times she used to make me toast and tea and sit and chat with me. I liked her and Mrs Kellett so much – the two of them did so much for me.

Once a week, Starting Point pupils visited a local old people's home. I enjoyed it because I loved elderly people – they reminded me of my grandparents. I felt so sad for these old people who had to live there, away from their families. Some had no family at all.

I think, during this time, I was overwhelmed by it all. After all the battles to survive, I couldn't quite cope with the fact that my life was now improving. At night I still woke in sweats and tears as the nightmares gripped my soul.

I tried to kill myself again.

This time I very nearly succeeded; Hazrat only found me because he came round to visit unexpectedly. He rang 999 and I was rushed to hospital.

As he cried by my bedside, he made me swear I would never do something so silly again. 'Did we go through all this just so you could die on me, Gulwali? What will I do if I lose you?'

I was so unhappy, I probably would have tried to kill myself again. But my mother's voice saved me. One of Hazrat's friends had been deported back to Afghanistan, and promised to make contact with our family. He emailed me with a mobile phone number for her, and we were able to speak, for the first time in two years. Just hearing her voice changed everything.

Starting Point went into battle for me over my age dispute. They observed me in the classroom and carried out their own age assessment on me. They told both Kent Social Services (who I was still listed with) and the Home Office that, in their view, I was a child of fourteen.

I was by now Starting Point's longest-serving pupil. Most kids came there for about six weeks, until they got a place at a local school. The whole idea of the centre was to immerse children in education and English language before they moved into mainstream schooling. But until I could prove I was fourteen, no school in the area could take me.

'You will stay here with us until we work this out, Gulwali. If you stay two years then so be it, but we will not let you down,' Mrs Kellett told me.

She and Mrs Brodie were the only two adults I believed and trusted.

Thanks to them I was able to secure a new interview to discuss my claim for asylum and to appeal the decision to reject me. My social worker, Nassi, from Kent was there, but the interview was carried out by Bolton Social Services.

The meeting was a similar format to the ones I had attended before: five officials sitting around a table with a translator to ask me questions. But this time it could have not have felt more different. This time I had people on my side. Nassi and Mrs Kellet were there, and an advocate from the charity, Action for Children.

After the meeting, Nassi went back to Kent to file a new report. By now she had my birth certificate and Afghan passport. Kent spoke to Starting Point, saying they were prepared to concede I was younger than they had previously said, but that they wanted me to accept I was born in 1992 not 1994, making me just under sixteen. It was crazy. How could I accept it? That was not my true age. But I found it funny now, and not so upsetting. This new offer meant things were at least beginning to move in the right direction.

Finally, after a lot of back and forth and pushing from Starting Point, Kent Social Services officially reassessed my age, and accepted what I had told them from the beginning: that my birthday was 11 October 1994. The Home Office also then wrote to me saying that they would reconsider my case.

It was like being born again – the happiest day of my life. And not long after that, Hazrat was allowed to become my legal guardian and we were able to rent a house together in Bolton.

Starting Point started to try to find me a school. I was sad to leave the place that had become my sanctuary but I was delighted to finally be allowed to go to a proper school. I was interviewed by Essa Academy in Bolton, by Mr Khaliq.

'Do you think you can cope with this, Gulwali?' he asked. I already knew him because I had seen him at Starting Point. He always used to joke with me that I'd come to his school one day but that I wasn't to expect treats like the tea and toast Mrs Brodie made for me.

'Yes, I do.'

There were only two months left of the academic year. I asked them to put me into year 9, the academic year below my actual age group so I could try and use that time to catch up.

When year 10 began, all of the other pupils were choosing their GCSE subjects. I was very frustrated to be told my English wasn't good enough for me to be allowed to sit any exams; instead, I was placed in entry-level groups in maths, science, English and other basic subjects. I was also working towards a certificate in care and social work. The school said that without any other qualifications, that would be one of the only future career routes open to me.

The hardest thing about starting mainstream school was making friends. I had gone from a centre with a maximum of fifty pupils to a school with 1,000 pupils. The other children scared me. I couldn't understand why some of them didn't want to learn and messed about instead, being rude to the teachers. I also hated sports and especially loathed getting changed in front of everyone during PE. That was a culturally difficult thing for me to do, and I cringed red with embarrassment as I put on my PE kit, the other boys laughing at my discomfort.

One of my favourite moments was a school geography trip to Scafell Pike, the highest mountain in England. We climbed it. As the other children huffed and puffed and moaned, I strode up like a champion. After so many mountain crosses and treks on my journey, it was a breeze.

CHAPTER THIRTY-TWO

Slowly but surely, I settled in and made friends. I was still living with Hazrat. I threw myself into school life and activities, doing my Duke of Edinburgh bronze and silver certificates. As part of this I learnt to swim, which was a huge challenge for me after nearly drowning. After six months of year 10 my English had vastly improved. I went to see the head teacher and persuaded him to let me sit my GCSEs.

'OK, Gulwali, you can take them but don't be disappointed if you fail them.'

I chose IT, maths, Urdu, religious studies and geography, as well as the core subjects of English, maths and science.

I had come so far but I wasn't there yet. I had stayed in touch with my friend Mrs Brodie from Starting Point; I visited her once a week, and she cooked me dinner. Her family – her husband and two sons – were lovely to me and I loved going there to see them all. One son was a keen rugby player. I told him I wanted to learn how to play it but that I didn't want to get hurt.

'Gulwali, I love your enthusiasm, but if you don't want to get hurt and you hate changing in front of the other boys –' he laughed – 'I don't think rugby is the sport for you.'

In the second year of my GCSEs I started struggling again. The subjects were hard and my depression was eating away inside me.

I decided to try and help myself stay positive by doing something positive for others.

The school appointed me the school ambassador for international arrivals. I had been one of those lost, scared children from a foreign land, and I knew how hard it was to fit in. I could assist them. With the help of my teachers, we devised a school plan to give extra moral and academic support to the arrivals, ensuring that immigrant pupils would swim not sink when they got there.

The plan worked so well that other schools in the area copied it. That made me so proud. I also became a member of the school council and pupil volunteer librarian. For me that was a joy: I would much rather spend my free time in a library than anywhere else.

In October 2010, when I turned sixteen, Hazrat and I had very bad news. Our mother was being threatened and was in danger. We both felt so helpless, in the end Hazrat decided he had to risk going back.

'What if something happens to her or the little ones Gulwali? How will I live with myself?' he pleaded with me. I was distraught. Social services were still officially responsible for me, and they wanted me to either to return to Kent, or to be placed in foster care.

I had been desperate to be in foster care the year I had arrived, when I was scared and alone, but now I was a star pupil, and I had friends. I had learned to live on my own, yet they were insisting I couldn't because I was still at school.

In December 2010, Mrs Brodie drove me to meet a potential foster family. Their house was a large, former vicarage in the countryside near Bolton.

'It's the middle of nowhere,' I complained. 'Let's just not bother going.'

As gently encouraging as ever, Mrs Brodie insisted we at least go and meet the family before I made my decision.

It was very cold and snowing heavily on the day she drove me there. I had by now been living by myself for two months, without Hazrat and with no heating. I think it was the cold that made me agree to go and look at a foster family.

They were a married couple called Sean and Karen. They had a son of their own, who was grown up and lived away from home. They also had two other foster children, a boy and a girl, both British.

As Sean showed me around the house and where I might sleep, I was polite but firm: 'Thank you, but I am not coming.'

I was still insisting that I be allowed to live on my own. But Mrs Brodie knew me well enough by now to know I was my own worst enemy at times. She badgered away at me until she convinced me to give it a try.

Just before Christmas, I moved in. What I couldn't get my head around was that Sean was cooking the dinner, not Karen. I had changed so much and had my eyes opened to the world, but in some places, deep inside, I was still the same conservative village boy I had always been. I struggled to understand why any married man would cook when he had a wife. I thought this made Sean less of a man and, rudely, I didn't want to eat his food.

But that night, as he made sure I settled in, I was touched to see they had bought me a desk for my room. It was old, made of solid oak. I ran my fingers over it, thinking what a nice gesture it was.

The next night I ate Sean's food and told him it was delicious. I meant it. He offered to give me cooking lessons, which I accepted. Over the coming weeks he showed me how to cook curries, and Italian and Mexican food. He explained to me that he did all the cooking because he loved it and because Karen, or Aunty Karen as I called her out of respect, worked very long hours. He said marriage was about partnership and about being a team. As I observed Sean and Karen, who seemed very happy and in love, I began to think differently. I began to see that my views were borne of a different culture, a culture I still loved and believed passionately in, but that it was not how people lived here. I respected that. And I got it.

I continued studying hard, and Sean helped me. One night, not long after I moved in, I handed him a piece of paper with a time-table on it: 'Here you are. This is my homework schedule.'

'This is for you, right? You want me to help you stick to it?'

'No, it's for you. These are the times I need you to help me with my homework.'

He laughed so hard I thought he might fall off his chair. 'Gulwali, this is a first. I've never had a foster kid give *me* my homework schedule before.'

Living with Sean and Karen really helped me to settle at school and into life in Britain. I had love, warmth, and people to speak to each evening.

By now, I was in year 11, and about to sit my GCSEs. I was made an ambassador for the whole of Essa Academy, a prefect, a school councillor – I threw myself into school life and I felt that I really belonged.

I surprised my teachers with my GCSE results: I got an A in Urdu, and Bs and Cs in the other subjects. My head teacher, Mr Badat, couldn't believe that I had managed a C in GCSE English; I was the only person in all of my core subject classes to get a C or above in everything. When I received a B in maths, having covered the whole syllabus in six weeks, the head of maths, Mr Hussein, named our year 'Gulwali's Year'.

There were two other staff members who really helped me: Mrs Reid, one of the directors, and Mrs Bolton, the PA to the principal. They were really proud when they saw my results.

In September 2011, I moved to Bolton College to take my A levels in politics, economics, philosophy and Urdu. I also took an extended research project in the issues young refugees face around education.

I pursued my political activism outside school, too, becoming a regional advocate for children in care, mainly refugees. I stood for the UK youth parliament election. I lost but, as a result of it, I was asked to join the National Scrutiny Group, recruited by the British Youth Council, which had been set up to advise the government on policy and how it affected young people. I was one of only fifteen young people nationally on the panel. I also joined the youth wing of the Labour party.

I don't know how or why I was so driven at that point – it was just my way of giving back to British society. I had been given so much from the UK, I wanted to do something in return for my new country. And I also wanted to help other young people. I knew what it was like to have no one. I knew that, after all my awful experiences, I didn't want to waste a single second. And I wanted to suck up every opportunity, every chance that came my way.

On my weekends I attended an access course at Manchester University. It was designed to help get young people from disadvantaged backgrounds into top universities. If I passed that, it would add to my entry score. I was worried I might not get the grades I needed to follow my dream of studying politics, so it was my way of ensuring I got the place I wanted.

In October 2012, I turned eighteen. I was now an adult in the eyes of the state and so I was no longer able to stay with Sean and Karen. It was time to move on again. I was given independent accommodation in Bolton town centre.

I had spent two years with Sean and Karen and didn't want to leave; it had been the happiest time in my life since I'd left home. But they remained very supportive and encouraged me to continue with my studies.

In the end, my A level grades were better than expected: I was thrilled with one A and two Bs. I also got an A star for my extended study project on refugees, and was awarded a sixth-form excellence award. Not bad for a boy who just four years earlier had spoken only a few words of English and came to England in the back of a banana lorry.

And then, finally, came the news I had been waiting for: I had won my appeal. I had been granted asylum. I wept with joy as, hands trembling, I read the letter over and over again.

We have a saying in Pashtu: '*Pa jamoo kai na zaydam.*' It roughly translates as: 'Feeling too big for our clothes due to pride.'

A full five years after that boat nearly capsized, I stood in Burnley town hall with my foster parents, Karen and Sean, by my side. I had clean, fresh clothes now, and I was definitely feeling too big for them. I, the once scrawny refugee, had been selected to carry the 2012 Olympic torch through Britain ahead of the London Olympic Games.

Mrs Brodie, who by now I was so close to I called 'Mummy number two', had suggested I apply to do it: 'Well, what have we got to lose, Gulwali?'

I loved how she always referred to me as 'we'. It made me feel special, loved.

When I learned I had been selected I was so proud I thought I might burst, but also felt incredibly humbled.

The day had begun early, with a forty-five-minute drive from Sean and Karen's home in Bolton, to meet the rest of the Olympic relay team. The streets were lined with people cheering and waving flags. At that moment, I don't think I could have loved my adopted country more. It was a day when Britons of all ages came together as one.

As I set off, Karen warned me to walk slowly and savour the moment. Police were on all sides of me, the crowd ecstatic. I tried to walk slowly but in my excitement I was bouncing along. I kissed my torch, beaming with pride, with love, with recognition that this life-changing moment was one of the most special things I would ever do. At so many times on my journey to freedom I had felt hopeless, despondent and afraid. Many times I considered giving up and going home. But at those moments of weakness one thought had kept me going: my mother sent me away to save my life.

My mother sent me away so she didn't have to bury another person whom she loved. In doing so, she had made the ultimate sacrifice any mother could ever make.

As I ran through the streets of my adopted second home, the torch burning brightly, with people cheering and taking photos, I thought only of one thing – her.

At that moment I knew, beyond all doubt, that I hadn't failed her. I had made it.

EPILOGUE

There is another Pashtu saying: 'There is not enough time in this life for love – I wonder how people find time for hate?'

I could all too easily have lived a life of hate. I was twelve years old when my father and grandfather were massacred. All I cared about, loved, respected and was influenced by was torn away from me in a single instant.

It would have been easier for me to choose anger. It's in my genes. As a Pashtu, the notions of honour and family are at the heart of my identity. We are attached to the concept of revenge and blood feuds, which can go on for generations.

And then other men, soldiers from both sides of a conflict I was too young to understand, wanted to use my brother Hazrat and me as pawns in their game of war. Whichever side we would have chosen to work with, the result would have been the same – in all probability we'd be dead, and more people would have died with us. My mother would have had to bury more of her loved ones, more families would have wailed in grief, and my country would be no further along the road to peace.

Violence begets violence.

The choice to go away was not mine; it was my mother's. She proved her wisdom beyond doubt when she sent my brother and me to Europe. She knew that, were we to stay, the outcome would have been bloody and ugly – not a thing of beauty, honour or justice. Yet, so many times, in my most desperate and loneliest moments, I was left bewildered, despairing and angry at her decision, my childhood a brutal game of survival. So many times on that awful journey I nearly didn't make it – jumping from the speeding train, coming so close to drowning in Greece, on those endless treks without food or water when my young, exhausted body wanted to give up and fade into blackness.

In part, I was saved by the warmth and kindness of the friends I made who looked out for me. More than anything, this book is about faith, hope and optimism. I hope too that it is about dedication and commitment towards fellow human beings. A story of kindness, love, humanity and brotherhood.

Baryalai, the kind and lovely man who truly took this lost child under his protective wing, did make it to the UK. We found each other again in 2008 and we met up a few times. We lost contact about three years ago. He simply disappeared, and I fear he may have been deported or gone into hiding. His is one of the few names in the book that remains unchanged because I hope he will somehow read this, and that through his doing so, we may meet again.

Mehran, the constant joker who kept me going with his humour, lives in Greater Manchester and works in hospitality. He's doing just fine.

Sadly, I haven't seen or heard from Abdul, the fourth member of my original group, since the day I escaped from the police prison bus in Iran. I don't know if he made it to safety or not.

Nor have I seen Shah or Faizal since the day they were put into a separate vehicle from us, in Turkey.

Tamim reached the UK in 2009 but I last saw him in 2012, and I don't know how he is now. I fear he may also have been deported.

Jawad I haven't seen in person since he was left behind in the *musafir khanna* in Istanbul, but we are in contact by email. He made it as far as Greece, where he now lives and works.

Hamid, ever the smart one, lives in London. He is also at university, studying to be a doctor, and I know he will go on to be a high achiever one day. He and his friend Ahmad arrived in the UK at the same time, having managed to stay together since I got into the back of a truck in Greece and they did not.

Ahmad also lives in London and is awaiting the final Home Office decision on whether he will be allowed to stay in the UK.

Jan, Qumandan and Engineer also made it here. I last saw Engineer in Manchester, in 2009. He had done OK and was studying at college, but then the Home Office refused his claim for asylum and he left Britain.

Qumandan currently lives in Kent and also continues to fight the Home Office for the right to stay here.

Shafique arrived in the UK one month after me and we were reunited in the Appledore immigration centre for unaccompanied children. We are still very close friends but, as yet, he does not have a final decision from the Home Office, and I am trying to help support him with that.

Hazrat returned from Afghanistan in 2014. He hadn't been able to protect my mother because a few weeks after getting back he had been kidnapped and forced to go to a Taliban training camp. He had managed to escape and somehow made our terrible journey all over again. It took its toll and he's not the same boy he once was. We share a house once again, he works long hours in a restaurant and now it's me who tries to look after him.

I call my mother once a week. But perhaps the hardest thing of all that I have been through is that when we talk, we have so little understanding of each other. I try to talk to her about my political work, my university exams and my campaigning, but my life here in Britain is like a different planet from our old life in Afghanistan.

By sending me away, she definitely saved her son, but she also lost him. She, of everyone, paid the heaviest price. But she will always remain my inspiration, as will my beloved grandmother, who passed away a couple of years ago. We were able to speak on the phone when she was dying. She told me she loved me, and I her. I ached to be able to hold her and stroke her hair as she breathed her last. In 2015 my little sister also passed away. To not be there at a loved one's funeral is one of the most agonising pains for any refugee.

Hopefully the opportunities and education I have been given here will allow me to get a job with something like the United Nations. I am currently studying politics at the University of Manchester. From that position, I hope to begin a slow reverse journey back home. If it becomes safe enough for me, I want to return to Afghanistan so I can help to rebuild it.

I truly believe faith and fate brought me to this land, and I want to thank Great Britain from the bottom of my heart. I have done all I can to give back to it since I got the opportunity to do so. Through my political activism and community volunteering I hope I have helped to improve other young people's lives and to help the public understand the plight of refugees and asylum seekers.

Ultimately, that is why I wanted to write this book.

But there are some days, even now, when I wake up after a particularly bad nightmare and it's all I can do to get through the day. The nightmares will never leave me; nor will the memories of those I have lost, nor the faces of the terrified and vulnerable migrants I met on the road. Did the tiny little girl in the blue bobble hat I saw on the mountain crossing into Turkey ever reach safety? I have no idea who she was or what war-torn country her family had fled from, but her tear-stained, grubby face and scared eyes are for ever seared into my soul.

On those days hate, bitterness and anger whisper my name, their tentacles stirring in my core, willing me to succumb to their poison. It would be so easy for me to do so. And that is when I must fight *jihad*.

Jihad as 'holy war' is one of the most manipulated concepts in Islam today. A false and twisted version of it has been used by terrorists acting in the name of Islam to commit violent acts, aimed at the indiscriminate killing of innocent people.

The literal meaning of *jihad* is 'struggle' or 'effort' – the holy war within oneself.

I suppose you can call this the battle within all of us: it is a fight we all must fight in different ways – whatever faith we may come from.

I fight my *jihad* so that I can go on loving.

The enemy of love is not hate, it is indifference. The enemy of love is turning away from those in need. The enemy of love is doing nothing when you can help your fellow man.

The refugee crisis, the greatest global crisis since World War II, has been caused by conflict, wars, poverty, injustice and oppression. It is our moral duty to treat these fleeing human beings with dignity and respect. We cannot shy away from the fact that recent wars in Iraq, Libya, Syria or Afghanistan have exacerbated this crisis. Nor can we pretend that the Western desire to buy cheap products or possess the latest must-have items at a bargain price does not contribute to poverty and inequality.

True freedom and democracy demand that people educate themselves about the world around them. That requires an honest and inquisitive mind – one that questions all opinions, yet hates none. If a person wishes to be free then they must understand the shackles that bind them. The internet, and the age of social media, makes the dissemination of ideas very easy. There is no way we can turn back the clock on this reality; instead, we must learn to live with it. It can be empowering, or it can be destructive. Causes are powerful – and now they travel vast distances instantly.

Many extremists are drawn by the romantic notion of fighting, and maybe even dying, for a righteous cause. Perhaps that's why young people from every walk of life are at risk of radicalization: whether they are a frustrated white male who walks into a black congregation and starts shooting at innocent people, a desperate Somali fisherman's son who opens fire in a Kenyan mall, or a French schoolgirl born of migrant parents who resents the strictures of life and seeks adventure and fulfilment in what she believes is the exciting new world offered by the false prophets of the so-called Islamic State – a group of people who in no way represent Islam.

Assumed thinking creates assumed responses. Our world is a fast-changing place – but more and more people are becoming entrenched in the same mind-set as previous generations. I don't see how this can be helpful.

My journey nearly killed me, and it left mental, physical and emotional scars that I will bear for the rest of my life. Those moments that I was at my lowest, when I felt as though I could not keep going – those truly painful moments when death seemed the only solution – those moments almost entirely coincided with periods when I struggled to move forward. And so it is in life.

I have had so many great friends on my journey who have helped me, and continue to do so. None of us travel alone in life. We all have the power to help those around us, or to harm them. It is the choices we make that define our walk, define our own personal journeys and make us the people we are.

I want to thank you for reading my book and for being a part of my journey. Truly. Thank you. But please don't change the world for me. Do it for the other children out there alone in the world, lost, afraid and trying to find safety. Do it for the mothers who would rather send their children into the unknown than to see them die of starvation or from bombs raining from the sky. Do it so that no other child has to wake up to another lightless sky in the way I did.

If I have one single dream it is this: that a child in the future will read this book and ask, 'What was a refugee?'

We can change the world. All of us together. We can.

We can end this.

ACKNOWLEDGEMENTS

I would like to thank everyone who has helped me along my life journey. But special thanks go to:

All those I travelled with who helped to keep me safe. The staff at the children's home in Italy who tried so hard to help me. My social worker Nassi; and my caseworker Ryan and all at Greater Manchester Immigration Aid Unit who represented my asylum claim at the Home Office. Zia, my support worker at Kent County Council, who was so supportive and helpful. All the teachers at Starting Point but especially Katy Kellett for believing in me and fighting for me; and Chris Brodie, my mentor, best friend and second mother. Thanks to all the staff at Essa Academy, in particular Mr Badat, Mrs Reid and Mrs Grills for helping me find my political and campaigning voice. Also Mrs Bolton, who I always went to whenever I felt down and upset. Thanks to everyone at Bolton Sixth Form College, in particular Mr Hindle and Mr Ivory, who both taught and encouraged me. And to all at the University of Manchester, especially Dr Julian Skyrme. To Kath Evans at NHS England, who has been an inspiration. To Ciara Steele at Bolton Children's Services, who first got me involved in youth representation work. To the various youth workers and organizers I have met through different committees, commissions, forums and groups – you are amazing. To Julie Hilling MP and others, for their letters in support to the Home Office.

Thank you to Roya, for all your emotional and moral support, and to Sahrish, for your friendship, thoughtfulness and admiration.

I am for ever indebted to my wonderful foster parents, Sean and Karen, for their warmth, love and support, and for allowing me to share their home and family.

To the inspirational Nadene Ghouri, without whom I wouldn't have written this book. Her passion and enthusiasm kept me going to the end, helping me through the stress and pain. Thanks also to her husband, Sam Robertson, and everyone at Gladstone's Library for nurturing us during the writing process.

Finally, thanks to my lovely agent, Brandi Bowles, and everyone at Atlantic for believing in this book and making it a reality.

There are so many others who have been a part of my journey. I am sorry if your name isn't here, but I hope you know who you are and how important you are to me. I am in debt to so very many people.

CO-AUTHOR'S NOTE

Making his journey over the course of a year, and through eight countries, Gulwali saw more and suffered more than any twelve-year-old child should.

He is not alone. Today more than half the world's refugees are children.

In 2014, there were 23,100 asylum applications made in the twenty-eight European Union member states by unaccompanied minors (defined as persons under the age of eighteen who enter without an adult, be it a parent or guardian).

As we wrote this book, in the summer of 2015, a UNHCR Global Trends report, 'World at War', revealed shocking new statistics which showed that the worldwide displacement of people is at its highest level ever recorded. By the end of 2014, 59.5 million men, women and children had been forcibly displaced by persecution, conflict, generalized violence or human rights violations. That is one in every 122 people globally.

If this number of people was a country, it would be the world's twenty-fourth biggest nation. Around a third of these people have fled their home countries and are refugees.

The reasons why people flee the countries they come from may shift and shape at any given time. What does not alter is the way in which people smugglers operate. It is perhaps simplest to describe the business of smuggling by looking at its structures as though it is a corporation:

At the top level are powerful yet rarely seen national agents, the 'CEOs', men who control smuggling in certain countries. They use a variety of aliases. Gulwali only knew his as Qubat. His family only met Qubat once and paid US$8,000 – the amount agreed to get Gulwali as far as Italy. Money was lodged with a third party agreed upon by both sides, and only after Gulwali made it across each border was the next tranche of money paid to Qubat. Agents at this level build repeat business by reputation: it is not in their interests to cheat or to fail. But it must be pointed out that had Gulwali died along the way, no refund would have been given, and payment would still have been required to be made to Qubat in full. I have in the past interviewed many families with dead children for whom this was the case.

Underneath this are the regional agents – the men who control a certain area of a country, akin to senior management level. Malik, the besuited and briefcase-carrying man Gulwali met in Turkey would fall under this category. Men like Malik, who also owned the brothel where Gulwali briefly stayed, are very often where the cross-over between smuggling and trafficking collides, profiteering from both.

Migrant smuggling – reportedly a $7 billion global industry today – is defined by the UN and Amnesty International as 'procurement for financial or other material benefit of illegal entry of a person into a state of which that person is not a national or resident'. On the other hand, human trafficking is characterized by exploiting another human being against their will. The UN definition of human trafficking includes the recruiting, transporting or harbouring of people by means of force.

The next level on the rung is effectively middle management: the guest-house owners or men who can offer specialist logistical solutions, such as a fleet of cars. Black Wolf falls into this category.

Underneath that is the operational level, the myriad networks of smugglers, boat captains and drivers who are paid to move people from place to place. This is where things become increasingly unstable and most often go wrong, and where migrants can be at their most vulnerable.

At the very bottom of the smuggling business are people like Serbest, the man who provided Gulwali with a horse and guided him over the border into Turkey for the second time. Gulwali has a great deal of sympathy for many of the people he met who worked at this level, because so often they were fighting to survive in situations of great povery and conflict in a way not dissimilar from himself.

Names and certain details throughout the book have been changed to protect identities and some characters have been omitted. We have sought to be as accurate as possible, but it must be stated that these are the sometimes hazy memories of a twelve-year-old child. Dates and times blurred into one another on the road. Gulwali had a sense of the months based on the weather, but his journey took him from high mountain passes to stifling basements, making it hard for him to tell at times.

What are described as detention centres in the book may have been prisons, and vice versa. Often it simply wasn't clear to him where he was being kept, only that he was incarcerated. Many of the support services that were available to Gulwali in the UK no longer exist due to cuts. Starting Point has closed down.

Gulwali, like most Afghans, is a natural linguist and picks up phrases quickly. As he says: 'I had to, in order to survive.' His English developed rapidly because it is the common language used across Europe by many police and officials in their attempts to communicate with migrants. However, at certain points within the book, we have taken small liberties with his understanding of language in order to maintain the narrative.

We simply could not include every story, every voice or every person he met along the way, as much as we would have liked to. There were many characters who sadly remain unheard or unwritten about. Above all else, Gulwali and, I hope, this book will give voice and a human face to the refugee crisis. The very fact that this book exists ensures that these people have not been forgotten.

At the time of writing – August 2015 – over 2,000 men, women and children are known to have drowned in the Mediterranean this year alone. The unofficial figure may be far higher. Their story ended in the way that Gulwali's book begins. Gulwali could so easily have been one of them, his voice snuffed out in the depths of a cold sea.

I leave you with that thought.

Nadene Ghouri, August 2015

NOTE ON THE AUTHORS

Gulwali Passarlay was sent away from Afghanistan as a young boy, fleeing the conflict that had claimed his father's life. After an extraordinarily tortuous journey across eight countries, Gulwali arrived in the UK a year later and has devoted his new life to education. Now twenty-one years old, he is set to graduate from the University of Manchester with a degree in Politics. Gulwali is a member of many prestigious political, aid, and youth groups, each a stepping stone to his ultimate goal: to run for Presidency of Afghanistan. In 2012 he was invited to carry the Olympic Torch.

Nadene Ghouri is an award-winning journalist and a former correspondent of both the BBC and Al Jazeera English. She is a former writer in residence at Gladstones Library and is the co-author of the *New York Times* bestseller *The Favored Daughter*, and *Born Into the Children of God*. Nadene has also advised several major charities and the UK Foreign Office on media and peace-building communications across Africa and Asia.

"The first day I picked up a Regina Brett book, my life got a little brighter. Her words are soooo good...I'll confess I have stolen a quote or two! Her books are my go-to gifts for friends and family—I like to pass them on."

—Hoda Kotb, cohost of the *Today* show

PRAISE FOR *GOD NEVER BLINKS*

"A rousing inspirational collection...Brett employs a veteran writer's knack for keen observation and thorough self-knowledge, delivering hard-earned wisdom with deceptive ease."

—*Publishers Weekly*

"Both wise and moving, and a remarkable testimony to the power and love of God."

—*BookPage*

"Provide[s] humor, good advice, and an instant mood booster...enough to cover just about any situation you may face in your daily life."

—BookLoons.com

"This book is a jewel...sprinkled with life mantras to keep you ticking no matter what situation you face. An amazing book! I surely will be passing this little treasure on."

—MomLikeMe.com

ALSO BY REGINA BRETT

God Never Blinks: 50 Lessons for Life's Little Detours
Be the Miracle: 50 Lessons for Making the Impossible Possible

GOD
IS
ALWAYS
HIRING

50 Lessons for Finding
Fulfilling Work

REGINA BRETT

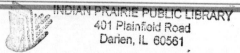

GRAND CENTRAL
PUBLISHING

NEW YORK   BOSTON

Grand Central Publishing
Hachette Book Group
1290 Avenue of the Americas
New York, NY 10104
grandcentralpublishing.com
twitter.com/grandcentralpub

Originally published in hardcover and ebook by Grand Central Publishing, April 2015.

First Trade Paperback Edition: April 2016

Grand Central Publishing is a division of Hachette Book Group, Inc.
The Grand Central Publishing name and logo is a trademark of Hachette Book Group, Inc.

The publisher is not responsible for websites (or their content) that are not owned by the publisher.

The Hachette Speakers Bureau provides a wide range of authors for speaking events. To find out more, go to www.hachettespeakersbureau.com or call (866) 376-6591.

Library of Congress Cataloging-in-Publication Data has been applied for.

ISBNs: 978-1-4555-5637-3 (pbk.), 978-1-4555-5635-9 (ebook)

Printed in the United States of America

RRD-C

10 9 8 7 6 5 4 3 2 1

To Bruce—
My husband, my cheerleader, my forever boyfriend

Contents

GOD
IS
ALWAYS
HIRING

Introduction

In the past five years, I've had the pleasure of speaking in front of thousands of people at countless appearances and book signings. The question I'm most often asked is: "What's your next book going to be about?"

When I tell audiences I want to write a book to help people find more meaning and passion at work and in their lives, they cheer and want to read *that* book right now.

So here it is.

God Is Always Hiring is a collection of inspirational essays, stories, and columns with lessons to help people look at their work and their lives in a new light.

It's for people who no longer love the work they do.

It's for people who love their work but want to find more meaning outside of work, in the rest of their lives.

It's for people who are unemployed, underemployed, or unhappily employed.

It's for people who have been derailed, temporarily or permanently.

It's for people who are just graduating into the world of work and want to know what to write on that clean slate.

It's for people who have retired or can no longer work who want to live a more meaningful life.

It's for people who love the work they do so much, they want to inspire others to find their unique passion in life.

It's for people like me who once felt lost in life and wandered aimlessly along a broken road that ultimately led straight to the perfect place in life. I believe there is a perfect place for each of us. Our job is to find it. Or to relax and let it find us.

I wrote this book to help you find the work you love and create a life you love around your work. Regardless of who your boss is, what your income is, or what the economy is doing, you have the power to expand, enrich, and deepen your own life and the lives of others.

These lessons come from my life experience as a single parent for 18 years, from my perspective as a breast cancer survivor, and from the lives of others I've met at various jobs and in my 29 years as a journalist. My hope is that each lesson helps you jump out of bed in the morning, enjoy a lunchtime boost, feel tucked in at night, or simply gives your life a jolt or a bit of sparkle to make your work and your life matter.

When you don't get what you want, you get something better—experience.

Most résumés don't show the broken road life takes you on or the names people called you along the way. We pretty up our résumés, rename the jobs we had, leave out the parts we wish we could have skipped.

My résumé used to change every six months. Early on in my life, that's about how long I lasted at most jobs. Six months. I was a work in progress. I just wasn't making much progress.

The song "Take This Job and Shove It" was the sound track to my life. I could relate to that other country song, "It's Five O'clock Somewhere," which describes a time when the boss pushes you over the limit and you'd like to call him something, but you'd better just call it a day. One day I didn't. I stormed out of the restaurant and quit my waitressing job. I didn't even stop on my way out to empty the tip jar.

Some people climb the ladder of success. I walked under it. For years I didn't seem to have much luck, and the luck I had seemed bad. My first boss was a real bitch. Seriously. She was a poodle named Mam'selle who lived next door. My first paying job was to walk the neighbor's dog. Mam'selle wore bright red nail polish and a bow. After a long walk with that fluffy ball of white, she finally did her business and I brought her home. The owner lifted up the poodle's puffy Q-tip of a tail.

"You...didn't...wipe her?!" she gasped.

I swear Mam'selle gave me an evil grin. I didn't last long at that job. I thought I was hired to be a dog walker, not a dog wiper.

My next job was to be a personal assistant at a dinner theater that had just opened. The boss ran me ragged cleaning dressing rooms and bathrooms. I was in high school and didn't get home until after midnight. My parents fired me from that job. Then I upgraded to being a cashier at Clark's Pharmacy, where I spent most of my time dusting vitamins and trying to look busy and not get caught sneaking candy bars. Then on to waitressing at Widener's Family Restaurant, where people left me pennies for tips in a puddle of ketchup.

I moved on to the local hospital, where I wore a pink uniform and a hairnet. I stood in white shoes for hours putting prune whip for sick patients on trays on a long conveyor belt. The employee ID card I carried gave me the lovely title Kitchen Help. The title I put on my résumé read Dietary Assistant. I still have the hairnet and ID badge glued to my scrapbook to remind me of those days working 6 a.m. to 3 p.m. in the dish room hosing down trays and dishes that sick

people threw up and bled on. I'm not sure we even wore protective gloves back then.

For a while I worked as a secretary. That was BC—before computers. Back then, you were lucky if you were issued an IBM Selectric with eraser tape. I got ink-stained hands from arm-wrestling carbon paper. I used to be a Wite-Out wiz. I'm surprised my boss didn't find me passed out over the keyboard from the fumes. I hated the job. One day it took me all morning to type a three-page letter, only to have my boss hand it back to me after he drew huge circles of red ink around typos that Wite-Out would have covered. I had to retype the whole thing.

It took me many jobs to realize I wanted something more than a job. A job is where you work so you can pay the bills. A job is a place where you're penalized if you're five minutes late even if you stopped to help a stranded motorist. A job is a place where you call in sick so you have time to look for a better job. It might be stable and safe, but it's boring. You do what's expected and you go home. You call in sick every time you rack up enough sick pay because you're sick of the place.

A job is for making a living. A career is for making a life. A job is a paycheck. A career is a bigger paycheck. A career requires education, training, and taking risks. So I set out to get a career. I changed my college major six times, from biology to botany to conservation to English to public relations to journalism. Kent State University had mercy on me and applied its academic forgiveness policy to my GPA after I flunked chemistry and got Ds in zoology and child psychology. It took me 12 years to get a 4-year degree because I took time off to work and raise a child. I started college in 1974 and didn't graduate

until 1986, when I was 30. Then it was time to take that degree in journalism and find my mission in life.

I used to think only people like Mother Teresa and Gandhi had a mission in life. We all have one. How do you find it? You listen to your life.

All those dead-end jobs? There's no such thing. In God's economy, nothing is ever wasted. The dots all connect in time. As a kid, I used to love those coloring books with the connect-the-dot pictures. Each dot had a number, which made it easier to discover the final picture. In real life, the dots aren't numbered.

My zigzag route looked like a broken road for the longest time, until one day all the dots connected. As one friend told me, God writes straight with crooked lines. I love that Rascal Flatts song lyric that says, "God blessed the broken road that led me straight to you." God did bless my broken road. I was never lost. God always knew right where I was.

All those jobs I used to call meaningless and mindless vastly enriched me. I just couldn't see it at the time. That meager $200-a-week paycheck blinded me to the wealth of experience I was getting.

Jobs that some people call menial gave my life meaning. My tour of duty as a waitress taught me compassion for the blind man who came in every Wednesday for liver and onions and knocked people out of the way with his white cane as he shouted out his order.

The job at the funeral home taught me how to comfort people in grief so I could have compassion years later as a reporter when I interviewed the father whose son was shot riding home on his bicycle. Working as an emergency medical

technician, straddling that place where life meets death, taught me more about deadlines than any editor in a newsroom could.

Every secretarial job taught me how to type better and faster. My job as an alcoholism counselor taught me how to tell when people I interviewed were lying, like the client who served time in prison but didn't think killing a man while he was drunk had anything to do with having a drinking problem.

Working as a clerk in traffic court writing ticket information in court dockets helped me know where to find court records when I did an investigation into how a man with 32 DUIs kept getting his license back before he killed two college students with his car.

My job as a legal secretary typing long legal briefs helped me understand the court system, so when I wrote about an innocent man on death row, it led to a law being changed in Ohio so prosecutors could no longer hide evidence. After 20 years in prison, that man is now free.

They say, "Life is what happens when you're making other plans." So does your résumé. It takes on a life of its own if you let it. Some people try to map out their paths and plan every step, but in reality, life hands you something better. A dead end is really a detour to a new route you hadn't planned on taking. Every experience enhances your life now or later. Without my knowing it, each job I tolerated prepared me to do the work I now celebrate.

You can't always see the growth when your life is taking root. If you're one of those people who feel lost in life, take heart. Being lost could lead you to the very place life planned on taking you anyway.

LESSON
2

Everything changes when you change.

I t was either the key to the future or a deal with the devil. I wasn't sure which, so I wasn't sure what to do with the document in my hand.

At 22, I had become a parasite on my parents. I had no job and no prospects of one. As an unwed mother, I couldn't support myself or my new baby. It wasn't fair to live rent-free with my parents forever. Plus I felt like I was wearing an invisible scarlet *A*. It stood for Awful. Awful daughter. Awful sister. Awful mother.

Getting help from my daughter's father was out of the question. I wrote him off before she was born. I told him I didn't want to marry him, so I couldn't go to him now. What if he took her away? What if he told the courts he could give her a better life than I could?

I had dropped out of college after I got pregnant. I quit my

job working as an emergency medical technician when I was four months pregnant. Back then, the local funeral homes ran the ambulance services. In addition to saving lives, I had to make death calls at hospitals, nursing homes, and residences. Picking up dead bodies wasn't glamorous work, but it paid the bills, and, as we used to joke, no one complained. But after I got pregnant, I couldn't afford to hurt my back or my baby lifting people who weighed more than 300 pounds. The funeral home didn't want to pay for more than two attendants on duty, so I quit.

I didn't know where to get my next job. How could I leave my baby all day to work? She had only one parent. If I was gone all day, it would be like she didn't have any. Factory jobs were out. There was no flexibility. Working 7 a.m. to 3 p.m. meant she'd wake every day to spend the day with someone else. The 3 p.m. to 11 p.m. shift meant I'd never get to tuck her in. The 11 p.m. to 7 a.m. shift meant she'd never get to sleep at home.

I applied for jobs, but I had few skills. I couldn't even type. Buying a car seemed impossible, so I borrowed my dad's. When you're a single parent, it's hard to dream alone. You need money to go with dreams. Other than having a baby, my life was bankrupt. That's how I ended up with those papers in my hand.

Officially the document was called an application for Aid to Dependent Children. But in my small town, we called it what it was: welfare. I debated what to do with the 32-page form. Going on welfare seemed so much easier than finding a job and day care that wouldn't eat up every dollar. With welfare, I would also get medical care for me and my daughter. It seemed like the responsible thing to do.

But every time I tried to sign my name to the forms, I couldn't. I would have to legally name her dad as the father so they could go after him for child support. I didn't even name him on her birth certificate. In the end, the real reason I didn't sign the form was this: I was afraid if I ever got on welfare, I'd never get off. Welfare is a tricky benefit. It starts out as a lifeline to freedom that can become a rope that keeps you in bondage. Any time you want to earn any extra money by working, you risk losing all your benefits and health care.

It's hard to find work in a small town when you don't have a car. There's no bus or subway, no public transportation. Just personal transportation. You're limited by how far your two feet can carry you to and from work. The funeral home a mile away was walkable. I didn't want to go back to picking up bodies, but they offered me a job doing office work, so I took it.

I fell in love there. Not with the job, but with the boss. Bad idea, but desperation does funny things to you. It can make a raging alcoholic look like Prince Charming. I fell in love with everything he had: success, money, and happiness. He owned a gorgeous home. He wore suits to work. He ate out at restaurants. So he drank a little. Okay, a lot. Blackouts, driving drunk, missing work.

In the months we dated, I made it my job to save him. If I could save him, I could have my happily-ever-after. I would make him want me so much he wouldn't want to drink. We spent hours in deep conversations that he never remembered. We made plans to meet at 8 p.m. and he would call at 10 p.m. from a bar saying he was on his way. When the bars closed at 2 a.m. he would finally show up too drunk to stand and then pass out on the couch.

Finally, my friends who knew about Al-Anon told me I needed to detach with love, to stop counting the number of drinks he had, and to stop counting on him to change. There was no future with him, but there was no future without him. I loved his home. It had a breakfast nook and a big porch and bedrooms for all the imaginary kids I fantasized we would one day have. Before I could leave la-la land, though, he left me.

By then my daughter was a toddler. She was growing up even if I wasn't. I finally saved enough money to move out of my parents' house and into an apartment two blocks away from them. It was scary to depend on that meager paycheck for the $210 rent and the utilities. Plus, it was my first time on my own. I had never gone away to college, never lived in a dorm, never had to manage my own life.

All the pieces of my life that had shattered when I became pregnant were starting to fall into place. Every six months I moved to a better-paying job. I found new female friends, including a woman who took me on a retreat to help me get my life on track. There a priest advised me to change the pattern I had with men. I never got around to it. Two weeks later, I was in love.

David was six foot something, drove a Mazda RX-7, wore designer clothes, and didn't drink. He was a teenager emotionally, but so was I. One day he showed up with a souped-up Corvette and I drove 130 mph down the highway. We took off for weekends on a whim, with my mom stuck watching my daughter.

David sent me flowers, bought me clothes, and took me on vacations. He had money to blow all the time. When he blew it on me it was fine; when he blew it elsewhere, I got angry. I

didn't know that it wasn't his money; it was his parents'. After one vacation, the credit card company sent someone to his house to cut up the credit cards.

David was going to college for free on government aid. He was skipping classes to play poker and ride his motorcycle. I worked long hours at jobs that paid little. He drove a fancy car while I drove a used bright orange Ford Fiesta I bought for $2,300, every single dollar of which I had saved. It was held together with the duct tape and gutter seal my dad put around the windows.

My future? David was it. I wanted to finish my degree, own a house, have a family. Marriage to him would make all that possible. When we got engaged, the diamond was as big as my fantasy. I had it all.

I lost it two months later. While I was out trying on wedding dresses, he was sleeping with other women. The only thing worse than finding out he was cheating on me was finding out at a bowling alley. He had been acting strangely for days, so I bluntly asked, half joking, "What, are you cheating on me?" When he didn't answer, I stormed away. Then I decided, No, I'm not going home to boo-hoo all alone. I went back to him, yelled at him, even grabbed him by the collar and ripped his designer shirt. I didn't like him, but worse, I didn't like the person I had become.

It was over. I gave him back the ring and told him to give it to me when he wanted me and me alone. I never got that ring back. I got something better.

I got angry. Angry at him. Angry at me. Angry enough to get my own act together.

I was 26. It was time to grow up. When I broke up with

him, I broke up with the person I no longer wanted to be. It was time to take charge of me and my life.

Without David, the future was blank. It was up to me to write something on it. It was time to own my life. First, I returned everything he left in my house—including the *Playboy* magazines he had hidden in my dresser. I exchanged the sexy miniskirt and slinky black dress he bought me for sensible skirts and slacks I could wear to a career job. Then I got a college catalog and opened it. I had no idea what I wanted to be or do, but I did know this: I wanted to be happy.

That's when the world opened up. Everything in my life changed when I decided to change me. I didn't need to *find* the right person. I needed to *become* the right person.

Burying your talents won't make them grow.

One day in high school we all took an aptitude test to see what we were destined to be. We laughed at the results. I was supposed to be a respiratory therapist. My friend Betsy was supposed to be a truck driver.

Betsy ended up working as a nurse. I ended up a writer.

Who knew?

Somewhere inside, we did.

Somewhere inside, we all know.

We just do a great job of burying our deepest passions.

I did everything in my power to avoid using my talents. I buried them as deep as I could and I resisted anyone who came at me, with a shovel. In ninth grade, my English teacher, Mr. Ricco, made us write a paragraph each week. I balked. I wrote mine right before class and picked the most boring subjects to wear him down. Instead, he wore me down and polished me into a writer without my knowing it.

Still, I resisted. I never wrote for the high school newspaper or yearbook or took any creative writing classes. I was too scared of the one thing I desperately wanted to be: a writer. So many of us know deep inside that one thing we were meant to do, would love to do; but it's too scary to actually do it because we might fail at it, so we leave it buried inside where it will be safe, untouched and untapped. The dream and desire to do it seem so much safer than actually taking action and risking failure and rejection.

I wrote in secret, filling diaries and journals. One day, out of bravery or ignorance, I let my sisters read them. Later, when I realized what I had done, I took the diaries to the metal trash drum in the backyard and burned them. As the flames ate my words, it seemed they were putting out the fire in me.

The embers still burned. In tenth grade, when I read Henry David Thoreau, something in my soul expanded. It was like I could take in more breath. I didn't have enough money to buy my own copy of *Walden*, so I copied the text from the school's copy word for word, starting with why he went into the woods.

To avoid writing, I almost ended up in the woods for a living. We've all heard that saying "Man plans, God laughs." Had my plans been blessed by the gods, I would have ended up a forest ranger. I was too scared to be a writer, so I turned to conservation for a college major when I turned away from writing. How ironic that I ended up as a journalist filling newspapers and books with words. I pray that those forest rangers preserve enough trees to keep me in business.

I have loved newspapers ever since I was a toddler sitting on the floor near my father's steel-toed work boots as he buried

his face in the daily news. I pretended to read whatever section he dropped on the floor, curious about what mesmerized my dad after a long day spent patching up a hot roof. When my mom had time to read, which was close to never while raising 11 children, she loved newspaper columnist Erma Bombeck. Erma made writing look so easy. And it was, in my diary. There it stayed, safe and sound, for years.

I buried my talents out of fear they would never be good enough. I ignored the call to use my talents. I kept telling God I wasn't ready, until one day it hit me: What if God stopped asking? What's scarier than God calling you to use your talents is the thought that God will stop calling you and go elsewhere.

The parable of the talents in the Bible haunted me. A nobleman gave one of his servants five talents, another one two, and another man one talent. As time went on, the man with the five talents traded with them and made five more talents. The one with two talents doubled his as well. The man with one talent dug a hole in the ground and hid the money out of fear. When the master came back, he rewarded the first two men. The man who buried his talent returned it unused. The master was angry, took the talent, and tossed the servant out. The master told the first two men: "To everyone who has will more be given, and he will have an abundance; you have been faithful over a little, therefore I will make you lord over much" (see Matthew 25).

When you have been faithful with what you have been given, you get more. You won't get more talents until you use what you've already been given.

We're all gifted, but some people never open their packages. We each have a calling, a vocation, a particular unique tal-

ent. Your calling isn't necessarily your job title. It might not be written on the business card you carry, or on your job description, or on your résumé. It's more likely written on your heart. I worked a lot of jobs before I found that place in life that writer Frederick Buechner calls "the place where your deep gladness and the world's deep hunger meet."

What does God want you to do with the gifts He gave you? Use them. Not hoard them. When the Israelites got hungry on their way to the Promised Land, God dropped manna from heaven. Free bread! Out of fear, the people hoarded the bread for the next day. It grew moldy. God wanted them to have faith that each day's grace would be enough.

No hoarding. You have to use up all you have learned, uncovered, and discovered, or you don't get more. My writing had to have life beyond my bedroom. But who would want to read it? Who would publish it? Who would buy it? That was all none of my business. It was time to take action. In prayer I might have been saying yes to God, but a yes without action isn't truly a yes.

What are you called to do or be? The answer is in you. Instead of conducting a survey of family and friends about what you should do, survey the inner landscape to find the spiritual interpretation of your life. God has already whispered it to you. Most of us keep our lives too busy and noisy to listen.

Many of us stay clueless not because we don't know, but because we're afraid of knowing, because then we'll have to take action. I was at a party once and listened to a woman complaining to the small crowd around her that she had all these career options and just couldn't choose. Every time someone offered a great piece of advice, she rejected it instantly and

said, "I don't know what to do." She was getting a lot of attention and mileage out of not knowing, out of being helpless.

I felt that tug of the Spirit, looked her in the eye, and gently asked, "Do you *want* to know?"

She looked appalled. Everyone grew quiet. Then she softened. "Yes," she said, and proceeded to tell all of us exactly what she loved but was afraid of doing.

Someone once told me this beautiful story: Before we arrive in this world, we each possess all the wisdom we will ever need for this life and beyond. But right before we're born, an angel comes and touches us on the lips, as if to silence us, and leaves an imprint there, causing us to forget everything we knew. We spend the rest of our lives recovering the lost data.

Sometimes I place my finger on my upper lip, right in that little groove, and listen.

Try it. It will remind you to stop talking so you can listen to the wisdom you already possess.

What they call you is up to them. What you answer to is up to you.

People do it all the time. Ask someone, "What do you do for a living?" and they'll use that nasty four-letter word *just*.

"I'm just a janitor."

"I'm just an orderly."

"I'm just a bus driver."

"I'm just a secretary."

Just?

I love when I run into people who can't wait to tell you what they do for a living. They create their own job titles and celebrate who they are. The woman who paints nails who calls herself a Nail Technician. The guy who repairs pianos whose business card identifies him as Director of Piano Technology. The man at the amusement park who fixes the merry-go-round and sees himself as a Ride Technician. The person who cleans the city pool who calls herself the Aquatics Manager.

The hotel security worker who calls himself Director of Loss Prevention.

What's in a title?

Nothing and everything. It all depends on what the title is, who gave it to you, and whether it expands or limits you. Instead of shrinking to fit a job title, sometimes you have to expand the box you're in and create a title that fits.

The key is to do what's in the job title you have and squeeze in room to do what matches the job title you want to have.

When I was hired to be a business reporter at the *Beacon Journal* in Akron, I cried the whole drive home. I wanted the salary and benefits, but I didn't want to be a business reporter. I didn't want to write about sales figures, annual meetings, and quarterly earnings reports. I hated numbers and data. They didn't fit the mantra pounded into us in journalism school: "Bring me humans!" Where were the humans in the stock listings and statistics?

It was my job to find them, so I did. I wrote business news but also created a side beat spotlighting people who worked interesting jobs. I wrote about a chimney sweep, a cement truck driver, and a blimp pilot. I did magazine stories on third-shift workers and farmers, and followed a woman all the way through the police academy.

Not everyone appreciated my zeal at first, but they usually liked the final product. Too many bosses put people in a box. Whatever box they put you in, expand it. Better yet, break down the sides, smash it to the floor, and turn that box into a wide-open blank slate and write whatever you want on it.

Don't ask. Just do it. As they say, it's better to ask for-

giveness than to ask permission. Every morning before work, decide who you want to be and go be it. It's up to you, no one else. No one except you is in charge of building your résumé, or giving you challenging work, or making your nine-to-five day meaningful.

Before I got the dream job of being a newspaper columnist, I used to tell people, "I'm a columnist without a column." It helped me see past the position I had as a reporter to the position I wanted. I love those famous words by poet Lucille Clifton: "What they call you is one thing; what you answer to is something else." That part is up to you.

When I was growing up, my next-door neighbor, Thelma, worked in the kitchen at the hospital. She was my mom's age, and I felt sorry for her because she spent her whole career in a hospital kitchen wearing a pink uniform and a hairnet, until I realized why. Her job title might have been Kitchen Help, but Thelma considered herself so much more than that. She made the best piecrust in town. What a treat for patients. It didn't matter what her title was. She considered herself a baker.

I thought of Thelma when I was asked to speak at a cere- mony honoring Cleveland Clinic employees with 25 years of service. It could have been a boring night; it could have been little more than an assembly line of handshakes, photos, and watches handed out. It could have been a ho-hum night of identical thank-yous to 200 workers. They could have been treated like cogs in the massive medical machine that is the Cleveland Clinic.

Instead, it was like opening a treasure chest filled with something more valuable than jewels. Each person was seen

for what they were: a vital player in saving lives and enhancing the quality of patients', families', and coworkers' lives.

They had all started at the hospital before computers, when bills were hand-typed, when nurses wore white caps, when no one paid for parking. Back then, offices were the size of elevators; some actually were in old elevators.

On this night when they were honored, you couldn't tell the doctors from the medical-records workers in the ballroom. It didn't matter what anyone's paycheck or title was. On this night, everyone was equal. Everyone had given their 25 best years. The program carried a bio on each employee, but it wasn't the stuff of résumés. It was the stuff that truly matters: *Consistently jovial. Pleasant conversations. Boundless energy. Wonderful storyteller. Humble.*

The program mentioned that one department coordinator for the Cancer Center was often found at her desk late into the night trying to schedule patients. One person whom we'd call a custodian didn't just clean offices; he helped visitors find their way. The fire marshal was more than that. He was a human alarm clock who drove every day from Columbus to Cleveland his first year of work and was always on time. That's a two-and-a-half-hour drive—one way.

A pediatrician was praised for his "Daffy Duck" voice that quieted the most frightened child into laughing through medical exams. He was also praised for his work getting bicycle helmet safety legislation passed. One nurse was referred to as an actor, comedian, and published author. She was also known as the Nurse Whisperer. What did she whisper? Probably, "Get well, get well, get well."

They talked about a dentist whose specialty was facial pros-

thetic replacements. He gave patients a new way to face life with new eyes, ears, noses, and mouths. Because of him, patients could enjoy a drink, a meal, a kiss.

The man who maintained dry-goods storage and ordered supplies made sure the babies didn't go hungry. He was vigilant about making sure there were always enough tube feedings and infant formula on hand.

I left the celebration knowing that the custodians of the world matter as much as the heart surgeons, that it doesn't matter what the world calls us. We get to decide who we really are. And it's up to each of us to take the word *just* out of our job titles.

In this drama of life, there are no small parts.

Thinking small stops too many of us from doing great things. We talk ourselves out of doing a kindness because we figure someone else will do it or because we doubt we can pull it off.

Folks on the bottom rung sometimes feel that way: the invisible workers in cubicles, the title-less people in accounts receivable, the nameless voices on the phones in billing. But a handful of those people changed a man's life one week. Changed it forever.

It all started when Marty Kenny lost his right hand in a car accident one summer night back in 2003. One friend left him to die on a bridge in the industrial Flats of Cleveland while another friend stayed and saved his life.

That summer day in June started out as a celebration of friendship. Marty and Dean Stecker spent the day hanging

vinyl siding, pounding nails in the hot sun. They ended up at a party and left with Marty's friend Greg.

Greg drove them all to a bar in the Flats. When they left the bar at 11:30 p.m., Greg revved the engine and spun in the gravel. The car was going 60 in a 25-mile-an-hour zone when he floored it. Marty yelled for him to slow down, then gripped the door with his hand and held on for dear life. The car hit a dip in the road and went airborne on a lift bridge.

BAM!

The car slammed into the wall of the bridge so hard, it flipped over and skidded on the passenger side across the steel bridge. It screamed across the serrated metal like a train. When the car stopped 240 feet away on its side, Dean crawled out a window. Marty was stuck under the car. His right hand was gone.

Dean pushed hard to flip the car over, back onto its wheels, to free Marty. Greg walked around dazed, his business cards falling through the grate into the water like confetti. Dean tore off his shirt and wrapped it around Marty's arm. He screamed for Greg to call 911. He watched in shock as Greg paused to pick up the side mirror to his car, then drove away with the only cell phone. Hope faded as the red taillights disappeared into the night.

Dean wrapped both arms and legs around his bleeding buddy as they sat on a bridge suspended over the Cuyahoga River. Marty lost so much blood, it drained through the steel bridge like rainwater. Dean cradled Marty, rocking him as if that could stop the bleeding. Both of them were soaked in his blood.

On that dark, lonely bridge in Cleveland's industrial Flats,

Dean screamed at Marty to hold on, to stay conscious. When Marty fell silent, Dean rocked him and told him everything a dying man should hear: "Your wife loves you, your son loves you, and I love you."

Then he heard a rumble and saw headlights. Dean set Marty down and jumped in front of the vehicle and started screaming for help. The driver called paramedics. Dean's tourniquet saved Marty's life, but there was no hope for his hand.

Later on in the courtroom, the judge held up photos of Marty's injured arm as Greg stood with his two good hands cuffed behind his back. Marty stared at those hands with envy, with anger, with sadness. Greg was convicted of aggravated vehicular assault. In the courtroom, Marty reached over to hold his wife's hand, only he didn't have one, so she laced her fingers over the stub of his arm and held it.

For four months, the 21-year-old struggled to tie his shoes, write a check, diaper his newborn daughter, have a catch with his 4-year-old son. He lived off the money he and his wife had saved to fix up their house.

I stood on the bridge where he lost his hand when he visited the scene for the first time. He ran his fingers across the serrated grating of the bridge, studied the skid marks, and peered through at the river.

"I'm looking for my hand," he joked, only I could tell he wasn't completely joking. He had left a part of himself there. Marty can't remember much about that night. Dean can't forget.

I wrote a long article about the accident, about their friendship, about Dean's efforts to save him. The two celebrated the

court case being over. They sat at Marty's dining room table and shoved aside stacks of medical bills that Medicaid would cover as long as Marty didn't work and his wife didn't earn too much at her day-care job. But he wasn't sure how to cover the prosthetic hand he wanted. His son wanted his dad to get a robotic arm so he could give him a high five. Dean worried that Marty would get discouraged that he couldn't swing a bat, tie a fishing lure, or hold both of his children's hands at once.

When the story about Marty went public, the paper-pushers and phone operators in the gray cubicles at Hanger Prosthetics & Orthotics in South Euclid, Ohio, couldn't forget his face. And that missing hand. When Lisa Kowardy first saw Marty's picture in the paper, she felt awful. "It was a terrible inhumanity done to him," she said. "We wanted to show him some humanity."

Who is Lisa?

She shrugs. "I'm just the billing manager."

Just?

Her job was to juggle accounts receivable. She never saw the patients, only their bills.

After she read about Marty, she and the women around her, women crammed into a small office above a storage room, approached management to do something about it. Lisa copied the news article and gave it to Kimberly Reed, the woman in charge of fitting prosthetics. Another woman tracked down Marty.

All of the women upstairs—Charon Speights, Alida Van Horn, Irene Flanik, Rose Johnson, and Annette Phillips—wanted to help Marty swing a bat with his son and be able to feed his baby daughter a bottle.

Because of their diligence and dedication, Marty got a $58,000 robotic hand for free.

The TV cameras captured Marty trying out his new hand, picking up a tissue, signing his name, lifting a bottle. The cameras didn't stay to capture Marty thanking the women who made it happen. The women oohed and ahhed when Marty came up to show off his hand.

"All you lovely people, this is just amazing," Marty said. "You guys are great."

Marty couldn't stop opening and closing his hand and talking about how powerful it was, with 22 pounds of pinch pressure.

"Do that guy thing and scratch yourself," Lisa joked.

"Not with this hand." Marty laughed.

He rolled up his sleeve to show it off.

"Oh my God, it's beautiful," Irene said.

"This is more than I could ever imagine," Marty said as they all fought back tears.

He promised to come back with his wife and two kids, then raised his new hand and waved good-bye, as if it were nothing at all.

LESSON
6

Give others a second chance to make a first impression.

T hey always say, "You never have a second chance to make a first impression."

Thank goodness people have been gracious enough to give me a slew of second chances.

I've made a lot of bad first impressions. The first time I stepped into a newsroom as a student guest to meet with my mentor, I wore a black blouse with silver glittery stripes, a ruffled collar, and sleeves that poofed out at the shoulders like balloons. A white gauzy skirt, a pair of black hose, and bright white shoes completed the ensemble. Someone should have called the fashion police to throw the book at me.

I came back two years later for a job interview there. This time, I meant business. I wore the only suit I owned. So much was riding on that interview at the *Beacon Journal* in Akron. I was 30, a single mom with no money and big dreams. I wanted to be a real journalist, the kind that could pay the rent

from a writing job. I had blown my first impressions when I tried to get an internship. At the *Pittsburgh Press*, an editor asked about my hobbies and interests. I told him about my love for violin music but choked when he asked me about Isaac Stern an hour later. My mind went blank. I had also blown a shot at an internship at the *Detroit Free Press*. An editor liked my résumé and asked me to write an essay. I wrote a powerful essay on a lousy typewriter. I had to pencil in corrections. The editor never called back. Finally, after 30 rejection letters, a small paper in Lorain, Ohio, the *Lorain Journal*, gave me an internship in 1986 that turned into a job.

Sometimes we're the ones who need a second chance; sometimes it's up to us to grant one. Sometimes it's both. That was the case with the toughest boss I ever had.

The stories about him were legendary. Most of them were true. Trash cans flew. Heads rolled. Grown men cried. My first editor, John Cole, was Lou Grant on steroids. He gave me the desk that sat under a warning bell that went off when we were on deadline. That bell wasn't as bad as sitting right outside his door at the *Lorain Journal*. Everyone feared the wrath of John. He fired people and hired them back, sometimes in the same day.

One day he hated what he saw in the newspaper so he stood on a desk in the middle of the newsroom, let loose a long rant about how he might as well just give up and die, then lay down on the floor.

One time a photographer showed him a feature photo of a nun in full habit splashing around Lake Erie.

"What do you think of this?" John asked me. Trick question. Did *he* like it?

"Um, it's interesting?" I answered.

"No it isn't," John said. "It's a cliché." Then he tore the photo to shreds and let the tiny pieces fall on the photographer's feet.

John was tough. He made us tougher. He was the kind of boss who changes you forever. Years later, you still bear the imprint—and the scars. He became editor of the paper when he was 29. The people who worked with him used the same words to describe him: *mercurial, demanding, smart, fearless, passionate, no-nonsense, gruff.* They called him a crusader with contempt for corruption, who celebrated the truth and never cowered before anyone.

John stood up for us. I often heard him on the phone yelling to a source, "Those are my reporters. If you have a problem with my reporter, you have a problem with me."

End of problem.

When I was still brand-new, one day another reporter dumped a story in my lap that he had been assigned but didn't want. It would involve working another late night on top of my assignment to cover city hall. I wiped away tears at my desk.

"Brett, get in here," John yelled.

He challenged me to get tougher. "There's no crying in my newsroom," he barked. Oh, if he only knew how much crying went on in his newsroom.

"Don't let people push you around," he yelled.

Strange, but I left his office feeling better, like he had given me an espresso shot of courage. Then he called that reporter in. I tried not to smile as I heard the screaming. A few minutes later, the reporter came to my desk and, without looking at me, asked to take back his assignment and told me, "John said you can go home."

John cared about the right things. He taught me that you're never too small to make a difference and never too big to be gracious about it.

I'd worked for him only six months when the phone rang one day on deadline. John sat the new person under the warning bell. The bell was ready to go off when a secretary handed me a phone message with a name I didn't recognize. I called back and John Greenman from the *Beacon Journal* answered. He wasn't part of the story I was writing, so I told him I was on deadline and hung up.

Then it hit me: *Oh no, I just killed my future.* I had just hung up on an editor who worked for a newspaper I wanted to work for. Another terrible first impression.

When I called back, he told me he was impressed that I put the deadline first and wanted me to come in for an interview.

That year, 1986, Akron's largest employer, Goodyear, was in the midst of a takeover attempt by Sir James Goldsmith. The paper directed all its best business writers to cover that big story. The paper needed another business writer to cover the less important news.

I knew nothing about the business world. I'd never read a business section before, so I was completely unprepared. I showed up in my one and only business suit to look as smart and professional as possible. No black-and-white disaster outfit this time. They ushered me into the editor's office. It was full of men wearing yellow power ties. The interview went well until the editor of the newspaper asked me how I would write a profile of Martin Marietta.

I'd never heard of the guy, but gave a detailed account of how I would gather background on Mr. Marietta. Then I no-

ticed the editor looked like he was ready to deliver a kidney stone. They were all cringing as I went on and on about Mr. Marietta. Finally, one of them broke the news: Martin Marietta wasn't a person. It was a major defense corporation.

Arghhh! I felt so stupid. I had prayed going into the interview and all through it had held my right hand open and pretended to be holding on to God's hand. Now what? I prayed, took a deep breath, and said something like, "Well, it's obvious I don't know the business world, so if you need an experienced business writer, I'm not the one to hire. But I do know how to report and write, and I'm willing to learn anything I need to know for the job."

They were kind and shook my hand. One of them escorted me to the elevator. As I pushed the button, my heart sank. I'd probably just blown the best chance I would ever get to work for a great newspaper. Before the elevator door opened, the managing editor came over and asked when I could start work.

What? They were going to hire me anyway?

And they did.

I found out later they hired a copy editor who spelled her name wrong on her résumé. So much for first impressions.

It was hard to break the news to my editor in Lorain that I was leaving after just six months on the job, my first real career job.

When I left his newspaper, John Cole wished me well but didn't say much. A week later, my mom called. John Cole had sent my parents a letter, telling them what a great job *they* had done.

Every job is as magical as you make it.

What's the worst job you ever had? That's always a great conversation starter. Go ahead, ask people. But you have to be careful. Your worst job could be someone else's best job.

Wouldn't it be great to have a cosmic job swap? If everyone gave up the job they hated, someone who truly loved that job could step in and be happy.

My worst job? Picking up bodies for a funeral home.

When you work at a funeral home, you do a little bit of everything. You print memorial cards, wash hearses, work viewing hours, and go out on death calls. You never forget your first dead body. The first time I was "on call" I had no idea what to expect. You just go to sleep at night and the phone rings if they need you. The call came at 3 a.m. It was eerie driving a hearse in the dead of night (pun intended) to claim a body.

The woman was in her 40s and had thick black hair.

Decades have passed and I still remember her face. She was in bed and her eyes were still open. She had been ill for some time, and the family doctor had already been to the house to pronounce her dead. The family was present, so I had to act like it didn't bother me in the least to touch her. I didn't realize how hard it was to lift a dead body until I tried to lift her. It gave new meaning to the word *deadweight*. Back at the funeral home, we had to undress her, rinse off her body, and position her head and hands for viewing hours.

At times, the funeral business can be deeply disturbing. Week after week, you're immersed in death and grief. You have to handle decomposing bodies that hadn't been found for weeks that no longer look human. You have to cover the holes left in bodies by guns but are helpless to fill the holes left in the survivors of those suicides. The smell of death makes you gag until it's replaced by the smell of embalming fluid, which makes your eyes water. But nothing bothers you more than the tiny coffins. The newborns, the stillborns, the hopes and dreams for a lifetime that ended with an empty nursery and numb parents who aren't sure they can still call themselves parents.

The magical part?

Seeing death up close gives you a deep appreciation for life. One day an embalmer allowed me to assist him. He showed me how years of unhealthy eating can narrow the artery in your neck. I've never forgotten seeing the cross section of that man's thick artery. I think of it every time I'm tempted to eat a French fry.

One day I walked into the embalming room to be greeted by a man whose chest was spread apart like an open book.

His body had been autopsied and the embalmer had opened it to prepare it. For a brief second I was horrified and jumped back. Then I was completely fascinated. I stepped closer and examined each rib and the tissue that had once held his beating heart in place. It was a beautiful moment. How often do you get to peer inside a human body?

Over the years, I've interviewed hundreds of people, from blimp pilots to migrant workers and everyone in between. They all had jobs one person might love and another person might hate. I spent weeks talking to migrant workers at a muck farm in Hartville, Ohio. They had a job I assumed most people would hate.

The women I talked to said they preferred to be called field-workers. They didn't call themselves migrants. They didn't like the stigma that job title gave them. One woman told me the word *migrant* conjured up images of poor, dirty, uneducated people to be pitied. "They call us migrants, but I don't see us as that. I like to cut lettuce. It's an honest pay," she said. "If I don't want to work, I don't have to. I just get paid less."

The workers came from as far as South Carolina, Florida, and Texas to work the muck fields at the K.W. Zellers & Son produce farm in Hartville, Ohio. They brought their children, their work clothes, and their Bibles. They moved into old farmhouses, shanties, and trailers. They wore bright yellow waterproof overalls that matched their yellow rain slickers and rode old school buses deep into the fields on the 400-acre farm. They planted and cut Bibb lettuce, romaine, and endive that glowed fluorescent against the black earth. They tucked their hair into bright bandannas and wide straw hats, squeezed fingers into orange latex gloves, and rubber-banded their an-

kles to keep bugs from crawling up their pant legs, then shoved their feet into black rubber boots.

Every day they were one with nature. Their music was the crunch of knees crawling in unison, the swish of cold knives against warm green lettuce, and soft songs to Jesus rising from the sombreros. I heard row upon row of hearty laughter.

I spent one day picking onions with them and came home with a killer backache. When I blew my nose, dirt came out. I couldn't last a day doing that work. They never complained. They rejoiced over a bird's nest they found in the field. They checked on that nest every day and shared updates on the mother bird and the babies.

They used rubber bands to create bouquets of red radishes. They never stopped for rain, no matter how hard it fell, or the sun, no matter how hot it felt. When the baking sun was too much, the women giggled and ran through the irrigation sprinklers. They tossed handfuls of lettuce at one another. They chattered about love affairs on soap operas. They talked about where they would spend their money at the mall. They told me they preferred the sun, wind, and sky to any indoor job. They pitied people stuck in an office all day with a glass window between them and the world.

"It makes you feel like you are free, like you're not locked up all the time," Willa Mae told me.

They taught me that every job is as magical as you make it. Sometimes the magic isn't in the paycheck or perks. It's in the mark you make or leave behind, from the nest in the field to the bouquets of red radishes that end up in the grocery store.

LESSON
8

There's a time for everything but not always at the same time.

Early in my career as a journalist, a boss gave me a rude awakening about my dual roles. I was a single mom and an aspiring journalist, and I wanted to excel at both.

An editor came up to me in the newsroom one day excited to offer me an incredible opportunity to go out of state to cover a big breaking news story. He assumed I'd jump at the chance. What journalist wouldn't?

Me.

My daughter had one parent. Her dad wasn't involved in her life. I alone had to figure out child care. To find someone to spend a few nights watching her at a moment's notice seemed insurmountable. I told the editor that I couldn't give him an answer right that second. He gave me a sour look, shook his head, and said, "Brett, you're going to have to choose between being a mother and being a reporter."

Did I? How could I? I needed that job to support my daughter.

It was easy for him to compartmentalize his life and stay 100 percent focused at work. He had a wife at home running the house and caring for their child.

Way back then, I wanted to be a powerhouse in the newsroom, but I also wanted to be the best mother in the world. How could I do both? It seemed like the two didn't match. Juggling parenting and work is hard. Just when you have it down, it seems like someone tosses you a bowling ball and a raw egg to juggle in the mix.

I had already been passed over for one job because I was a single mom. Years before I was a journalist, a paving company needed a secretary who doubled as a dispatcher. I was made for the job. I had used a radio as an emergency medical technician and had been an office manager. Perfect. The company called my current employer and asked only one question: Does she miss work to take care of her child?

I didn't get the job.

How do you become a great parent and a great employee? Do you have to choose?

It wasn't until years later that I got clarity from a woman who told me, "You can have it all; you just can't have it all at the same time." Or maybe you can, just not in the same hour or day or week.

I once spoke at a retreat called BREATHE at Camp Robin Hood in, of all places, Freedom, New Hampshire. The women's weekend offered all sorts of healthy activities including hiking, biking, swimming, and canoeing. I ended up with a rifle in my hands at the shooting range. *Bam! Bam! Bam!*

It wasn't so much the power of the gun that thrilled me, but the focus and concentration that it took to hit that target 20 feet away. I gathered a handful of targets and used them for my presentation about how to stay focused on the bull's-eye and not get lost aiming for the outer rings of the target.

Jamie Cole, who organized the retreat, said she struggled with the idea of having just one target when it seemed she had so many targets that popped up at different times in her life, sometimes in the same day or hour. Her job, her children, her various passions. I thought about that dilemma we all share. What do you make your priority when everything and everyone seem to be the top priority?

I went back to the shooting range and found the answer. There was a target sheet that had not just one target printed on it, but five small ones. Each target had its own ring and its own bull's-eye. Sometimes you have to switch targets. Jamie loved it.

Instead of feeling as though she had one target in life and had to put her children or her work in the outer rings, she could put them all in the bull's-eye, just not on the same target.

We talked about how, when you're at work, you aim for the work bull's-eye. You stay focused on the task, the project, the job, the bottom line. We often do have different targets at the same time, and sometimes they're all moving at once.

I've learned to stop and assess which target just showed up in my life. I pause and reenter my life with different intentions hour by hour. When I used to host a weekly radio show, I paused, rebooted, and reminded myself I was about to interview someone so I needed to listen carefully and be present.

When I visit my grandbabies, I pause, reboot, and remind myself I am their wickedly fun grandma who is here to play, read, wrestle, and build forts.

Each time I enter a new segment of my life, I pause, reboot, and claim that identity. I make sure I'm in the right segment, being the right me, hour by hour, chunk by chunk. It's a way of consecrating my life, to make myself present and to make each encounter a holy one.

Each time I reaffirm: What is the bull's-eye on this particular target? Best parent. Best boss. Best grandma. I no longer bring work to do when I visit my grandbabies. I no longer check e-mail while playing LEGOs. When you're at home, you aim for the parenting bull's-eye. When you're with your children, you're with them, 100 percent. Turn off the Black-Berry, iPhone, iPad, and e-mail, and be fully present.

When my brain gets jumbled over priorities or jolted back and forth between them, I pause and decide which target is top priority at that very moment, then focus on that one with all the energy and passion I have in me to hit the bull's-eye.

None of us will ever do it all, or do it all perfectly. I'll never forget the tsunami of scorn that hit over presidential candidate Mitt Romney's wife, Ann, who raised five sons. Some women scoffed and said Ann "never worked a day in her life." The Mommy Wars heated up, even though we all know that anyone with five sons worked *every* day of her life.

It hit that nuclear button: Am I enough? There's a war waged within every mom. Am I doing enough for my children if I work outside the home? Am I doing enough for myself and for the world if I don't?

If that wasn't bad enough, one week *Time* magazine had

the audacity to ask on its cover: *Are you mom enough?* It didn't help that the cover photo was of a sexy, young mom in skinny jeans nursing a three-year-old son pressed against her bare breast. The picture of the woman disturbed some people, but the question the headline posed should disturb us all.

Are you mom enough?

Many days the answer we would give ourselves would be no.

Like the day my little girl held up her spoonful of Cheerios to show me the little worm wiggling on it. *Oh no, when did that box of cereal expire?* Or the afternoon I took a moment to sit in a lawn chair to crack open a book and my toddler bolted into the street. Or the time I went to get her out of the crib and found her playing with what had rolled out of the diaper I failed to seal shut. Or the morning I found her eating a stick of butter for breakfast after she learned how to open the refrigerator door. Or the time I had to pry her fingers off the car door in the grade school parking lot when she developed a fear of going to school. She didn't know I cried harder than she did after I pulled away to go to work.

If we're keeping score on parenting, it might seem that we're all failures some days. My daughter is parenting more perfectly than I ever did. She taught her babies to self-soothe, swaddled them like burritos, hand-painted onesies, and sewed ribbons onto burp cloths. She even decided to leave her career to be a full-time mom.

There are days she calls in tears, sometimes from the joy, sometimes from the guilt over mothering a three-year-old and a ten-month-old. Is she a good-enough mom when a tired

Asher cries for his "striped blankie" and begs her to turn the car around to get it and she doesn't? Or when she lets Ainsley cry herself to sleep because sleep is what that tired baby needs most?

There's no perfect parent. Not the ones who stay home all day. Not the ones who go to work. Not the ones who carefully sterilize every bottle and nipple. Not the ones who breast-feed until the child is taking the SAT.

I remember one day my mom gave herself an F for parenting. She was fretting all day because my little brother forgot his lunch and she blamed herself. I remember thinking, *Wow, she cares that much about us?* My mom did the best she could raising 11 children. Some days she hit it out of the ballpark. Some days she hit a single. Some days she struck out. But she always got up to bat, no matter how exhausted she felt.

Baseball offers a good way to measure success. A great batting average is .300. That means 70 percent of the time, you fail. Even the greatest home-run hitters strike out. Some of the greatest players of all time are included in the list of the 100 major-league players with the most strikeouts: Reggie Jackson, Hank Aaron, Willie Mays, Babe Ruth, Mickey Mantle, Sammy Sosa, and Barry Bonds. The year Babe Ruth set the record for most home runs in a season, he also struck out more times than any other player in the majors. How comforting.

Every mom is playing in the major leagues. We have the most important job in the world. The reason we strike out is because every day we step up to home plate and swing with all we've got.

Are we mom enough?

You bet.

Every single one of us is doing the best we can.

So let's call a truce in the Mommy Wars both around us and inside us. No more judgments about what we "should" be doing. Let's stop "shoulding" all over ourselves and one another.

Let's just do the best we can and call it enough.

LESSON
9

Only you can determine your worth.

"Would you like fries with that?"

You get used to asking that with every order.

I worked at McDonald's for only one week, but it left an imprint for life.

Since one out of every eight Americans have worked at a McDonald's, a newspaper editor asked me to get hired at McDonald's and write a story about it for Labor Day.

I was honest with the manager at the nearest McDonald's and told her I was a newspaper reporter. I asked her to treat me the same as everyone else. No special privileges. That meant I had to go through the interview, sit through orientation, and wear the McUniform, which was two sizes too large.

It's hard to get nervous about applying for a job when the flip side of the application is a Ronald McDonald summer fun

safety maze to color. The place mats doubled as job applications. I got hired to work the hours of 7 a.m. to 2 p.m. At orientation, I got a McDonald's bag with two uniforms. We watched training films on how to wash our hands and on how to treat customers. TLC meant "think like a customer." We were never to use the term "fast food." We were a "quick service" restaurant.

Once home I opened the bag and pulled out the black polyester pants; a red, gray, and blue striped polo shirt; and a bright red hat with a huge *M* and the words "We Got the Power." The hat stuck up five inches off my head. My daughter laughed hysterically and dared me to put the uniform on in front of her. At least it was one outfit she wouldn't ask to borrow.

Each day I had to clock in five minutes before my shift. The small employee lounge had signs all over to remind us: Talk To Our Customers, Smile, and Learn Customers' First Names.

The manager popped in a video for me to watch called *Serving Up Smiles* on how to make breakfast. Everything I fixed was supposed to look like the pictures and be served in 59 seconds or less.

I ended up working at the drive-thru window. Robbin trained me. She wanted to change the world and used her 30 seconds with each customer to do so. She could tell who was in a hurry, who needed a compliment, who needed to feel important. She knew the names of the regulars and punched in their orders before they gave them. She looked past the yawning, grumpy, unshaven faces and smiled.

"I usually look into their eyes and watch them for the ex-

pression on their faces to tell how they're feeling and what they're thinking," she told me.

When people found out she was 31 and worked at McDonald's they pitied her. She didn't see why. She was proud of her work. She was saving up to buy a house.

It was hard work. My knees and feet ached from standing all day. There was nowhere to sit. To amuse myself, I looked into people's cars, checking out what was hanging from the rearview mirror (fuzzy dice, air fresheners, clocks) and what oddities were in the backseat (a vacuum, a roll of carpet, golf clubs). We could never sit except for our 30-minute break. My feet felt like they would explode. My hands smelled like grease. My uniform stuck to me. Before going home I filled fry baskets with frozen potatoes. I left exhausted.

The next day I worked the front counter. We were supposed to greet everyone with: "Welcome to McDonald's. May I take your order?" But we got so busy, I started shouting, "Next!" The person training me that day was Carlos, who was 17. He was 20 years younger than me but never made me feel small. He knew too well what that can be like. He rolled his eyes when one manager told him to send me to the dining room to clean tables. "I won't send you, I'll ask you," he said. He refused to be a hen in the pecking order where I was the smallest chick. To him, we were all equals on a team.

Carlos wanted to be a doctor one day and work with crack babies in the neonatal unit. He was saving money for medical school. He worked 35 hours a week and graduated from high school a year early. McDonald's taught him responsibility, he said.

Between orders we stuffed dwarfs into Snow White Happy

Meal boxes and endlessly wiped off the counter. The motto was, "You lean, you clean." You can't afford to not look busy. I did that once and ended up cleaning the women's restroom. How solid waste can end up on the wall—the wall!—is beyond me. It was my job to scrub it off. I left that day smelling like bleach.

That night I attended a mandatory crew rally. It was like a pep assembly, complete with balloons, crepe paper, and food—from McDonald's of course. It was a chance to point out problems (like customers not getting condiments in the drive-thru); win prizes for McTrivia questions (What is the weight of a McDonald's sundae? Five ounces); and get answers to rare questions (What if a customer wants 18 packets of croutons for one salad?). They reminded us to use Mr. Tongs and Mr. Gloves, not fingers, to pick up food. They discussed the courtesy cards; 95 percent of the customers said the restrooms were unclean. (The cards must have been filled out before I cleaned.)

The next day at Mickey D's was meat day. They put me, a vegetarian, on the grill. I stared at sizzling sausage and bacon all morning. Then I moved to toasting muffins but kept forgetting to take them out when the machine buzzed. There were so many timers and buzzers and bells going off, I couldn't figure out which one went to which machine. It sounded like a science-fiction movie with a meltdown every ten seconds.

Sarah, the Grill Queen, showed me how to speed things up. She picked up four sausages at a time, using her fingers to keep them from falling. She had scars from her fingertips to her elbows from splattering grease. She opened the place at 4 a.m. and left at 1 p.m. She was 37 and had started at McDonald's

as a teenager. Her dream was to own a restaurant. She loved working the grill.

"It's hard. It's nonstop. It'll make you or break you," she said.

At lunch, I assembled burgers, Big Macs, Quarter Pounders, and Triple Cheeseburgers. I thought a Triple Cheeseburger meant three pieces of cheese on one burger. Who in the world eats three beef patties?

Between 11:30 a.m. and 1 p.m. we were slammed. People called back special orders for dozens of burgers at once. We were supposed to use tongs to pick up the meat, but they slow you down. I tried wearing plastic gloves, but my fingers stuck together. So I used my bare hands and burned my fingertips.

The next day, they put me at the front drive-thru window where people picked up orders. All I had to do was hand food out a window. What could be easier? No one told me about the language barrier. The computer screen above me read: SACHBI, SAMFEG, SAEGBI. It took an hour to decipher the code: SA = sausage; BI = biscuit; MF = muffin; EG = egg; CH = cheese. What was a VANCON? Vanilla cone. For breakfast? Yep. I wasn't the only nutritionally challenged person who liked ice cream before noon.

Kay, my trainer for the day, reminded me to fold the bag tops, not crumple them, and not to lean on the window. She didn't even yell when I dropped an order between the car and the window. Kay was 37, had two kids, and had worked at McDonald's for 12 years.

"I love it," she said. "It's tough, but living on welfare doesn't make it."

Turnover is high. Most employees quit to go to college or

find other work. Some can't handle the stress. On my last day, I could see why.

One customer plopped his toddler son on the counter and ordered a triple cheeseburger. Then he told me I got it wrong. He wanted a value meal. So I got that. Then he said I got that wrong. He wanted the value meal without cheese on the burgers. Then he complained about that. The manager had to unjam my machine five times. I nearly violated number 7 of the McDonald's Ten Commandments: "Our customers are not people to argue or match wits with." This guy was lucky I didn't violate one of the original Ten Commandments: "Thou shalt not kill."

That customer saw me as some loser because I was working a fast-food job. It's a mistake many people make. They're wrong. It's noble work to feed people and lift the spirits of strangers. Martin Luther King Jr. was right when he said that all labor that uplifts humanity has dignity and importance.

Everyone I worked with at that McDonald's gave humanity a boost. They also knew to hold on to their own dignity. This wasn't menial work. It was a foundation for their dreams. Just ask former burger flippers Jay Leno, Star Jones, Shania Twain, Rachel McAdams, and Jeff Bezos, the founder of Amazon.

When my fast-food career at McDonald's ended, the owner asked me what I thought of working there. I told him to get rid of the hats, put a stool at the drive-thru window so employees could rest, and give everyone a big raise.

Even the mistakes belong.

Every creation starts with a lump of useless clay.

The potter leaves a part of himself in every creation.

Only the potter can hear the clay. He listens to know its breaking point, to learn its limitations, to reach past them or to accept them and make them a thing of beauty.

I've never tried my hand at clay but got to watch as Tom Gedeon sat at the potter's wheel, took a block of burnt-orange clay, squeezed it down then up, trying to keep it smooth and centered on the wheel. That's the key, he told me: stay centered.

The people who visit the Jesuit Retreat House in Cleveland seek the gift of the potter: staying centered and letting go as the Potter shapes your life.

At 78, Father Gedeon, whom everyone called Tom, still saw himself as the Potter's lump of clay. He could probably quote

Jeremiah 18:6: "Behold, as the clay is in the potter's hand, so are you in my hand." But he let the clay speak for him, not the Bible.

Ordained as a Jesuit priest in 1956, Tom ran the retreat house for 16 years, then traveled the country as executive director of Retreats International for 20 years. He started the professional organization that now connects more than 500 retreat houses in the United States and Canada.

After he retired, he joked that you can't say you're retired in religious life, so he called himself "an artist in residence." He puttered around this 57-acre sanctuary and tried, through his art, to help others hear the "universal call to holiness."

When he was the director there in 1962, he hung traditional religious art in the halls, Rembrandt-like depictions of Mary, Jesus, and churches.

"That's stuff I forced on people," he said, cringing.

When he returned in 2000, he took down all those "holy" pictures and hung his photographs. A lily pad in bloom, rowboats moored in a foggy cove, a flower poking through a drab gray fence: proof that even in the bleakness of life, beauty persists.

"These are the real holy pictures," he insisted. "Nature is God's greatest message of beauty."

Each captured a moment that delighted him, that he froze with his camera to delight others. He had taken pictures all his life, but he'd never touched clay until a nun suggested it a few years before. What a thrill to turn a mess of clay into a vase, a bowl, a teapot. He called art "the most primitive experience of God."

Off the garage, in a room the size of a toolshed, he had

just enough space to sit at the potter's wheel. His white wispy hair refused to behave in the humidity and poked out like Einstein's as he finished a bowl. The dish ended up with a slight dent only he could see.

"It's got some limitations," he said, but he wasn't disappointed. He was intrigued. It's been said that the Amish leave an imperfection in every quilt they create to remind them that only God creates with perfection. Tom didn't try to be perfect. He took joy in the imperfect.

Tom could tell by the coolness of the clay that it was time to flip the bowl over. He hesitated. It was the biggest one he had ever made, and he wasn't sure he could trust his aging hands with eight pounds of clay.

"If you want to see a grown man cry...," he warned as he flipped the bowl over. It didn't crack.

Even if it did, there's no such thing as a mistake to a potter. Or the Potter.

Once, when Tom used a stick to form a long neck in a vase, the clay bent, grabbed the stick, and wouldn't let go. A failure? Not at all. Everyone wanted to buy the disfigured vase.

The spinning clay pulls sweat from your hands, so the potter leaves a part of himself in every creation. Maybe that's why Tom always hated to let them go. He used to take a picture of each one, to hold it in his memory. He could have fetched more than the $20 or $30 he asked for each creation, but he wanted art to remain affordable to all. As the wheel turned slowly and another bowl spun, he talked about how grateful he was to delight others in his "closing years."

"Another ten years would be a great gift," he said.

He got only two more. He died in 2005, at 80. When I look

on the shelf in my living room at the vase he gave me, I think of how beautiful our flaws can be when we surrender like clay in the hands of the Potter.

It's hard to surrender. I keep striving for perfection as if it's attainable in all things when, in reality, most of the blessings that come to me, and most of the blessings that come through me, come through the imperfect. It is through our mistakes, our misses, our almosts, that we bless the lives of others. All of that mess belongs. There exists, as William James called it, an "unseen order" in my disorder.

What a relief. Still, it's hard to *feel* that relief when someone points out my flaws at work, not just because I have so many, but because I so want to be perfect. I have a constant need to prove that I'm not flawed because deep down, that's how I felt through most of my childhood. I was one big fat mistake. There's a core of that leftover shame inside me that gets activated now and then when someone criticizes my work. There's still a lingering belief that when I make a mistake, I am a mistake. Not just what I did is flawed, but who I am is one big flaw.

I've always loved that one of my daughter's blue eyes has three brown stripes running through it. She always colored in those stripes in every drawing of herself. She never saw them as a flaw, but as a unique imprint God had left on her alone. If only we could see our flaws that way, as something beautiful and useful.

The potter reminded me that on everything we create there are two imprints: ours and God's. Both are good. Both belong.

If you're going to doubt anything, doubt your doubts.

A college professor once gave me a short, simple prayer to help conquer fear:

"Lord, I take refuge in You from cowardice."

Those are the words Zeki Saritoprak uses to silence his fears. He's a professor of Islamic studies at John Carroll University in Cleveland, where I got my master's degree in religious studies.

Most of us don't call ourselves cowards, and yet we constantly doubt ourselves instead of our doubts. I used to think being brave meant having no fear. When I heard this definition, I laughed out loud: *Bravery is being the only one who knows you're afraid.*

We're all just faking courage. Some of us just do it better than others. "Fake it till you make it" has carried me along for years. My friend Vicki taught me one better: "Faith it till you make it." That will carry me along forever.

Many years ago, I met a mom outside a church hall in Wadsworth, Ohio. She told me about her daughter, Diana, who wanted to be a writer. This mom was so proud of her daughter for knowing what she wanted to do with her life. Her face lit up when she talked about how Diana was always writing in journals, how she worked on her high school yearbook and got a story printed in the local paper.

But she said everyone was discouraging her daughter from pursuing what she loved. I heard the same discouraging words when I started my career:

There are no jobs in journalism, people told me.

There is no money in writing, they warned.

There is no room in the world for your voice, they challenged.

If I would have listened to all their doubts—and mine—I never would have ended up working nearly three decades as a professional journalist. I remember how worried I felt when I heard people tell me: Don't become a writer, you'll never be able to pay the rent. Don't become a writer, newspapers are a dying industry. Don't become a writer, the world already has too many.

It was hard not to listen. What did I know? I was a single mom who was broke and years behind my peers. They graduated from college at 21; I graduated at 30. I had more desire than actual talent, so I simply listened to the desire and let it rule me.

It was hard because my doubts often shouted down my desire.

Who do you think you are?

Who are you to dream so big?

Who cares about what you have to say?

The road was rocky at first. My first job barely covered the rent. All along, people kept warning me that newspapers were dying. They told me that in the 1980s when afternoon papers were folding across the country. They're telling me that now as digital news replaces print news. No one knows for sure what lies ahead.

The same kinds of people who cautioned me were older and wiser than me and made me fearful of my career choice. They understood the economy, the laws of supply and demand, the complexities of the job market and global economy.

So what.

I had to do what was in my heart, and they didn't know what that was. No one else really knows what's in our hearts but us. No one knows how loud your own heart sings or pines or aches to do what it alone loves.

There are scores of others out there like me. Not all of them want to be writers. Some want to be painters or architects or carpenters or dentists or undertakers. Someone out there is discouraging them or has already discouraged them from going after their hearts' desires.

I knew a man who wanted to be a funeral director with all his heart but got stuck taking over the family grocery business, until decades later when he broke free and became an undertaker. I worked for a funeral director who wanted to be a jazz musician but, to his dismay, spent his life running the family mortuary business. He never broke free of it.

Diana's mom told me she had wanted to be an artist but ended up studying chemistry and hated it. Finally, when she

hit middle age, she went back to school and started working as a draftsman. She loves it.

You can't listen to the critics. The world is full of them. My guess is the critics are the same people who didn't go after their own dreams and feel that pain every time someone else goes after a dream.

There's room in the world for your desire, whatever it is. Someone out there needs your gift. There is room in the world for your voice. Someone out there needs to hear it. I finally told myself, *Writing is like music*. There can never be too many songs. Someone out there who hates country music loves rap, and vice versa. The person who is moved by Shakespeare may hate John Grisham. The readers who hate my voice may love yours.

People will tell you the world is full of writers, but most of them talk away their words, talk away the plots of their unwritten novels while downing shots at a bar because they're too afraid to risk failing. They embrace their doubts instead of going after their dreams.

To go after what you want in life, you have to silence the critics, starting with the biggest one: you.

Sometimes the job you want is the job you already have.

The day I was hired to work at the *Beacon Journal*, I cried the whole way home. An hour's worth of tears. Buckets.

Why? I had just accepted a job to be a business reporter. I hated business news. What if I had just made a horrible mistake? After six months of writing sales and earnings reports, I did get bored and restless. A local magazine offered me a job as a feature writer. One wise soul in the newsroom encouraged me to stay put to build a résumé, pension, and life experience.

"You've only been here a few months," he said. "Give this newsroom a chance. Give yourself a chance here. You'll never regret it."

He was right. That "boring" beat they gave me? It was a mix of leftovers no one wanted: farming, health insurance, and the blimp. This is how boring it was:

So I'm flying the Goodyear Blimp...

What?!

Yep.

I proposed a story to follow the Goodyear Blimp with a photographer. We drove from Akron to South Bend, Indiana, and I got to fly in the blimp while it was covering a Notre Dame football game. I spent days interviewing the rope crew, the guys on the ground, who are an amazing bunch. They don't get the glory of the pilots, but they greet the townspeople in the area and make them feel welcome when they line up to see the blimp.

There's nothing like riding in the blimp. It doesn't feel like flying. It feels like riding in a boat. You sort of bob along on the sky. It's uplifting but noisy. The TV camera crew took the door out to shove in a big camera to cover the game. It was so noisy we had to wear headphones. We were flying over Notre Dame, waving to Touchdown Jesus, the Golden Dome, watching the Fighting Irish against Michigan State. At halftime, the pilot turned to me and said, "Here, you drive."

Me? Me at the controls of the *Spirit of Akron*?

Whoa.

How could I say no? I was still pinching myself that I got to fly in the Goodyear Blimp. It's a rare treat usually reserved for corporate bigwigs who are the best clients of the tire company.

Flying it? WOW.

He explained how simple it was and pointed to two gauges. An altimeter with numbers and a dial that was split across the middle. The top half was blue. "That's for sky. Keep it in sky," he said. He warned me not to let the needle on the altimeter

rise too much or the blimp would float up and the skin would get hotter and expand. He also told me to keep the blimp in the blue part. Don't let it head south to the ground.

No problem. How hard could it be?

I was doing great. Then he left to go to the bathroom. Yep. There is a bathroom on the blimp. Sort of. There's no toilet, just a tube. The fluid just "dissipates" into the atmosphere. At least that's what the pilot told me. (Tip: Never stand directly under the Goodyear Blimp.)

He walked down the gondola to the back of the blimp and I was alone at the controls. It was halftime. I was watching the band when all of a sudden, the altimeter needle jumped. So I pointed the blimp down, just a tad. The needle rose higher, so I pointed the blimp down more. The front of the blimp gondola is all window, so I was looking at the ground and bracing my feet so I wouldn't fall through the glass. Yikes! The blimp was no longer in the blue.

From the ground, it must have looked like a scene from a disaster movie with the blimp preparing for a crash landing on the 50-yard line. The pilot had to hold on to the seats as he walked back to me and grabbed the controls. He righted the blimp and said, "It's hard enough to use that thing without standing on your head." He also promised I would never, ever fly another blimp.

What an experience—at a job I thought I would hate.

That job gave me many opportunities far beyond covering business news once I decided to raise the bar for myself. I volunteered to go to El Salvador to write about the end of the war through the eyes of a boy who had lost his leg and got a prosthetic leg in Ohio. I flew to Northern Ireland to write about

"the troubles" through the perspectives of children who came to America for the summer to escape them.

The secret to any job isn't to leave when you get bored or restless or irritable, but to stay and make it better. Sometimes we simply need to stay put and call it holy ground. A dear friend of mine used to change jobs every six months. She always ended up hating every job. Her solution was the geographic cure. The only problem was, she always took herself along. We all know people like that. The solution to every problem is to move. Moving will solve their marital woes, their drinking problem, their employment dilemma, their financial mess, their lack of passion, their surplus of boredom. A better solution is to change you, not the job. When you change you, the job automatically changes.

Moving might be the solution for some, but as the old story goes, the new guy in town asks an old-timer, "What are the people like in this town?" The old-timer asks, "What were they like in the last town?" The man says, "Mean and nasty." The old-timer answers, "Then that's what you'll find here." The next day, another new resident walks into the bar and asks what the people in this town are like. The old-timer asks, "What were they like in the last town?" The man says, "They were kindhearted and giving." The old-timer tells him, "Then that's what you'll find here."

You attract what you are. Or as Mr. Brady, father of the infamous Brady Bunch, once said, "Wherever you go, there you are."

The simple idea of staying put was transformed into a sacred vow by the monks of old. Saint Benedict had the idea of making a commitment to remain in one community to

keep the monks from wandering off in search of the perfect place to serve God, as if such a place existed. The Trappist monk Thomas Merton struggled more with his vow of stability than his vow of poverty. He constantly fought the desire to leave the monastery for more solitude and a deeper experience of God. He ended up spending his life in a Kentucky monastery writing books about the holiness in the ordinary life around him.

You don't have to be a monk to figure out that the search for happiness takes place on the inner landscape, not in filling up a U-Haul every year. I have never lived outside of Ohio. My restlessness always found an outlet in changing the scenery of my workplace. I've been a journalist for nearly three decades. I went through phases and fads of wanting to leave for more money, more prestige, more fulfillment.

Maybe it's middle age that cries out, "Enough!" Or the not-so-subtle daily reminders that convince me to stay, like the postcard of the red ruby slippers my husband gave me. Dorothy's shoes remind me, "There's no place like home," and to not go searching for my heart's desire any farther than my own backyard.

I've heard reporters grumble—and I've been one of them—that if we were real writers, we'd be in New York City writing novels or for the *New York Times*. But one photographer I worked with, Robin Witek, showed me that we don't need to be anywhere but in the present moment to find fulfillment.

Her approach to life and to taking pictures was to choose a spot, wait, and let life happen around her. When she covered a basketball game, she didn't chase after the action, running up

and down the court. She chose her spot and captured the action around her.

Once you choose a place to stay put in life, a job, or a town, the landscape will never fail to amaze you. No matter where you decide to sink your roots or grow your branches, you are already standing on holy ground.

LESSON
13

Most of the time, the only person in your way is you.

I used to keep a yellow sticky note posted on my computer that read "Think like a man."

Men seemed to figure out how to get up the career ladder faster, earn more money at the top, and never complain about a glass ceiling or a sticky floor holding them back. I threw the sticky note away after the YWCA honored me with a Women of Achievement Award. The motto of the event was "A career ladder can be climbed in heels." I don't know about you, but I can't even walk in heels, much less climb a ladder in them.

Both women and men have given me a lot of tips for getting ahead. How do you climb up the ladder? You start by getting out of your own way. Some of us—insert my name here—come up with every form of excuse to avoid climbing over, under, or around the hurdles life throws at us.

We blame the boss, our dad, our seventh-grade teacher. We

blame the system; the economy; the people above us, below us, around us. We let all those buts get in our way. *Yeah, but this is the way we've always done it. Yeah, but the boss will never allow it. Yeah, but the board won't approve of it. Yeah, but I'm too old...too young...too inexperienced...too overqualified...too unskilled.*

It's time to get rid of your big but.

I have an entire excuse catalog for things I'm too scared to do or don't really want to do. Most of them start with the words *I can't.*

I can't; I'm too busy, too tired, too overwhelmed. I can't use LinkedIn, Facebook, Twitter, Excel, PowerPoint; it's too confusing and difficult. I can't; I'm not good with money, statistics, numbers, technology, machinery. I can't; I'm not smart enough to figure it out by myself and I'll do it all wrong.

Then there's the mysterious "they." "They" won't let me. Who exactly are we talking about?

Someone once told me, "If you don't want to do it, you'll find an excuse. If you want to do it, you'll find a way." It really is that simple.

We all know people who spend 15 minutes explaining why they can't do a task because they didn't have the time, yet the task would have taken 10 minutes less to complete than giving the excuse. I've been that person. I either didn't want to do the task or feared I'd do it wrong, so I didn't do it. My husband loves to remind me that I once said I'd never use e-mail. I resisted technology because I hated feeling powerless when it didn't work. My husband always tells me that when you're complaining or defending, you're losing. I finally stopped complaining and defending my weaknesses. Instead,

I learned how to embrace technology to empower me. I now love the freedom e-mail gives me to work from home. I once hated Facebook and Twitter until I hired someone to teach me how to use them.

We often hold ourselves back simply by believing we're being held back. My friend Michael used to tell me if you tie up a donkey long enough, once you untie him he'll stay there. You can get so used to being stuck you don't move once you're free.

What's keeping you stuck? It might not be a glass ceiling or a sticky floor. Usually it's the person standing between them: you. There's usually a payoff for being stuck. If you can blame someone else, you never have to be responsible for anything that goes wrong. The flip side is, nothing ever changes to improve your life.

I'm constantly amazed by people who refuse to excuse themselves from life. Victor Riesel was a newspaper columnist who keeps me from making excuses. I never met him, but I saved his obituary and read it often.

He was a syndicated labor columnist who wrote about corruption by gangsters and labor unions. One day he stepped out of a restaurant in Manhattan and a man threw acid in his face. Victor was blinded for life. His career could have ended that night back in 1956. But the person who wanted to silence him only made his voice stronger. Victor kept writing and typing his own columns. He woke early and his wife read the paper to him cover to cover before he went to the office. When he was attacked, his column was in 193 papers. Before he retired in 1990, it was in 350 papers.

Gee, how can I call in sick after reading that? How can I

whine about anyone holding me back? How can I complain about work conditions?

I can't.

I've known parents who banned the word *can't* from their kids' vocabulary. Strike it from your own. That's the first step in getting out of your own way. Here are a few more:

Preserve your power. Live a blame-free, no-fault, victim-free life. No one can make you feel or think or do anything that isn't right for you.

If you can't change a person, place, situation, or institution, change how you think, feel, or respond to it.

My friend Bob used to tell me, "If life stinks, check your own diaper first." It might not be the boss or a coworker who messed up. You could be sitting in a mess of your own making, or it could simply be your attitude that stinks.

Be you, but be the best version of you. Like it or not, people make judgments about your age, education, credibility, and expertise based on midriff tops, low-cut blouses, miniskirts, tattoos, nose rings, and flip-flops. If you want to stand out in a memorable way, make sure it's how you want to be remembered.

Take the action you know to take. My friends in recovery love to tell the frog story: There are four frogs on a log. Three decide to jump off. How many are left on the log? Four. Those three only made a decision. They didn't take action. Take one small step that will propel you forward. Make the call. Send the e-mail. Ask for the raise.

Become teachable. It's hard for me to learn new things because I lack the humility to ask for help. Not knowing how to do something taps into that childhood core of shame inside

me that tells me I'm stupid. I can now give myself permission to be a student of life. There is an endless supply of people to teach you anything you need to know. Pay them if you have to.

The best way to get out of your own way?

Take 100 percent responsibility for your own happiness and success. Stop believing that you're being held back. You can make an excuse or you can make it happen. It's always your call.

14

God is still speaking.

It's hard to imagine anyone willing to answer this old employment ad:

> We offer you no salary; no recompense; no holiday; no pensions, but much hard work; a poor dwelling; few consolations; many disappointments; frequent sickness; a violent or lonely death.

The job? Join the Sisters of the Presentation of the Blessed Virgin Mary.

As you might guess, nuns are a tough breed. The Dominican nuns taught me for eight years at Immaculate Conception School in Ravenna, Ohio. I never quite appreciated the contributions of nuns until I saw the national *Women & Spirit* museum exhibit that showed all they did to build schools, hospitals, and charities.

Catholic sisters created the country's largest private school system. They started some 110 universities. During the Civil War, they cared for both Union and Confederate soldiers. One nun started an insurance company for loggers so they'd have medical care coverage. Another one helped develop an incubator for newborns. One nun helped start the Mayo Clinic. Sister Henrietta Gorris, who helped rebuild poor neighborhoods after the race riots in Cleveland back in 1966, lived by a motto every inner city could use now: "Don't move, improve." One nun helped start Alcoholics Anonymous in Akron. Sister Mary Ignatia Gavin sneaked drunks into beds at St. Thomas Hospital to help them sober up.

And yes, some of them beat multiplication tables into us. I still have the scars on my knuckles. Even that was gently addressed. One exhibit stated: "Memories of Catholic school graduates vary widely, from affectionate to painful." I looked but didn't see a yardstick on display.

At every twist and turn of history, nuns helped and healed others. A giant cylinder bore the names of every order from Adorers of the Blood of Christ to Xavier Sisters. They changed the world not by force, but by prayer and a loyalty to their mission to serve others, a mission that constantly changed.

The nuns I had throughout grade school taught me how to read, write, add, subtract, and tell time. They also taught me that we might have more than one mission in life. I used to wonder what God's will was for me, used to struggle with finding out that one perfect thing God chose for me alone. What was my personal mission in life? The nuns taught me by their own lives that a person's mission in life might constantly change.

Sister Mary Ann Flannery used to be a college professor. Then she became director of the Jesuit Retreat House in Parma, which I call my spiritual home. She told me that the exciting thing about being a nun is: "You go where the grace leads you. You let the street be your chapel. You let your love of others be your vow." She's not boxed in by any one calling. She knows God is still speaking and listens daily for that day's direction.

The hardest part of being a nun, at least according to the ones I've talked to, isn't the vow of chastity. You don't hear scandals about nuns running amok and having affairs right and left. The hardest part is letting go of all they have loved about their sisterhood as convents merge and close. Nuns, I fear, are on the verge of extinction.

Nuns have taught me not to let the last word of God get in the way of the next word of God. God is still speaking. God's will might be one thing, or it might be many, or it might change as life changes. They constantly reinvent themselves as the inner evolution unfolds.

Sister Evangeline Doyle was my sixth-grade teacher. She did her best, but she didn't seem to love teaching a bunch of hormonally challenged boys and girls. I found out why when she stopped teaching.

She was an artist who felt like she was going to explode if she didn't create. She was small and frail but could attack a 5,000-pound chunk of limestone with a mallet and chisel like no one else. She traded in her habit for a pair of faded jeans and a torn sweatshirt. For years she was a hidden sculptor, making creations in the convent basement. She finally quit teaching and dedicated herself to her art. She stayed a nun

but signed her work as Vang. She made endless paintings and sculptures in wood, limestone, and clay, including a massive one in front of the public library in Akron. Her goal was to help others appreciate the beauty in all things, to find God in everything.

I saved the prayer card from her funeral. It carried this quote by her: "There is a certain mystery of life in stone, it is so strong and enduring. Within the stone the artist comes into contact with the mystery of God's own creation."

I never got to thank her for showing me how to say yes to my dream. That's why it was important to thank my second-grade teacher. Sister Eleanor Wack didn't just teach us to read; she taught us to read the face of God. She taught us that God's face wasn't just in the man hanging on the crucifix, but in nature, in one another, and in every experience life would hand us.

When she shared her love of the stars with one class, a child stayed up late to see what the fuss was all about. The next day the breathless boy told her, "Sister, I saw Orion last night."

Sister Eleanor saw God everywhere, especially in the toothless grins of six-year-olds whose noses she wiped and whose shoes she tied. For 50 years, she taught hundreds to read Dick and Jane and Dr. Seuss. Adults came up to her in restaurants all over Akron to thank her for their love of reading.

She started her first day of teaching as Sister Dismas, back when I had her. She finished her last day as Sister Eleanor. At 74, her knees gave out. I went to say good-bye, and to thank her.

She was the last Dominican from Our Lady of the Elms in Akron to teach full-time. At one time the order had almost

220 sisters, nearly all of them teachers. She spent her last day hugging children, comforting weeping mothers, and greeting former students. A deputy chief from the Akron Police Department showed up to say good-bye. So did I. The report card she gave me in second grade says she taught me phonics, spelling, and arithmetic. It doesn't say that she taught me to love learning.

Back then, she was wrapped in a Dominican habit that revealed only her face and hands. They were enough. In those blue eyes and gentle hands, we caught more than a glimpse of how much God loved us.

The report cards her students glue in scrapbooks don't say that she taught them to say "Pardon me?" instead of "What?" or to spend at least four minutes in prayer every night—two minutes to talk to God and two minutes to listen.

"I try to teach them for life, to become what God planned them to be," she said.

After the children left, she took down the sign in room 109 that read SISTER ELEANOR'S ROOM.

"I'm not a crier, but in my heart I'm crying," she confided.

Before the final bell, she reviewed one last lesson. "What do you say when someone isn't nice to you?" she asked.

One boy recited, "You're not my friend, but I see God in you."

Sister smiled and told him, "That'll last you a lifetime."

It will. It did for me.

Make gentle the life of this world.

The Lost Boys of Sudan stood in the big medical supply warehouse early one morning waiting for the chance to send help back home.

At one point they broke into song, singing words in Dinka that had renewed their spirits back in 1983 when they were boys fleeing the civil war in Sudan. As children, they ran from bullets, crossed rivers infested with crocodiles, and walked thousands of miles under the blazing sun from Sudan to Ethiopia to Kenya.

As they sang in the MedWish International warehouse in Cleveland, one of them, Majier Deng, explained to me the song's meaning. "It's a God song," he said softly. "When we went from place to place, God always bless us, protect us, wherever we are, whatever we do."

Peter Manyiel nodded. "God helped us survive," he said.

"We always put everything in God hands. Today, we giving back."

The Lost Boys of Sudan are no longer lost and no longer boys. The six men sang to bless the medical supplies bound for South Sudan as a forklift hummed around them. Six of the Lost Boys came to help pack 10,000 pounds of medical supplies into a 40-foot-long cargo container bound for South Sudan. It is so poor there, one in seven children die before turning five. People walk two hours to a clinic or wait for help under a tree. There is no hospital, no equipment, no beds.

Majier said the shipment will show the people of Sudan that someone cares. "That is true love, to care about someone you don't know," he said.

Dr. Lee Ponsky started MedWish International in 1993 when he was just 20. He wanted to be a doctor and ended up working one summer at Mt. Sinai Hospital in Cleveland. He wanted to go somewhere else and make a difference. He has made it his life's mission to collect local medical supplies that would end up in landfills and send them to poor countries all over the world to save lives.

As a medical student working in a clinic in Nigeria, he saw doctors make their own saline, use fishing line for sutures, and run out of clean water during surgery. It was Lee's job to wash, powder, and sew up medical exam gloves to use again.

Lee graduated from the University of Rochester, and then he got his medical degree at Case Western Reserve University. He started the nonprofit MedWish in his parents' garage. He later became chief of urological oncology at University Hospitals in Cleveland.

He calls MedWish his hobby. Some hobby.

The Cleveland Clinic donates the use of the 38,000-square-foot warehouse that he has transformed into an international medical supply depot. MedWish collects and distributes medical supplies from 50 hospitals and nursing homes from Cleveland to California. MedWish ships to more than 90 countries, from Belize to Zambia. It takes no government funding and runs solely on donations.

It costs from $5,000 to $10,000 to ship one container. Each container is customized for what that country needs and what limitations it may have regarding clean water and electricity. MedWish vets every recipient. The containers are filled in Cleveland, put on a train, taken to a port city, and sent out by sea. MedWish helps deal with customs, impassable roads, changing political climates, and rules that vary from country to country. The organization is able to match good intentions with practical realities on the ground. MedWish tracks when the container arrives and when it is released.

People drop off walkers and wheelchairs, unopened gauze and gloves. Most donors prefer to be anonymous. One nursing home donated beds. A hospital donated sleep sacks for babies and burn dressings. The warehouse is full of hospital beds, incubators, operating room lights, mattresses, examination tables, IV poles, infant airways and bottles. There are stacks of beds, wheelchairs and dialysis machines, incubators and operating lights ready to go.

"Everything you see in this warehouse would be thrown in a landfill," Lee told me. "What we throw away is gold in other parts of the world."

I love the small sign attached to the office refrigerator: THE

Person Who Says It Cannot Be Done Should Not Interrupt the Person Doing It. MedWish runs with the help of donors, volunteers, and special-needs students paid to sort items.

Huge banners on the wall remind everyone of the mission. Each shows the face of one child from Africa, Central America, the Middle East, and South America. When I met Dr. Ponsky, I thought of those powerful words by Robert F. Kennedy: "Let us dedicate ourselves to what the Greeks wrote so many years ago: to tame the savageness of man and make gentle the life of this world."

That's what Lee Ponsky is doing here. A manual resuscitator sent to Laos saved the lives of five babies. A defibrillator considered outdated by U.S. standards is saving lives in Gabon, Africa. A heart valve MedWish sent to Honduras saved the life of a 16-year-old girl. A group of 67 volunteers took supplies to Nicaragua that treated the back pain of poor farmers. The patient who came in with bad arthritis and a knee brace made of wilted cabbage leaves held together with rags left with an elastic band and a smile.

There's a map of the world and a large wipe board that reads "Currently shipping to: Honduras, Ghana, Nicaragua, Peru, Uganda." It lists the "hot items" needed most: gauze, gloves, antibiotic cream, tongue depressors, and stethoscopes.

If you're going on vacation, you can take a box of medical supplies with you and turn your vacation into a lifesaving medical mission. Doctors traveling overseas stop in and get supplies. One doctor visiting Vietnam filled his suitcase with nebulizers.

Donors can adopt a room: pediatric supplies, wound care,

maternal health care, sutures, instruments, IVs, personnel protection—gloves, masks, and the like. There are tubs of breathing tubes, infant airways, baby bottles, catheters, maternity pads, and suction devices. Maternal packs include everything midwives need to deliver a baby.

The Lost Boys smiled at the pallets of bandages, gauze, ointments, IV poles, exam tables, wheelchairs, stretchers, gurneys, beds, and mattresses headed for South Sudan. They walked past a wall with a map of the world full of stickpins where containers have gone, to Central and South America, Africa, and beyond. A map of Ohio bulges with stickpins showing where the volunteers come from.

"Thank you, thank you," the Lost Boys said, almost in song.

They wanted to tuck something else into the shipment. They sat at a table and wrote letters to put inside the cargo container. Slowly and carefully, they printed words of hope for people on the other side of the ocean.

"This gift from MedWish is just a beginning," Majier wrote. "Keep praying and trusting in God Almighty. This gift, I hope, will make a difference."

Lazarus Makhoi paused a moment, then wrote the words he had wanted to hear all those years ago when he was that boy in a refugee camp:

"I didn't forget about you."

To help make a difference, go to www.medwish.org.

Sometimes your mission is revealed moment by moment.

Life always gives us exactly what we need at every moment, and in every moment, we get the chance to bless life back.

There's a lovely quote by American Zen pioneer Charlotte Joko Beck that I keep on my desk to remind me that every bug, every problem, every traffic ticket, every boss, every bump, every bruise, every breath teaches us something. "Every moment is the guru," Joko Beck said.

In every moment lies your mission.

How long is a moment? I don't know, but I once heard that a minute is a moment with handles. It takes a mere 60 seconds to make a difference. Cancer taught me that.

The nurses and doctors who cared for me didn't have a lot of time to comfort me while they cared for me. They had other patients to juggle, but they took care to make every moment matter.

When I woke up from a surgical biopsy, the surgeon came to answer my questions. Right before Dr. Leonard Brzozowski left my bedside to check on the pathology report to see if the lump he had taken out of my breast was cancer, he did something I've never forgotten. He squeezed my toes. It was a small moment of human connection, but a powerful act of grace. I was wrapped in a surgical bra, tucked in a thin hospital gown, and wearing those little hospital socks. I felt so vulnerable. That little squeeze helped me trust him then and down the road, the day we shared a big moment.

The day he peeled off all the layers of gauze around my chest so I could see what I looked like for the first time after a double mastectomy, he sat next to me on the hospital bed and unwrapped me slowly and tenderly, as if opening a fragile gift. He created a sacred moment for me to see my new body. He did it in a way that put both me and my husband at ease with my blank chest.

Then there was the nurse who called me at home after surgery. She said she wanted to check in on me to see how I was doing. It might have been a routine call, but she did it with compassion that I could feel through the phone. She told me she was sorry I had to go through cancer.

In my work and in my time as a patient and as an EMT, I've talked to nurses from recovery rooms, coronary care, pediatrics, geriatrics, and ER and trauma units. They've shared the comedy and tragedy of the job, how they're pushed and pulled in 100 ways, how they barely get a chance to use the bathroom, how they end up wearing blood and vomit home.

Nurses are the patient's advocate, the doctor's eyes and ears, and everyone's scapegoat. They can page your doctor but can't

make the doctor magically appear. My sister is a nurse and wears a T-shirt around the house that reads "Be kind to nurses. We keep doctors from accidentally killing you."

What do they get in return? They're greeted with "Hey you...Yo...Lady...Nurse Ratched" and choice words they're too kind to repeat. They also are called IV leaguers and the heartbeat of health care. The few times in my life when I've had the misfortune to be a patient, nurses came through for me.

I wasn't always a compliant patient 16 years ago when I was diagnosed with breast cancer. When it came time to set up my chemo appointments, I wanted to schedule them around my volleyball games. I hadn't yet wrapped my brain around the concept that I had a life-threatening disease. I kept trying to delay setting up the chemo because I was scared. Finally the nurse looked at me and said firmly, "You need to get your priorities straight." I threw a fit and demanded a new nurse, but deep down, I knew she was right.

When the antinausea drugs weren't working, my chemotherapy nurse, Pam Boone, spoke up for me and pestered the doctor for better medicine to put in my IV when I lacked the energy to speak up.

I met him only once, but a nurse named John in radiology called me honey and promised I would get through six weeks of daily radiation in no time, and I did.

Countless others, whose names I never knew, watched over me. Anonymous blurs in scrubs, those angels in comfortable shoes left behind an imprint of compassion in the squeeze of a hand, the caress of a cheek, the fluff of a pillow.

Nurses are up there with grandparents and guardian angels.

They are dedicated to the weak, the confused, the broken of body, mind, and spirit. They don't care if you throw up on them, miss the bedpan, or hit the call light in the middle of the night just because you're scared and don't want to be alone. They will go to bat for you against disease, track down doctors on golf courses, and stay late just to check on you one last time. And they do it all, minute by precious minute.

Oh, the things they put up with. The fights from the Jerry Springer families who smuggle in beer and bring diabetics doughnuts, then demand more insulin and threaten to sue if they don't get it. They mistake a hospital for a hotel and the nurse for a housekeeper.

Nurses get yelled at, kicked, slapped, punched, spit on, and sexually harassed by people in various states of mental illness, intoxication, and just plain arrogance. The paycheck doesn't begin to cover the endless miles nurses walk, the meals they skip, the holidays they miss with their families. They stay on their feet for 12-hour stretches to wash blood and glass off a car crash survivor, stabilize a broken neck, teach a mother to nurse a newborn, save a diabetic's leg, help a hospice patient let go.

Nurses have told me about family members who have started fights, untied restrained patients, poked around gunshot wounds, brought in babies and let them crawl on the floor, ordered pizzas and left the mess behind.

People don't go into nursing because they love the paperwork or the pain-in-the-neck patients, families, and doctors. They go into nursing because they want to help people. It isn't a job. It's a calling. A minute-by-minute, moment-by-moment calling.

Nurses have taught me that it takes only a moment to make a difference, to make the mother of a newborn feel celebrated and the mother of a stillborn feel comforted.

It takes only a moment to help the homeless and lonely feel at home in the world. To make a teenager with cancer feel confident she can face her classmates bald at the senior prom. To give senior citizens their dignity when they have to use a bedpan, a catheter, or a diaper.

It takes only a moment to make a woman who just lost both breasts believe she is still whole. To make a stroke patient who can no longer speak feel understood. To dry some tears, hold a hand, or tell a son that his mother forgave him before she took her last breath.

Nurses help newborns take their first breaths and grandparents take their last. In between those bookend breaths, nurses make scared children feel safe and scarred people feel beautiful. They fulfill their calling in life every time they answer a call light.

They constantly remind me that each of us can be the light, even if all we do is shine for a moment.

When things fall apart, they could actually be falling into place.

There's an old saying: "Some years ask questions, some years answer them." Most of us would rather be living in a year with answers.

Sometimes you go through months or years of uncertainty, where everything on the outside looks stagnant. You're stuck in a winter where you can't see the growth. When you look back on those periods of time, you were growing roots.

Some years you see the fruits of your labor, you flower, you bloom, you strut your stuff, and the world sees a bouquet and celebrates. Root years aren't so attractive. There's not much to show for them until much later in your life when you realize that those were the most vital years of all.

I thought of that when I heard about Mary Ann Corrigan-Davis. She had a dream job, then lost it and found a more perfect dream. She graduated from college with a degree in

French and planned to go into international business. She got her MBA from Case Western Reserve University and expected to get the perfect job in international business as soon as she graduated.

It took a year of interviews to find a job, and when she did, it was in sales at American Greetings, the card company. She planned to stay briefly and then move on to pursue her dream job. She stayed for 27 years. She ended up as president of the Retail Division in charge of 440 stores across 40 states, worked in Australia, and climbed the ladder all the way to the rung called Senior Vice President of Business Innovation. Then it all came to a screeching halt.

She got downsized. Then her dad died. Then she got breast cancer.

All in one year.

She said, "Lord, You have my attention. What is it You would like me to do?"

It looked muddy and messy at the time, but looking back, it's clear what that time was for.

She got to be with her dad in his final days.

She got to heal and make getting well her full-time job.

She got to strengthen her faith when she went through chemotherapy and radiation, a faith that was deepened by her years at Saint Joseph Academy, an all-girls Catholic high school.

After Mary Ann survived the storm, she found a huge rainbow. She ended up in the job of her dreams, one that didn't exist until she got downsized. She's now president of Saint Joseph Academy, the school she always loved. She likes being in a workplace driven by a sense of mission, not profit.

"Life is like a roller coaster," she told me. "Sometimes you do want to throw up. You just have to believe it will get better."

How do you keep believing?

You make denial work for you. You believe in spite of the statistics. You believe past your doubts. You believe anyway.

When I was diagnosed with cancer in 1998, once I got past the fear, cancer seemed like such a big waste of time. I was practically useless as far as work was concerned. Or so it seemed. I spent endless hours at doctor's appointments and medical procedures. Everyone else was busy completing to-do lists and conquering the world, and I was conquering the next MRI, CAT scan, or side effect from chemo.

Cancer sucks. There's no polite way of saying it. Cancer sucks away your energy and enthusiasm. Even when you feel good, you don't yet feel normal. It's like having the flu for a year. Cancer put me in the slow lane of life. A lane I resented at the time but am grateful for today. The whole cancer experience deepened every area of my life and forced me to grow spiritually, emotionally, and physically. I always wanted to be able to inspire people to live their best lives. So much of what inspires me came from that slow lane I traveled in. The slow lane of life teaches you to do what is necessary, then do what is possible, and pretty soon, you're doing the impossible.

It was a scary time. In my family, cancer was fatal. Everyone who got it before me had died. My aunts Veronica, Francie, and Maureen all died from breast cancer. I got breast cancer at 41. A year later, two cousins were diagnosed with it. That's when we all decided to get genetic testing.

I found out I carry a mutation called BRCA1. It raises the

lifetime chance of getting breast cancer to 85 percent. Five of my cousins have been diagnosed with breast cancer. My sister Patricia was tested for the gene. She had it and decided to do something about it.

She tells everyone, "I cheated cancer."

Boy, did she.

With courage and grace and grit.

She's the youngest girl in our family of 11. She remembers going with my dad to visit his sister Veronica in the hospital when she was fighting cancer. He brought her wigs. Veronica died at 44, leaving behind six children, ages 2 to 14.

Patricia decided to be proactive and not wait for cancer to show up. She had a preventive bilateral mastectomy with reconstruction at the age of 39. Her son was just 2.

Then we found out my daughter carried the gene. I had passed it on to her. Oh, the sadness over giving her a gene that could threaten her life. And yet having that gene changed her life and shaped it.

A year after she found out that she carried the BRCA1 gene, Gabrielle started a job at University Hospitals working with the National Cancer Institute. She had been working in human resources and saw the job ad. It sounded like the perfect fit. As partnership program coordinator for NCI's Cancer Information Service, she worked with organizations to share the latest cancer information and help people learn about lifestyle changes, screening, and clinical trials to reduce their cancer risk and increase their survival odds. Part of her job was to make cancer information and treatment available to those who didn't have insurance. She was saving lives.

When she couldn't find a support group for young women

with the gene, she helped start one. She connected with other women in online support groups for "previvors," women who haven't had breast cancer but have the gene for it. Having the breast cancer gene both scared and empowered her. Educating others gave her a sense of control over what she couldn't control. She looked out for the family. She collected everyone's diagnosis and surgery history to put into a family tree to pass along to all cousins. She became our family's personal educator and sent us the latest on studies, conferences, clinical trials, and online resources.

She, too, had both of her breasts removed. It was sad at first, but now that she's the mother of three, she's just grateful every day to be alive to see them grow up. Once she had children, she decided to quit her job and become the full-time CEO of her home. She's never been happier.

Another gift came out of all this. Back when I was looking for a dress to wear to my daughter's wedding, it was hard to find something elegant that wasn't strapless or low cut. The dress had to hide the thick industrial-sized straps on my mastectomy bra that holds my prosthetic breasts. Other survivors had told me to make friends with my new bosom buddies, so I named them Thelma and Louise. Patricia helped me look for a mother-of-the-bride dress and was struck by how hard it was to find the right clothes after having a mastectomy.

Then, when my daughter had to make peace with her surgery and sadness over having to wear mastectomy swimsuits for the rest of her life, Patricia got to work. She pulled out her sketchbook and began to draw swimsuits. My sister the architect started to design luxury swimwear for women who have had mastectomies. She named her line of suits Veronica

Brett, in honor of our aunt. Patricia wants every woman to feel beautiful and elegant and special. I love how I feel and look in her suits.

The tagline on her swimsuits is a perfect fit for the suits and for anyone facing the changes ahead with courage: "LIFE NEVER LOOKED SEXIER."

When you fail, fail forward.

My husband is a perfect failure.

He's great at falling down. He's even better at bouncing back up.

Before we met, he had many different careers. He came to the marriage with a good solid résumé of failures behind him.

He was always an entrepreneur. In high school, he made and sold bumper stickers and buttons with messages of love and peace.

He tried other things. He worked at a steel factory. For one whole day. The foreman handed him a hard hat and told him to go empty that truck and pointed to the biggest tractor trailer Bruce had ever seen. It was full of boxes of aluminum siding. They were so long, the boxes bent in the middle when he lifted them. It was 120 degrees in the shade. It took all day. At the end of that day, Bruce handed the foreman his hard hat. "This isn't for me," he said.

He spent a summer working in a catalog showroom near home. The manager looked at him and said, "You're the only kid in the neighborhood I'm gonna hire. You're the only kid whose father didn't call ahead. You walked in on your own." Bruce never forgot that lesson.

He went to college, got married at 20 to a woman whose dad owned a jewelry store. Bruce took over the costume jewelry side of the business. For seven years. He hated every minute of it, but he learned how to sell. He liked owning a business, he just didn't like that business.

"I learned how to take pleasure in the margins," he said. "I found an avocation."

He had a flair for organizing and getting involved in local politics. He ran a huge street fair attended by 60,000 people. He filmed a documentary on it for the local cable access channel.

But he was paralyzed when it came to changing jobs. It wasn't until his hand was forced that he took action, when interest rates went up to 20 percent and inflation skyrocketed. No one was paying him what they owed and his suppliers demanded cash. He took a second mortgage on his house to get out of debt. One day he saw an ad in the paper for an executive director of a large Jewish synagogue and applied. He was only 27 and knew nothing about running a 1,200-family synagogue, but he had learned how to recruit and use volunteers at the street fair, and he had balanced books for his jewelry business. Somehow he got hired.

The first year, he was so lost he felt like he was in an aquarium. He could see people talking but couldn't understand a word they were saying. He oversaw 15 employees, 25 active

committees, 2 cemeteries, and a catering operation. He lasted three years. Then one day the president fired him. The board rehired him, but he knew it was time to move on.

Bruce had been selling the remaining inventory of his costume jewelry business on the weekends at flea markets and to retail stores trying to cover his second mortgage until the phone rang and his mother-in-law said, "Come to work right away. Your business is gone."

All that costume jewelry inventory he kept in the basement of his father-in-law's store? A water main broke and the basement flooded. Eight feet deep. The jewelry fell apart. Bruce lost everything. He still remembers the stench and mud and mold. He lost thousands of pieces of jewelry. The insurance company offered 50 cents on the dollar. "If you don't like it, sue us," they said. Bruce had no money to sue. He took the money.

He went on to sell car phones, which back then were used only by the wealthy. They cost over a thousand dollars each. He was salesman of the month for three months. The fourth month, he missed his quota. The next month he missed it again and got fired.

He's never forgotten that day when he was standing at a pay phone with tears running down his face and he had to call his wife and tell her, "I got fired." They had two kids and no income.

Bruce ended up doing public relations and property rezonings for a chain of car dealerships. Then, one day, he took his biggest gamble and opened his own public relations business. He starved for six months, maxed out two credit cards, and took out a third to borrow money to make the minimum

payments on the first two cards. He was $25,000 in debt and terrified. His wife kept saying, "Just get a job." But he didn't want a low-paying job. He wanted to be the man who signed the front of the check, not the back. The business grew. He got a partner, and it grew more. Then he got divorced, which felt like a failure.

Two years later, he met me.

When I met my husband, he owned the small public relations firm, which specialized in everything. He did it all, from political campaigns to rezoning issues. He made a great living until the terrorist attacks of September 11. Those attacks scared business owners all over the country, and they trimmed any nonessential costs out of fear. The phone stopped ringing at my husband's firm. Business evaporated. For six months, he didn't have one billable hour. He lost so many clients, he lost the business. He had to shut the doors.

He came home that last day of work beaten down like a whipped dog. While he was emptying his office, my daughter and I turned a spare bedroom into an office for him. He would need to remake himself in time. I figured he'd look for a job. A few weeks later, he announced he was ready to start another business. Was he crazy?

He wanted to use our home equity line to fund it. Was he crazy?

After much prayer and counsel with friends and confronting my own fears, I agreed. Was I crazy?

A good friend, Bob Smith, CEO of the large investment firm Spero-Smith, told Bruce to quit trying to be all things to all people and focus his business in one area. For years, Bruce had lurched from project to project with no plan. Bruce decided to

make this time the last time. What were his skills? What did he love? Crisis communications. That would be his brand. It sent his adrenaline rushing. He would choose one thing, go narrow and deep, and do it better than anyone.

For a few months I paid all the bills and trusted all would be well. Within two years, he had paid back all the money. Within five years, he was earning more than he had before and still worked out of that bedroom office. He got a new business partner. By year ten, the company had grown so big that they moved the business out of their homes to down-town Cleveland on the 32nd floor of Terminal Tower, the heart of Cleveland.

The year the economy was the worst, they had their best year. They created a business that is recession-proof. Hennes Communications now has clients all over the country.

"I love what I do," he tells people. "I haven't worked a day in thirteen years." That doesn't mean he doesn't work hard. He works harder than anyone I know. Some would say too hard. (Me.)

A mystic named Julian of Norwich said, "First there is the fall, and then we recover from the fall. Both are the mercy of God." Or as my friend Bob always says, "I fall and I rise up. Both are the grace of God."

He's right. Failure can be your best teacher. If your life looks like a mess, it could be because you're still in the middle of it. The middle always looks messy. It's simply too soon to tell how it will all turn out. It turned out better than Bruce ever imagined.

"Every person I met, every job I held, every sale I ever made, every experience I ever had, gave me the happiness and

success I have today," Bruce said.

The benefits of failure are endless. Failure strips away fear. Once you've failed, you have nothing left to lose. You realize that you're still alive, still breathing, still you, and life goes on. When you strip your life down to survival mode, you realize you don't need all that much to survive or to serve others. You discover what you're truly made of, and that you're tougher than you ever knew.

Choice, not just chance, determines your destiny.

How do you make the right choice to take a new job or to stay where you are, to choose one college over another, to choose one calling over another?

It's easy to decide when one choice is obviously good and one is clearly bad. It's tough to choose when both options appear equally good or bad.

I had been working at the *Beacon Journal* in Akron, Ohio, for 14 years. During that time, I got married and moved to Cleveland. My life was no longer centered in the Akron area. When you're a newspaper columnist, it's important to live near the people you write about to capture the feeling of the city. It was time to get my life in one place.

I approached the *Plain Dealer* in Cleveland and they offered me a job as a columnist. Should I take it? To make it more complicated, the editor at the *Beacon Journal* found out and of-

fered me more money to stay than the *Plain Dealer* had offered me to leave.

What should I do?

There's no secret formula, no one-strategy-fits-all solution to use to make decisions. Or maybe there's a different one for everybody.

There's the easy way out. I could turn over a Magic 8 Ball and ask again later, consult my horoscope, throw darts at a board, flip a coin, or play Bible bingo. That's where you open the Good Book, point a finger to any random passage, and—voilà!—there's the answer.

There's the old standby: write down the pros and cons of each choice and go with the longest "pros" list.

Another option is to pick the two best choices and try them on for a day like a pair of new shoes to see how they fit. Let's say you want to move to Kalamazoo or Chicago. You choose one city and imagine living in it for one day. You pay attention to how it feels in your head, heart, and gut. The next day, you try on the other choice. Usually by noon of the second day, you know which to choose.

I've heard that it helps to separate fact from fiction. Once you've done that, discard the fiction. Once you have all the facts, separate the relevant facts from the irrelevant ones. Base decisions on those alone. Don't assume anything. As one journalism teacher taught me, any time you assume, you might make an *ass* of *u* and *me*.

My friends in recovery taught me to apply the Four Absolutes of Alcoholics Anonymous: honesty, purity, unselfishness, and love. They ask themselves these questions when confronted with a choice: Is it true or is it false? Is it right or

wrong? How will this affect the other person involved? Is it ugly or beautiful?

You could just take a shower. Seriously. Sometimes your subconscious will take over and hand you the solution.

Or take a poll. Consult your inner circle of friends. Form your own board of directors of people whom you respect most and run the decision by them.

You could just let fate decide for you. "It is what it is," people say all the time. They don't realize that not deciding is a decision.

What I try to do most often is move from the outer methods of choosing to the inner ones. The priests I met at the Jesuit Retreat House in Cleveland shared a formula they learned from Saint Ignatius of Loyola, who started their religious order. They suspend all fear, anxiety, and doubt and stay focused on their mission to praise and serve God. They make themselves indifferent to health, wealth, fame, and longevity. They desire and choose only what will help them be of the utmost service to God and others.

I like the idea of thoughtful discernment. To consciously ask for clarity and then wait for it. You usually have to wait until the noise clears. Some days it feels like recess at a day care in my head, with so many toddlers running around in so many different directions.

The key is to discern which voice is God's and which one isn't. One priest described the Holy Spirit speaking the way water falls gently on a sponge, while what isn't God comes to us like water pounding violently on rocks. The voice that isn't God becomes easier to recognize over time. For me, it's the noise and static inside that makes me feel sad, guilty, or con-

fused. The voice that makes me feel weighed down by life, or restless and irritable, isn't God's voice. Confusion, noise, and frustration are my three signs to stop ruminating. My friend Ruth often reminds me, "Don't believe everything you think." I need to wait for the quiet, clarity, and peace to catch up. Sometimes I actually hold up my hand and yell, "Stop!" and the noise does.

When I'm feeling beat up from within, it isn't God holding the club, it's me. My God isn't armed. My God is a loving, joyful, gentle God. The clarity of God's love comes to me through a calm peace that creates either an opening or a closing. Then, no matter what I choose, I confirm it with the people I trust the most: my husband, children, and closest friends.

When I feel lost, I've learned to wait it out. The confusion and doubt will pass, like turbulence on a plane. I might be in for a bumpy ride, but I stay the course. I can't let noisy passengers be my guide. The best thing for me is to wait. I don't make any changes until the clarity comes. I pray for clarity, then meditate to receive it. I've learned not to make any decision under the influence of despair or fear or fatigue.

I'm not saying that you should do nothing while you wait. Keep praying, meditating, journaling, talking to those who have your best interests at heart. Naps help, too. Sometimes, just before I rest, I pray for a spiritual awakening. As they say, the answer will always come—if you want it.

The answer came to me when I stopped wrestling with the decision. While struggling with whether to stay at the *Beacon Journal* or take the job at the *Plain Dealer*, I decided to stop thinking about it for 48 hours. I had done enough intro-

spection and prayer. I had already asked for the clarity and inspiration. It was time to relax, take it easy, and trust that the answer would come when I was ready to hear it.

I drove four hours away to visit my daughter at college. We had a great weekend wandering around campus and shopping and laughing with her friends. As I packed up my things to leave, suddenly, I just knew. The answer came with total peace.

When I left that morning, I borrowed a blouse from her so I could drive straight to the *Beacon Journal* to break the news that I was leaving. I didn't know it, but my coworker and closest friend, Sheryl, who also had the chance to leave the *Beacon Journal* for the *Plain Dealer*, had made the same decision. Sheryl told our boss the same day I did. We even ended up wearing the exact same outfit to work: black slacks and a white blouse.

That sealed the deal.

And we've never looked back.

It's not about what you can do, but what God can do through you.

Some days the bad news of the world can overwhelm you.

Poverty. Unemployment. Wars.

Who is going to fix everything that's wrong with the world?

Then you hear about guys like Rick Burns who decide to simply change their corner of it.

Burns Auto Service sits on a corner in a small town called Bay Village, Ohio. People bring in their cars for muffler repairs and oil changes, but one day, they started dropping off cash to help give one life a tune-up.

The sign outside Burns Auto Service advertises mufflers and tune-ups. The sign inside on the bulletin board tells what really happens here.

Rick Burns has curly hair the color of butterscotch candy. He wears blue work pants that look black from the oil and grease they absorb as he slides in, around, and under cars.

Rick's dad bought the gas station, then pulled out the pumps and made it a repair shop. Rick bought the shop from his dad ten years ago, right around the time Brian showed up.

Brian is 37 and lives with his mom. Most everyone in Bay Village knows him. They give him free haircuts at the barbershop and free coffee at the restaurants. Brian was born with cerebral palsy, which hampers his muscle control. Brian works at City Hall three days a week. He empties trash and stocks the bathrooms. City Hall is across the street from the auto shop, which is just a mile from his home.

Brian's world is small, but it's also deep because of people like Rick.

Brian used to sit in the front seat when his mom brought her car in for an oil change. That's how he met Rick.

Brian can't drive a car. He used to mope around the house. He started calling the auto shop for rides. Brian limps slowly. His body tilts to the left. He shuffles and drags his left foot. He keeps his left arm close to his side, where his hand lies curled up. It made Rick nervous every time he saw Brian cross the street, so one day, Rick placed an ad in the *Villager* newspaper:

Everyone in Bay Village knows Brian. Brian needs a good trike to get around town. Rick Burns of Burns Auto Service at Dover and Wolf roads wants to trick out a great new trike for Brian. Stop in at Burns Auto and make a donation for Brian's trike.

He didn't include a phone number, website, or address. He didn't need to.

People drove by and dropped off tens and twenties. In three weeks he raised $200.

Rick bought a cobalt-blue Schwinn three-wheel adult sports trike, a canopy to keep Brian out of the sun and rain, and a hundred dollars' worth of accessories. One lady dropped off a headlight. The police gave Brian an orange light stick and a pole with a reflective handicap logo on the top that spins. Someone gave him an American flag. Another person donated a reflector.

Jason Tuneberg, who works with Rick, put the bike together. It has headlights, taillights, front and rear brakes, a basket that folds down, tire valves that light up, a speedometer, racing pedals, and, of course, a bell.

"It's perfect for parades," Rick said.

Rick reached into the basket and held up a bike lock and key. "This is his security system," he said. "We keep the other key here in case we need to go save him."

The rearview mirror broke off.

"I hit the side of my garage," Brian confessed.

So far the fastest he has driven is eight miles per hour.

"I try not to go downhill," Brian said.

Inside the shop, repair orders are lined up neatly in a row on the counter. Rick has set toy trucks on a shelf at toddler eye level for children who have to wait with their parents. The bulletin board above is filled with news clippings of Cleveland Indians victories.

Rick pinned up the card Brian's mom sent thanking him for the bike. Underneath the card, a sheet of white paper with these typed words clarifies the mission of the auto shop. It isn't just a place to get mufflers and tune-ups.

Definition of Life: Life is not the number of breaths you take. Life is the number of moments that take your breath away.

"We got him out of the house," Rick said. "He's back on the road."

And back into life.

After I wrote a column about Rick, people filled envelopes with cash and shoved them through the key slot at Burns Auto. One anonymous donor gave $200. One man donated $100 and left a note asking Rick to buy a windshield and snow tires for Brian's bike. One man sent a big box with a bike helmet, gloves, radio, and a water bottle.

Everywhere Rick went, people said, "You're that guy." Women gave him hugs; men shook his hand. He collected $1,200. What would he do with the extra?

Then Jeannette drove up on her old trike, the one with the tires that go flat, the chain that falls off, the seat that wobbles without duct tape. Jeannette is a single parent with a son in high school and a daughter in third grade. Jeannette moves and talks slowly, enunciating words in her own unique way. She holds her hands behind her back and sways unless she needs her hands to sign words because she is hard of hearing. She's 41 and tells anyone she trusts that she was diagnosed with a developmental disability.

Jeannette rides a trike to get groceries, to go to the bank and the doctor. She can't drive a car because she has seizures. When she saw the trike Rick decked out for Brian, she started praying for one. God answered through Rick.

He bought her a trike like Brian's. He added a pink horn, headlight, pink tassels, radio, side mirror, two American flags, and a safety spinner. When he gave her the trike, she covered her face and started to cry.

Inside his shop he keeps a three-ring scrapbook with all the cards and letters people sent. One page is full of sticky notes on which he wrote down the gifts:

$50 Mrs. Camry

$50 walk-up lady

90-year-old man $100

Walgreens lady in line $20

$5 Dan landscaper

Rick took the lid off the blue coffee container on the counter. "Look at this," he said, pulling out a handful of bills. "The money is still coming in."

What's next?

Rick continues to give away new and used trikes that he and his team restore, paint, and customize. "I love doing it," he said. "We're blessed."

We all are, by people like him.

One evening I pulled into a parking lot and walked into the building where I was to give a speech and sign books. A woman stopped me and told me the back tire on my car was growing flat. Was it a slow leak or a fast one? What should I do? My talk would end around 9 p.m. By then it would be dark. As I stared at the tire, a man walked over and said, "Looks like you need help."

It was Rick. He just happened to come to my talk and just happened to have an air compressor in his trunk. He filled my tire and we went inside. After my talk, I found a note on my

windshield. He had drawn a cross and written: "Your tire is fine. Check it tomorrow."

He took my breath away one more time when I opened the mail a few days later and found a box with this note: "Here's your own air compressor so you won't get stranded in the future. You might also be able to help someone else in need some day."

Instead of trying to be the best in the world, be the best for the world.

W hat journalist doesn't want to win a Pulitzer Prize?

It's the greatest height a journalist can reach. Or so they say.

In my field, they tell you that once you win the Pulitzer, the first line of your obituary is already written.

I've come close to winning twice. Editors have nominated my work for the coveted prize many times, and I was actually chosen as a finalist twice.

The first time I was one of three finalists across the country for a Pulitzer Prize in commentary, I was giddy. I had written a series of 40 columns on inner-city violence. The judging is supposed to be a secret, but information often leaks out of who the three finalists are in each category. Two days before the winner was to be announced, I was sitting in a movie theater on a Saturday night when my editor called. I went out into the lobby to take the call. She told me I didn't win. I was crushed.

When I went to work that Monday, friends and coworkers didn't even try to console me. They were so excited and proud of me for being a finalist it didn't seem at all like I'd lost anything. They were right. It should have been enough, but my ego wanted more. My husband threw me a party. My friends, family, and coworkers gathered to celebrate that I was one of the top three columnists in the country that year, but deep inside I was disappointed that I wasn't Number One.

The second time, I was a finalist for columns I wrote that helped change the law in Ohio so prosecutors could no longer hide critical information from defense attorneys. For the category of commentary, you can submit up to ten columns, so we also sent columns I wrote about my daughter's decision to have a preventive double mastectomy at age 29. She inherited from me the BRCA1 gene for breast cancer, and sharing her journey was excruciating. I wanted to win for her, and, of course, for my ego.

I couldn't imagine losing this time.

But I did. This time, I found out in front of everyone in the newsroom as we gathered around to celebrate a victory as the Pulitzers were announced. Again, everyone said, "You didn't lose. You were a finalist!" They served cake and punch and everyone offered kind words. But I have this strange ego: If I don't win, I've failed. There's no middle ground. It's A or F. There are no other grades like B, C, or D.

The truth is, no prize can put that kind of ego to rest. Not even the Pulitzer Prize. My friend Bob, one of the greatest reporters in the business, won a Pulitzer Prize. It did nothing to silence his inner-doubt demons. Bob was always my personal monk in the newsroom. He often repeated to me a quote by

Bill Wilson, the founder of Alcoholics Anonymous, who said: "I had to be number one in all things because in my perverse heart I felt myself the least of God's creatures."

Bob helped me realize that once you become unattached to the world and its applause and don't depend on it for definition and affirmation, you're finally free to serve the world. Instead of trying to be the best in the world, be the best *for* the world.

One of his favorite sayings is: "I'd rather stand in the dark than in a light of my own making."

Can't I just stand in the light of the Pulitzer, too?

Deep down, I wanted to be famous, important, complimented, noticed, needed, respected, nurtured, praised. Every time I got some of that, it wasn't enough. Whenever I set a goal and reached it, I reached for another one that was out of reach. It was a chase for the horizon.

As much as I'd like to win a Pulitzer, the place that really means the most to me is under a refrigerator magnet. I'm honored that people cut out my columns and stick them on the fridge next to their son's A in science and their daughter's artwork. Readers open weathered wallets and unfold faded columns they'd tucked in there that touched them. A judge once called me into his chambers after a court hearing to show me the column of mine he kept under the glass on his desk. At one book signing, a woman brought a scrapbook of her little boy's life. I'd never met her, but I had seen her son's beautiful grin in a photo that ran on the obituary page when he died. I mentioned that smile and his name in a column and she never forgot. She asked me to sign that column she so carefully glued into her precious book about his brief life.

How humbling.

A quote from Isaiah 49 reminds me what truly matters: "I shall be glorious in the eyes of the Lord and my God shall be my strength." That's the glory I seek. When you are one with God, you don't have to prove your worth. I now aim to write for the greater glory of God, not for the greater glory of Regina.

Ego is a tricky thing. Some see it as a bad thing and call it easing God out. A coworker once told me ego isn't all bad if it motivates you to be of service. God might even find it useful. People with big egos can get a lot accomplished to help others. You can turn that famous Nike slogan into "Just Do It...for the glory of God." The key is, What's in it for God? I love Mother Teresa's answer to the person who said he couldn't do her job for a million dollars. She said she couldn't either. She did it for Jesus.

The goal isn't about being the best, but being the best for others. One reader never lets me forget the true worth of what I do. One year I was invited to a job fair for minorities at a prestigious law firm. I went and chatted with people there and wrote a column about some of the men and women looking for work. It wasn't a dazzling column. It wasn't great. I'm not even sure it was good. It definitely wasn't Pulitzer material. It was simply the best I could do with the material I had at the time.

It wasn't award-winning, but it turned out to be life-changing.

In the column, I mentioned that Tony Morrison, a commercial photographer, appreciated a chance to get a foot in the corporate door by attending the job fair. As a black man, he

found it hard to break into the old established white guys' network, although he never used those words.

He expressed his gratitude for the job fair when I interviewed him. "You finally got past the receptionist," he said. "If you can show your product, you have a chance. It's like David against Goliath. By doing this they sort of leveled the playing field."

In a column of some 600 words, I used 50 to mention Tony.

Those 50 words changed his life. From that column on, he was hired all over town to take photos. Every year I see him at Cleveland's Chamber of Commerce Public Officials Reception where hundreds of movers and shakers gather to network. Tony is the official photographer, taking shots of senators, mayors, and CEOs.

Every year he comes up to me, sticks out his hand, and thanks me for his career.

And I thank him for reminding me about what matters most about mine.

If you can help someone, do; if you can hurt someone, don't.

F or years the bumper sticker on my office cubicle offered this message: *And what difference do you make?*

I posted it one day to give myself a boost after hearing too many newspaper readers complain about a column advocating for the poor and powerless.

That bumper sticker became a reminder for me to stay focused on my true calling, to make the difference that Regina Brett is supposed to make. A job isn't just to make a living or a life. It's to make a difference. What imprint will you leave at the end of the day? Is that the imprint you want to leave on coworkers, clients, customers?

Someone once told me, "One day you will be just a memory to people. Do what you can now to make sure it's a good one."

I don't always know if it's a good one. When I was a news-

paper reporter, I was often assigned to call people for comments on breaking news. Once, I called a workplace to gather information about a man who had been killed in an accident. The person I spoke to had not yet heard that her friend was killed. I felt awful that she hadn't heard in a more graceful, gentle way from someone who knew her.

Another time, we were all covering the aftermath of the riots at a prison in Lucasville, Ohio. The National Guard had been called in to break up a riot at the Southern Ohio Correctional Facility that killed seven. An editor wanted me to call the victim of one of the inmates who had died in the riot. He had been convicted of kidnapping and raping her at knifepoint ten years earlier.

I dreaded making that call. Wouldn't it just stir up more pain? I prayed before dialing her number. When I asked for her reaction to his death, she screamed. She didn't know he had been killed in the riot.

She started to laugh and cry. Ever since he had attacked her, she'd been afraid of the day he would be free. "I wake up screaming and have headaches. I have nightmares every day," she told me. She was relieved he was gone. "What a blessing."

She thanked me for telling her and for changing her life. She hadn't paid any attention to the news of the riot and no one in her immediate life knew about that rape that had happened ten years ago.

Sometimes it isn't clear if you're doing good or harm. I once wrote a column praising a child for calling the police when she found her mother's drugs. Maybe that mom could get help and not end up like another mom, a drug addict who was murdered and left behind two sons. Unfortunately, I named those

kids. Their names had already been used in the newspaper, but I didn't need to use them again.

I saved two of the angry letters I got. One was from a fifth-grade teacher of one of those boys: "Your article not only rehashed the gruesome details of his mother's death (details that the child wasn't aware of) but made the assumption that the boys knew what their mother was doing and should have turned her in…I ask you to please use better judgment when dealing with the feelings of children in the future."

The principal also wrote me. He agreed with the argument I made, but wrote, "You have assisted in victimizing these children…Listing the boys' names has undone what months of work by counselors, teachers, family members and friends have tried to heal."

They taught me a great lesson with that column: If you can help someone, do; if you can hurt someone, don't.

I once wrote a lighthearted column about a dilapidated house my daughter lived in on a college campus with eight guys and one woman. The refrigerator had such a horrible odor, I joked that its previous owner might have been Jeffrey Dahmer. I got a call from an angry reader who reminded me that Dahmer's first victim was from the Akron area. I wrote an apology in my next column.

Now when I'm done with a column, I send it through my "spiritual scanner." I pray over it. I say the Saint Francis prayer and ask that God's grace keep me from hurting anyone.

When one of my columns helps people, they carry it in their wallets, post it on the refrigerator, tuck it into Bibles, mail it to their aunts and uncles, quote it in sermons, and reprint it in newsletters and blogs.

One factory worker called at 3 a.m. after he read a column I wrote about my dad's blue-collar work ethic. The man said he knew he couldn't leave his kids much in terms of money, but when he saw his own values reflected in my column, he knew that's what he was passing on. "I loved that column you wrote about your dad," he said. "I taped it to the inside of my tool-box to remind me why I do what I do."

One woman sent a card that read "If I were a writer, I'd like to know what people thought of my work. Someone on stage can hear the applause; you should know there is a 70-year-old grandma in Wooster clapping for you."

One father invited me to come into his home just hours after his son was gunned down. He trusted me, a stranger, to tell the world what a good son he had lost. I'll never forget how this big electric company lineman broke down weeping as he opened up his worn wallet to hand me the photo of his son.

One woman in blue jeans thanked me for blasting a police chief who had been accused of beating his wife. I didn't know she was an off-duty police officer until she whipped out her badge and told me the officers on her shift appreciated the columns, too.

One woman called to say she found my column of life lessons in her husband's pocket after he died. He lived just 45 days after being diagnosed with cancer.

In every walk of life, there are people who do their best not to hurt others, and people who don't care. I met a public defender who called his clients "dirtballs" and others who worked overtime for free to keep defendants out of prison. I've met police officers who love to hand out tickets to boost

their quota and I've met officers who won't ticket cars with expired plates in poor neighborhoods because they know that $100 ticket covers food for a month.

I've met judges who took pleasure in shaming people by giving them absurd sentences to carry out publicly just to get on TV. I've also met judges like Joan Synenberg who were tough yet thoughtful. One defendant wept in her courtroom during sentencing because he had no family and no one to write to him in prison. She promised to write to him and did every month.

It's not about how much power you have at work, but how you choose to use your power. I'll never forget the e-mail I got from a woman named Barb who shared this story with me: She had challenged her granddaughter, Calista, who was eight, to learn how to spell "supercalifragilisticexpialidocious." Within two days, the little girl called and spelled it for her. Barb decided to take her to dinner to celebrate at Macaroni Grill.

She called the restaurant before they arrived and asked if the server could come to their table and ask, "Are you girls celebrating something special tonight?" The person could have said, No, we don't have time for that. Instead, a man named Jim agreed to after he heard about Calista's achievement. When they arrived at the restaurant, he came to their table and asked if they were celebrating anything special.

When Calista told him about her spelling achievement, Jim asked if she knew what movie the word came from. Calista said, "Yes, *Mary Poppins*."

"Do you have the movie?" he asked. She didn't. They had rented it from the library.

"Well, you have the movie now," Jim said, and handed Calista the DVD with a pink bow on top.

Before they left, Calista asked her grandma how the man knew what they were celebrating. The little girl thought he might be a spy, then she decided he was an angel.

He was.

Bottom line?

Be one of the helpers. My daughter grew up watching Mister Rogers. She was glued to the TV every day watching that boring man in the boring cardigan sweater talk slower than molasses. One day I listened. The man spoke like a minister. I didn't know until he died in 2003 that he was an ordained Presbyterian minister.

I never realized the power of his message until we lost 20 children in the shooting at Sandy Hook Elementary School in Newtown, Connecticut. What should we tell our children? How could they ever trust life again? How could we?

People everywhere started quoting, of all people, Mister Rogers. He once shared that when he was a boy and saw scary things in the news, his mom would tell him, "Look for the helpers. You will always find people who are helping." His words helped us all remember that the world is full of helpers.

That's where you find your comfort. You turn your attention away from the hurters and look for the helpers.

Better yet, be one.

*It's important to know both your superpower
and your kryptonite.*

One person can change the world.

How do I know?

I work with Clark Kent.

Seriously.

Michael Sangiacomo is an energetic, curly-haired guy who has the wonder and joy of a ten-year-old boy. Mike is a mild-mannered reporter at the *Plain Dealer* who refuses to grow up. He still reads comics. He writes comics. He still believes in superheroes. Still believes Superman can fly.

Good thing.

A while back, Mike took on something brave and bold and slightly crazy. He believed he could save Superman's house. The real thing. The real, live, bricks-and-mortar three-story blue house with the red trim at 10622 Kimberly Avenue.

The Man of Steel was born in Cleveland, Ohio, more than 75 years ago.

The house nearly died of neglect despite its occupants' efforts to maintain it. Then one day a writer came to town. Novelist Brad Meltzer wanted to see the very room where two kids in the Glenville neighborhood created the biggest superhero known to man. The owners granted Brad a tour. Brad shared that tour in a video he made to help save Superman's home at www.OrdinaryPeopleChangeTheWorld.com. There he told viewers, "I believe ordinary people change the world."

Ordinary people? Not superheroes?

"Want to know how the world got Superman?" Brad said. "Because two kids, Jerry Siegel and Joe Shuster, who were so poor that they used to draw on the back of wallpaper, came up with the idea for a bulletproof man that they named Superman."

In the video, he walks into Superman's house and shows us room by room how Cleveland, Ohio, failed to preserve the famous house decades ago. The walls and ceiling rotted away. Red tape holds up a light switch. It's sad as the music on the video plays the song lyric "Even heroes have the right to dream."

He made me think of those nights I spent as a child imagining a bigger, better me while reading those comics under the covers.

"People think that Superman is the important part," Brad said. "The best part of the story? Clark Kent."

The mild-mannered reporter?

"Wanna know why?" Brad asked. "'Cause we're Clark Kent. I love the idea that all of us, in all our ordinariness, want to do something better, want to be something better, that we can tear open our shirt and try and help people."

We all have a superpower. We all possess some ability that defines us. We also have our own kryptonite, something that confines us, something that robs us of our strengths, drains us of our powers, weakens us in an instant. Usually our greatest strengths and our greatest weaknesses are cousins.

For Superman, it was kryptonite. A slice of his home planet, Krypton, made him crumble. He could leap tall buildings in a single bound, race a locomotive and win, and spin the world back to yesterday, but expose him to a bit of kryptonite, and he couldn't walk around the block.

My greatest power is speaking up for others. My kryptonite is not ever feeling worthy enough to speak up. All through my childhood, I couldn't speak up to my dad to stop him from hitting my brothers and sisters. I couldn't speak up to the kids at school who made fun of me for being skinny, for having hairy arms and big ears and glasses. I couldn't speak up to the kids who teased and tormented a girl in eighth grade because she didn't know to use deodorant. I couldn't speak up for the boy who got shoved into lockers and pushed around in high school because he was gay.

As a columnist, I've used my voice to speak out against child abuse, bullying, and all sorts of social injustice. I've taken on judges, prosecutors, and governors. Still, some days it's hard to find my voice when I need to return a sweater and don't have the receipt.

My friend Beth found her superpower in helping babies in medical distress. She has spent her entire career as a child life specialist at Rainbow Babies & Children's Hospital in Cleveland, advocating for children before, during, and after medical tests and procedures. Her kryptonite? Deep down, under all

that joy helping parents and children feel safer at the hospital, is a terrible sense of powerlessness over losing her own newborn son whom she never brought home from the hospital. Beth had diabetes, which weakened her body so much she couldn't carry her baby to full term. Her son was born too early. The loss of the only child she ever gave birth to is where Beth gets both her superpower and her kryptonite.

A good friend of mine is a perfectionist. That is both his superpower and his kryptonite. He suffers from obsessive-compulsive disorder. When we go on vacation together, he brings cleaning supplies to spray down the bedroom and the bathroom. The plus side? Here's what he does for a living: he's paid to find errors in commercial leases.

My husband runs a crisis communications firm. He absolutely loves to help people get through their worst moments. A chemical company had a spill one night and called at 2 a.m. Bruce stayed on the phone for hours and calmly walked them through who to call and what to say to the employees, media, and residents who had to be evacuated. He's great in a crisis, but is constantly weakened by his own worst moment, by the one crisis in his life that he couldn't stop.

He got the call that his mom died when he was 22. She had been talking on the phone to a friend when she suddenly dropped dead. Barbara was just 45. The coroner called it atypical pneumonia. No one knew she was sick. It was a crisis that rocked the family. He had a brother who had recently graduated from college and a brother and sister still in middle school when she died. The family had just sold their home and was planning to move the week she died. Not a day goes by that he doesn't miss her; not a week goes by that he doesn't wish he

could have done more to help his siblings through that awful time.

His brother Gary never got over losing his mom and his home all in the same week. He owns and operates Gary Hennes Realtors and specializes in finding people the homes of their dreams in South Beach. He wants them to find their sense of place in the world, something he still struggles to find for himself. His superpower is to bring beauty into every building and condo he encounters and help create a home for the right owner. His kryptonite? A lovely woman named Barbara who tugs at his heart so hard, it's difficult to let anyone else into it.

We all have a superpower, even the most ordinary among us.

That's how the video on saving Superman's house ends. The people trying to save Superman's house are just ordinary Clark Kent types.

"You know who's going to save it?" Brad asks. "We are. Regular ordinary people."

People like him. People like Mike. People like us. The video ends with a string of ordinary people proclaiming, "I am Superman."

We all are.

Inside of me, inside of you, inside of us, we all have the power. The power to change the world, or at least our small corner of it.

God completes our work.

The emergency call came while I was inside the ambulance restocking bandages on the shelves above the cot: *possible heart attack*.

The victim was in Atwater, a farming community 15 minutes away. We flew at 80 miles an hour with lights and sirens, zipping past cornfields and barns, past women hanging out clothes and children chasing collies. The training I received as an emergency medical technician flooded my head as the adrenaline flowed through my body. Clear the airway, check the vital signs, check for history of heart disease, et cetera. When we got to the scene I was ready for this man and his heart.

What I wasn't ready for was a little boy.

People flagged us down at the scene and led us to a back-yard where a small crowd clustered around a body. I pushed

my way through them and someone pulled the blanket off. I expected an old man. The first thing I saw was a sneaker smaller than my hand. The boy was about seven years old, had blond hair, and was wearing blue jeans. He wasn't breathing. I lifted his small head and put my fingers on his neck; no pulse. I tipped his head back, pinched his nose, and blew into his mouth. His chest rose like a balloon. Another ambulance attendant started CPR and counted out loud, "One thousand one, one thousand two..."

I scanned the backyard. There was a rope at the foot of a nearby tree. No one there knew who the boy was or what happened. My heart was silently screaming, *Where are his parents? What is his name? Who is this little boy?* I wanted to stroke his blond hair and hold him, talk to him, love him into life, but I had no free hand for comfort, no free breath for words. When I tilted his head back, I saw a half-inch-wide red ring across the front of his neck. It stretched from ear to ear. I checked his pupils and looked into the bluest eyes I had ever seen. They were quickly dissolving into black. His skin was still warm, and so, so soft.

With every breath, I breathed in a prayer: *God, don't let this little boy die. Please, let him live.* If only I could will him to life, pray him to life, breathe him to life.

The ride to the hospital seemed like both an eternity and a mere second in time. At the hospital, three doctors and five nurses met us at the emergency room door. They hovered over the boy as I stood in the hall, praying for a miracle. I couldn't even pray for him by name. We had no idea who he was or what had happened. The doctors zapped his heart, pumped oxygen into him, rubbed his limbs for over an hour,

but the red ring on his neck never faded. It was as if death left a permanent smile, mocking us all. My ambulance crew didn't leave until we saw the white sheet of surrender cover him.

I thought of his parents coming home or getting the call. The world would end for them. It wouldn't matter what they owned, what jobs they held, what their income was. Their son was dead. In the bathroom outside the ER, I punched the wall with one hand and wiped away tears with the other. The next day I read in the newspaper that the child had been accidentally strangled on a rope while playing in a tree.

Every October, I think about that boy. The breath that left his lips had smelled like tomatoes ripening in the sun. Every autumn, when that scent brings him back, I blow him a kiss, wherever he is, and pray for his parents.

There are times in your life when you do the best you can and your best isn't enough. You don't get the happy ending. You don't get the job you wanted or the raise you deserved or the promotion you earned. You don't get the high fives and pats on the back and fist bumps. You go home broken and sad and exhausted and wonder what the hell happened. And you don't get an answer. You just have to go back to work and do your best again and again, without fail, no matter how you think you failed. God completes our work, makes it complete in ways that sometimes remain a mystery to us, a mystery that isn't ours to solve, but ours to accept.

In my career as a journalist, it has often been my job to interview people about their worst day. I'm not talking about the bad day at work because the copier broke or the boss

yelled at you or the vending machine ate your dollar. I'm talking about when the patient dies or the plane doesn't land the way it's supposed to or the bad guy can't be stopped in time.

I've never forgotten a flight attendant who shared her story of survival with me. She showed me the uniform she wore the day that United Airlines Flight 232 crashed in a cornfield in Sioux City in 1989. I spoke to her six months after the crash, the week she was to return to work. She held up the uniform she had worn the day of the crash. She wouldn't wash the dirty white blouse with the gold-and-navy epaulets. The blood on it wasn't hers. It was the imprint left when a wounded passenger hugged her.

Susan talked about the faces of those who died. They weren't strangers; they were the women she had chatted with on the plane, the men she had comforted with pillows, the children she had poured sodas for and smiled at. She remembered all those people whose tears she couldn't stop, who kept crying, "Are we going to die?" Susan kept telling them, "I don't know. Keep praying." There's no way to understand why 112 people died that day and why she lived.

Then there was the police chief in Brimfield, Ohio, who told me about his worst day at work. "January 21, 2005," David Oliver said. "It wasn't just the worst day of work. It was the worst day of my life."

A woman in his small town of 10,000 people had tried to flee her abusive boyfriend. Renee Bauer had her coat on, a bag packed, and was ready to escape with her son, Dakota, who was seven. James Trimble stopped her with his gun. She tried to shield her son, but the bullets went through her and killed him, too. Renee and Dakota are buried in the cemetery be-

hind the Brimfield Police Department. The chief goes to the gravesite every week.

"It makes me feel I'm taking care of them now," he said.

The man who killed them fled the scene before police arrived and took a Kent State University student hostage. Chief Oliver remembers trying to negotiate for her freedom. He can still hear the woman slowly spelling her last name for him over the phone. Sarah Positano was shot and died before the police could reach her. Trimble was arrested, tried, and sentenced to death.

The chief told me he still loves his job, but to love it, you have to make peace with the things you can't change and summon the courage to change the things you can. You simply keep doing your best to make a difference wherever you can. He works hard to catch the bad guys, but he also goes to the elementary school every morning to high-five every child who walks in the door. He organizes events like Shop with a Cop, where a hundred children each get $100 to buy anything they want. Or Fill-a-Cruiser, where police park cruisers at area stores and people fill them with toys and food for the local food cupboard. He has breakfast with hundreds of senior citizens so shut-ins don't feel so alone.

Your worst day at work might scar you for life, but it doesn't have to scare you away from the work you love. If you let that scar make you stronger, then, in time, it will make the world around you stronger, too.

LESSON
25

Not everything that counts can be counted.

Most of us won't end up famous, but wouldn't it be great to be unforgettable?

Or to leave a mark behind that is?

Those people are called teachers.

Andy Rooney used to say that most people don't end up with more than a handful of people who remember them, but teachers have thousands who will remember them for the rest of their lives.

I once wrote a column encouraging readers to write a six-word memoir. These entries were penned by teachers:

Making a difference. Leaving a legacy.

Shaping the future in the present.

Teachers wanted: Patience mandatory, sanity optional.

Hoped to make difference. Was transformed.

I just want to teach. Period.

The last one could be echoed by teachers everywhere.

Unfortunately, tests have taken over teaching. The way we measure the worth of a teacher is no longer by the impact or imprint they leave on a student's life, but by the grade the student leaves on a test score. Too often the worth of a student is reduced to a number on a state proficiency test, graduation test, GPA, SAT, or ACT.

I love the apology that Principal David Root wrote to parents of students at Rocky River Middle School in Ohio after the report cards came out one June.

The children did well on the 2008 Ohio Achievement Tests that were required to be given each year to assess math, reading, science, social studies, and writing skills among all the state's public school students in grades three through eight. The school earned an "Excellent" rating and met the mandates for Adequate Yearly Progress. But what was the cost to the students and staff to focus so much on testing all year long? Where did they lose their focus? In far too many classrooms, teachers spent most of their time teaching children how to pass the state's proficiency tests. He lamented what wasn't getting taught, those experiences and the knowledge that can't be measured or counted in numbers.

For all those accomplishments, the principal had only one thing to say to the students, staff, and citizens of Rocky River: I'm sorry.

Mr. Root issued an apology. He sent it to me typed out in two pages, single-spaced. His apology made me think about how we can lose focus on what really matters when we insist on using measuring sticks to evaluate success.

He was sorry that his teachers spent less time teaching

American history because most of the social studies test questions were about foreign countries.

Sorry that he didn't suspend a student for assaulting another because the attacker would have missed valuable test days.

He was sorry for pulling children away from art, music, and gym, classes they loved, so they could learn test-taking strategies.

Sorry that he had to give a test for which he couldn't clarify any questions, make any comments to help in understanding, or share the results so students could actually learn from their mistakes.

Sorry that he kept students in school after they became sick during the test, because if they couldn't finish the test as a result of illness, the students would automatically fail it.

Sorry that the integrity of his teachers was publicly tied to one test.

He apologized for losing eight days of instruction because of testing activities.

For making decisions on assemblies, field trips, and musical performances based on how that time away from reading, math, social studies, and writing would affect state test results.

For arranging for some students to be labeled "at risk" in front of their peers and put in small groups so the school would have a better chance of passing tests.

For no longer focusing as a principal on helping his staff teach students but rather on helping them teach test indicators.

Mr. Root isn't anti-tests. He's all for tests that measure progress and help set teaching goals. But in his eyes, state

achievement tests were designed for the media to show how schools rank against one another.

When I spoke to him, he had been a principal for 24 years, half of them at Rocky River Middle School, the rest in the cities of Hudson, Alliance, and Zanesville, Ohio. He loves working with sixth, seventh, and eighth graders. "I have a strong compassion for the puberty-stricken," he joked.

His students, who are ages 11, 12, 13, and 14, worry that teachers they love will be let go based on how well they perform. One asked him, "If I don't do well, will you fire my teacher?" He cringed when he heard one say, "I really want to do well, but I'm not that smart."

He wants students to learn how to think, not how to take tests.

"We don't teach kids anymore," he said. "We teach test-taking skills. We all teach to the test. I long for the days when we used to teach kids."

The way we judge teachers makes me think of that beautiful quote attributed to Albert Einstein: "Not everything that counts can be counted and not everything that can be counted counts."

That's so true about teachers. But it's true about the rest of us as well.

Too often employers create ways to count, quantify, or measure our worth, yet those methods barely come close to valuing what really matters. We're measured by performance reviews, evaluations, critiques, the number of widgets produced, sales figures, customers served, or clicks on a website. I remember an editor who used to do a byline count to see how many stories a year every writer produced. It made reporters

cringe. Was it really all about numbers? Accountability is important, but you can't quantify everything.

It's not always the boss who tries to quantify our worth. Sometimes we do it to ourselves. We constantly find ways to measure our worth outside of ourselves and we never measure up. We obsessively check the number of friends and followers we have on Facebook and Twitter. I used to count the number of calls and e-mails I got on a column to see how much it mattered. The truth is there is no way to measure the love that goes into the work that we do or the worth that others see in us.

Not everything that counts can be counted. Early in my journalism career, an editor passed along a story that I've never forgotten. It's been handed down to countless journalists. A reporter named Al Martinez was working late one Christmas Eve for the *Oakland Tribune*. He was writing about a boy who was dying of leukemia. The boy's greatest wish? Fresh peaches.

Such a simple, small wish.

It was a perfect tearjerker story for readers to wake up to on Christmas. The reporter was typing away on the story when the phone rang around 11 p.m. The city editor asked what he was working on. The reporter told him about the dying boy and the peaches and how there weren't any fresh peaches, but it was a good story. There was space reserved on the front page for it, the prime real estate every reporter shoots for every time, the true measure of greatness achieved in a newsroom.

The editor asked how long the boy had to live. The reporter said, Not long. Days. After a long pause, the editor told him, "Get the kid his peaches."

The reporter had tried. He had already called all over. Peaches were out of season. The editor persisted. Call all over the globe if you have to. Do whatever it takes.

The reporter made hasty calls as his deadline neared and finally, magically it seemed, he found peaches and arranged a plane to fly them in so the boy could receive them. There was barely time to write the story. Deadline was looming large when the editor called again and asked him to deliver the peaches to the boy. The reporter said time was running out; he had to start writing the story to get it in the paper.

The editor told him, "I didn't say get the story. I said get the kid his peaches."

The boy got his peaches. The readers got the story. The reporter got his byline. And the rest of us got the message: what counts most isn't our work, but the humanity that goes into it.

Don't confuse your work with your worth.

It's strange how Father's Day sneaks up on you after you've lost your dad.

You forget the day is coming, then, *bam!*, it's there. You pass the greeting card section in the store, stop and pull out a card, then realize there's nobody to send it to.

My dad has been gone for 16 years, but I can still hear his voice and feel remnants of him everywhere. I've never forgotten the winter night I borrowed his car and was driving home late. Snow was coming down so hard you could hardly see the road. I was just a block from home when I saw a ghostly figure walking in the middle of the road. What nut was out walking on a night like tonight?

My dad.

He was carrying a space heater to a family a few blocks away. They had no heat. They called him to fix their furnace

but he couldn't get it working, so he took them one of our space heaters.

That's the kind of dad he was.

His sister Kate once told us that our dad never had a childhood. He always worked, even as a child. He was the oldest son, which meant the burden always fell on him. He got yelled at for feeding the horses extra grain when they were dying of starvation during the Depression. It must have broken his heart to see them wither away.

My aunts told me about the day they lost the farm. They were in the house and listened as the auctioneer sold everything they owned and loved, from the house to the horses to the corn in the fields. My dad, Tom Brett, had planted that corn. He was just 20 years old. The auctioneer said the $690 for the crop would go to my dad.

He used the money for a down payment on a shack by the railroad tracks on Sycamore Street in Ravenna, Ohio. It was the only place the family could afford. The neighbors couldn't believe anyone would move into it. My dad and his brothers scared out all the critters and then dug out a basement. The second floor had one bedroom. They turned it into three.

As time went on, my dad and mom lived in that house. Dad kept adding more rooms as he added kids.

My dad never worried about furthering his education. He quit school after eighth grade to support his family. He spent his life in blue-collared shirts with a red bandanna in his back pocket to wipe off his sweat. The only time he left his small town was to fight a big war. He was a tail gunner in World War II and flew more than 30 missions. He cried every time one of us left for big cities like New York, D.C., Phoenix, Chicago,

and even Cleveland. If he'd had it his way, we'd all still be living in Ravenna.

Dad was a workaholic. He had no hobbies. He never stopped working. He expected us to do the same.

When our punishment wasn't the belt, it was work. Sweep the floors. Mop the dining room. Sort nails in the Shop. He always called his garage the Shop. It was the original Home Depot. Somehow he knew where every screw and bolt and nail belonged. So did my five brothers. Anytime they committed a misdemeanor, like breaking a lamp while wrestling in the living room, Dad would bark, "I've got some nails for you to sort," and lead them to a workbench with a giant pickle jar full of every size of nail known to wood.

If we were playing, he'd yell, "Go help your mother." If we were reading, he'd say, "You'll never learn anything from those." We dreaded these words: "I've got a job for you."

Work defined him. When he lost his job, it shattered him. I still don't know what happened. He had me type page after page of angry rants to the union, the company, whoever it was that took away his livelihood. He never got it back. I watched my six-foot-two dad shrink before my eyes. He was lost. My mom got a part-time job working nights at traffic court to help pay the bills.

It killed my dad. His wife was working and he wasn't.

When she took on more hours to help clean the church, he got angry. He accused her of spending too much time there. He was bitter. His reaction was almost like she was having an affair. With who, God?

Finally, he went into business for himself and the world righted itself. He recruited my brothers to help with roofing

jobs, ductwork, and fixing furnaces. Somehow he always out-worked them.

My dad never took a vacation. Ever. When we got spring break, we didn't get a vacation either. Ever. There were no trips to the beach or Disneyland. Ever. We spent our week off cleaning out the freezer in the basement, scrubbing the dining room chairs, all 13 of them, or washing down the wood panel-ing in the living room.

Did he like his work? We never knew. You never asked that kind of question back then. He liked not being poor. He liked not being hungry. He liked making our lives better than his ever was.

When he had a heart attack in his 70s, he took the wooden ladders off the roof of the station wagon before driving himself to the hospital so my mom wouldn't have to drive home from the hospital with them on the roof.

As much as I admired his work ethic, it was both a blessing and a curse. It still is. Sometimes your parents teach you lessons that you have to unlearn. It took a long time for me to realize my work wasn't my worth.

I still find it hard to relax. I still feel guilty taking a vacation. I still struggle with calling out of work when I'm sick. If I do call in sick, I usually end up doing the laundry, dusting the furni-ture, or cleaning out a drawer just to feel useful. Even the year I had breast cancer, when I had two surgeries, four months of chemotherapy, and six weeks of daily radiation, I missed just two weeks of work. I scheduled my chemo around my job, so I would be sick on the weekend and able to recover for work on Monday. I sobbed when I finally had to call out from sheer exhaustion. Who was I if I wasn't working?

Who was I? A child of God who was already worthy enough. I remember how I balked when a priest told me God didn't care a whit about all my doing. "God delights in your presence," he said.

But I could give God so much more than that, I thought.

"Your presence matters more than your performance," the priest kept telling me.

That's what mattered most about our dad. His presence, not his work.

When he was present pulling us on the metal saucer sled through the snow, or taking a break from work to run the bases with us in a game of kickball, or taking us fishing with those bamboo poles and bobbers, and all those times he came home from work happy and yelled as he opened the door, "I'm home, you lucky people!"

Yes, we were lucky.

I thought of that as I walked through the Shop one day and caught a whiff of the sawdust from the lumber he helped us turn into birdhouses and caught sight of those fishing poles and that old beat-up sled. I poked around his workbench and found a big grocery bag. I couldn't believe what was inside.

Every Father's Day card we ever sent him.

I used to worry that as time wore out the roofs and furnaces he installed, my dad's work would be gone. Whenever we went for a drive, he used to point out every roof, as if it was a work of art he had created. But his work wasn't his legacy.

Blue-collar guys like my dad didn't worry about leaving a mark on the world. They never focused on climbing a career ladder to reach some lofty goal or holy grail. They were too busy climbing real ladders to keep roofs over their families'

heads. My dad held the ladder for us to climb higher than he ever got to.

We were his grail.

He left his mark on us, and because of that, he is in every mark my siblings and I leave on the world.

Clear the path for the person who comes after you.

What advice do you wish you had known before starting your career?

Jessica Thomas answered that question in a handbook she wrote called "Advice for College to My Little Sister." She typed it up and gave it to her younger sister as a high school graduation gift.

Jessica was 23 and a graduate student in biomedical engineering at Ohio State University when she decided to clear the path for her sister. Rachel was 18 and an incoming freshman at Ohio Wesleyan. They're both from North Olmsted, Ohio. Jessica took everything she learned in four years and condensed it into five pages.

"The most difficult moment is when your parents leave," Jessica wrote. "But remember, it's like when you were 2 and were left with a babysitter for the first time—you freak out for

about 10 minutes, then you're fine." When your parents drive away, you panic for a few minutes in fear: "Oh, no, I'm on my own." Then the excitement kicks in, and it becomes "Oh, wow, I'm on my own!"

The first year you can feel lost and confused. The second year, you own the place. You catch yourself telling your parents, "I'm going home," and by "home," you mean your dorm.

As the protective older sib, Jessica wanted to make the transition easier for her sister. It was all the stuff she wished she would have known. Reading Jessica's handbook made me wish I had both received one from my four older sibs and written one for my six younger sibs.

After I got pregnant at 21 and dropped out of college, I worked a series of jobs to pay the rent and ended up as a secretary. I've never forgotten the day my oldest sister, Therese, challenged me to finish college. She did it with one single sentence: "Do you want to be a secretary the rest of your life?"

Now, if you love being a secretary and are great at it, your answer might be a joyful, resounding "Yes!" But I sucked at it and hated the job. Still, I got mad at her for making me feel so small. How dare she insult me. The truth is, no one can make you feel small. What she did was remind me that I felt small because I was settling for something smaller than my own dream.

We weren't taught how to dream. We were taught how to survive. My dad never got to dream. He dropped out of school after eighth grade to support his family after they lost everything in the Depression. He spent his life carrying shingles and spouting up ladders in the hot sun. In the winter, he fixed fur-

naces full of asbestos, which ended up killing him. He had hoped his five sons would take over the Brett Sheet Metal family business. They didn't want any part of that backbreaking work that paid so little and took so much out of them.

My mom never went to college. She worked as a nurse's aide until she met my dad. He was a handsome bachelor who was a patient in the hospital. She either accidentally or on purpose burned him with a hot water bottle so he had to stay longer. They married, agreed to have 10 kids, and ended up with 11. One was an accident. They never told us which.

It was hard on them when the first child left for college. I think they felt abandoned or betrayed. They wanted us to live at home or at least in our hometown forever. When my sister Patricia got a scholarship to Yale, they spoke about it in hushed tones, whispering, "Why does she have to leave Ohio?" They had no idea what an incredible achievement it was for her.

My siblings forged their own paths. I remember my sister Therese in that unflattering matronly uniform she wore at the Acme grocery store in our hometown as she worked her way through college ringing up groceries. She was the first to attend college, but she commuted from home. She ended up with several careers. Her last one was saving lives as an ICU nurse before she retired.

My sister Joan was the first to move out to live in a dorm at college. My parents wanted us to go to the closest and cheapest university, Kent State University, which was six miles away. Joan was the pioneer who set her sights on Ohio State University, two and a half hours away. It meant moving out and supporting herself. Joan ended up with a PhD in organiza-

tional psychology from New York University and is a professor at Arizona State University.

My brother Michael got his MBA at Ohio State and became a CPA. Mary, who worked a factory job at General Electric for years to pay for college, got two master's degrees and has saved countless souls who have suffered from domestic violence and drug and alcohol addictions.

Tom spent years working on roofs with my dad, graduated from Kent State, and does real-estate appraisals and works for the Ohio Department of Transportation.

Maureen went to Bowling Green State University and got a degree in journalism. She ended up marketing homes and services for a retirement community that makes seniors feel at home in the world.

Patricia went to Ohio State, then got her master's degree in architecture at Yale. I love walking past the building she designed in New York City. Then she went on to design her own line of Veronica Brett swimwear that was featured in O, Oprah's magazine.

Mark got a degree in physical therapy from Ohio State, earned an MBA, and now oversees several hospitals in Michigan. Jim got an accounting degree from Kent State, joined the Peace Corps, and served in Uzbekistan. He's now a CPA in Washington, D.C.

Matthew, the baby, spent his childhood drawing comics. Being the last of 11 made him bolder. He once told my parents he was going camping and drove to New Jersey to see Bruce Springsteen. Another time he told them he was going fishing and went skydiving. He graduated from Kent State with a degree in graphic design. I never realized how hard it was for

him to pave his own way until years after he opened his own graphic design firm in Chicago called Substance.

Back when he was still living at home with Mom and Dad, he got an interview in Chicago. When it ended, they said, "Can you start in two weeks?" He said yes, not having a clue how he would break the news to our folks that he was moving out in two weeks. How would he tell them that after raising 11 children, they would soon be empty nesters? How would he find an apartment? How would he get there? How would he get around? Moving from Ravenna, Ohio (population 12,000), to Chicago (population 2.7 million) can seem like a trip to the moon when you're the first one to do it.

I wish I could have helped him, but back then I was too lost to know how to clear the way for the next traveler. I didn't even know it was my job to do so. Now I do. We all do. Each of my siblings has helped clear the way for the nieces and nephews that came after us.

My husband and I have used the third floor of our old home as a launching pad, first for our own kids, then for our niece Rachel, who left a job in Dayton to come to Cleveland. She ended up getting a job at the Rock and Roll Hall of Fame. She got an apartment, met the love of her life, and lives nearby with her husband and son.

My nephew Michael is pursuing a PhD. He knows it's possible because his aunt has one. His sister Leah played in the marching band in her high school in Garrettsville, Ohio, population 2,329. She ended up in the marching band for Notre Dame, playing in the band on national TV in front of millions. She just got a master's in dance therapy in Boston. Her brother Luke starred in high school theater productions, spent a sum-

mer living in our house to work at a theater camp, wrote a play, then spent a summer studying theater at the Stella Adler Studio in New York City. He graduated with a theater degree from Baldwin Wallace University.

I'm still in awe that each of my ten siblings left home and pursued their dreams. That old adage "Reach for the moon; even if you miss you'll land among the stars" describes them all. They are all stars to me, and a light for the next generation of stars.

Just because someone isn't on your path doesn't mean they're lost.

When my daughter was 23, she fell into a funk.

Her friend who lived in Manhattan was talking about moving to L.A. Her friend who grew up in Kent was heading for Atlanta. Her friends who were getting married were into couplehood. Her friends who were having babies were into motherhood.

Gabrielle found herself stuck in the quarterlife crisis. It hits sometime in the 20s, when you're trying to get a life but everyone else's life looks better than yours. At first I thought my daughter was alone in this quandary. Then she showed me an anonymous e-mail circulating among her friends. It answered the question: How do you know you've moved into adulthood?

"You keep more food than beer in the fridge. You hear your favorite song on an elevator. You don't know what time Taco

Bell closes anymore. You no longer take naps from noon to 6 p.m. You go from 130 days of vacation time to 7."

That last one was killing my daughter. She used to work every summer—on her tan. For the first time in her life, she had a real job, a nine-to-five that didn't allow for tanning between noon and two o'clock. She loved the job; she just hated the concept of working nine to five for the rest of her life. I remember the day the realization of finishing school for good hit her and she said to me, "You mean I'm going to have to work every summer for the rest of my life?"

My daughter graduated from college engaged to a great guy. The plan was to get a career job using that $50,000 communications degree and live at home to save money for a fall wedding. As they say, life is what happens when you're making other plans. Life happened. After four months, she quit the job that required her to work 12-hour days for 8 hours' pay. Then somewhere between booking a reception hall and shopping for a wedding gown, she wasn't ready to get married and gave back the ring.

She got a new job, but she wasn't sure what would happen next. She looked for an apartment but couldn't afford much. She struggled to build a life that no longer came with a blueprint. Basically, she was adrift.

I tried to be her anchor, but that didn't help her move on. It was great having her around the house to watch reruns of *Friends*, try new recipes, and take long walks together. Then one week she scared me by checking out flights to Atlanta and New York City. Worried that she might be tempted to move, I suggested she might want to get an apartment here first.

"I don't want to be stuck in this town forever," she sighed.

Stuck in this town? This is Cleveland, I reminded her, land of opportunities, home of the Rock Hall, the Flats, the Tribe, not some Podunk small town with nothing to do. She rolled her eyes. Anywhere your parents live is a town too small.

Living at home too long can make an adult child regress. Parents, too. Hover too long, and you hurt the child's social life and motivation to move on. I thought I was giving her a financial cushion to help her. It turned out that cushion was suffocating her. I wanted to tell her it was okay to fail, to take a risk, to choose something—a city, a career, a guy, a hobby—and build a life. It won't be perfect. No life is.

Life is messy. The five-year plan is highly overrated. Most of the things I planned in life never took. Most of the things that took, I never planned. So far, it's turned out to be a life better than anything I could have imagined. One day she would realize that the world is her oyster. But back then, my pearls of wisdom were useless. It was time for her to discover her own, and she did, without me writing out a map for her. She forged her own path by listening to her own heart, not mine.

Sometimes you have to get lost to find yourself. My nephew Michael did just that after he graduated college. He had a plan: three guys, a van, and a map. It didn't sound like much of a plan to me, but Michael counted on it to carry him all the way from Ohio to the University of New Mexico. He was setting out for graduate school. The 26-hour drive from rural Garrettsville, Ohio, to Albuquerque would take a mere three days, he said.

I've seen too many independent films to think it was a good idea. A lot can happen between here and New Mexico to a guy with Ohio plates, long hair, and three guitars. I wanted to save him from breaking down, going broke, or getting lost. So

I made him an offer. As a graduation gift, I would fly him to New Mexico. I was giddy when I presented the offer.

He turned me down flat. He and his buddies wanted to take a road trip in his friend's van.

How many miles were on it?

He didn't know.

Was he covered under the insurance?

He didn't know.

What kind of shape was the van in?

He didn't know.

I kept picturing him lost in the middle of nowhere.

But I couldn't stop him.

Then I left for my own road trip to the beach. My husband wanted to make sure we didn't get lost the way we did the previous year while I was driving, so he bought a GPS. How could I argue? I'm the one who missed the exit and drove a half hour before realizing it.

The GPS looked like a tiny TV stuck to the windshield. The map unfolded on screen as you drove. If you took a wrong turn, it told you to take a U-turn. A female voice told you where to go. "In 800 yards, turn left onto the motorway," she said. After about 20 minutes, I wanted to tell her where to go. I don't like someone telling me how to drive every five minutes, especially some stranger with a British accent who called every interstate "the motorway."

"Isn't this great?" my husband chirped.

No. I hated it. He snored away in the passenger seat, trusting our ride to an anonymous compass.

It's not so bad getting lost, I pouted. It merely extends the vacation. One year we ended up lost but found a lovely view of

the Shenandoah Valley. One year we found ourselves on a tiny road no wider than a hair on the map. We saw a sign with a large *L*. Lost? No. It signaled the old Lincoln Highway. My husband perked up. His great uncle, Mike Singer, hiked from New Jersey to San Francisco on it in 1914. His uncle was 18. What a wild trip that must have been. The massive mountain in front of us didn't look so daunting when we pictured him climbing it.

Unfortunately, the next year, our GPS kept us on track and on time. My husband was happy, but I felt robbed by the perfection of it all. There's so much of America to explore. With MapQuest, Google, or a GPS, the art of getting lost is becoming a lost art. I miss the old days when you trusted a map and the man at Texaco to be your guide. Or you just hopped in the car and followed your inner compass.

I thought about that when I said good-bye to Michael. By then, his plans had changed. Three guys and a van turned into two guys and a car. The guy with the van had backed out. But instead of giving him advice, I gave Michael my atlas full of states I've only dreamed of seeing. I was no longer worried that he would get lost.

Truth is, I envied him. He squeezed everything he owned in the back of a Dodge Neon and no one was telling him where to go on the motorway.

He did end up getting lost an hour from home before he even left Ohio. Then the power steering and air-conditioning broke and they melted all the way to Albuquerque.

He got lost, but he found himself on the journey. He is finishing a master's degree in philosophy and is ready to tackle his PhD. He's not sure where that will happen, but he'll forge his own path and do it his way.

Expand your comfort zone to make others more comfortable.

Minutes before I walked onstage to give a keynote address at a business conference, a woman approached me to ask a question.

She was the interpreter for the event at a local university and asked if it was all right if she signed my speech for anyone in the audience who was hearing-impaired or deaf. She didn't want to be a distraction but wanted to share my message.

Of course it was fine, I told her. I warned her that I talked fast and might be hard to follow. She laughed.

We had a few minutes, so I asked what got her interested in sign language. I thought she might have been raised by a deaf parent or had someone hard of hearing in her immediate family.

She told me a lovely story I've never forgotten.

She was just 14 that summer she worked at the ice cream shop. One day a man walked in and held up a sign: *one large chocolate cone*. She thought he was a bit odd, but she scooped the cone and handed it to him. Whenever he came in, he always held up the sign for the same order: *one large chocolate cone*. It finally hit the young girl that the man was deaf.

So she got a book out of the library and taught herself some sign language. It took her half an hour to learn one question for her customer. The next time the man came into the ice cream parlor, she signed the words: *How may I help you?*

He was stunned.

So stunned he left the store without even getting his large chocolate cone. Did she sign the wrong words? Did she somehow offend him?

Minutes later he came back. He brought with him a carload of deaf friends.

They came into the ice cream shop, he looked at her then signed to them, they looked at her, and they all started to cry. I cried when I found out the woman became a professional interpreter and a college professor who teaches sign language for a living.

Incredible things can happen for us and others when we expand our comfort zones to make someone else comfortable. Instead of searching for our career paths, sometimes the paths find us outside of our comfort zones.

Annette Fisher was comfortable running a bridal store until she volunteered to take care of a friend's farm animals while the woman was on vacation. While Annette was feeding the animals, she noticed a dark corner of the barn stall full of cobwebs. She brushed them away and discovered

a crippled pig. The potbellied pig had been neglected and looked as if its legs had been broken. The pig had no hair and couldn't walk. It turned out the pig had once been fat and happy until someone dropped her while unloading her from a truck.

Annette's career path had taken her into graphic design. She owned an advertising agency for 11 years, got married, bought a few acres, and owned the bridal shop. She had reached all her goals at age 26, but something was missing. Her "aha moment" came the day she took that sick pig to work to give it medicine. A bride-to-be was upset that the Alfred Angelo gown she was trying on didn't match her shoes and purse. As Annette watched the woman in the designer dress, she looked at the pig and realized she'd rather be working with the pig.

"When you look at the big picture, no one really cares if your shoes match your dress," Annette told me.

When the farm owner returned and asked how much money she owed Annette for taking care of the animals, Annette told her, "How about you just give me that crippled pig?"

That pig haunted her. Annette wondered how many other farms had animals like that, abused, neglected, or forgotten in dark musty stalls. Annette closed the bridal shop and opened Happy Trails Farm Animal Sanctuary.

Annette pampered the pig until Janice died seven years later in 2007. She calls Janice the founder of Happy Trails. Annette fed the pig peppermints, and Janice lived out her last days in a tiny log cabin with heat lamps. She slept under a thick pink comforter beneath a piggy pinup calendar on the wall.

Annette has since expanded Happy Trails Farm Animal

Sanctuary in Ravenna, Ohio, the town where I grew up. Once word got out about her refuge, the Humane Society, Animal Protective League, and law enforcement officers started bringing in abused and neglected animals. She has barns full of hogs, horses, ducks, geese, and chickens. Happy Trails has rescued more than 4,000 animals. The nonprofit finds foster and adoptive homes for farm animals. Volunteers clean stalls, repair fences, build shelters, and unload hay. The farm's mission is to rescue, rehabilitate, and adopt out animals removed from abuse, neglect, or abandonment situations by law enforcement officials, like the 40 roosters police rescued from a cockfighting ring in Cleveland.

A man who was camping found Wilbur, a piglet who looked as if he had been drop-kicked like a football. Bronson the chicken was dumped on a highway in Cleveland. Barney, a logging horse for the Amish, developed a bad back and couldn't work. A piglet named Maria escaped a slaughterhouse in Mogadore. A pig named Mr. Bojangles was dumped in a school parking lot in the middle of winter.

Annette gave me a tour of the ten-acre farm. She showed me a pig tucked into a sleeping bag. Asbury had a groove around her belly left by a water hose. Someone tied it around her and never took it off. As she grew, the hose became embedded in her body and had to be removed.

I met Joy, a Holstein heifer who thinks she's a pony. At five weeks old, she was found frozen to the ground. Part of her tail broke off. It's heartbreaking until you see how Annette's heart expands for each one. She loves them back to life and finds someone to give them a permanent home.

Annette is forever grateful to Janice the pig, who changed

her life by expanding her comfort zone. Annette wears shiny pink lipstick, dark eyeliner, silver earrings, a dusty blue coat, and work boots covered in, well, you don't want to know. She's come a long way from the bridal shop, but she loves it. You might say she's in pig heaven.

LESSON
30

There's no whining on the yacht.

Before you complain one more time about the daily grind called work, consider this: What would your life be like if you couldn't work?

We've all heard the adage "I've never met anyone on his deathbed who said, 'I wish I'd spent more time at the office.'" I used to say that until I actually met one person who vowed those won't be among the last words she utters.

All her life, all Susan wanted to do was work. When other teens were fantasizing about how they'd look in a wedding dress, she was busy visualizing herself in navy blue pumps, a plaid skirt, white blouse, blazer, and carrying a briefcase.

"A leather monogrammed briefcase," she corrected. "That's who I wanted to be. I never wanted to be somebody's mother or a traditional wife, not that there's anything wrong with those."

Susan got degrees in communications and history from Ithaca College in New York, then enrolled in graduate school in 1976 to get an MBA from the University of New Hampshire. Four weeks before graduate school started, a doctor told her she had multiple sclerosis. She was 25.

"The earth opened up and swallowed me whole, in one bite," she said, enunciating every syllable like a punch to the gut.

Her life was never the same.

When I met her she was 49 and scrunched up in a black wheelchair in her home in Shaker Heights, Ohio. She bore little resemblance to the vibrant career woman who loved shopping for briefcases and Jos. A. Bank suits with bow ties. She looked almost girlish, wearing a dandelion yellow dress, matching socks, and bright white sneakers without a scuff. Since she can no longer talk with her hands, her brown eyes and dark eyebrows leaped to punctuate her sentences.

"My limitations? I don't even know where to start. I used to be right-handed. I now eat with my left hand. I can't stand. I have home care. I cannot cut my food. I haven't been able to button my shirt since 1982," she said.

Susan can't push her own wheelchair, can't open her own mail, can't drive a car, can't pick up a pen if it falls. She paused and took stock of her abilities and delivered the summation like a punch line: "I have a big mouth and one hand.

"Look, I am not a victim. This just isn't my first choice," she clarified. "I was robbed, but life isn't fair. You do the best you can. I don't envy anybody their own life, but I wanted mine."

She did get that MBA and used it in the computer department of the Cleveland Clinic. Her parents had to come over at

6 a.m. to help dress her, then pour her into the car. At work, someone had to take her out of the car and into the office. "The people in my department were extraordinary," she says. "I never would have made it without them."

She quit working more than ten years ago when it became too difficult.

With work no longer the centerpiece of her life, Susan volunteers all over town. When asked what she missed about the world of work, a peace settled over her face like sweet memories of a lost lover.

"There was a dignity and an elegance...and pearl earrings, little ones, tasteful ones. You had authority. You were good at what you did," she said as if talking about another person. In a way, she was.

"You need someplace bigger than you to belong to. You miss the ideas, the stimulation. You miss having to decide. Work legitimizes you. I miss the connections. I miss the normal."

She offered one piece of advice for those who get to complain about rush-hour traffic, long hours, and crabby bosses: "Treasure what you have."

After meeting her, I had a new perspective on work and a renewed sense of gratitude. I wonder what our jobs would look like solely through the eyes of gratitude.

What if we all went on a gratitude binge every day, and saw everyone and everything as the gift that it really is? We probably would realize that most of us are sitting on a yacht compared to the rest of the world.

A lot of what we complain about is what someone else would love to have. That slow drive to work through rush-

hour traffic? That arrogant boss? That annoying coworker? That small paycheck? To someone who can't work or find a job, those are all gifts.

Someone created a great video of people from third-world countries reading the complaints of people from first-world countries at www.waterislife.com. A boy sitting in a pile of dirt says, "I hate when my leather seats aren't heated." A woman standing by a river where women wash their clothes says she hates "when I leave my clothes in the washer so long that they start to smell." A boy with a goat laments, "When I leave my charger downstairs." The video ends with the words: "First-world problems are not problems."

My friend Connie always reminds me, "There's no whining on the yacht." That's where a lot of us are sitting compared to most people in the world, especially those who are unemployed and treading water. There are days when I whine about an editor making changes to my writing when I'm blessed to be paid to write for a living. There are times when I moan about the hassles of filling out a monthly mileage form when I'm lucky to get reimbursed for travel expenses.

Through the eyes of gratitude, the job you have is still worthy of praise and thanks. It might not seem like a yacht. It might look more like a small powerboat or a canoe or a life raft, but if you're employed, your head is still above water. If you keep your chin up, the view is bound to get better every day.

No one can drain you without your permission.

The gas bill to heat our old house kept getting bigger, so we decided to find out where we were losing heat so we could put more insulation in the walls to stop the leaks.

My friend Bill came over with his special infrared thermometer. It looked like a small yellow gun. Everywhere he pointed it, a red dot appeared on the wall and the temperature of the area near the red dot registered on the meter.

Bill aimed the gun at the back-door landing. The temperature near the floor was 43 degrees. Cold air was seeping in around the door. The temperature on one wall was 53. The temperature on a nearby wall was 68 degrees. The energy leaks were easy to find with that gun.

Once we found all the leaks in the house, we caulked and insulated and added weather stripping. Our budgeted gas bill dropped from $185 to $118 a month. We stayed cozy and warm all winter.

Wouldn't it be great to have a little gizmo like that to point all over your life to see where the energy sneaks out? Imagine how much more productive you could be if you could get rid of all your personal energy leaks. Imagine taking on only projects that energized you. Imagine how you would feel if you chose only friends, partners, and coworkers who fired you up instead of blowing out your pilot light.

There are some days I feel like I'm having my own personal energy crisis. Days when I can feel the life force leave me, when I catch myself saying, "I'm so overwhelmed...I'm so exhausted...I feel so drained."

I've heard it said that how you spend your energy matters more than how you spend your time. Instead of time management, people now focus on energy management.

So where does all that energy go? Once you find the leaks, you can plug them up. It didn't take me long to identify my leaks once I became willing to look for them.

I fritter away energy checking and rechecking e-mail, Facebook, and Twitter. I lose energy when I skip breakfast and lunch.

Energy pours out when I gossip, complain, criticize, blame, and doubt. Energy sneaks out when I react and give in to drama instead of waiting and thoughtfully responding to someone. It leaks out when I handle the same papers over and over and keep reshuffling them on my desk. Energy seeps out in all the unfocused and unnecessary brainstorms that clutter my thinking and my desk.

I get drained by staying up late playing sudoku or watching a movie I've seen 20 times before, like *The Proposal*, *Sweet Home Alabama*, or *My Best Friend's Wedding*. By constantly saying yes

and adding more demands on my depleted self. By reading horrifying news stories that still disturb me hours later. By listening to drama that isn't mine.

I constantly try to squeeze more out of me and more onto my calendar, as if each day will expand beyond 24 hours and each week beyond 7 days. I'm not alone. We tend to respect our electronics more than our own bodies. We plug in our cell phones to recharge them every night but barely get enough sleep to recharge ourselves.

The good thing is, once you find your personal energy leaks, you can plug them up. Here's what works for me:

Prayer and meditation. The most important thing I do, every morning, is to tap into divine energy, that endless source of energy.

I post positive affirmations on my desk, car, and mirror to remind me how to be my best self.

It's important to choose the right sound track to your life. I'm a big fan of country music. It used to be so full of heartache, lying, cheating, and somebody-done-somebody-wrong songs. We used to tell this joke: What do you get when you play a country music record backward? You get your dog back, your truck back, your wife back. The country songs I listen to now fill me with hope and laughter.

Also, I try to do just one thing at a time. When I eat a meal, I eat the meal. I no longer read the paper or flip channels while eating or eat while on the Internet, iPhone, or iPad.

Fake deadlines are great. If there isn't a real deadline, I make up a fake one for myself. That way I don't waste time meandering around a project or column or book chapter for weeks or squander hours surfing the web if it's not needed.

H.A.L.T. Don't get too **hungry**, too **angry**, too **lonely**, too **tired**. My friends in recovery taught me that. Too many people skip lunch every day. They're too busy to eat. There's no such thing.

I consult my "no" coach before saying yes to another new project, brainstorm, or major commitment of time. My sister Joan helps me stay grounded in facts, not fiction, about my ability to do what I want and not what "should" be done. I love Anne Lamott's words: "I live by the truth that 'no' is a complete sentence." Amen, sister.

I'm learning to say no to my biggest time and energy drains when it comes to work:

E-mail: Instead of checking it compulsively when I don't have time to answer it (which means I'll only have to read it again), I read it once, then respond and delete.

Paperwork: How does it grow so high so fast on a desk? Someone taught me this tip: Every time you touch a piece of paper, put a staple in the corner. If you find a paper with a zillion staples, that means you're avoiding the subject of the paper. Either act on it, file it, or toss it.

Crazy-makers: Every workplace seems to have a few characters who suck up all the oxygen in the room. You feel them before you see them. They constantly create problems where none exist through gossip and envy and want you to join forces with them to defeat the imaginary enemies in their heads. Stay clear, stay sane, and stay away.

Saying yes just to please someone else: I used to suggest projects just to impress others during meetings, then left realizing I didn't have the time or the interest to complete those projects.

Procrastination: Too often I avoid the most important thing

to do out of fear. The anxiety over completing it grows like a storm in my brain and the clouds of doubt keep me from getting clarity on anything else in front of me. Now I blast through the toughest thing first and get them over with.

If you can't say no, do a cost analysis of what it will mean to say yes. It always costs something, either time or energy or both. When I was getting overwhelmed giving speeches (on top of writing two columns a week, hosting a weekly radio show, and writing my next book), I consulted Joan about how to say no to some of the speaking requests. Joan listened to my concerns about how hard it was to say no to important groups and organizations and friends and family members who all had a worthy cause and wanted me to support it by being their speaker. But too much of a good thing is still too much.

My husband once said to me, "Too many chocolate bars." What? "One chocolate bar is great. Two looks better. Three is a little much. Four is too many. Five is a stomachache." Even if I could do all the talks, it wouldn't be good for me. I wouldn't be living, I'd be performing for a living.

There's only so much "you" to go around. Joan gave me a solution using simple math: What will it cost you, from door to door? Include driving time, preparation time, greeting people, signing books, thanking people, and so on. Then look at what you are giving up: time with the grandbabies, spouse, or hobbies, et cetera. Then list the benefits. For example, How many people will you touch? If it doesn't make sense to say yes but guilt is tugging at you to do so, measure the guilt factor. Draw a timeline that goes from one to ten. Mark where your guilt falls. When you do, you see clearly that you are letting

guilt make your decisions and drain the life out of you. Guilt is a terrible tyrant that never lets up.

She also suggested I draw another timeline, this one to gauge my passion. Write NO on one end and YES on the other. Does saying yes to this particular task make my heart sing or my face fall? Where is the "wow"? If there is no "wow," the answer is NO. Period.

I'm not there yet, but I'd like to get better at using these, too:

Set a specific, limited amount of time to check e-mail, voice mail, Facebook, and Twitter.

Feed myself healthy, live nourishment every day instead of food that isn't actually fuel for my body, like soda, chips, and ice cream.

Spend more lunch hours with friends just to catch up, not to do business or network.

"Stop multi-tasking and start multi-asking" is a great tip from motivational speaker Colette Carlson. "The solution isn't time management. It's *you* management," she said at a conference I attended. She suggested making a not-to-do list and put down all those "shoulds." Instead of calling it selfish, focus on the *ish*: **I** stay **h**ealthy. I also like her version of a sit-down family meal. "Cereal works," she said. "Or McDonald's. They're called Happy Meals for a reason."

Stop micromanaging the husband, kids, and coworkers. I don't have to oversee every detail. No, they won't do it perfectly, which is to say, my way. They might actually do it their way, which could actually be better.

Tame the takers. Who are the takers? All those people who want more and more time. It could be your spouse, child, or

boss. Whoever it is, get better at saying no. If you can't say no, practice saying "Wait." No one can drain you without your permission. Be with people who complete you, not people who deplete you. I love these words a friend e-mailed me: "No one can drive you crazy unless you give them the keys."

A friend on a retreat taught me to get my own physical flow of energy going by tapping different places on my body. You know how gorillas pound on their chests? Try it. It's incredibly energizing.

Once you figure out where you squander your energy, you can start plugging up the leaks. Once you do, you'll have more time and energy for the work and the people who matter most—starting with you.

There's more to life than making it go faster.

The poster stopped me cold: *Never confuse having a career with having a life.*

It doesn't matter what we do for a living if we don't take time to have a life.

Sometimes the best thing you can do for yourself and others is to hit the brakes and slow down. I'm all for more downtime. There's an actual International Day of Leisure to celebrate it. Every year I miss it. I'm too busy.

It's a great idea to take a day off to pause, reflect, and have fun. How about a season of leisure? Wait. Isn't that what summer is supposed to be?

Life flies by so fast, you wonder, Did someone speed up the rotation of the earth? Short-sheet the calendar? The way we live, you would think one of the Ten Commandments was "Thou shalt not rest."

Even God took a day to rest.

Most of us don't.

Whether you honor the Sabbath on Saturday or Sunday, it used to be a time to silence the noise. Albert Schweitzer once advised people not to let the Sabbath be taken away, that if your soul doesn't have a Sabbath, it becomes an orphan.

We are a nation of orphans.

Our kids play in baseball, soccer, and hockey leagues on the Sabbath. Our stores sell liquor and beer during sermons. Our malls, grocery stores, convenience stores, and strip centers fill with shoppers. When I was a kid, you couldn't find a gas station open on the Sabbath and most stores were closed to honor the commandment "Remember the Sabbath day, to keep it holy."

We'd go to church, come home, and sit down for a big family meal. We didn't call them sit-down dinners; it was a given that we sat around the dining room table and didn't get up until everyone finished. If the phone rang, it was treated like a misdemeanor. "Tell them to call back. We're eating," my dad would bark.

Then we would spend the afternoon visiting Uncle Joe or driving out to see Grandma and Grandpa on the farm. We would snap beans. We would press blades of long grass between our thumbs and whistle. We would eat tomatoes and cucumbers warm off the vine. No one was in a hurry. There was nowhere to go because nothing was open.

Now the Sabbath day is just another day. People run errands, shop, and work. They're getting too busy to read the Sunday paper. Whatever happened to a day of rest?

We fill Sunday with work and projects. We boast about

what great type A's we are all the way to the cardiac-care unit. We talk incessantly about our multitasking until we suddenly remember that we forgot to pick up the kids from soccer.

We overschedule our kids, bragging about how many sports leagues Jason plays in and how many classes Bethany attends to learn ballet, gymnastics, German, and piano before she starts kindergarten. We're teaching our kids multitasking. We're teaching them to fill up every weekend, to postpone joy until retirement.

When was the last time your kids played a game of capture the flag? Spent a night on the front stoop studying the stars? When was the last time they caught lightning bugs? Climbed a tree? Read a comic book? Had a grass fight? Ran through a sprinkler? Have you ever taken them fishing? For a walk to get ice cream? In the woods exploring?

If we don't teach them the fine art of wasting time, who will?

What if we stopped scheduling every minute and let them be bored long enough to discover their own imaginations? We might also discover our own.

If you've already got a strong work ethic, it's time to strengthen your play ethic. Forget about where fun fits in your five-year plan. Where does it fit in your five-hour plan?

A while back an anonymous e-mail made the rounds with advice on how to maintain a healthy level of insanity. It suggested putting your trash can on your desk and labeling it "In." Skip instead of walk. Wrap mosquito netting around your cubicle and play tropical sounds all day.

Why not add to the list? Stick a drink umbrella in your coffee at work, kick off your shoes and go barefoot in your cu-

bicle. When you get home after a long day, sit in a hammock and appoint yourself in charge of Cloud Patrol.

Unplug the TV. Turn off the computer. Confiscate all cell phones, video games, and iPads. Kick the kids out of the house. Kick yourself out, too.

Round up the neighbors for a game of flashlight tag. Hold a scavenger hunt, a pet show, a talent show. Play charades on the front lawn. Make musical instruments out of clutter from the kitchen and garage. Don't lecture the kids on how great it was back when you were a kid. Get out and show them.

Don't call it downtime.

It's called living.

Instead of planning a better life, start living one.

One day I was having a pity party that no one else attended but me. My writing was at a standstill. A finished manuscript sat on my desk, but I was too scared to send it to an agent or publisher for fear it would be rejected. I wanted to know God's perfect path before I'd take one wobbly step down the wrong road.

My husband said, "You're looking for a sign, but the sign is in you. It's up to you. You haven't done anything to get it published. You haven't taken any action. You keep waiting for God to tell you what to do. Maybe I am your sign: send the book out."

I did, and I'm still stunned that it ended up in 26 countries.

An old Amish guy used to tell me, "You can pray for potatoes, but grab a hoe." One of my friends in recovery used to say, "God will do for us what we cannot do for ourselves, but God won't do for us what we're supposed to do."

Most of us don't procrastinate because we're lazy. We delay action because we're afraid of taking the wrong step, so we don't take any step.

It's like the guy who prayed to God again and again to win the lottery, but he never did. One day in the middle of that prayer, he heard God's booming voice yell down from heaven, "Buy a ticket!"

If you want to win the lottery, buy a ticket. If you want potatoes, you can pray all you want, but you'd better grab a hoe. You can have faith in God, but you have to back it up with action, even the smallest bit of action. You have to do what you can do.

Part of me rebels and resists action. I want a better moment, a perfect story line delivered from beginning to end before any word is typed. I want assurance that this is the right idea from the start all the way to the end. How can I act before I'm ready? But maybe there is no "ready."

I often fool myself into thinking I am actually taking action when I'm only planning and organizing and reading about taking action. I've bought countless books on how to exercise and have read them all without stretching a muscle.

Whenever I want to learn something new, I take a class or read a book instead of just jumping in and doing it. I once read four books on how to play piano better. I put all my notes in a three-ring binder. Did I play any scales or songs? Nope. Not a note.

So many people who tell me they want to be writers take endless classes and go to countless conferences but won't move a pen. It's safer to stay in the dream of writing a play or novel and enjoy all the possibilities instead of trying them

out and failing. I admire people who are willing to risk doing something imperfectly instead of perfectly doing nothing.

One of the prayers I heard on a retreat included these words: "I have spent my life, Lord, tuning up my lyre instead of singing to You." My guess is God just wants to hear us sing, even if we're off-key. Father Clem Metzger was a director at the Jesuit Retreat House. I savor this precious moment when he asked a woman to do a reading for Mass. She looked scared as she reviewed the Bible verse. Then she asked him for help on how to pronounce a few words beforehand. "Oh, stumble through it," he told her.

Stumble through it.

What great advice.

We're all stumbling through life. Some of us are just better at covering it up.

I once attended a retreat where Dr. Francoise Adan gave a talk called "Bringing Peace Inside Out." She was born in Italy and grew up in Belgium. She got her medical degree and decided to specialize in helping people take care of their minds, bodies, and spirits. She is co–medical director of the Connor Integrative Medicine Network at University Hospitals and assistant professor at Case Western Reserve University Medical School. People call her a wellness champion. I can see why.

The room was packed with busy women who took a day off, but many were cheating, tapping away on BlackBerry devices and iPhones under the table. She urged all of us to cease our endless doing. First she had us breathe, and make our exhale longer than our inhale. Breathe in four counts, breathe out six counts.

Then she had us pose this question to ourselves: *What will most benefit my well-being?*

The room fell silent. What came to me was this: Stop planning and start living. What would it take for me to trust life and embrace it 100 percent right here and now? What if I could let go of the quest for perfection and believe that completion, not perfection, is good enough?

That quest to live life perfectly keeps me from actually living. I overthink. I plan too much. I organize too much.

Then she had us all participate in an exercise I'll never forget. She held up a feather boa and described feathers as light and airy, versus goals, which are weighty and bog us down. She asked us to picture a set of scales with what we wanted to do on one side and what we didn't want to do on the other side. Instead of burying ourselves under the burden of endless goals, what if we just did one action, one feather-sized bit of action? If you add a feather to the scale, it doesn't make much difference at first, until you add another, then another.

Just one feather will tip the balance in your favor. What is your feather? Your one thing that will tip the scale? What is your feather today?

She passed the boa around the room and had us each pluck one feather off and share what feather, what action, we were going to take or stop taking to change our lives.

One by one by one, we took turns and shared our feathers. Women resolved to reach out to friends, to write down one thing they appreciate about themselves, to ask for help, to leave work by six every night. They vowed to check e-mails less often, go to yoga, hire a personal trainer, schedule half an hour of "me" time on the work calendar. They announced

they would set time for margaritas with girlfriends, morning affirmations, and naps.

I left the retreat with a simple blue feather and a vow to stop putting more on my to-do list. And what I do add to that list has to be worthy of my life, because that's what my time is—my life.

The world needs people who are fully alive.

Always saddle your own horse.

I thought of that cowgirl's motto as I tugged at the leather straps, making them as tight as possible so I wouldn't fall. This was no horse, but to me, it was just as scary.

After reading an obituary on Connie Douglas Reeves, the country's oldest cowgirl, I decided it was time to get busy living. The Texan cowgirl, who was 101, hard of hearing, and nearly blind, died after her horse, Dr Pepper, threw her.

Amazing. She was still on a horse at 101.

Too many of us never even get on one. We live life too carefully. We're afraid of getting hurt. I used to think the best way to die was to grow old, fall asleep, and never wake up. The cowgirl changed my mind. Don't tiptoe to death. Go out with a bang. Go out living.

Not that I planned to go out anytime soon, but I did plan to

go up. About 800 feet in the sky, strapped in a powered parachute that looks like an industrial fan attached to a go-kart fitted with two seats and a parachute.

I had just finished reading yet another book that urged me to get out of my comfort zone, to feel the fear and do it anyway, when my friend Hal Becker called. He'd been calling for weeks leaving chirpy messages on the answering machine: "The weather's just right...Looks gorgeous out...Call me."

I wanted to go up—well, I wanted *to want* to go up—but I don't even go on Ferris wheels, cable cars, or roller coasters. But because of that dang cowgirl, I said yes.

Nothing stopped her. Internet stories told how she would brand cattle, castrate sheep, and kill rattlesnakes. She broke her leg in '86 when a horse kicked her. A horse threw her after riding into a hornet's nest when she was 91. She broke her wrist and five ribs and punctured a lung.

She once told an Associated Press reporter about her sister-in-law, who was a decade younger, wasting away watching TV. The cowgirl grumbled, "What kind of living is that? You have to get out in the world and look at all the wonderful things."

That's what Hal promised. A wonderful view.

I trusted Hal's view of the world.

Hal Becker was diagnosed with stage 3 cancer at 28. They gave him three months to live. The testicular cancer had already spread to his abdomen, chest, and brain. That was back in 1983. He carries a photo of himself when he weighed 83 pounds and had burn marks on his arms from the chemotherapy.

He became an author, sales training guru, and international speaker. But he plays as hard as he works. Maybe harder. Being

a cancer survivor, he knows there are no guarantees about having a long life, so he has the time of his life all the time. He plays in a band, takes aerial photography, and soaks up every sunset he can from the sky. He makes the most out of now. As he says, "Now will never come again."

How could I say no to Hal? As we stood in a high school football field, Hal tossed a handful of grass into the air to check the wind, grinned, and said, "It's a great night for flying."

He unpacked the rainbow nylon parachute, untangled the strings (mere strings!) attached to the go-kart, then handed me a helmet.

"Anything in your front pockets?" he asked, not wanting anything to fall into the propeller. I quickly dumped out the contents of my pockets.

I tightened the straps of the shoulder harness, put on the helmet, and took a deep breath. Hal climbed into the front seat and we bounced along the grass on three small tires. Suddenly, we were floating on air.

Hal warned me that the first minute might "disorient" me. I'd have used the word terrorize. But he was right. After a minute, my body got used to the rush of wind around me, the feeling that there was nothing to hold on to, yet nothing to fear.

We floated over lush treetops, blue swimming pools, emerald ponds, brown slivers of deer, and into the setting sun. When we landed gently on the grass, Hal asked, "Do you feel it?"

Some would call it a rush of adrenaline. I think it's something else. A flush of joy running through every vein. I bet

it's how that cowgirl felt after every ride. She'd told reporters she'd never quit. "It's in my blood."

She wasn't talking about riding. She was talking about living.

One way to jump-start your life is to write your obituary and live it while you're alive. That's what Nancy Lee Hixson did. I never met her, but I wished I had after reading her obituary that ran in the *Plain Dealer* where I work.

She actually wrote her own obituary and kept revising it for seven years. Nancy packed as much life as she could into her 65. She died at sunrise on June 30, 2009. Here's what she had to say about her life. Her family said it was all true:

> In addition to being a tee-totaling mother and an indifferent housekeeper...she often volunteered as an ombudsman to help disadvantaged teens find college funding and early opened her home to many children of poverty, raising several of them to successful, if unwilling, adulthood.
>
> She also enjoyed a long life of unmentionable adventures and confessed she had been a rebellious teen-aged library clerk, an untalented college student on scholarship, a run-away hippie, a stoic Sunday school teacher, a Brownie leader, a Grange lecturer, an expert rifleman, a waitress, a wife once or twice, a welder, an artist, and a writer.
>
> She was the CEO of the Cuyahoga Valley Center of Outdoor Leadership Training, where she lived in a remote and tiny one-room cabin in the Cuyahoga Valley National Park. Despite the lack of cabin space and dining table, she often served holiday dinners to friends and relatives and could seat twenty at the bed.

She lived the last twenty-three years at Winter Spring Farm near Danville, Ohio, where she built a private Stonehenge, and planted and helped save from extinction nearly 50 varieties of antique apple trees. Her homemade cider and wine were reputed to cause sudden stupor.

She befriended countless stray dogs, cats, horses, and the occasional goat. She was a nemesis to hunters, and an activist of unpopular, but just, causes. In short, she did all things enthusiastically, but nothing well. After moving to Danville, she bravely suffered with a severe and disabling disorder and a ten-year battle with lymphoma that ultimately took her life.

She was often confined to the home where she continued to tirelessly volunteer and donate her limited resources to needy teens in the area, always cheered by their small and large achievements. Sympathy and big donations may be extended at this time.

After listing the survivors, Nancy's obituary read, "She was a long-time card carrying member of the ACLU, the Democratic Party, and of MENSA. In lieu of flowers, please pray for the Constitution of the United States."

What a life.

It reminded me of that powerful quote by Howard Thurman, who said: "Don't ask what the world needs. Ask what makes you come alive, and go do it. Because what the world needs is people who have come alive."

What makes you come alive?

It might not be work. It could be everything else that surrounds it.

The best use of your life is to love.

My daughter married a man who grew up with 63 brothers and sisters.

His parents, Elsie and Kevin Sullivan, had 3 children but were foster parents to 60 babies.

They made a career out of loving other people's children. They were emergency foster parents for babies who were taken from parents because of abuse, neglect, or medical emergencies. I can't even begin to imagine all the diapers and feedings and fevers they soothed. My son-in-law got a PhD in love in that house.

I once interviewed a boy who wanted to be adopted. There's still a huge crack in my heart from Maurice. I met him years ago, when he was 12, when he was running out of hope. He knew he was running out of childhood. He knew that most people wanted a baby or a toddler to adopt. Still, he

got excited when his picture ran in the *Plain Dealer*'s weekly feature, "A Child Waits." His personal ad seeking new parents described him as a bright, creative, artistic boy who was in residential treatment for abuse and neglect, who wanted at the time to be the first black president of the United States.

Only no one called.

Maurice was old enough to know that no one wanted him.

"It's kind of hard to be patient when years just flow by," he said softly. "Why won't anybody call?"

What would he say to someone who would consider taking him? He grinned so wide his huge cheeks squeezed his eyes into black slits holding onyx jewels. "Come on," he said, sounding like a salesman. "You're making a good choice. It's an opportunity you can't miss!"

From a kid's point of view, it's easy to feel like you're being punished for your parents' mistakes when no one wants to adopt you. The anger takes over, you act up, and then it's even harder for someone to want you. When I met Maurice, he was living with 42 children at Beech Brook in Pepper Pike, Ohio. He had been there the longest—going on two years. I asked him how many foster homes he'd had.

"Whoa," he said as he did the math. "Twelve, at least."

Maurice was taken from his parents when he was seven. His two sisters ended up in foster homes. He wished he were in one, even though they scared him.

"You get all nervous," he said, wringing his hands. "You don't really know anybody. You don't know where the kitchen is, where the bathroom is. It's kind of like first being born. You don't know what it's going to be like."

And you never know how long you will last there. He

thought the last foster parents would keep him. "They said they wanted to adopt me," he said. "I guess I just jinxed myself."

He talked dreamily about how he got to play hide-and-seek there, and how on the day he left, they threw him a party and his foster mom cried. "I don't even remember the phone number or address," he said, staring at his sneakers.

Before getting therapy, Maurice disrupted foster homes. In time, he learned not to throw a chair or swear when he was angry, but to talk about why he was upset. His history scares people from seeing who he is now and who he could be.

He did have one piece of hope to cling to. Maurice had a mentor to help him practice his new skills in the real world. Dave, an archaeologist with the Cleveland Museum of Art, took him out every Saturday.

"He's delightful," David told me. "He's real smart and fun to be with. He's dying for affection. He'd get along with anybody."

Before the mentor came along, Maurice felt hopeless. He told his therapist, "I don't want to live anymore. I'd be better off in heaven." Maurice wasn't choosy about the kind of family he wanted. "I want a family that doesn't do drugs, that's nonviolent," he told me.

It was hard for him to see other kids get adopted and leave. Each time that happened, the hurt deepened.

"Man, everybody is leaving me," Maurice said, shaking his head. "Every time my best friend leaves, I just try to make another best friend."

As far as I know, Maurice never got adopted and aged out

of the system. I don't know where he is, but he has a heart full of hurt. He's not the only one. I once interviewed a group of children at a camp for kids who were getting too old to adopt. They were 13 to 17 years old, and they talked about the Good Life, back when they had dads and moms, brothers and sisters, bedrooms and backyards that never changed.

They talked about when they got the bad news. A parent died or got arrested and wasn't coming back. They talked of how they reacted to the news. Some screamed. One threw up. Another couldn't speak. One confided, "I still can't believe it." They talked about the anger of leaving behind younger siblings and friends; about not being told a sister was adopted until a year later; about being watched constantly in foster homes; about cousins, aunts, uncles who never called or came for them.

They shared the bargaining they tried: *If I get straight As, if I behave, if I'm quiet, maybe then I can go back home.* Each one shared how they didn't feel good enough for anyone to love them. The camp volunteer had each one light a candle to remind them they could still choose hope and that no one else could make that light go out. She wanted them to reach a place of acceptance that they might never return to the Good Life, but they could create a new one.

If only there were more people like Jean and Chuck Harrell, who offer children a new life. They've been married for nearly 60 years and have taken in 300 children. Loving other people's children became their mission in life. They call it their ministry. It was her idea.

"We had to pray a *lot*," she said.

They had three of their own children, then decided to be-

come foster parents. Any resistance Chuck might have had, Jean prayed it away.

One day he said, "Okay, let's do it," and they've never stopped.

When I last spoke to them, he was 81, she was 78.

What a journey it has been.

They've had nine children living in their home in tiny Rootstown, Ohio, a town with two traffic lights. Their home became an oasis for children who had been abused and neglected. One time they took in an entire family at a moment's notice. The family was driving through from another state when they were in a car accident. The parents ended up in the hospital; the children ended up at Jean and Chuck's. The day the children were to leave, one of the boys went exploring at the park down the road. He discovered an outhouse, took a look inside, and fell in. He came back a stinking mess. Jean had to hurry to clean him up before his aunt arrived.

"We just laughed," Jean said.

And sometimes they cried.

"They come in with problems. Some are medical, some are physical, some are behavioral," Jean said.

All the children have touched them, but a little guy named Isaac left the deepest mark. One day the county children services called and asked them to take a baby. He had been shaken and his brain was badly damaged. Jean and Chuck went to the hospital to see the baby to decide whether they could care for him. They were told the baby probably wouldn't live. They decided to take the baby anyway.

"The only instruction they gave us was who to call when the baby died," Jean said.

They just poured love all over him, every moment they could.

"We prayed and prayed and worked as hard as we could with the baby," she said.

Isaac had lost part of his vision. He couldn't talk or sit. He had endless doctor appointments. They had to feed him through a tube, take him to physical therapy, give him medicine all day. His immune system was so weak, they gave up going to church so they wouldn't expose him to harm.

"That baby was God's special child and God didn't mind us missing church," she said. "We were doing what the Lord wanted us to do."

"All he could do is lay on his back, but he had the most beautiful smile you ever saw," Jean said. "He'd wave his arms and legs and coo. He was the happiest baby."

He could still feel love. That's what saved him. Their love.

They had him for almost three years. He left when another family adopted him.

"He was just pure joy," Jean said.

And now he is someone else's joy.

To find out who you are, let go of who you aren't.

If you grew up watching the TV game show *Let's Make a Deal*, you know how hard it is to choose the right door.

Contestants on the show are given the option to trade in a prize they have already won, like a TV or an oven, for what is behind door number 1, 2, or 3. They usually gamble all their winnings for one of those mysteries, even though a booby prize waits behind one mystery door.

What's behind door number 1? It could be a trip to Hawaii, a luxury car, or a dining room set. Or it could be a donkey, a jalopy, or a year's supply of furniture polish.

In real life, we usually want to cling to what we know and have for as long as we can. Too often when one door closes, we stand at that door and keep pounding away on it, as if more noise and effort will force it open. Meanwhile, another door might be unlocked or even standing wide open, but we refuse to budge from the closed one.

For years, I hosted a public affairs radio show on an NPR affiliate in Cleveland. I loved doing radio. I loved it so much I hosted for free every Friday during the 9 a.m. hour. But in time, I ached to do more topics that focused on the heart and soul, on topics I call "internal" affairs. So I wrote up a plan to create an entire radio show called *Internal Affairs*. I listed page after page of topic ideas for the show. I couldn't wait to present it to management.

No one wanted it.

No one.

Instead, they wanted to tighten the focus of the existing show even more on topics related to business, the economy, and politics. None of those topics made my heart sing or my passion meter fly off the scale. One week we did a show on auto industry workers but our guests were analysts for the car industry, not real live auto workers, which is what I suggested.

One week I was given the choice to do a show on Asian carp in Lake Erie or the building of the Innerbelt Bridge. I chose the bridge and hosted a rousing discussion, but it wasn't a topic I would have tuned in to as a listener.

That's when I knew I was the proverbially square peg trying to fit into a round hole. I should be hosting shows I actually wanted to listen to, and management should be presenting shows they believed in. We were no longer a match. It was time to go. So I left.

What to do with my big brainstorm? I took it to another nearby public radio station. WKSU-FM loved it. They gave me my own weekly show, *The Regina Brett Show*. I found my match. The tagline was: "Smart...with heart." They kept telling me, "Be you. We want more of you in the show." More

of me? Wow. That's clarity. That's how I knew I was in the right place.

Sometimes the slam of one door reverberates so loudly in our ears it's hard to hear the quiet opening of the next door. We often hear the quote "When God closes one door He opens another." We rarely hear the words that follow it. Helen Keller added another important part when she said when one door of happiness closes, another opens; but instead of walking through it, we stand stuck at the closed door and miss seeing the one that has swung open for us.

Sometimes we have to let go of who we are to find out who we are being called to be. We have to give up the good for the great. My friend Adam Shapiro traded the good for the great. He was at the top of his game in Cleveland with a coveted spot as the anchor of WEWS-TV's (ABC) show *Good Morning Cleveland*. He did the early evening newscast called "Live on Five." He won awards for his work as an anchor and a reporter.

His friends—including me—were stunned when he quit that plum job and headed for the Big Apple. He didn't go there for a job. He went there for the possibility of one. He always wanted to live in New York City. He ended up being a general assignment reporter in New York for the WNBC-TV morning show *Today in New York*, then landed a job at FOX Business Network.

Midlife crisis?

Not at all. He called it a midlife correction.

Sometimes life corrects your life for you. For years, my column ran on the front of the Metro section. But I had gradually quit writing local metro columns about crime and corruption to focus on columns that would uplift and inspire. They say,

"Success is doing most what you do best." It was time to do my best work, the work I felt most passionate about.

I came in one day excited about my new book *Be the Miracle*, a collection of inspirational essays. I brought signed copies for each editor. When I handed one to the managing editor, he asked me to sit down. He broke the news that my column was being moved. He said it no longer fit the local metro page. It would go on page A-2. It knocked the wind out of me for a few seconds. Oh, no, my writing would no longer be on a section front, the prime real estate in the newspaper. Then I realized, *Wait a minute, this is a gift.*

A new door was opening. Behind this new door, I was free to write more inspirational columns and wasn't limited by local news. I would no longer be expected to write commentaries about crime and corruption. I was free once I released my old job with this prayer:

"God, thank You for all You have given me, thank You for all You have taken, but mostly, thank You for what You have left me."

I see myself now as an inspirational writer, not a journalist. No more apologizing for who I am or for who I am not. I'm getting better at saying no to what I know clearly isn't my calling. If there's no joy in it, no smile in it, it's not mine to do.

You don't have to be good at everything. If you try to be, you'll probably end up mediocre at everything. Leo Buscaglia used to tell a great story about why we should treasure our uniqueness. He told how the animals got together and created a school. To paraphrase his story, each animal played a part in designing the curriculum. The rabbit wanted running on the curriculum, the bird wanted flying on it, the

fish wanted swimming, and the squirrel wanted perpendicular tree climbing.

What happened next? Everyone was expected to excel at everything, which ruined everything for everybody. The rabbit was great at running, but fell out of the tree trying to climb it and got injured. That hurt his running, so when it came report card time, he no longer got As in running and he flunked tree climbing. The bird broke a wing trying to burrow in the ground and ended up with a C in flying and flunked burrowing.

The moral of the story for me is this: If you try to be a second-rate version of someone else, you will fail to be a first-rate version of you. All God wants for me to be is me, the very thing I hold back because I believe I'm not worthy. God already knows that and doesn't care.

Whenever I feel like an oddity in the world of journalism, I read this e-mail a reader sent me. Paul wrote it after reading a column I wrote about a soldier who died. At his funeral, his daughter carried his Purple Heart:

Dear Ms. Brett, Each person is born with a gift from God. Some people can cook, really knock your tongue out. Some sew or woodwork. Some people are natural born Mommies, that know when to wipe a tear or bake a pie. You my friend, can paint. I have never considered the keyboard the tool of an artisan, and yet, in your hands, a picture is painted of an event, or an every day occurrence that becomes a piece of the heart of the person reading it.

Your capabilities of reaching out and plucking exactly

the right heartstring is astounding to me. You pierced me today. Understand that the gifts I mentioned from God are not ours to possess. They are meant to be shared to make life whole and fuller for as many others as possible. In my opinion, God is well pleased with your use and sharing of his gift.

When I stop trying to be someone else and settle for being me, great things come to pass for me and for others. I love this quote: "In a world where you can be anything, be you."

Just be you. That's all God is calling you to be. And that's always enough.

Align yourself first, then take action.

It was a rough day at archery.

My arrows were flying everywhere except where I wanted them to go: smack in the center of the bull's-eye where the tiny X is.

I stood with my recurve bow in hand, quiver full of arrows, aiming for the center of the yellow bull's-eye 18 meters away. Each time I drew back the string, had my sight on the target, and it felt right to let go, I scored well. But every time the shot didn't feel right, instead of putting the bow down and starting my shot over, I fired anyway. I let go even though I heard the word *Stop* in my head. Each time, the arrows landed far from the inner circle. Damn. Why was it so hard to shoot today? Shot after shot made me more frustrated.

A woman a few archers down kept hitting the bull's-eye. From the looks of her target, it was as easy as breathing.

She even hit the X. Twice. In a row. What did she know that I didn't? What secret technique was she using? I had to find out.

After taking my three shots, I studied her. She stood at the shooting line, drew back, paused, then stopped and set the bow back down. Again and again, she put the bow down without releasing the arrow. That's the one thing I resisted doing. She stopped herself, got realigned, and started over. That's how she hit so many bull's-eyes. She never once let go of the arrow until she knew she was aligned.

We both knew when we weren't ready. One of us listened and got realigned. The other one, me, shot anyway.

In archery, they say every shot starts with your feet. Your stance has to be right before your shooting will be. Before any action is taken, you need consistent alignment. You want your body to develop muscle memory. In archery, you learn to shoot well by repetition. You find out what works, then keep repeating the same steps over and over until your body remembers them. You no longer have to think about your shot; your body just does it. And once you release the shot and it hits the target, you're supposed to forget about it, clear your mind, and get ready to shoot the next one.

You are storing and releasing energy into the bow, which then releases it into the arrow. The best archers visualize each shot; they see it before they release an arrow. They practice alignment first, then action. When I remember that and practice it, my score is higher and I have more fun shooting.

It's true about life, too.

When I am aligned, when I am spiritually centered, emotionally calm, and mentally focused, nothing rocks me. When

I'm not aligned, the smallest speed bump will knock me off balance, the smallest insult will crush me.

How do I stay aligned? Mostly through daily prayer and meditation. I call them spiritual exercises. They build muscle memory so you always know your true center and aim in life when life surprises you. Once you're aligned, in life and in archery, it's a lot easier to hit your target, because you actually know what you're aiming for.

When I worked at the *Beacon Journal* as a reporter, some editor decided we all needed to get more focused in our writing. The paper instituted a rule that every time you turned in a story, you had to write a two-sentence summary at the top of it to help the headline writers choose their words. When you think about it, the headline is the most vital part of the story. It attracts people to read it or to turn away.

At first I grumbled and resisted writing that stupid two-sentence assignment. Then I grew to love it. When I got lost writing long columns or stories, I'd often go back to the top and consult those two sentences to make sure I hadn't lost my focus. It helped me trim away the nonessential information that didn't advance the story or serve the reader.

Companies do the same thing by writing a mission statement. It serves as a compass point so everyone travels in the same direction, from CEO to secretary.

My husband once owned a PR firm whose motto was "We build relationships." His business card was the most confusing one I'd ever seen. It listed everything they did: government relations, community relations, public relations, media relations, business relations. He did so many things, no one, not even his kids or I, knew exactly what he did for a living. His "elevator

speech" was fine, as long as you were going from the lobby to the 32nd floor and had 20 minutes for him to explain his line of work.

Once he decided to specialize in one thing, crisis communications, his business took off. If you try to be all things to all people, you end up not mattering much to anyone. When you do one thing and do it well, you make yourself essential.

It helps to have a focal point to keep you centered on what that one thing is. When I hosted my own radio show for three years, I didn't want to lose sight of what I wanted *The Regina Brett Show* to be. To help me stay focused on my personal mission, no matter what the topic or guests were, I wrote my own Ten Commandments for the show:

1. Be interesting. Surprise the listener.
2. Be original.
3. Be you. Sound 100 percent like Regina Brett.
4. Have fun.
5. Ask the tough questions in a respectful manner.
6. Honor the listener first.
7. Inspire all involved to find and use their inner power to create a greater life for themselves and others.
8. Give people hope.
9. Work as a team to do only what we can do well and consistently.
10. Do the best you can every week, 100 percent, then release it.

Before we started the show each week, I went into the restroom and got aligned. I held my hands together in prayer,

touched them to my forehead, and asked God to bless all my thoughts with clarity; then touched my hands to my mouth and asked God to bless all my words with compassion; then touched my hands to my heart and asked God to bless my guests, staff, and listeners. Once I aligned myself, I no longer worried about what happened next.

My friend Terry Pluto is a sports columnist who also writes a column on faith for the *Plain Dealer*. We also worked together at the *Beacon Journal* many years ago. He used to write the most powerful columns about his dad, who spent his life working in a warehouse, then retired and had a stroke that left him unable to walk and barely able to talk. All he could do was grunt or say one word: "man."

Terry came on my radio show and told a powerful story about his dad, himself, and the importance of staying spiritually aligned. In 1998, Terry spent a few days with his dad in Florida and had helped him leave the hospital and get settled back home. A caretaker took over after Terry had to go back home to Akron.

Terry was supposed to go to Japan that February to cover the Winter Olympics as a sportswriter. It's a big honor for any sportswriter and a big commitment for a newspaper to make. The paper had already bought the airline ticket and paid for the accommodations. Before Terry left for the airport, he called the caretaker. Everything was the same. On the drive to the airport, Terry was praying for his dad when he heard a voice say, "Don't go."

It was as clear as if someone had said it out loud. The words stuck with him; so much so, he pulled over and called the caretaker to check on his dad. Everything was fine. Terry closed

his eyes and prayed for clarity. He heard those same words, "Don't go." So he called his boss at the newspaper and said he didn't think he should go to Japan. It was an awkward call to make, since his dad was the same as before, wasn't in the hospital or near death's door, and the paper had spent thousands of dollars to send Terry there. Terry told his boss he just didn't feel good about leaving. The boss said, Don't go.

Terry drove back home and called his dad before going to bed. Terry talked to his dad, who just said his usual, "Man, man." Terry fell asleep.

At 4 a.m. his brother called. Their father had died.

I think Terry heard God speak because he constantly aligns himself to hear God. He practices prayerful listening, so when God does speak, he hears. Those two words, "Don't go," could have easily been drowned out by the noise of busy thoughts if he hadn't been aligned.

Aligning myself every morning in meditation is the best thing I do for me. One day I was just about to merge onto the interstate from the on-ramp when I heard a voice say, "Stop!" I hesitated for a brief second and then hit the brake. Good thing. Just then, a semitruck flew past. It had been in my blind spot. Had I sped ahead, I would have been crushed.

Another day I was driving down the road with too many to-do items buzzing through my brain. What should I do first? Then I looked up and saw the license plate in front of me: BE CLEAR.

It doesn't get any clearer than that.

The most important boss to answer to is the small, still voice within.

Have you ever worked for an arrogant boss?

Who hasn't?

There's actually a scale created to measure how arrogant your boss is. It's called the Workplace Arrogance Scale, WARS for short.

Stanley Silverman is an industrial and organizational psychologist at the University of Akron. Every time he asks a roomful of people, "Have you ever worked with an arrogant boss?" every hand goes up. I wonder how many of those hands belong to bosses who don't realize *they're* the arrogant ones.

Think your boss is off the scale?

Now you can verify it. Stanley and researchers at Michigan State University developed the scale after interviewing hundreds of people and collecting all the traits they saw in their bosses as arrogant.

According to the scale, your boss is arrogant if he or she: Makes decisions that impact others without listening to their input. Glares or stares to make people uncomfortable. Criticizes or belittles. Shoots down other people's ideas in public. Makes unrealistic time demands on others. Here are a few things the rest of us would add: Yells. Curses. Blames. Shames. Acts omnipotent, invincible, superior.

Everyone has a bad-boss story. I once had a boss who made one worker sit in a closet to work to punish her for being slow. The boss would order us not to talk to the woman. It was degrading for everyone. The poor woman was doing her best to keep up.

Early in my journalism career, I worked at a newspaper where we learned from a competing newspaper that our paper was for sale. We lost confidence in the owner of the paper when we realized he had no confidence in us. He held a staff meeting in the newsroom and told the roomful of journalists, "You can't believe everything you read in the paper." Great. We reporters were working for a newspaper publisher who didn't trust reporters.

Some bosses like to micromanage. I'm rarely productive for that kind of boss. I want to crawl out of my skin when I see them coming. I feel suffocated in every conversation and want to scream, "Just leave me alone and let me do my work!"

Some bosses want to correct your work before you're even finished with it. In one newsroom, one editor read electronically over my shoulder. I was typing away on a story at my desk and sent her the final version. She sent an e-mail commenting on the earlier versions, the ones I had deleted. It turns

out she had been reading my writing from her computer without my knowing it. It was like Big Brother was watching.

One editor took joy in deleting my most poetic lines. He earned the nickname Captain Strike Through. Before he even read through the whole story, he started making changes in your copy. What a contrast to one of the best editors I ever had, Stuart Warner. He created a whole new model of what an editor, and a boss, could be. Whenever I turned in a story, he read it all the way through, made a few suggestions, then he got out of his chair and invited me to sit there. Together, we made the changes, but it was my hand making them. What a difference. Every story improved with his delicate touch.

It took me a long time to believe I could trust a boss. I haven't always been the easiest person to work with. I used to have a bumper sticker over my desk that read: QUESTION AUTHORITY. And, boy, did I.

For the longest time I hated any authority over me. Every boss became the father I couldn't please, and my dad was tough to please. No matter what I did growing up, it was never good enough for him, and he let me know with his belt or his rage. His constant refrain still reverberates through my head: *What the hell is wrong with you? Can't you do anything right?* My guess is he heard that from his own dad his whole childhood. As they say, when you know better, you do better. My dad just didn't know better.

If you haven't resolved your dad or mom authority issues, every boss becomes that unpleasable, unpleasant parent. One day at work a coworker was having a tough time with the boss. She complained to a reporter next to her that nothing

she did could please him. The reporter laughed and said, "Daddy doesn't love you. Get over it."

It has taken me a long time to trust that every boss isn't out to punish me. To this day, if the boss asks, "Do you have a second?" my heart races and I fear the worst: *What did I do wrong? How am I going to be punished?*

It doesn't help when that is what happens. One day many years ago, the editor wanted to see me. Before walking into his office, I paused and prayed and reminded myself that it could actually be for something good, like a raise. It wasn't. Someone had written a nasty letter about my work and the editor called me into his office to tell me he was going to run it. He didn't go to bat for me; he didn't have my back. I left feeling battered and bruised, which is how I felt as a child.

When I left my job as a columnist at the *Beacon Journal* to become a columnist at the *Plain Dealer*, I gave myself a fresh start. I figured it would be easy. I was already a columnist; I knew how to write, how to meet deadlines, and had already won national writing awards. So why did I get hit with a wave of anxiety a week before I started my new job? It made no sense. I would be doing the same job, just for new people.

Bingo. Would I be able to please that new boss? It hit the old childhood button: fear of Dad's disapproval. Then a friend in recovery shared this passage from the "Big Book" of Alcoholics Anonymous. It gave me a new perspective on who's really boss. The passage describes AA's third step:

Made a decision to turn our will and our lives over to the care of God as we understood Him...

We decided that hereafter in this drama of life, God

was going to be our Director. He is the Principal; we are His agents. He is the Father, and we are His children...When we sincerely took such a position, all sorts of remarkable things followed. We had a new Employer. Being all powerful, He provided what we needed, if we kept close to Him and performed His work well.

The book even offers a prayer to go with that step. I use the prayer often, especially when dealing with work. Here are a few lines that guide me often: "God, I offer myself to Thee, to build with me and to do with me as Thou wilt. Relieve me of the bondage of self, that I may better do Thy will."

Once I surrender, I have nothing to fear. With this new way of seeing it, I always have the same Boss, a God who loves me and wants the best for me.

Every day, I consult God for my assignment, my marching orders, my perfect good. The clarity doesn't come down like a hammer or a hurricane. It comes to me, not through any earthly boss, but from that most important Boss of all, the still, small voice within. For me, that voice is God. For others, it's that inner clarity and peace that comes from knowing, accepting, and loving who you truly are and honoring it above all other voices first, last, and always.

Power is an inside job.

The speaker onstage didn't care if anyone saw her sweat.

She wiped her brow but promised she wasn't having a hot flash.

"This is a power surge!" she bellowed.

We all felt the energy at the Spirit of Women in Business conference at Kent State University. More than 300 women attended the daylong conference about how to harness your power. First we heard from DeLores Pressley, a motivational speaker and coach who urges women to be "undeniably powerful."

"Women take care; men take charge," she said. "Men are taught to apologize for their weaknesses; women are taught to apologize for their strengths."

How true. I remember sitting with a group of fellow writers at a national conference of columnists when the man next to

me asked what my plans for the future were. He was about ten years older and had been writing a column a few years longer. I told him I hoped to have a syndicated column one day, give inspirational talks, and write books.

"That's awful ambitious," he scoffed, then turned away and started talking to the men at the table. From the tone of his voice, his words didn't sound at all like a compliment. It sounded like one of those "Who do you think you are to dream so big?" kind of messages. It left me feeling small.

I wish I could have sat up taller, held my head higher, and said, "Yes, I'm excited and grateful to be blessed with so much ambition and passion and enthusiasm to spread my message to anyone in the world who needs or wants it."

Unfortunately, I was too dumbfounded and shamed to make a quick comeback. If only I could have quoted Timothy Leary, who said, "Women who seek to be equal with men lack ambition." Or shared Marianne Williamson's words that everyone should commit to memory: "You are a child of God. Your playing small does not serve the world. There's nothing enlightened about shrinking so that other people won't feel insecure around you."

She's right. Your smallness doesn't make the world a grander place. My success benefits everyone and everyone else's success benefits me. It's not just our shadow selves and weaknesses we need to stop fearing. We all need to stop being afraid of our own light, stop being afraid of our power and what it might mean to tap into it, all the way down to the core of that nuclear reactor that is the indwelling Spirit of God most alive in us.

Yes, we were all born to glorify the God who lives and dwells in each of us. We're here to use up every bit of that power and energy and passion and light. When we shine, the world gets brighter for everyone, not just us.

People like DeLores remind us of that. She urged all of us to get a mentor and a coach. The more people on your side, the better. Get rid of the silent beliefs, those voices in your head that keep telling you, *You can't do it . . . You're a fraud . . . You're going to fail.*

Toss fear overboard. "When fear knocks on your door, don't give it the key," she said.

I needed to change my locks.

We heard from other great speakers at the conference. Barbara Blake, from Longview Associates and Sherpa Coaching, taught us how to coach ourselves. Leadership is a state of mind, not a job title. See yourself as a leader even if no one else does.

You always hear people say, "Get out of your comfort zone." Barbara said, "Grow your comfort zone." That sounds more inviting and less scary.

She told us to ask ourselves, *What should I stop doing?* "The power is in the stopping," she said. I used to think it was in starting more projects and plans. For starters, we could stop whining, complaining, and doubting. Stop interrupting others, talking over people, and being afraid of success.

Barbara urged us all to stop using the f word.

No, not that one.

The female f word: *feel.*

Don't tell your board of directors, "I feel like we should

invest more." Don't tell your client, "I feel we can increase sales." Don't tell your employees, "I feel we will succeed." Don't tell your boss, "I feel like we're doing the best we can."

Cut the f word out and make your point forcefully: "We should...we can...we will...we are."

Then Leslie Ungar, president of Electric Impulse Communications, told us how to develop the diva within. I never before had anyone give me permission to be a diva. It felt wildly exciting.

Diva is Italian for "female deity." It used to be reserved for the celebrated singer, the outstanding talent. I like the idea of celebrating your inner goddess and letting her out.

Find out what you need to feel empowered. We all need something, Leslie said. It could be shoulder pads, power ties, red lipstick, pearls, or a tattoo. She told the story of a man who remarked on her high heels. She told him she wore them to feel powerful. He said he didn't need anything to make him feel powerful.

She asked him what kind of car he drove.

"A BMW," he answered.

"That's what you need to feel powerful," she told him.

We laughed. A pair of Manolo Blahniks are soooo much cheaper.

What's it mean to be a diva? Whenever you get the chance to be onstage, own it. Own your real estate, your office, your cubicle, your workstation. Make people believe they can't do without you. Be confident enough to ask questions, to speak up, to ask for what you need to be your best self at work and beyond. Know your brand and communicate it. Stand out.

Whenever you are in the spotlight, shine bright. That doesn't mean just focusing on you, but rather focusing on how others are better off having heard or met you.

And if they see you sweat, they'll know it's because of your power, not your fear.

It's up to you to launch your life.

My favorite greeting card shows a biplane in the air with this quote above it:

Orville Wright didn't have a pilot's license.

Open the card and it reads, *Go change the world.*

That's what the Wright brothers did. They changed everyone's world when their plane left the ground. They were the first real pilots breaking new ground—the air.

I think about that every time I look at my vision board. There's a picture of their plane on it.

I believe we all can fly. Why? I'm from Ohio.

We're not just first in flight; Ohio is first, second, and third. It's the birthplace of aviation. Orville and Wilbur Wright built airplanes in Dayton. Ohio gave birth to John Glenn, the first American to orbit the earth. Then the Buckeye State produced Neil Armstrong, the first human to walk on the moon.

In my home state, we put the possible in impossible.

In eighth grade, I had the honor to meet John Glenn. Back then, that freckle-faced astronaut was the biggest hero around. In Ohio history, we learned about those restless brothers who opened a bicycle shop in Dayton. Orville and Wilbur didn't just build bicycles. They built gliders and kites, motors and propellers. They built the first wind tunnel, to test the wing surface of the airplanes they invented.

After the historic flight at Kitty Hawk, they returned to Ohio to perfect the plane, which led to the creation of the first dependable airplane. Their original airplane bears this inscription at the Smithsonian Institution:

The world's first power-driven, heavier-than-air machine in which man made free, controlled, and sustained flight. Invented and built by Wilbur and Orville Wright. Flown by them at Kitty Hawk, North Carolina[,] December 17, 1903. By original scientific research the Wright Brothers discovered the principles of human flight. As inventors, builders, and flyers they further developed the aeroplane, taught man to fly, and opened the era of aviation.

They opened the door for Neil Armstrong, who got his pilot's license at 15, before he learned to drive. He was born in Wapakoneta, Ohio, population 9,843. The quiet, humble man was an engineer and a Navy fighter pilot who flew 78 combat missions in the Korean War. He was in college when someone else broke the sound barrier. He was disappointed to miss out on what he thought was the greatest adventure in flight. Little did he know what was ahead of him.

In 1969, he took us all to the moon with him on Apollo 11. I'll never forget those words when he landed the lunar craft: "Houston, Tranquility Base here. The Eagle has landed." Or when he took that first step and said, "That's one small step for man, one giant leap for mankind." On that flight, he carried with him a piece of the original plane the Wright brothers flew.

Armstrong was a reluctant hero who hid from the media spotlight and rarely talked to reporters. He became a professor, bought a farm in Ohio, and disappeared back into his life. He knew he had completed his mission in life.

How do you know what yours is?

I once saw a poster at church and knew instantly it was my job assignment for life: *Inspire the world. Live your vocation.*

Inspire the world. That was it.

I keep a tiny plaque on my desk that bears this definition of inspire: *To affect, guide, or arouse by divine influence. To fill with enlivening or exalting emotion. To stimulate action; motivate. To affect or touch.*

Underneath it is my personal mission statement: *To inspire men and women to find and use their Inner Power, to find and complete their Sacred Mission, to create a greater life for themselves and others.*

If the word *mission* scares you away, call it something else. Søren Kierkegaard described it this way: "God has given each of us our 'marching orders.' Our purpose here on earth is to find those orders and carry them out."

I heard the call to carry them out near Kitty Hawk where the first flight took place on a remote stretch of sand.

Almost every year we vacation in the Outer Banks of North

Carolina, but I never visited the memorial until my friend Beth joined us back in 2007. I barely knew her, but my husband knew her husband and invited them to join us for a week on the beach. As soon as she arrived and we saw each other's inspirational books we had brought along, we knew we were soul mates.

At the end of a wonderful week together sharing our deepest dreams, we went to the Wright Brothers Memorial to launch our new life. We joked that we were the Right Sisters. We walked up to the official memorial, a 60-foot monument, and the words blew me away: "Dauntless Resolution. Unconquerable Faith." Those were the qualities the brothers had. Those were the qualities I wanted.

There are four stone markers to commemorate the four flights made on December 17, 1903. The first flight traveled just 120 feet; the second made it 175 feet; the third made it 200 feet. The last attempt was the best. The plane flew 852 feet.

A wonderful breeze blew through me as I stood on the flight path that first plane had taken. I walked from the starting point, the liftoff point, to the first marker where the first flight ended. There, I gave thanks for the first part of my life's journey that I had taken as a single parent with Gabrielle. That unplanned pregnancy, which once seemed like such a big mistake, had been the greatest gift of my life.

As I walked to the second marker, I gave thanks for the journey I had taken with friends in recovery who helped heal my childhood wounds. On my way to the third marker, I offered thanks for the journey I had taken with my husband. His undying love and loyalty saw me through cancer. He also

helped launch my career as a columnist. He believed in me before I could.

I stood at the third stone and looked far down at the last stone. It was time to really and truly embrace my writing. There at Kitty Hawk, where man first took flight, I let go of my fear of success and my fear of failure. I was afraid to release being a journalist to become an author, that earliest of all my dreams. I had been afraid to let go of who I had been to fully embrace who I could be.

I stood at the third stone with the breeze as my only companion. It was time to say yes. Yes to all the writing that was in me to release. I felt the Spirit move through me. I opened my heart and offered all of me to God. I launched my dream life: to write all the books in me, to tell all my stories, to share everything life taught me to inspire others. I held my arms out like wings, and I swear the Holy Spirit supplied the lift and carried me to that final marker. I felt a new freedom and a new happiness.

I once read that there's the thing you do for a living and then there's the thing you were born to do. I was finally ready to do the thing I was born to do.

Once home, I taped the brochure from the Wright Memorial with the black-and-white photo of that plane on my vision board. I made the covers to all the books I wanted to write and posted them there. Then I wrote at the top: *This or something better.*

Was it okay to tell God what I wanted? Should I seek my heart's desire or God's will? Then I remembered what Beth told me: God's will is your heart's purest desire. They are one and the same.

Was it okay to post it there in the open? I knew it was when Beth sent me this quote from Habakkuk, a chapter of the Bible that I had never even heard of:

> Then the Lord answered me and said: Write down the vision clearly upon the tablets, so that one can read it readily. For the vision still has its time, presses on to fulfillment, and will not disappoint. If it delays, wait for it, it will surely come, it will not be late.

Wait and it will surely come.
God is rarely early, but God is never late.

Things don't happen to you; they happen for you and for others.

One of the hardest parts of getting cancer is losing your hair to chemotherapy.

When you're bald from chemo, you feel powerless. To the world, you're a patient. People stare. Friends cringe. Children flee.

When I had breast cancer 16 years ago, I planned to go right from my hair to a wig that looked just like me. No one would know I was bald from chemo. My husband took me shopping. We went looking for a wig while I was still under the influence of the cancer diagnosis. It wasn't pretty. Wig stores should carry a warning: Do Not Shop Until the Shock Has Worn Off. I felt paralyzed by anger, grief, and fear. I ended up outside the store sitting on the steps crying.

I was scared and sad and had no idea how to buy a hairpiece. We spent $500 on a human hair wig. The owner of a fancy sa-

lon guaranteed he would make it look just like my real hair. He even took a photo of me to guide the styling of the wig. He held my hand and promised it would be ready before my hair started to fall out.

Instead, he ruined the wig.

When my hair started falling out, he wouldn't return my phone calls. When the salon owner finally agreed to meet with us, he showed me the damaged wig and blamed me for bringing him an "inferior" wig. No apology, no refund. He charged me $190 for "styling" it. I was too weak from chemo to argue.

The wig was so overpermed, it looked like roadkill. I wore it for a whole two hours. It looked like hell, felt like hell, and reminded me of the hell that creep put us through. I threw it in the closet and never wore it again. It has become a Halloween costume.

The man left us no time to buy another one. Patches of hair were falling out. I looked like a dog with mange. My husband, my prince, helped me shave my head the day I was eating breakfast and saw bangs in my Cheerios. I ended up walking around bald for six months.

I can laugh about it now, but, boy, did I cry back then. Rivers.

No other woman should go through that, I vowed.

But I didn't do anything about it. What should I do? Report him to the Better Business Bureau? Sue him in small-claims court? I was so focused on the problem, it never occurred to me to be part of the solution for other cancer survivors.

Years passed. One day I went to Fort Wayne, Indiana, to speak at a cancer tribute dinner for Cancer Services of North-

east Indiana. I walked into their agency and nearly fell over. They had an entire wig salon with more than 150 beautiful wigs on display, organized by hair color. When I found out the wigs were free for the borrowing, I cried.

Women bald from cancer treatment can check out two wigs at a time, like you would books from a library. When they're returned, the wigs go straight to the salon, where volunteers shampoo and style them for the next woman.

The room felt warm and inviting, like a real beauty salon.

Then I heard about Debra Brown and knew I had to act. She came to the Fort Wayne agency one day to find a wig, but there were only two wigs for African American women. She didn't like either one. She already felt depressed and discouraged from cancer treatments and losing her hair. The lack of diversity at the salon made her angry—angry enough to do something. She called her family, her friends, and every church that would listen. She got the Fort Wayne Urban League involved. She asked them all to donate money or wigs. Her goal? One hundred wigs. She didn't want any other African American woman walking out of that salon disappointed.

In three months, Debra had 200 wigs to donate. She told everyone, "It's not about me. God put it on my heart."

That's when it hit me to create a place where women who are experiencing hair loss from cancer treatments can get free wigs. The Gathering Place, which offers free help to anyone touched by cancer, got on board.

As soon as I shared my idea, they started creating a salon at their Beachwood location. They made a cozy, private space with a big mirror and bright lights and lots of shelves for all the wigs we were going to collect.

I wrote a column that we needed wigs. Wigs for brunettes, blondes, and redheads. Wigs for women with gray hair. Wigs for women of all races. Wigs of all shapes, colors, and styles. Wigs of synthetic hair, since human hair is harder to maintain.

I asked people to get their church, school, or family to donate new and "pre-loved" wigs to The Gathering Place. We needed money to buy new wigs and wig hair products. We also needed beauticians willing to donate time to clean and style wigs.

We decided to send a message to every woman touched by cancer: losing hair doesn't mean losing hope. We wanted to give them peace of mind. We called the salon HairPeace.

Within weeks, more than 500 wigs were donated to The Gathering Place, along with more than $38,000. People all over Greater Cleveland wanted in. Philanthropist Sam Miller donated $3,000. "I'm in for a couple hundred wigs," he said. "I know what this disease does to people." He's been fighting cancer for more than ten years.

Students at the Academy of Saint Bartholomew in Middleburg Heights collected more than $700. In one kindergarten classroom, children got to pin hair on wig heads when they donated money. On Saint Patrick's Day, students donated a dollar to "dress down" for the day. The Knitting Angels of Bainbridge, from the Church of the Holy Angels, donated wigs. A visiting nurses agency sponsored a drive to collect "pre-loved" wigs.

Dozens called in tears and offered to donate the wigs of their wives, mothers, and sisters who had died from cancer. The response was so big, The Gathering Place opened another wig salon in its center on the west side of Cleveland.

Before we were open for business, an older woman came to The Gathering Place for a massage wearing a baseball hat over a long gray wig. When she saw the wigs, she asked if the staff could set one aside for her until HairPeace opened. Eileen Coan, the medical librarian, didn't want her to wait. Eileen loves to tell the story:

"We closed the door, she took off her wig, and she pointed hesitantly to a short curly one and whispered, 'I always wanted *curly* hair.' She put it on, had an ear-to-ear grin and the beginning of tears. She whispered, 'I *love* it.' I started to put her old wig in the bag. 'Oh no,' she stated confidently. 'That one stays here; this is all I need!'"

Another young woman, who was thin from chemotherapy, came in to meet with a nutritionist. Her short, perky wig looked good but was too big. Every time she sneezed she feared it would pop off. Eileen described her joy in this e-mail:

I got her set up with a cap liner and told her to take her time looking. She chose a more sophisticated straight look with some subtle highlights. One look in the mirror and she clapped. "THIS is the one I want!" She stepped out into the library and told the room full of eight strangers, "Look at my new hair," and they all clapped, too. She told us to give her old one to someone else, and she headed out to show her mom her new look.

A couple came in together, eyes red from crying. They had been to wig stores and were ready to give up. The wife's hair was scheduled to fall out within days. Every wig they tried had too much hair until the woman spied a little pixie blond

wig. It fit just right. Her husband smiled. They left holding hands.

Another woman came in with her husband. She was newly bald and reluctant to enter. Then she spotted a wig that looked like her original hair. She tried it on, loved it, and asked her husband to come in. He stood silently at the door, then said, "My beautiful bride is back."

One woman who had just found out she would need chemo stopped by. She wanted a wig that was thin and wispy like her hair. Sure enough, she found one. She tried it on then told the staff, "I'll come back when I need it and hope that it is still here." They handed her the wig.

"It can't be that easy," the woman said.

Yes, it can.

To donate for wigs, send a check to: The Gathering Place, 23300 Commerce Park, Cleveland, Ohio 44122. Or visit www.touchedby cancer.org.

Don't die with your music in you.

Rocco Scotti is Cleveland's own Yankee Doodle Dandy.

He has sung the national anthem probably more times than anyone in the world. He sang it at nearly every Indians game for 20 years.

He sang it at a home opener an hour after he left a hospital with stitches from a car wreck that knocked him unconscious. He sang it for Presidents Gerald Ford and Ronald Reagan. He sang it at six public venues in one day. He sang it at stadiums in New York, Pittsburgh, and Baltimore; at the Football Hall of Fame in Canton; and at the Baseball Hall of Fame in Cooperstown, New York.

Rocco sang it for nearly every major league baseball team. He sang it at football games. He sang it nearly 50 times a year for 20 years.

He sang it so well, he received a Civilian Purple Heart for

"inspiring patriotism through his exceptional performing of 'The Star-Spangled Banner.'"

He believes God called him to make the national anthem his one-hit wonder. It wasn't what he set out to do.

Rocco was born in 1920 in Ambler, Pennsylvania, grew up in a family of 14 children, and moved to Cleveland when he was three. Like most kids back then, he dreamed of becoming a baseball player. He followed his dad into the construction business instead, carrying 100-pound bags on his shoulders. His dad sang around the house, so Rocco started singing, too. He worked with a voice coach. He met his wife, June, in 1945, and they moved to New York where he could study opera.

Rocco's career as an opera singer never took off, so he moved to Los Angeles and studied with a tenor. He sang pop tunes in nightclubs for a while. His singing career stalled, so he moved back to Cleveland. He worked construction, took voice classes, and sang the national anthem at random events. Back then, he sang it straight up, the same way everyone else did.

Then one day he decided to dress it up, to add something unique.

He was asked to sing the anthem for a Cleveland Indians–Baltimore Orioles game. As he was driving to the game, Rocco wondered what he could do to make it different. He added a high G at the end. He's not sure Francis Scott Key would approve, but the guys in both dugouts loved it when Rocco first tried it two decades ago.

When he gets to "the land of the free, and the home of the brave." He hangs on to the word *free* and the last *the* for as long as he can. No one had heard it sung that way. Everyone loved it. From then on, he was asked to sing it at every game.

His favorite time? He had just finished the song when he was told someone in the stands wanted to meet him. It was baseball Hall of Famer Earl Averill, a six-time All-Star and Rocco's idol. Rocco was so overcome, he sat next to Earl and cried.

That and singing for the presidents were the best times.

"They seemed to like it," Rocco said.

He hates that so many singers botch the national anthem. "Almost nobody does it well," he said. It's a hard song. Too many people try to wing it, and they start with a broken wing.

Roseanne Barr screeched it. Michael Bolton forgot it. Steven Tyler changed it. (At a racetrack in 2001, he closed the anthem by singing "and the home of the Indianapolis 500.") But those weren't the worst versions. "Robert Goulet," Rocco said, shaking his head. "He was too drunk to finish it."

"Do it well or don't do it at all. It means something," Rocco said.

Some performers sing the national anthem for an ego trip, to get in front of a crowd on TV, Rocco said. "They don't care enough about it. You have to treat it with respect." He always did. Before the words left his lips, a prayer did.

And you have to practice. Rocco used to practice in his car until the day he hit a high note and cracked his side window. In three places. From then on, he practiced with the windows down.

He has sung other anthems, too. The Polish national anthem for boxing team matches. He sang the Hungarian national anthem for basketball games, the Italian national anthem for soccer games, and the Israeli national anthem when the assistant prime minister of Israel was in Cleveland.

But he never tired of the old "Star-Spangled Banner." Every time, he felt a connection to his country. "It's a challenge every time to do it well," he said.

Rocco and his bride, June, have been married for more than 60 years. He was 89 when we talked. By then, he had been retired from the majors. When the Cleveland Indians started playing at their new stadium, the team brought in new voices. Rocco is a good sport about it.

"Things change. Life goes on," he tells people. "Everything comes to an end."

He has no regrets, no hard feelings. But if they called, would he sing it for them?

Rocco grinned and said, "I'd ask, 'What time?'"

Every so often there is talk of changing the anthem from "The Star-Spangled Banner" to "America the Beautiful" or "God Bless America." Reporters call Rocco and ask his opinion.

"They're pretty songs, but they don't have the built-in drama of 'The Star Spangled Banner.' It has character. It creates patriotism. It demands such attention," he said.

He loves "The Star-Spangled Banner." "The rockets' red glare, the bombs bursting in air" aren't just words to him. They're family history. His brother Nicholas died in World War II. Nick was a sergeant in the infantry. He was only 19.

Rocco was 24 when his brother died. It hit him hard. When Nick went into the service, he told Rocco, "I'm not coming back." Rocco shared a verse from a poem he wrote about Nick: "Now there are white crosses lying one next to each other; every night I say a prayer for them, for among them is my brother."

The difference between the way Rocco sings the national anthem and the way everyone else does is this: every time Rocco belts out those final words, "O, say does that star-spangled banner yet wave, O'er the land of the free, and the home of the brave?" he knows the answer is yes.

Rocco grew quiet when he talked about how that song turned into his gift to share with the world. "It's strange, but something happened that made it that way," he said. "It's like someone said, 'This is gonna be your thing.'"

And once you find your thing, you treat it with respect.

"Work very sincerely with it," Rocco urged. "Make it really mean something to you and those who will hear it."

His life story is a great reminder that we all have music in us, even those of us who can't sing a note. I used to attend a church where the music director urged everyone to sing, even those who weren't sure they had it in them. "If you sing off-key," he'd always say, "then sing even louder."

We all have a song to sing. A song that someone out there needs to hear, just the way it comes from our hearts and our lips.

Nothing you want is upstream, so stop struggling.

Got a crisis? Call my husband.

That's his specialty.

Not only does he talk me down from the ledge of whatever small speed bump I'm dangling from, certain I'm on the verge of a catastrophe, but, as I mentioned earlier, he owns a crisis communications firm called Hennes Communications in Cleveland. He has made it his specialty to help people and companies all over the country respond during a crisis.

When people hear what he does for a living, they often think he helps companies and executives spin their way out of trouble. Not at all. Bruce tells everyone you can't spin your way out of bad behavior. His mantra is "Tell the truth, tell it all, tell it first."

There's never a shortage of companies in crisis, so business is good. A few years ago, a man approached Bruce and his

business partner about a job. They made the decision not to hire him. Months later, the man was hired by a competitor who owned a much larger full-service PR firm that wanted to go head-to-head with them. Then Bruce read in the newspaper that the firm had hired two others to create a crisis communications unit to compete with Bruce.

At first my husband was worried. What would it mean to have competition? How much business would this new venture take from them? Would there be enough business for both companies to succeed? Would they have to struggle neck and neck to compete for clients?

Then he did something that made me admire him even more than I already did. He relaxed. He made a decision not to give in to fear, not to believe in scarcity or competition or the idea that you have to constantly struggle to get ahead in life and in business. He decided to keep doing what he did and keep doing it better. Then he wrote the owner of the business an e-mail congratulating him on starting the new business venture and wished him great success. Bruce even wrote that there was surely enough work for everyone. Then he went over the top and said, "If I'm ever in a position to send you business, I will."

The man was stunned when he received such a gracious note from the person others might see as his biggest competitor. The man called my husband and left a message on voice mail expressing his deep gratitude. The man's voice broke as he told Bruce what that e-mail meant to him.

Bruce taught me that we don't have to struggle to attract more of what we want. There is no competition, no scarcity. What about the global competition? What about the person

in the other cubicle competing? Not your concern.

A friend once gave me a CD by Esther Hicks. These five words changed my life: *Nothing you want is upstream.*

I burst out laughing when I heard her say that. So often I find myself fighting against the current, working against all odds to get to someplace I think will make me happier than where the flow of life gently invites me to go. I waste a lot of energy and time before exhaustion forces me to surrender and float to the place life has prepared for me alone. Once you stop struggling against the current—because it is always going to win—you can align yourself with what is, rest, and allow the river of life to carry you along to the place where you can make the biggest difference with your life.

The Bible constantly reminds us to let go and let God handle whatever it is we're trying to control. As the Gospel of Matthew says, the lilies of the field don't labor or spin:

> If that is how God clothes the grass of the field, which is here today and tomorrow is thrown into the fire, will he not much more clothe you—you of little faith? So do not worry, saying, "What shall we eat?" or "What shall we drink?" or "What shall we wear?" ... Your heavenly Father knows that you need them. But seek first his kingdom and his righteousness, and all these things will be given to you as well. Therefore do not worry about tomorrow, for tomorrow will worry about itself.

All that worrying and extra work doesn't buy you a smidge of serenity, according to Psalm 127: "In vain is your earlier rising, your going later to rest. You who toil for the bread you

eat, when he pours gifts on his beloved while they sleep."

For years I was baffled by the saying "Take the path of least resistance." It's hard to see which path that is when you're resisting them all out of fear. Then I finally got it: stop resisting. As they used to say on *Star Trek: The Next Generation*: "Resistance is futile." It really is. God does the real work, we don't. All we have to do is simply cooperate with grace, without struggle or strain. My old way was to suffer, try, work, agonize, worry, sweat, and struggle. My new way? Release, allow, surrender, trust, believe, and relax. The shortcut is God.

You don't have to try so hard to be great. One day I was all in a tizzy over which column to write. My problem normally isn't coming up with an idea, it's that I come up with too many and struggle over which one to choose. I had asked God for clarity and got it when my daughter called and said, "Do what is easy."

I wrote that on a sticky note that smiles at me every day. God does the heavy lifting. I'm always awed when I see the work of Michelangelo, who simply released the figures from the marble. All I need to do is move my fingers and release the words that God gives me. That doesn't mean everything comes easy to me, but writing comes out of me when I let it.

What's easy for one person isn't what comes easy for others. Math comes easy for others. Not me. I have the proof. My college ACT scores. I got a 17 in math. Back then, the high was 28. At first I was ashamed of it. Now it's a reminder to stick with what comes easy, and math isn't it. Writing is easy when I just try to write like Regina Brett. It gets complicated and messy when I try to write like someone who I think is better than me.

My friend Barb used to tell me there is no competition.

When you lie out in the sun to get a tan, you aren't competing with anyone for the rays. There is enough sun for all. God's love and direction is enough for each of us and for all of us.

I remembered her words when I first became a newspaper columnist. The good news was that the editor gave me a column. The bad news was, he also gave three other people in the same newsroom a column. Would there be enough ideas to go around? I've been writing columns for 19 years and have yet to run out of ideas. The goal isn't to be better than the other writers. The goal is to be better than the last column I wrote. Success is never about undercutting others to get to the top. The top of what?

There was a brief period when I suffered from terrible envy of another writer. I envied her talent and awards and success, even though I had my own. How could I get her off my radar screen? Instead of booting her off, I made her my prayer partner. Every time I thought of her or heard her name or read about her success, I saw it as a call from her soul to mine to pray for her. So I kept throwing Hail Marys at her. She became even more successful, which drove me crazy until I realized her success was blessing the world, and so was mine. The world needed us both.

There's room for all of us in our own particular spot. My divine assignment has my name on it, no one else's. So does yours. When you live the life you alone were created to live, there is no competition. There's enough for everyone and no reason to struggle.

Create a pocket of greatness right where you are.

You want to change the world?

Change the workplace and you change the world.

People spend nearly a third of their lives working. Every boss and business owner, large and small, can have a huge impact on that third. You can change the world one employee at a time. One customer at a time. One client at a time. One patient at a time. One coworker at a time. When you change their world, you change the world for their children, spouses, and pets.

How?

When people have a bad day at work, they go home and take it out on their spouses, who take it out on the children, who take it out on the dog. When people have a great day, they send out ripples of joy.

Imagine if each boss took a good, hard look at what they

paid their staff. On paper, those things look like simple benefits that cost the company. But in real life, they're so much more. A salary increase means someone can afford to buy a house instead of renting an apartment. It means the difference between a car that breaks down and a car that can get a family all the way to Grandma's house for Thanksgiving.

What a person is paid determines what's under the tree at Christmas, whether a child gets to play in the band at school. I remember in eighth grade when I wanted to play the flute. My dad went with me to the band meeting. He shook his head and told me, "You'll pass out." He didn't tell me the truth: we couldn't afford it.

Employers have a lot of power, like the power to provide funeral leave. When my dad died, no workplace kept my five brothers and five sisters from traveling in from Arizona, New York, Indiana, Florida, and Michigan to be in that front row at Immaculate Conception Church to hold up my mom as she let go of my dad.

The power to provide personal days means you can take the day off to be with your mother on her birthday, the first one she spends alone after your dad died. Maternity and paternity leaves mean new parents can bond with a baby. Vacation time means a family can create memories for a lifetime.

Sick leave, what a gift. When I had cancer in 1998, I had to worry about losing my hair and losing my lunch to chemotherapy, but I never had to worry about losing my job if I took too much time off. I didn't need to skimp on the daily radiation treatments, because my company offered good insurance coverage.

Dental insurance will determine whether a child with

234 • God Is Always Hiring

crooked teeth turns into an adult who can smile. The braces the company insurance provides show up in all those family pictures in every album. That smile? Imagine being the boss who provided it.

Some companies offer insurance that covers fertility. How powerful to make it possible to turn a couple into parents for life.

Flexible hours and scheduling mean a mom can get off work in time to see her son hit a home run. It means a daughter will know that her dad saw her kick the winning goal in soccer. Companies worry about the global marketplace but shouldn't lose sight of the importance of the backyard catch with Dad.

And finally, there's retirement. Because of good benefits, seniors won't have to cut their high blood pressure pills in half or be shamed into asking their children if they can move in.

All because of the risks a boss takes, the choices an employer makes. It's not about creating jobs or even creating great jobs, it's about creating great workplaces so employees can create a great world.

Employers have incredible power over people's lives. Two of the most powerful words in the English language are *You're hired*. Remember how powerful those words were to you? Remember the day that call came and you heard those words? You called your spouse, your kids, your parents. Or these words: *You got a raise*. The relief. The celebration. The pride. The gratitude. The bills you could finally pay.

It's amazing what companies can do to make work a joy for others. I once gave a keynote address at the NorthCoast 99 honoring the 99 best places to work in Northeast Ohio. The

program was developed by the Employers Resource Council, which is dedicated to fostering the best HR practices, programs, and services. I was amazed at all the things companies did to celebrate and honor their workers. Some places offered aerobics classes, a yoga room, fitness centers, or gym memberships. Others provided on-site day-care centers and tuition reimbursement. I love that Hyland Software offers surprise visits from the ice cream truck. The eight-month-old daughter of an employee of one company got a piece of plastic stuck in her throat and couldn't breathe. Her mom saved her life because she had learned the Heimlich maneuver at work.

At ADP in Independence, Ohio, employees visit the elderly with Alzheimer's and those in hospice care. They adopt seniors, serve meals, and collect for school supplies for children. At Weaver Leather in Mount Hope, one year each employee adopted a foster child for Valentine's Day and stuffed duffel bags with items from a wish list. For some children, that bag was the only personal item they owned.

MCPc Inc., a Strongsville IT company, holds chili cook-offs, Hawaiian shirt day, Easter egg hunts, and car washes where the bosses wash the cars.

It was fascinating to hear that some companies provide dry cleaning and laundry service, an on-site hair salon and barber, access to a doctor or nurse at work, and free mammograms. Others offer free oil changes, travel agents, and tax preparation.

I left the event hoping more employers might be creative and give people a paid month off every five years, an all-expense-paid vacation every 20 years, discounts on computers or cell phone service, or share access to company discounts at hotels, restaurants, and amusement parks.

Even at small businesses, it doesn't take a lot of money to fill a candy jar or provide doughnuts to make a boring meeting go a little faster. It won't break the bank to let employees leave a few hours early on Friday, or to stock a refrigerator with fresh fruit or create a coffee bar with free coffee, tea, and hot chocolate.

The best employers make it possible for people to make a living and a life, and better yet, a difference. By changing the workplace, they change the lives of all those around them, which means they're changing the world.

Even when you feel invisible, your work isn't.

It's easy for some people to feel invisible at work.

Every time we went for a drive in my small town, my dad used to point out every roof he'd repaired or replaced. He had a story to tell about every house we passed in Ravenna, Ohio. He would tell us who lived there, who they were related to, how many children they had, and what they all did for a living. The people who lived in those homes probably forgot who climbed that ladder, carried that spouting, and hammered those shingles under a burning sun, but my dad never did.

Turns out they didn't either. When he died at 83, the funeral home was full of people grateful for the roofs over their heads and the man who put them there.

The world is full of people whose work matters long after they've touched it. Some of those people were at my dad's funeral, like our mail carrier, Tony. He was steady as clockwork

on Sycamore Street, showing up at 10 a.m. every day. He cushioned the blow of the gas bill with a grin and a story about his latest win at the bowling alley.

Those people are everywhere in our lives. People like Doctor Neely, the family physician who still made house calls and rarely ever sent a bill to my parents. People like my appliance repairman, Sruly Wolf, who comes at a moment's notice when the rinse cycle stops on the washer or the dryer quits when it's full of wet clothes. He trims a few bucks off the bill and sends us a turkey and a basket of food every Thanksgiving to thank us for being faithful customers.

In his other life, he's a humble rabbi and a police chaplain in Cleveland, Ohio. He once received an award for saving the life of an unconscious off-duty police officer. Sruly, who was in Chicago on business, was walking down a street and saw the officer in a smoke-filled car and pulled the unconscious man free. When a reporter interviewed him, he downplayed it, saying, "Look, I just went to Chicago that week to attend a trade show."

Everyone leaves a mark. It's up to each of us how we leave it and where. When my husband and I had our fireplace tile replaced, the man who did the work spent long hours trying to get the fireproofing wall in place to protect us. Our home was built in 1920 and the brick was nearly 100 years old. It gave him major headaches, breaking every nail he drilled into it. When he finally got it right, I asked him to sign the fireboard. He smiled as he scribbled his name, Donovan, on that wall in marker. No one would ever see it once the tile went up, but it truly was a work of art and I wanted him to know it.

We tend to measure our worth by the big highlights that mean the most to us, not the small moments that mean the most to others. I had the privilege to hear about one of those moments from a man who spent 28 years as a firefighter.

There were calls that made Tom Schultz cry, calls that made him laugh, and calls that made him fear for his life.

One time a tired new mother fell asleep on her couch with her one-month-old baby. "One woke up and one didn't," Tom said softly.

Another time, an old woman stopped answering her phone and picking up deliveries. Neighbors called her, but no one answered. They called her son in Toledo. Her son called her, but no one answered, so he called 911. The firefighters banged on her windows. No answer. They looked in the window and didn't see anyone. Their supervisor told them to break down the door.

When they did, they saw the old woman sitting in a chair with the phone next to her. They said, "Ma'am, the neighbors called and your son called; why didn't you answer?" She looked up and said, "It's my phone and I'll answer it if I want to."

Then there was the woman who fled after the sausage she had left burning on the stove caught the house on fire. She got her children out and slammed the door behind her. That cut off the flames but left the fire smoldering.

A fire can double in size every minute. When Tom opened the door, black smoke poured out. Tom was at the tip of the hose, the first one in, with the next firefighter six feet behind him on the hose. He couldn't see him, but he could hear him. They walked through the pitch-black house. The air from

opening the door reignited the fire. The third firefighter coming in mistakenly yanked on the hose. It flew out of Tom's hands.

Oh no, he thought. *The hose is your lifeline out. You can't see a door. The hose is the only way to find your way back out.*

It was the longest ten seconds of Tom's life. He thought about the wife and kids he'd never see again. Then he heard the voice of the firefighter behind him: "I still have the hose." They got out safely.

No one touched him more deeply than the old lady with the plums.

He tried to share the story with the firefighters at his retirement breakfast, but the words couldn't get past the lump in his throat. He cried as he told it to me.

Early in his career he got a 911 call one summer: *lady down in backyard*. The woman was in her 90s and had fallen off a stepladder near a plum tree. It was late summer and all the plums were ripe. She had a compound fracture of her ankle. The neighbors had called for help. Tom helped dress and splint the wound, then transport her to the hospital.

A doctor said she would need surgery to fix the break. She would have to spend the night. Tom didn't remember her name, but all day long she was on his mind. He never imagined she'd stay with him the rest of his career.

He wondered, *Why would an elderly lady with all her wits put herself in danger on a ladder to pick plums?* The next morning when his shift ended, he drove back to her house, still in uniform, and picked her a bag of plums. He took them to the hospital.

When he found her room, he introduced himself and

handed her the plums. She was quiet for a minute, then told him why those plums were so important to her.

She said she had no family. She had outlived everyone. She was picking the plums to make plum jelly to thank all the neighbors who looked out for her, who were her family.

She thanked Tom for the plums. "I made her day, but she made my career," Tom said. "I'm just an average guy. She showed me I could make a difference in people's lives."

Before being a firefighter, Tom had worked a job he hated at a machine shop, where he felt like a machine. He loved the outdoors and hated punching a time clock and working inside all day for ten hours.

Tom was the oldest rookie when he started as a firefighter on May 7, 1984, at age 35. He retired at 63. He planned to tell the plum story at his farewell breakfast but got too emotional to finish. He wanted to leave behind more than his picture hanging on the wall of the fire station. He wanted to leave the rookies with that plum story.

He wanted them to remember to treat everyone with the utmost respect, dignity, and compassion at every emergency.

He wanted them to know the thing that mattered most in life was simply to make a difference in someone else's life.

You make a living by what you get;
you make a life by what you give.

Want to be rich?

Share what's in your pocket. It's not your money anyway.

Sounds absurd, doesn't it?

That's what I used to think. Not anymore.

One of the richest men in the world became rich only after he gave away all his money. Millard Fuller was famous for saying, "I see life as both a gift and a responsibility. My responsibility is to use what God has given me to help His people in need."

He set a goal early on: get rich.

His marketing business made him a millionaire at 29. It also made him miserable. After his marriage and health suffered, he sold the cars and the boat and gave his money to the poor. Then he started building them houses all over the world. His wife, Linda, worked for free. Fuller's salary was $15,000.

"God's money is just in the pockets of people," Fuller used to say. "We've got to extract it."

When the founder of Habitat for Humanity International died at 74, God's money remained in the roofs, walls, and plumbing in the homes of 1.5 million people all over the world. I once heard someone say, "All God wants is for you to take good care of His children." Fuller did that. So did Laura Bickimer.

She lived a simple life, lived all her life in the same home she grew up in. When the retired math teacher died at 93, she left $2.1 million to Baldwin Wallace University in Berea, Ohio. She graduated from there in 1936 and had attended on a scholarship. She never forgot the power of someone else's generosity. Part of her gift will go toward scholarships.

Bickimer never earned more than $40,000 a year. Imagine living on that when you have $2 million in the bank. She saved it for others.

She once wrote, "I have discovered that one's life can be quite simple and unspectacular, yet full and worthwhile!"

Hers turned out to be a simple and spectacular life.

Small donations can make big changes in the world. My friend Kevin Conroy is a Catholic priest serving the poorest of the poor. I once wrote a column about how he left Cleveland to work in Cambodia with the Maryknoll missionaries. He helps the Little Sprouts, 270 children orphaned by parents who died of AIDS. The children are all HIV-positive. He sometimes travels to the garbage dumps where families forage for food and things to sell.

After reading about his work, readers sent him checks for $10, $20, $50. One person gave $1,000. All the donations

went toward building ten classrooms in a two-story building. The public school dedication was held on International Children's Day.

"Originally, we were just going to build one story and pray that in the future we could find the money to finish the job," Kevin told me. "I used the $10,000 that I raised from your column to help build the school."

The school principal asked Kevin what names he wanted to put on the school. "I am thinking of something like 'Friends from Cleveland, Ohio, USA,'" Kevin said.

You don't have to give millions. It's about giving a genuine gift from the heart. Before I met my husband, Bruce was just 35, struggling financially and barely making ends meet, when he had a moment that changed his life. He had just opened up his own public relations business when he attended a fund-raising event for the Jewish Community Federation. The meeting was at the home of one of the largest property developers in the country. After the 30 guests had dinner, they went into a room where Sam Miller, one of the most generous philanthropists in Cleveland, gave a passionate speech about the importance of helping the Jewish community.

People were so moved, one man stood and said, "I want you to know our family gift this year will be 1.2 million dollars." My husband gasped. Another man stood up and said, "My gift this year to the Jewish Community Federation will be $750,000." My husband gulped. They were going around the room, and everyone was going to announce their gift. Bruce broke out in a sweat. There were some rich people in that room, but he wasn't one of them. Most of them were 20 years

older than him and 20 years further down the road of financial success.

When it was his turn, Bruce stood up and said, "I'm the youngest person here and I just opened my own business. I'm in debt up to my eyeballs, having financed my business with credit cards. I'm clearly not in the same caliber in business with all of you, but how could I not be moved by your generosity? I don't know how I will do it, but I gave $100 last year—and this year I will double my donation."

He got a standing ovation. They slapped him on the back in wild congratulations. They knew that he had dug the deepest to make the biggest stretch. What he learned from their reaction was that what matters isn't the size of the gift, it's the quality of the gift.

Quantity is nice, too. Bruce once worked at a car dealership for Lee Seidman. Lee opened the Motorcars Group in 1958. One year he decided to take a gamble on an automobile franchise no one else wanted. People thought he was nuts. It was called Toyota. Lee became one of the nation's largest auto dealers. He made millions. Then he gave it all away.

He could have left a hefty estate to his children and made them all multimillionaires. He could have spent his retirement taking cruises around the world. Instead, he went to Harvard and learned how to give his money away.

He gave $17 million to the Cleveland Clinic to create an endowed chair in functional neurosurgery and to help pay for medical research and build the clinic's heart center. He gave $1 million to University Hospitals Rainbow Babies & Children's Hospital for pediatric cancer innovation. He gave $6 million to Hillcrest Hospital so they could expand. Then he

outdid even himself. He gave $42 million to University Hospitals to build a cancer hospital. The Seidman Cancer Center is ten stories tall and has 120 beds. It is the only freestanding cancer hospital in Northeast Ohio.

When his wife, Jane, looks at the building, she thinks of her dad, who died of cancer at 56. He never got to see his own grandchildren. Their gift will allow countless grandparents to live to see their grandchildren grow up. The Seidmans are spending their autumn years encouraging others to give their money away while they're still alive to see and shape its impact. He loves watching his bank account balance fall as each hospital grows. He's never felt richer.

When you share what God puts in your pocket, you realize you're richer than you ever imagined. Giving away money actually ensures that you will get more of it. I believe there's always enough to go around. I tell myself every day: *My abundance benefits everyone and their abundance benefits me.* The more I earn, the more I can give away, and as soon as I give it away, more shows up.

Years ago when I was a single parent with no money, my friend's family lost nearly everything they owned in a house fire. I wrote her a check for $80. It was all I could donate back then. That $80 sounds meager now, but back then, when I had nothing, it was a lot. Weeks later, I received a check for $80 from the college I attended. They had made an error in my financial aid and sent me the balance.

Recently, I felt that tug of the spirit to be more generous. It's time to put more abundance in the world. So I wrote out some checks to charities and to my niece and two nephews in college. It felt good to give back into the world.

An hour later, my cousin called. "Congratulations! Your phone must be ringing off the hook!" she shouted.

"What are you talking about?" I asked, puzzled.

"Your book was on TV!" she screamed.

What in the world was she talking about? It turns out that while I was writing out checks from abundance, *Today* show host Hoda Kotb was holding up my first book, *God Never Blinks*, to her TV viewers and urging them to read it.

When I got off the phone with my cousin, I paused, shook my head, and said, "Wow, God, You are *so* good!" I didn't even know it then, but that 30-second gush from Hoda sent my book to No. 11 on Amazon. *God Never Blinks* was No. 3 in self-help books, No. 2 in religious books, and No. 1 in spiritual books. The book had come out three years earlier.

Then God did one better.

That same week I learned that my friend's husband was going to Paris for a book signing. I called to congratulate her. How exciting that they were going to Paris. She had taken care of him when he had cancer and heart surgery and deserved a big bonus from life. She said she wouldn't be joining him. They hadn't yet received any royalties from the book, and things were stretched thin at home.

How could I not share my abundance with one of my dearest friends? So I got off the phone and went online. I found out the cost of a trip to Paris and wrote her a check and popped it in the mail. It felt so good to send more abundance into the world.

She called two days later. First she thanked me a million ways to Sunday, and then she said, "I tore up your check." What?

She didn't need it. The same day my check arrived, so did his royalty check. She was going to Paris. All I ended up giving her was a ride to the airport, but what a joyful ride it was.

I swear it's like a chain of giving that takes off and doesn't stop.

The more you believe in abundance, the more it believes in you. When you share what God puts in your pocket, you're always richer than you thought.

LESSON
47

Be somebody's hero.

I once heard someone pose this question: What is your heroic mission on Earth?

Whoa.

That's a powerful question.

Do we each really have a heroic mission? *Hero* is a word usually reserved for firefighters, paramedics, and police who save lives or for those who die serving their country. *Hero* is also a word too often squandered on guys who win at basketball, baseball, and football.

I was lucky to know a true hero, although he didn't look like one. Strangers driving down our street might have mistaken him for a tired old man. That's what he looked like hunched over in a chair sunning on the porch like a content cat, his dark glasses shading eyes weakened by 96 years and by the terrible things he saw on that beach at Normandy.

No matter how he was feeling, Joe kept his humor, his humanity, and his humility.

The life of Dr. Joseph Foley started out small. His parents were poor Irish immigrants. His dad was a garbage collector in Boston. When Joe's appendix ruptured at 14, a kind doctor left a big imprint on Joe and sparked his interest in medicine. Joe ended up studying neurology.

He had a collection of titles: Emeritus Professor of Neurology, former Chair of the Division of Neurology at Case Western University Medical School, past President of the American Academy of Neurology and of the American Neurological Association. He constantly urged doctors to listen to patients; to keep the patient as the center of their focus, not the disease.

Joe taught doctors to look every patient in the eye and greet every patient by name. One time a woman came to the emergency room complaining of crushing headaches. When no one could find any cause, they sent her to the psych ward. She died before she got there. It turned out she had a brain tumor that had ruptured. No one caught it.

Those who had examined her were beating themselves up for missing the medical diagnosis when Joe pointed out that they missed something else. They neglected to treat her with compassion. He told them that she died without anyone to comfort or console her, without the full measure of compassion that every person deserves.

Joe once went with his former classmates to visit an ill classmate who was in the hospital. The man suffered from depression and had been institutionalized. He was unable or unwilling to communicate. The visitors told endless stories about the good old days for a half hour. Joe made sure they in-

cluded their sick friend through all of it, even though the man never said a word or responded. He hadn't even opened his eyes during the entire conversation.

When it was time to go, they all stood to leave and each one squeezed the man's hand. Suddenly, he opened his eyes and said, "That was the best half hour I've had in months!"

Joe lived by the words of Winston Churchill: Never, never, never give up. Always communicate with the sickest, weakest person in the room. You never know what hope that person might be able to hear, see, or feel during an examination, conversation, or prayer.

After I mentioned Joe briefly in one of my newspaper columns, a woman from Nashville sent this e-mail:

Dr. Foley was my neurologist many years ago. I vividly remember him. It was the summer of 1968 and I had a grand mal seizure and was hospitalized for a week. I was eight years old and my parents had four other children at home to care for.

Much of the week in the hospital I spent by myself, a very frightening experience for me. Dr. Foley was a gem, kind and caring. Just the kind of doctor an eight-year-old needed. I have his kind face and calm voice imprinted in my brain. He was a big blessing to my eight-year-old self in July 1968.

I spent six years as a pediatric speech-language pathologist before returning to school for my PhD. In my years of clinical work, I worked with many, many children. I realized many years later that my ability to be compassionate and help families as well as children grew from

the interactions I had as a child with Dr. Foley and other kind and caring professionals like him.

I sent the e-mail to Joe's family. They read it to him and he laughed.

"There, you see," he said with a grin, "I wasn't all bad."

No, he wasn't. He never even sent the family a bill.

Joe planned to write back to the former patient, but he never regained his strength. That strength was something we thought he'd never lose. He had beaten cancer five times, survived a stroke, a heart valve replacement, and the loss of most of his vision to macular degeneration.

But that scene on the beach never left him. Joe was one of the first doctors to prepare the beach at Normandy before the D-Day invasion. At 28, he was one of the youngest doctors treating the wounded and dying at Licata, Palermo, Termini Imerese, and Normandy. He was with the first unit that went ashore. He ran fast and ducked bullets. He received the Bronze Star and the French Cross for the D-Day invasion. He was able to laugh about that Bronze Star when he told people the citation read: "He exposed himself repeatedly."

Joe talked about how he got off a small boat that morning, waded through the water to get up onto the sand, then ran from machine-gun fire dripping wet. He never forgot the wounded he pulled to safety by the scruff of their necks or the men who perished in the sand or in his arms. He told people that he never saw a dead man without wondering about the parents, wife, or children who would mourn.

When Joe died, hundreds showed up at the funeral, not to mourn but to celebrate the life he lived and all the lives he

touched. The Mass was celebrated by six priests and a bishop. My friend Father Don Cozzens gave the eulogy. He said Joe loved attention but saw the danger of being the smartest or funniest person in the room. He knew we are most alive when we die to our ego selves and live for others.

Don said that Joe, like Jacob in the Bible, wrestled with his faith, his God, and his church. He was a coffeehouse theologian who lived those words from Micah 6:8: "Act justly. Love tenderly. Walk humbly with your God."

Near the end of the Mass, these final words were read: "No one is really dead unless they are forgotten." It reminded me of the quote by philosopher William James: "The great use of life is to spend it for something that will outlast it."

That's what we all want. Immortality.

That's what a great life does. It makes you immortal. It lasts long after you are gone. Joe will live on in me, in his patients, in his friends, in his family. In the hospital maintenance worker who called to tell me Dr. Foley always made him feel important. In the countless children of the children of all those he saved on the beaches and in the hospitals.

Joe was married for 59 years, raised six children, and defined his life by love and service. He used to say, "Make sure you love people and behave in a way that you can be loved." That love guided him in everything he did, from the beaches, to the clinics, to the porch, where the man who saw too much war never stopped praying for peace.

Every time I pass by his house and see the empty chair on the porch, I wonder about my own heroic mission in life.

We all have one. And if we find it and do it, we, too, will live forever.

For networking to work, we all have to be the net.

The huge numbers don't hit you as hard as one single empty chair does.

Or one empty locker.

Or that empty spot at the lunch table.

Empty is how a lot of us have felt riding this economic roller coaster. If you haven't been laid off in the past five years, you know someone who has. We all do.

If you haven't lost your job, you suffer from survivor's guilt when you're among the last ones standing. You want to do something but feel paralyzed.

The *Plain Dealer* newspaper where I work as a columnist lost 27 people in one week to layoffs. It was eerie to pass an empty cubicle where my friend of 22 years sat, a friend who planned to retire as a journalist and suddenly found himself unemployed and unemployable.

We all silently wondered and worried: *Who's next?*

That same week, the Labor Department announced that the unemployment rate had hit 6.7 percent as 533,000 jobs disappeared that November alone, the highest in 34 years.

Like many people, I'm in a business that could one day be obsolete. We keep reading about the demise of newspapers, that our profession is teetering on the edge of oblivion. All across the country, jobs have been slashed at every newspaper. Papers are for sale, in bankruptcy, or have been sold countless times and whittled down to bare bones. Nothing is sacred, not even that sacred trust we call the Fourth Estate. Some papers have folded; some have cut out home delivery; others are publishing online only.

Our business model changed with the Internet. There are no longer enough advertising dollars to cover the bills. The real-estate ads went online, where people can watch a video tour of homes. Employment ads are better online. You can click and submit your résumé. Then there's Craigslist. How do you compete with free? It doesn't matter how great the writing is if there aren't enough advertising dollars to support the paper.

All around me in Cleveland, companies have cut or outsourced jobs. Banks, factories, steel mills, and auto plants have laid off workers by the hundreds. As a columnist, I sometimes joke, "I have the best seat on the *Titanic*." I plan to keep playing until the ship goes down. I hope the newspaper business stays afloat for a long, long time, but every time another paper cuts jobs, I wonder where the lifeboat is.

Who doesn't?

What do you do? Do you jump ship? If so, when?

I think you build a bridge, plank by plank. Then, when the time comes, you have something to walk across. You can build that bridge with others and for others.

That's what we did at the *Plain Dealer*. We couldn't stop the company from cutting jobs, but together we could form a safety net for those who lost their jobs so the landing wouldn't hurt so much. And we could help one another build that bridge.

My husband and I brainstormed an event we called a Media Career Transition Day. It grew into a grassroots effort, with staff in the newsroom providing career help to all those who had lost their jobs. It also prepared the rest of us for that day, should it happen to us.

The purpose was to provide career skills; to focus on the future, not the past. There would be no blaming, no bashing anyone for the situation we were in. The tone was important. We wanted it to be about empowering people for the future.

Our primary audience was the group of 27 employees who were laid off. The secondary audience was any *Plain Dealer* employee interested in acquiring additional career skills. We also wanted to help anyone else in the media facing the same situation.

We decided to make the day free for all those laid off and charge $25 for employees who weren't laid off. Any profits would go to a fund to help those laid off. We set up an online registration so people could pay by credit card or PayPal. We required registration to know how much food to get.

We picked a Saturday in January and found a church willing to donate space for free from 8 a.m. to 3 p.m. Trinity Cathedral in Cleveland had an auditorium, a large kitchen, and breakout

rooms. We spent a month setting up the event and recruiting a massive team of volunteers from the community and the *Plain Dealer*. One hundred people registered for the event and 40 presenters volunteered their time. No one received a dime for giving up an entire Saturday to help others.

The night before the event, it started to snow. And snow. And snow. It didn't stop. I worried that no one would show up. What a shock. Nearly everyone did. Some came from hours away, from Toledo, Akron, Elyria, and Columbus. Not only *Plain Dealer* employees, but journalists from surrounding newspapers, the *Beacon Journal*, Elyria *Chronicle*, Toledo *Blade*, *Sun* papers, and the *Cleveland Jewish News*.

People attended who were either laid off or feared they would be and wanted a plan B ready to build a greater career life ahead. We assembled a team of experts to be available all day. They would help people polish their résumés, figure out their next five steps, and find out how to get that second interview.

We gave each participant four tickets to encourage them to talk to at least four different career coaches. They printed their names on the tickets, and each time they met with an expert, they turned in the tickets, which were later pulled for prizes.

The day started with a breakfast of muffins and breads that our coworkers made. A motivational speaker at 9 a.m. got everyone jazzed, then we moved right into a session on résumé writing and how to write cover letters to make journalism skills transferable to other jobs.

The next session was on interviewing skills and how to negotiate a salary and benefits. We also offered a workshop on Internet skills and resources and how to use LinkedIn, Career-

Board, Monster.com, and other sites to find work. During lunch, we had a keynote speaker on networking, informational interviews, and how to make looking for work a full-time job.

The entire afternoon offered a menu of sessions that included the most likely areas in which laid-off journalists would find work: marketing, public relations, advertising, foundations, nonprofits, freelance writing, book publishing, radio, TV, and online work. We had professors, college career placement specialists, and a panel of former newspaper staffers who'd found successful jobs in other fields. Headhunters gave free one-on-one consultations.

We ended the day with a networking reception and desserts provided by our coworkers. We kept reminding everyone, this is *your* day. Make the best use of all the resources here. Don't leave with any regrets. The future is in your hands.

As I watched the room fill with hope, I thought about how my friend Barb used to tell me that life is a series of trapeze bars. You climb 50 feet to the top if you have the nerve, then you stand on the platform, take hold of the bar, and swing out into life. It's exhilarating and the ride is a breeze, until one day you look down and panic. Someone moved the net below. Or there never was one. Or something happens—a downsizing, a layoff, an illness, a divorce, a death—and life starts to pry your fingers off that bar you are holding on to.

It's hard to imagine life sending another opportunity your way as good as the one you have. So you cling tight to the bar you have. You can't see that other bar coming at you, or if you can, it's out of reach. And that's the scary part.

To grab on to the next bar, you have to let go of the one

you're holding on to. Once you do—you are in midair hanging on to absolutely nothing.

I looked around the room and saw people relax their grip on that bar and get excited as they explored what the next one might look like. At the end of the day, many were in tears as they thanked us for giving them hope.

Instead of dreading the unknown, they were looking forward to soaring toward it. They were ready to let go of who they used to be to discover who they could become.

If you don't want regrets at the end of your life, have no regrets at the end of each day.

The frail, white-haired woman came into my life more than a decade ago for only five minutes. It was summer and a friend introduced the two of us. Her name was Olga, and I never saw her again. It could have been one of those thousands of brief introductions that are usually forgotten five minutes later.

Olga looked like an 80-year-old but had the energy of a 3-year-old. When she heard I was going on vacation, she was as excited as if she were going. She told me there were two rules for vacation and that if you follow them, you'll have a great time no matter where you travel:

Rule 1: *Speak up about what you want to do and do it.*
Rule 2: *Don't have any regrets at the end of any day.*

Good rules for vacation.

Great rules for life.

It made me wonder why we save our best living for vacation and spend the other weeks waiting, whining, and pining for the chance to live the way we really want to.

Rule 1 sounds easy, but too often we make people guess at what we want, so of course, we don't usually get it. Not just on special days like vacations, birthdays, and holidays, but on normal days, like Tuesday. We've all done it. You're in the mood for Italian food and your husband says, "Honey, what do you want to eat tonight?" You answer, "I don't care," and you get stuck eating Chinese. You want to watch a football game and your wife asks, "Honey, what do you want to do?" You answer, "It's up to you," and you end up getting stuck shopping for curtains.

If you speak up, there's a risk you may not get what you want. But if you don't speak up, you're pretty much guaranteed not to get it.

As for Rule 2, it's up to us to live a life free of regrets. We can blame our jobs, our bosses, our spouses, our parents, our children, or our genetic material for our limitations, but in the end, our lives are what we choose to make them.

Annie Dillard once wrote that how you spend your days is ultimately how you spent your life. That one line stopped me cold. It was like a death sentence. Or a life sentence. Was how I spent my days really how I would spend my life? Wow. It sounded terrible, until I changed how I spent my days.

I spent a lot of days whining about what I didn't have time to do, lamenting over what I wished I could do if only... What was I waiting for?

If it's true that how we spend our days is how we spend our lives, most obituaries aren't honest. They never say that Jane Doe spent her life eating bonbons and watching *One Life to Live*. But if that is how she spent her days, isn't that indeed how she spent her life?

How about John Doe, who spends his days at a job he hates and the rest of the time sitting on a barstool complaining about it? It may seem to him like one day wasted, but in the end, it's a life wasted. His obit will list the children he had, even the ones that stopped speaking to him years ago. It will list the grandchildren, even if he hadn't seen them in four years and never even knew their names.

I once read that you should write out your own obituary— the way you would want it to read—to find out what your real desires are. Try it. Spend an hour of your vacation or weekend or lunch hour writing down how you would have wanted to live. It could jump-start your new life.

I do two things that keep me from having regrets. After watching a video of Steve Jobs give a commencement address to Stanford University, I wrote down the question he asked himself every day. His words are on a card that I read every morning. When I open the medicine chest to get my toothbrush, there it is: "If today were the last day of my life, would I want to do what I'm about to do today?" Then I pause and make sure the answer is yes. If the answer is no, I rethink my day.

Then, at the end of the day, I practice the tenth step of Alcoholics Anonymous that my friends in recovery taught me: "Continued to take personal inventory, and when we were wrong, promptly admitted it." They taught me to do a quick

scan of the day before bed to see if I closed my heart to anyone by being selfish, dishonest, unfair, resentful, fearful, or angry. Was I kind and compassionate? Did I think of others or just myself? Was there anyone I hurt? Anyone I need to apologize to? It's just a quick scan, not a flogging. Then I ask God to bless anyone I hurt by my action or inaction, and I pray for the grace to make amends the next day.

Do it long enough, and you right your wrongs just before you veer off course. You catch yourself, apologize, correct your course, and move on. You don't drag any hostages to bed with you or wake up with them and drag them into the next day. Everyone is free. No more emotional hangovers.

Daily self-appraisal keeps you in check so your whole life doesn't get off course. Some people do a quick inventory during the day as soon as they feel something go haywire. You pause, step back, and examine your thoughts, feelings, and actions, not the other person's.

I don't want to get to the end of my life and be buried under regrets. Too many people do. Hospice workers have shared with me the regrets they hear from people in the last months of their lives: They were too scared to live the lives they truly wanted to live. They failed to make amends with siblings, parents, spouses, children. They worked too much and wished they could have those precious hours back. They worried too much about small details that didn't matter. They wished they had said "I love you" more and "I told you so" less. They lost touch with dear friends and let them slip away. They never figured out how to be happy with life on life's terms.

My friend Sarah Maxwell used to work as a music therapist at Hospice of the Western Reserve in Cleveland. She helped

people make peace with the past, helped them mend relationships before they left this world. One day Sarah asked if I could do one of her patients a favor. One woman wanted me to share her last regret. Mrs. R. was 80 and wrote this dying message:

As I lie in bed, numerous volunteers have brightened my days. As I see the joy that they give and receive, I have feelings of regret. I lived down the street from a nursing home and I never thought about giving of my time and going there to bring a smile to a lonely person's face. I will feel that I made a difference if I am able to convince others to give even one hour a week in volunteering. You can be a hospice volunteer or a visitor to a nursing home or a tutor in a school. There are so many good people doing good things. Be one of them.

That was her dying wish. Give one hour of time a week so you don't end up dying with the same regret.

At the end of life, what will be your one regret?

What is in the gap between the life you are living and the life you want to be living? Once you know it, you can start living the life you want to be living, the only one worth living.

Find your grail. Be who God meant you to be, and you will set the world on fire.

Every spring the parents start to panic.

As college seniors prepare to graduate, their loved ones call and write me for advice: *My daughter, [my son,] is graduating from college and there are no jobs. They spent all that time and money to prepare for a career that might not exist. What can I say or do to give them hope?*

Before you start making room in your basement for them to move in, give them the greatest graduation gift there is: believe in them.

Hope for the next generation isn't found in the want ads. You make your own hope. No job I ever had in my life was found in the want ads or online. They all came to me by aligning myself on the inside first and connecting with the right people already in my life. They all came to me when I looked past the unemployment rate and remembered that God is always hiring.

Don't believe the rejection letters. Believe beyond the statistics. Believe in spite of the facts. Believe in your place in this world even when the world doesn't believe in you.

You have to believe in yourself even when no one else does. You have to believe bigger than the disbelief around you. You have to believe in miracles, in what you can't see.

That might mean you have to create the job you want. You might have to design the life you want to live. Three years ago, I made a fake book cover and wrote my name down as the author. It inspired me to buckle down and write my first book. My real book is now on sale at bookstores near you.

Before I finished writing my first book, I printed out the *New York Times* best seller list and taped it to my office door. I boldly put the title of my own book on it. My first book made the real *New York Times* best seller list three weeks in a row.

My vision board has a photo of me chatting with Oprah. Okay, so I cut off Sally Field's head (sorry, I really do like you, Sally) and put mine there. Why not dream big?

You have to design the life you want to have. Name it, claim it, and start living it.

Stop telling yourself, *I don't know what to do.* You know something. Start with what you know. Ask yourself, *What do I know for sure?* Start there.

I used to tell myself, *I'm scared*, all the time, so I attracted more fear. A big wad of it, like those giant rubber-band balls. That was me. Layer upon layer, that ball of fear grew. No more. I told myself, *Snap out of it. Go make something possible.*

I'll never forget the first time I heard the students from the Baldwin Wallace University music theatre program sing

their hearts out at Nighttown in Cleveland Heights. They blew me away. They're all on their way to Broadway. Talk about a dream out of reach. The odds are against them. They don't care. Their joy was so contagious, my face hurt from smiling as they belted out these lyrics from a *Spamalot* song: "If you trust in your song, keep your eyes on the goal, then the prize you won't fail, that's your grail. So be strong, keep right on, to the end of your song. Do not fail. Find your grail."

The Holy Grail might be mythical, but a holy grail is what we each are, a sacred container for the holy, for God. Saint Catherine of Siena said, "Be who God meant you to be and you will set the world on fire."

You can tell when someone does that. Jeffery Zaslow did it. He was a vessel for the holy. You knew him through all the books he wrote. Jeff gave voice to Randy Pausch in *The Last Lecture*. He gave Gabby Giffords words to tell her story. He gave Captain Sully more than a moment on the Hudson in a plane in the water. He gave the girls from Ames a chance to share their friendship and inspire that same love for others all over the world.

I met Jeff in 2000 when he won the Will Rogers Humanitarian Award from the National Society of Newspaper Columnists. I was once president of the NSNC, a fun-loving bunch of columnists from all over the country. Jeff was chosen for the award because he did so much to spotlight good, decent people doing good, decent things for the world.

That's what Jeff always was: a good, decent human being. He looked out for others. He looked for the good in others. He captured it and disappeared in the process. He let others shine through his words. Trappist monk Thomas Merton once

wrote, "Let me at least disappear into the writing I do…The work could be a prayer."

Jeff's life truly was a prayer. A prayer for others.

He used to write a column in Chicago called "All that Zazz" and held an annual Zazz Bash for singles. Thousands attended. He helped 78 couples find their soul mates to marry.

Jeff was writing columns for the *Wall Street Journal* the year he heard the last lecture by Randy Pausch, a computer science professor at Carnegie Mellon University in Pittsburgh. Randy had pancreatic cancer. Half of those diagnosed die within six months. The odds of surviving an airliner crash are 24 percent; the odds of surviving pancreatic cancer are 4 percent.

He had mere months to live when Jeff shared his story with the world. Randy died on July 25, 2008, at 47. He left behind a wife and three kids, ages 6, 3, and 2. I watched the last lecture online and cried at the end. The day he gave his last lecture was also his wife's birthday, the last one they would ever celebrate together. When they wheeled out a giant cake, she rushed onstage, threw her arms around him, and whispered in his ear: "Please don't die. The magic will go out of our lives."

I don't know if the magic went out of their lives. I do know the magic went into our lives, thanks to Jeff. The book has been translated into 48 languages and millions have watched that last lecture online and are busy climbing walls instead of being stopped by them. Jeff gave us a foot up to climb ours.

"Go hug your kids," he said. "Go love your life."

The last time he was in Cleveland, we talked before and after his book event. He said traveling was brutal and he couldn't wait to get home to his wife and children.

I still can't believe that he died in a car accident on his way

home from a book signing one snowy day in February 2012. He was 53.

Jeff helped me many times when I was stuck. We chatted on the phone or by e-mail, and he was never too busy to return a call or urge me on into the amazing world of authordom that he inhabited with such humility and grace. He even gave me a blurb for my first book, *God Never Blinks*, which I treasure now more than ever.

He still inspires me every day. I keep his business card next to my computer where I write: *Jeffrey Zaslow, Senior Special Writer, The Wall Street Journal.* It's next to one of the quotes by Randy Pausch: "Inspiration is the ultimate tool for doing good."

Jeff once told me after a book signing that he was tired of being on the road, that he just wanted to hug his kids and kiss his wife. His last book was inspired by his love for his three daughters: *The Magic Room: A Story about the Love We Wish for Our Daughters.*

The Magic Room.

I imagine he is in one now, interviewing everyone there, fascinated by every story.

Acknowledgments

There is no way to thank everyone who makes a book possible, especially a book about work. Countless bosses and coworkers shaped the person I am. It's impossible to list them all, but I am grateful for their fingerprints all over my life.

My first and greatest teacher about work was my dad, Tom Brett. He worked harder than any human being should work. He instilled in all 11 children a work ethic stronger than steel. My mom, Mary Brett, worked harder than any mother should, changing diapers, cooking meals, washing mountains of laundry day after day, year after year. I owe them both a debt of gratitude that can never be repaid.

I also want to thank...

My siblings, in-laws, and their children for loving me more than I deserve.

All my teachers at Immaculate Conception Elementary

School, Brown Junior High School, Ravenna High School, Kent State University, and John Carroll University for opening my mind and filling it with wonder.

All the people who hired me over the years at jobs great and small and gave me the chance to meet so many wonderful colleagues who taught me so many of these life lessons.

The loyal readers who read my columns, attend my talks, buy my books, send e-mails, and trust me to tell their stories. Thanks for sharing your experiences, strengths, and hopes.

My Polish publishers, Tomasz, Maria, and Pawel Brzozowski at Insignis Media, and the many readers in Poland who made me a best-selling author in their lovely country. Dziekuje! A special thanks to Dominika Pycińska for making my trip there a joy and a blessing.

The many writers whose love and support have lifted me for decades, including Sheryl Harris, Thrity Umrigar, Bill O'Connor, Dick Feagler, Ted Gup, Susan Ager, and Stuart Warner.

Two great mentors who left this world too soon, Gary Blonston and Jeffrey Zaslow.

Minister Joyce Meyer, whose tweet inspired the title of this book.

The *Plain Dealer* and the *Beacon Journal* for giving me the freedom to do my best work and for granting me permission to share it in this book.

My agent, Linda Loewenthal at David Black Literary Agency, for her great wisdom, laser clarity, and gentle honesty that guide me like a compass.

My team at Grand Central Publishing: Publisher Jamie Raab for believing in me and my writing with such zeal and

exuberance. Editor Karen Murgolo, whose kindness and passion make the editing process pure pleasure. Matthew Ballast and Nicole Bond, for spreading my writing all over the world. And to everyone else there who put their mark on this book.

My front-row friends, especially Beth Welch, Kay Peterson, Vicki Prussak, Sheryl Harris, Katie O'Toole, Suellen Saunders, and Sharon Sullivan.

To the joy of my life, my grandchildren, Asher, Ainsley, and River, who remind me to play hard and savor every morsel of fun in each moment by staying completely present in it.

To my children, Gabrielle, James, Ben, and Joe, for living such interesting, joyful lives that constantly open my mind and heart to new wonders.

To my husband, Bruce, who believed in me long before I did and absolutely cherishes me and celebrates everything life has given us.

And, as always, endless gratitude to the Source of it all, the God of my joy.

About the Author

Regina Brett is the *New York Times* best-selling author of *God Never Blinks: 50 Lessons for Life's Little Detours* and *Be the Miracle: 50 Lessons for Making the Impossible Possible*. Her writing has been translated into numerous languages and published in more than 26 countries.

Her famous 50 Life Lessons have traveled the world, but contrary to the popular Internet rumor, Regina is not 90.

Regina also writes columns for the *Plain Dealer* in Cleveland and for the *Cleveland Jewish News* and is syndicated through the Jewish News Service. Regina has twice been named a finalist for the Pulitzer Prize in Commentary.

Regina lives in Cleveland, Ohio, with her husband, Bruce.

She welcomes readers to visit her at www.reginabrett.com and to follow her on Facebook at ReginaBrettFans and on Twitter at @reginabrett.